*Unfolding
the City*

Unfolding

the City

WOMEN WRITE
THE CITY IN
LATIN AMERICA

ANNE LAMBRIGHT AND
ELISABETH GUERRERO
EDITORS

UNIVERSITY OF MINNESOTA PRESS
MINNEAPOLIS
LONDON

Chapter 10 was originally published as "Traperas y extranjeras en la Ciudad de México: Tina Modotti y Angelina Beloff como flaneuses en la obra de Elena Poniatowska," *Arizona Journal of Hispanic Culture Studies* (2003); reprinted with permission.

La lluvia es una piel by Delia McDonald Woolery (San José, Costa Rica: Ministerio de Cultura, Juventud, y Deportes, 1981) is excerpted with permission of the author.

Naciendo by Shirley Campbell Barr (San José, Costa Rica: Editorial Universidad Estatal a Distancia, 1988) is excerpted with the permission of the author.

Published by the University of Minnesota Press
111 Third Avenue South, Suite 290
Minneapolis, MN 55401-2520
http://www.upress.umn.edu

Library of Congress Cataloging-in-Publication Data

Unfolding the city : women write the city in Latin America / Anne Lambright and Elisabeth Guerrero, editors.
    p. cm.
  Includes bibliographical references and index.
   ISBN 978-0-8166-4812-2 (hc : alk. paper) — ISBN 978-0-8166-4813-9 (pb : alk. paper)
     1. Latin American fiction—Women authors—History and criticism.
 2. Latin American fiction—20th century—History and criticism.
 3. Latin American fiction—21st century—History and criticism.
 4. Cities and towns in literature. 5. Latin America—In literature.
 I. Lambright, Anne. II. Guerrero, Elisabeth, 1964–
    PQ7081.5.U64 2007
    860.9'321732—dc22

2006036913

Printed in the United States of America on acid-free paper

The University of Minnesota is an equal-opportunity educator and employer.

12 11 10 09 08 07   10 9 8 7 6 5 4 3 2 1

The city too has folds. . . . So you work the folds of that city. You work politically, aesthetically, linguistically, syntactically. You can bet on a possible city, that city which is not contained in the most official, or most institutional, or most dominant discourses . . . and inasmuch as you attempt to replace, restore, remake certain spaces, whether in a pleasurable or hyper-dramatic manner . . . you can in some way broaden the concept of city.

Diamela Eltit

Contents

Acknowledgments

We would first and foremost like to thank the contributors, who responded with enthusiasm to this project and with whom we have enjoyed invigorating intellectual exchange. Very special thanks go to Naomi Lindstrom and Marcy Schwartz for their incisive readings and suggestions for the introduction.

We appreciate the first-rate staff at the University of Minnesota Press for unwavering support of the project. We are also grateful for the thoughtful readings of the three anonymous evaluators; their comments decidedly enhanced the work.

On a personal note, Anne Lambright would like to thank her family, Guillermo, Corazón, Isis, Paloma, Mobey, and Maya, for enthusiastically applauding each successful phase of this project and for patience during stressful times. She is also deeply grateful to have been able to count on such a wonderful collaborator on this volume, which, without Elisabeth Guerrero, would not have reached this point.

Elisabeth Guerrero would like to thank her family, Oscar, Sophia, and Sebastian, for abundant affection, a lively sense of humor, and the ability to remind her that life is not all work and no play. She also expresses her warmest respect and gratitude to Anne Lambright for initiating our collaborative work. It has been an intellectual and personal pleasure, and I could not have hoped for a better partner in our joint effort.

Finally, the coeditors acknowledge the kind support of their colleagues at Trinity College and Bucknell University.

Introduction

ELISABETH GUERRERO AND ANNE LAMBRIGHT

As the Chilean writer Diamela Eltit implicitly recognizes in the quotation selected as the epigraph for this book, the city is not only a site built of towers of steel and glass but is also both a product and a generator of modern culture. This socially constitutive role of urban space is of growing interest in contemporary cultural studies. Theorists in a variety of disciplines—geography, sociology, anthropology, art history, literature—are debating the value of the city in modern life and its effects on its inhabitants. The city plays a particularly important role in Latin America, where urban areas hold a near monopoly on centralized political and economic resources and are home to a rapidly expanding majority of the hemisphere's population. Clearly, the city provides a panoramic vantage from which we can view the sociocultural landscapes of Latin America.[1]

It is clear that urban geography not only reflects social structure but also serves to create and sustain societal hierarchies. As geographer Nancy Duncan reminds us, "social relations, including, importantly, gender relations, are constructed and negotiated spatially and are embedded in the spatial organization of places" (5). For this reason, of special interest is how women belonging to the intellectual and professional elite, as well as to marginalized or disenfranchised groups, negotiate their dwellings and articulate their urban lives. As the studies included in this volume will show, women's views of the city, as expressed particularly through literature, are unique and revealing, as women writers propose new mappings of urban space; contemplate the vertiginously rapid transformations of the modern city; interpret race, ethnic, and class dynamics; and explore the place of their own cities in broader world dynamics. It is within these considerations that *Unfolding the City: Women Write the City in Latin America* situates itself, by examining the unique relationship between women writers of the nineteenth to twenty-first centuries and the cities that comprise their literary landscapes.[2]

This study arises in response both to gender studies research in Latin America and to an emerging body of theory and criticism focusing on the representation of urban space in the region. Mark D. Szuchman asserts, "no other people have paid more attention over the ages to their urban dimensions than Latin Americans. This preoccupation crosses nearly every genre of discourse, ranging from the self-conscious styles of academic scholars to the more freely expressed and popular forms of minstrels, street poets, folklorists, and essayists" (1). Whether or not we give credence to such a sweeping statement, we can certainly point to an abundance of theorizations and representations of the place of the city in Latin American culture in modern times, from Argentine thinker Domingo F. Sarmiento's nineteenth-century contemplations on European, urban *civilización* and Native, rural *barbarie,* to reflections by writers who rose to international prominence during the literary *boom* of the 1960s and 1970s, such as Julio Cortázar of Argentina, Carlos Fuentes of Mexico, or Mario Vargas Llosa of Peru, to, of course, the writers studied in this volume.[3]

In addition to these literary approaches, urban theory expands our understanding of cities both within and beyond the Americas. Scholars are ever more interested in how questions of power and resistance are played out spatially and socially in the planning, organization, architecture, and performance of the urban sphere and the lives within it. Among the most notable examples, Michel de Certeau's famous "walk" through New York City considers the practices and uses of urban space in everyday life. Henri Lefebvre's vast corpus of writings on the city considers, among other things, the ideology underlying urban planning and insists that "the city and the urban cannot be understood without *institutions* springing from relations of class and property" (106). Another prolific urban theorist, David Harvey, has dedicated a good part of his vast work to interpreting the role of capitalism in the formation of the city, writing in poignant terms that "the city is the high point of human achievement, objectifying the most sophisticated knowledge in a physical landscape of extraordinary complexity, power, and splendor at the same time as it brings together social forces capable of the most amazing sociotechnical and political innovation. But it is also the site of squalid human failure" (229). In Latin America, Ángel Rama's much-discussed model of the "lettered city," which we address later in this introduction, points out the role of lettered institutions in shaping urban dynamics. As these theorists recognize, municipal institutions show glimpses of their ideological roots as they carry on the business of the city and shape, control, or transform the lives of its inhabitants. For Lefebvre, the interpretive objective is "conceiving the city as a semantic system . . . arising from linguistics, urban language, or urban reality as a grouping of signs" (108). As will become clear, the literature studied in this volume is particularly engaged in decoding the signs of the city as interpreted through the lived experience and cultural imaginary of women.

Thinkers such as Edward W. Soja and Saskia Sassen provide theoretical tools for confronting specifically the city scene in the late twentieth and early twenty-first centuries. Soja's "postmodern geographies" attempt to come to terms with a restless megalopolis such as Los Angeles, which "seems too limitless and constantly in motion, never still enough to encompass, too filled with 'other spaces' to be informatively described" (222). In accordance with Soja's intention to formulate a "postmodern geography" that will provide insights into today's cities, sociologist Saskia Sassen postulates powerful international economic centers called "global cities" (a category within which she places such Latin American urban centers as Mexico City and São Paulo). Sassen's conceptualization of the "global city" serves as a space through which to analyze the workings and ramifications of an increasingly global economy. Several essays in this volume point to the concern of current women writers with the effects of these transformations. For instance, Debra A. Castillo contemplates the extreme velocity of urban life that makes the city virtually disappear in a novel by Mexican writer Margarita Mansilla, and Gareth Williams interprets the violent effects of capitalism as portrayed in Chilean writer Diamela Eltit's narrative. These analyses show how Latin American women writers are giving us new ways to "read" the city-text.

Along with these considerations of the city come explorations of its inhabitants and their responses to the urban milieu. Sassen, for example, considers issues of power and identity for women and other marginalized groups, finding that "the global city is a strategic site for disempowered actors because it enables them to gain presence, to emerge as subjects, even when they do not gain direct power" (*Globalization,* xxi). Geographers Steve Pile and Nigel Thrift propose new ways of "mapping" the subject, that is, of spatially situating and defining the subject, and remind us that "power—whether organized through knowledge, class, 'race', gender, sexuality and so on—is (at least partly) about mapping the subject; where particular sites—for example, the body, the self and so on—become 'points of capture' for power" (13). Indeed, contributions to this volume such as Marcy Schwartz's essay on short stories from Brazil, Puerto Rico, and Argentina, and Daniel Noemi Voionmaa's examination of Chilean narrative, will show that the relationship body–city serves as a powerful metaphor for many Latin American women writers; in their rendering, female bodies become texts on which new, alternative mappings of the city are drawn.

In this regard, current feminist geography is particularly useful in understanding the function of the city-space for the writers studied in this volume. As Doreen Massey states, "spaces and places, and our senses of them (and such related things as our degrees of mobility), are gendered through and through" (186). To give one example of this gendering of space, a woman artist or writer who traverses the city may not play the same role as a man. She may not have easy or secure access to certain streets or buildings, such as the soccer field, the pub, or a poorly lit avenue; furthermore, she cannot be a detached observer distanced from her surroundings, as she can rarely escape the gaze of others. On the other hand, as Elisabeth Guerrero observes in her essay on Elena Poniatowska's writings, these differences provide such a figure with the opportunity to more closely identify with the populace and to produce work that echoes this awareness.

In addition to social-science work such as Massey's that highlights the gendering of city-space there is also a great deal of current attention to combining the field of urban studies with literary and cultural studies, especially with regard to Latin America. The prominent Argentine-Mexican cultural theorist Néstor García Canclini contemplates the Latin American city as a multitemporal space in which the premodern, modern, and postmodern coexist, constituting the cultural hybridity to which the title of one of his major studies, *Hybrid Cultures,* speaks. García Canclini asks:

But how do we speak about the modern city, which sometimes is ceasing to be modern and to be a city? What was once a collection of neighborhoods spills beyond what we can relate to since no one can include all the itineraries or all the loosely connected material and symbolic offerings that present themselves. The migrants cross the city in many directions and, precisely at the intersections, install their baroque stands of regional candies and contraband radios, medicinal herbs and videocassettes. How do we study the cleverness with which the city attempts to reconcile everything that arrives and proliferates, and tries to contain all the disorder? (3–4)[4]

In order to answer the question he poses, García Canclini has particularly focused on the importance of media consumption in the hybrid cultural constructions of Latin American cities today:

More than an absolute situation of urban life by the audiovisual media, I perceive a *game of echoes*. The commercial advertising and political slogans that we see on television are those that we reencounter in the streets, and vice versa: the ones are echoed in the others. To this circularity of the communicational and the urban are subordinated the testimonies of history and the public meaning constructed in longtime experiences. (212)[5]

Many of the chapters in this volume recount how women writers are responding to the "disorder" of the contemporary city and the role of mass media in reflecting and communicating hybrid cultures. For example, Anne Lambright's contribution delves into how women writers negotiate the chaos of modern Lima, and Jacqueline Loss addresses the issue of global media in her essay on the role of the international publishing world in a recent novel by Cuban writer Ena Lucía Portela. In the "game of echoes" that García Canclini describes between mass communication on the billboards and giant screens and the more intimate exchanges in urban homes and neighborhoods, the cityscape rises all around us, dominating cultural experience today in the Americas and feeding the literary imaginations of women writers.

While social scientists such as García Canclini have paid critical attention to the Latin American city in general, historians, economists, and anthropologists such as Donna Guy, Linda Seligmann, Elizabeth Hutchison, Helen Safa, Félix Matos-Rodríguez, and Mercedes González de la Rocha have produced significant work focusing on women's experiences in the Latin American metropolis.[6] A handful of studies have also appeared critiquing Rama's "lettered city," but these volumes do not focus specifically on *women's* remapping of the literate urban centers. As this book makes clear, a lacuna remains regarding the convergence of women's creative writing with the impact of the city on women's lives. This volume shows that, while they face the same challenges of urban life as men—the population explosions brought about by internal migration, the rapid transformations influenced by globalization, the difficulties of movement and displacement imposed by insufficient infrastructures, the problems of attending to work and family exacerbated by the dispersion of the postmodern human condition—women intellectuals often provide novel approaches to these situations, as questions of gender, class, race, sexuality, or parental status deeply affect their experiences. As Eltit states:

> My literary, political, and aesthetic sensibility lies with the sectors that are, let's say, oppressed by the system. So there I have obsessive, fixed, absorbed points. I believe that I am always pointing to that part of the city. To those bodies, those histories, that part that is, in a way, annulled by the official discourses, or simplified by the official discourses.[7]

Because of intellectual sensibilities such as Eltit's that often identify with marginalized sectors and thereby tend to question official discourses, we have found, in women's writings, sophisticated interpretations of the workings of the city and its inhabitants from late-modern to postmodern times. The women intellectuals studied in this volume give us a look at the joys, the tribulations, the hopefulness, and the despair associated with inhabiting the Latin American city.

Although a number of critics have focused on women writers of the Americas, and pioneering social scientists have produced studies of the lives of women in the Latin American city, no book has been devoted to the juncture of these two areas: exploring how women themselves conceive the city and creatively articulate their lives within it. Nevertheless, several important works have addressed the role of literature in creating and sustaining discourse on the city and provide important theoretical frameworks for this volume. Raymond Williams's 1973 classic *The Country and the City* examines the history of the push and pull between the rural and the urban as portrayed in British literature. For Williams, "clearly the contrast of country and city is one of the major forms in which we become conscious of a central part of our experience and of the crises in our society" (289). Certainly the *campo/ciudad* dichotomy is of central importance in Latin American literature up through the 1950s, comprising one of the major foundations of national discourse. But recent critical inquiries have focused more exclusively on the city itself as object of literary creation. Among a quickly growing bibliography of resources, Joan Ramón Resina and Dieter Ingenschay's edition of essays, *After-Images of the City*, stands out for its considerations of how, in contemporary representations of the city in literature and film, "the city becomes a fetishized object for a gaze that is caught in the symbolic conventions of cultural or ideological consumption" (xvii). *Citizenship of Fear*, edited by Susana Rotker, uses a combination of scholarly essays and urban chronicles to contemplate the culture of violence and fear that defines major Latin American cities.

Of those volumes that particularly consider the contributions of women writers to portrayals of the city outside Latin America, we find of interest Deborah L. Parsons's *Streetwalking the Metropolis: Women, the City, and Modernity*. Concentrating on British and French writers, Parsons, drawing from Walter Benjamin's *flâneur*, theorizes a *flâneuse*, a female streetwalker/city chronicler whose perspective is "necessarily less leisured, as well as less assured, yet also more consciously adventurous" (42) than that of her male counterpart. Also of note are Deborah Nord's *Walking the Victorian Streets: Women, Representation, and the City* and Susan Merrill Squier's *Women Writers and the City*.

Although there are no studies focusing specifically on the contribution of female writers to discourse on the city in Latin America, some studies include the occasional female writer. Marcy Schwartz's *Writing Paris: Urban Topographies of Desire in Contemporary Latin American Fiction* includes a chapter on Argentine writer Luisa Futoransky; Julie Jones's *A Common Place: The Representation of Paris in Spanish American Fiction* examines Mexican author Elena Garro's *Reencuentro de personajes*. Héctor D. Fernández L'Hoeste's *Narrativas de representación urbana* has a section on Brazilian writer Clarice Lispector's *Hour of the Star;* and Gilbert M. Joseph and Mark D. Szuchman's anthology of writings on the city, *I Saw a City Invincible: Urban Portraits of Latin America*, offers portions of Brazilian Carolina Maria de Jesus's writings on São Paulo in her memoir *Child of the Dark: The Diary of Carolina Maria de Jesus*.

Yet, among all the recent discussions of urban space in Latin America, perhaps the most cited and discussed theory of the city in Latin American studies remains Ángel Rama's seminal theoretical work on the city in Latin American literature, *The Lettered City* (1984), which traces different "types" of cities-within-the-city throughout the history of Latin America, each with its own social function. Rama focuses on the religious, philosophical, and intellectual strata, which he calls the lettered city: "the lettered city acted upon the order of signs. . . . This was the cultural dimension of the . . . power structure, whether or not the people of the time conceived or experienced it as such" (17).[8] That is, the intellectual leaders of the lettered city—political, ecclesiastical, academic—control the symbolic order that defines a given national culture. Rama describes the reciprocity between the "real" city and the privileged intellectual metropolis, noting "the highly variable relationship between larger urban society and the elite city of letters" (27).[9] For Rama, the lettered city establishes order: "Only the letrados could envision an urban ideal before its realization as a city of stone and mortar, then maintain that ideal after the construction of the city, preserving their idealized vision in a constant struggle with the material modifications introduced by the daily life of the city's ordinary inhabitants" (28).[10] The task of these men of letters was to construct a city of words and ideas that would both shape and respond to the city constructed of stone and mortar and, later, of steel and glass.

In response to changes in publishing and mass media in recent decades, several reformulations of Rama's lettered city have appeared. In *The Decline and Fall of the Lettered City: Latin America in the Cold War*, literary theorist Jean Franco reads texts of such novelists as the Colombian Gabriel García Márquez and the Peruvian Mario Vargas Llosa to provide insights into Latin American writers' responses to the Cold War in their work. Franco argues that the lettered city has fallen into crisis following the destructive civil wars and military dictatorships of the 1980s and that, in a situation exacerbated by the mass-media explosion of recent decades, writers have lost their place of prominence in Latin America. Although Franco has done groundbreaking work on women writers, this recent book focuses primarily on the lettered city of men. Another book that addresses contemporary reformulations of Rama's lettered city is Edmundo Paz Soldán and Debra Castillo's edited volume, *Beyond the Lettered City: Latin American Literature and Mass Media*, which examines how mass media—cinema, journalism, comics, photography, Internet technology— oblige a reconsideration of Rama's concept. According to the coeditors, the introduction of mass media in major Latin American cities has created a Latin America that "abandons the territory of . . . 'the lettered city'" (3); they are especially interested in the effects of the changes brought about by modernity, especially its technologies, on Latin American literature. Although the introduction to the work mentions Rama's neglect of female perspectives, the volume's contributors do not address the issue of gender and study relatively few women writers.

Mabel Moraña's edited collection *Ángel Rama y los estudios latino-americanos* offers studies of Rama's theoretical corpus; of special interest here are the articles by Gustavo Remedi and Santiago Castro-Gómez, which dialogue directly with the "lettered city." For Remedi, one of Rama's greatest contributions to Latin American studies is his "spatialization of cultural analysis" (98), while Castro-Gómez looks to the earlier lettered city studied by Rama to find the seeds of the "processes of reflexivity and globalization in which . . . the majority of Latin Americans live today" (132). Finally, Silvia Spitta and Boris Muñoz's edited volume, *Más allá de la ciudad letrada: crónicas y espacios urbanos*, offers a mix of urban chronicles and literary studies that, according to Spitta, respond in one way or another both to Rama's formulation of the lettered city and to Alberto Flores Galindo's alternate articulation of the "ciudad sumergida," or the submerged city, in which less powerful residents such as slaves in colonial Lima also made use of written law to claim certain rights.

Unfolding the City aims to add to this debate on the lettered city by offering a glimpse of the *ciudad de letradas,* the city as conceived by lettered women. A careful reading of Rama's work reveals the masculine nature of his model of the lettered city, to the exclusion of women intellectuals, who were still rare during the periods that Rama studies (first the colonial era, and then the years of literary expansion following independence, particularly from 1880 to 1920). The government bureaucrats, lawmakers, and newspaper journalists who held the power of literacy and the written word during these times were predominantly white, upper-class men. John Charles Chasteen describes them tellingly in his introduction to the English translation of Rama's essay: "Imagine them: bearded and grave, the letrados of the colonial period are privy to the theocratic mysteries of empire" (vii). As our epigraph points out, the women writers studied in this volume are writing *against* this lettered city of a privileged few, conceiving other "ideal cities," or questioning the very concept of the "ideal" and replacing it with what Eltit calls the "possible" city.

This postulation of the possible city is timely considering the powerful effect that demographic changes have exerted on women, changes mirrored in the writings of many of the authors featured here, as, for instance,

Guillermo B. Irizarry observes in his essay on Puerto Rican novelist Mayra Santos Febres's representation of the breakdown of modernization in the illicit nocturnal activities taking place in San Juan. Although these writers produce works of fiction rather than social research, their novels and stories reveal many of the transformations of women's lives as the urban populace grows and adapts to this growth. At the beginning of the twentieth century, 90 percent of the population in Latin America resided in rural areas; in contrast, one hundred years later Latin America has become one of the world's most urbanized regions, with 75 percent of its inhabitants living in large urban areas, including such megacities as Mexico City and São Paulo, as well as in rapidly growing midsized cities such as Toluca, Mexico, and Valencia, Venezuela.[11] Although approximately half of the population in Central American nations still lives in rural areas, this transition from an agricultural to an industrial and service economy has been particularly pronounced in Mexico, the Caribbean, and most of South America; for instance, in Uruguay urban residents accounted for a whopping 90 percent of the population at the end of the twentieth century.[12]

Notably, roughly half of this burgeoning urban population is female, which will continue to increase in Latin America as more young men emigrate to the United States and Europe in search of work. It will also increase as the population ages, as women's life expectancies continue to exceed those of men. These demographic changes have widespread effects on the lifestyles of the inhabitants, creating a greater need for jobs, public services, housing, access to clean water and adequate sanitation, nutrition and health care, and education. In response to these needs, more women have entered the workforce, averaging 28 percent overall and reaching 60 percent in the low-paying, labor-intensive maquiladoras (assembly plants) on the Mexico–U.S. border (Brea, 30). Although their role in the public workforce grants women a degree of autonomy and economic power, the immense majority of these women still tend to earn low wages, have little opportunity for job advancement, and remain largely responsible for household chores and child care as well. In this volume, Sandra Messinger Cypess studies the literary representation of this phenomenon in her essay on Cristina Pacheco's skillful use of fiction to depict these challenges in women's work lives in Mexico City.

In addition to urban migration and increased participation in the workforce, the dramatic decline in birthrates, particularly in the city, has had a profound impact on women's lives in Latin America. Many countries, such as Cuba, Colombia, and Argentina, have drastically reduced average fertility, and in the Latin American region overall the total fertility rate has dropped from approximately six children per woman in the 1950s to roughly 2.5 children in the twenty-first century (ibid., 17).[13] It is generally understood that because today's city dwellers have smaller families, they are able to achieve a better quality of life for themselves and their children. Nevertheless, even with the advantages that come with fewer offspring, urban residents in Latin America continue to face many challenges, including those of a global economy in which a recession in the United States or Asia directly affects their own financial well-being. Furthermore, the infrastructure has been strained by rapid urban growth, and results include lack of adequate housing and sanitation and an increase in violent crime, a phenomenon that Lidia Santos acknowledges in this volume in her analysis of Brazilian writer Patricia Melo's novel of urban violence in São Paulo, *The Killer.*

It is within these contexts of rapid social change and demographic expansion, of grappling with modernity and postmodernity, and of reformulating local and global relations that many of the most important Latin American women writers produce their work. Repeatedly, we find within these literary creations attempts to map these transformations. The first set of studies in *Unfolding the City,* "Mapping the City," works toward creating a cartography of both city-spaces and the power relations within them as portrayed in women's narrative, addressing how women's spatial and cultural representations of the city are superimposed on more official mappings, becoming contestatory geographies in their own right.[14] Through literature, Latin American women are responding to the restrictive cartographies of their respective dominant national discourses, infusing the so-called universal with subjective, gender-specific experiences that belie hegemonic conceptions of the nation-space, specifically as it is reified in the city. Rather than fixing place as a site of nostalgia and stasis, these writers create mappings that acknowledge the dynamic transformations of space through time, particularly with regard to gender relations.[15]

As Marcy Schwartz observes in her essay "Short Circuits: Gendered Itineraries in Recent Urban Fiction Anthologies from Latin America," many recent editions of short fiction offer new manners of understanding the spatial configuration of the urban in Latin America. In Schwartz's reading, the implications of these collections for gender issues are of marked interest precisely because they do not focus on women writers. She examines short-story collections from and about Buenos Aires, Paris, San Juan, San José, São Paulo, and Rio de Janeiro that do not exclusively anthologize women's writing but where female voices significantly contribute to re-configurations of the urban in Latin American literature. Schwartz finds that in the women's stories three central themes emerge: a withdrawal to intimate and private places, a tribute to the body and sexuality, and a con-fronting of the "lettered city." Schwartz argues that the concerns narrated by the women writers included in the collections add a decidedly gendered perspective to these literary imaginings of the city.

Woman's evolving representation of city-space is the focus of Lidia Santos's "What Happened to the Cool City? Seventy Years of Women's Narrative in Brazil." Santos follows the presence of the city in Brazilian women's writing from the 1920s, in Patrícia Galvão's narrative of working-class São Paulo, to the 1950s, in Clarice Lispector's representations of the Copacabana neighborhood in Rio de Janeiro, to contemporary writers' rep-resentations of both cities in relation to their literary predecessors. Santos examines, for example, how the women of Sonia Coutinho's "O último verão de Copacabana" (The last summer in Copacabana) are trapped by consumerism and dominated by the popular cultural imaginary, while writers such as Patrícia Melo, through the depiction of the violence char-acteristic of the large Brazilian cities, destabilize Lispector's bourgeois narrators' lives and replace them with a hyperrealism that draws from the visual arts, transforming the city from place into protagonist.

The city also plays a protagonist role in current Peruvian women's writing, as Anne Lambright demonstrates in "On Being a Woman in the City of Kings: Women Write (in) Contemporary Lima," which explores the oppression and isolation experienced by women living in the Peruvian capital. Narrative from the 1990s to the present shows an urban geography that is hostile to and exclusive of women. On the other hand, these texts also propose ways in which women may both appropriate the current dis-tribution of urban space and escape these restrictive mappings through writing. This essay looks at a short story by Irma del Águila and novels by Carmen Ollé and Pilar Dughi in order to reveal how these women map Lima and the female subject within it, confronting hegemonic views of the city, challenging reigning topographies of gender, and creating geographies of resistance.

The redefinition of dominant geographies of the contemporary city in women's writing is the also subject of Guillermo B. Irizarry's "Failed

Modernity: San Juan at Night in Mayra Santos Febres's *Cualquier miércoles soy tuya* [Any given Wednesday, I'm yours]." Irizarry's essay comments on the act of staging a cityscape that illustrates the failure of a modernizing project in Puerto Rico and the Caribbean, and of narrating radically heterogeneous subjectivities and territorialities. *Cualquier miércoles soy tuya* maps the city's civic order, played out in heterogeneous locations (a motel, a gated community, housing projects, and abject slums) that mark the limits of state institutional administration. Irizarry argues that these sites, along with the dominant nighttime setting, articulate what has gone wrong with the modernizing project in Puerto Rico. For him, Santos Febres's novel illuminates alternative circuits of power and subjective articulation, a zone of radical heterogeneity where undocumented immigrants, Afro–Puerto Rican religious leaders, unknown writers, and drug pushers become the dominant social agents and embody the breakdown of a modern sociopolitical project.

Somewhat, though not entirely, in contrast to those studies that map the city, the essays in Part II, "The Restless City," respond to the rush of change in urban zones whose motion resists mapping. These essays address concerns with living and traveling within the briskly moving city and the particular difficulties writers envision for women and other marginalized subjects in this respect. The writers document the challenges faced both in Santiago de Chile, a growing cosmopolitan center, and Mexico City, a densely populated locus of international economic deal making. In the texts studied in Part II, urban centers provide a site for writers to depict the erasure of previous boundaries of the nation-space and historical time in the quickly changing world of mass-media technology.

In "Anna's Extreme Makeover: Revisiting Tolstoy in *Karenina Express*," Debra A. Castillo investigates how Mexican novelist Margarita Mansilla reimagines her own variations on Leo Tolstoy's classic novel *Anna Karenina*. For Castillo, Mansilla takes from the great nineteenth-century romance the metaphor of the train (its motion and speed as metonymy of modernity) and reifies it as a means through which to explore twenty-first-century urban life. As Castillo sees it, in this novel the city virtually disappears, becoming an indistinguishable blur where contemporary urbanites are not city dwellers but rather mass-transit passengers speeding through urban space. Mansilla's novel emphasizes movement—in the story of a literary journey—and in other meta-travels through international literary history and theory, as well as in references to trips from Mexico City to other hypermodern metropolitan urban sites such as New York City. In this novel, the city as we know it seems to vanish, and central tropes of modernity are called into question as the critical cluster of space/identity/authenticity gives way to time/contingency/("larger-than-life") performance.

Daniel Noemi Voionmaa continues the discussion of the function of time and urban space with an exploration of the city in contemporary Chilean women's narrative, specifically in short stories by Lillian Elphick, Andrea Jeftanovic, and Andrea Maturana, and a novel by Nona Fernández. In "The 'Uchronic' City: Writing (after) the Catastrophe," Noemi interprets the city as constructed in such a way that it reverts and annuls the very possibility of a determined concrete time and space. Thus emerges a "uchronic" city, one that is stigmatized by the continuous and always failed search for the possibility of a present. For Noemi, this is particularly evident in the trajectory of women's bodies in the texts; through their urban circulation, the body and the city mutually engender each other. Simultaneously, the text becomes a uchronic city itself; the writers are dealing with the ruins of history, and the postmodern cities and bodies are a key testimony of these ruins: the texts become the possibility of memory, but, at the same time, this is a memory that is erased again and again.

Navigating the impenetrable maze of the postmodern city is the topic of Gareth Williams's essay, "*The Fourth World* and the Birth of *Sudaca* Stigma," which analyzes the parameters of Eltit's critique of contemporary life, as well as the limits of that critique. According to Williams's reading of this text, if indeed, as others have argued, the novel is a narrative of female subject formation and empowerment, this very subjectivity and potential liberation is ultimately torn asunder by contemporary society's relentless drive toward commodification. For Williams, in Eltit's novel *El cuarto mundo* (*The Fourth World*), urban space no longer signifies the fundamental and productive biopolitical terrain of capitalist modernity. Rather, the city is portrayed as a site that remains under continual bombardment from the money that comes from the "most powerful nation in the world," fracturing and transforming permanently the social relations of the subsumed polis.

If the city is battleground for the excesses and violent transformations of recent years, it is also the stage for dynamic ethnic, racial, and class interactions. Part III, "Cities of Difference," explores how women writers represent conditions of marginalization from dominant society, as well as how cities become sites of both real and symbolic negotiations among diverse groups. The essays here take into account the lives of "outsiders" whose place in these centralized cities is uncertain: domestic workers, women of color, and foreign women.

Part III begins with Sandra Messinger Cypess's exploration of women's labor in Mexico in "The Cultural Memory of Malinche in Mexico City: Stories by Elena Garro and Cristina Pacheco." In her analysis of the female protagonists of Garro's and Pacheco's stories, Cypess emphasizes their Malinche-like qualities as traitors and forgers of a new culture as they relate to aspects of the urban Mexican environment as a space in which they act.[16] Garro's story, "La culpa es de los tlaxcaltecas" (It's the fault of the Tlaxcaltecas), is set in urban spaces of the bourgeois world but is intimately related to the city's indigenous past. In contrast, Cristina Pacheco's stories reveal much more of the harsh reality of the poverty and powerlessness suffered by servants and other workers in Mexico City. For Cypess, what links the urban narratives of these two writers is their evocation of aspects associated with Cortés's translator and lover, La Malinche, as a pathway to understanding the lives of today's disadvantaged women.

Dorothy E. Mosby further traces women's agency in the poetic construction of a dual identity in Costa Rican cities in "Writing Home: Afro–Costa Rican Women Poets Negotiating Limón and San José." She examines the articulation of cultural and ethnolinguistic tensions in the poetry of Eulalia Bernard, Shirley Campbell Barr, and Delia McDonald Woolery, where bodies and memories shift between Puerto Limón, the "black capital," and San José, the "white capital." For Mosby, in the poetry of these three women, Limón is constructed as a real and imagined space of "cultural authenticity" that represents the stable "home" for an identity that is continually in the process of "becoming." The port city is presented as a site central to the expression of Afro–Costa Rican identity, while San José is configured as a city that is replete with opportunity, but also as a hostile space that has yet to fully embrace Afro–Costa Ricans as part of the nation. While Bernard's perspective as a second-generation Afro–Costa Rican often elevates Puerto Limón to mythic proportions, the younger two poets reflect on the urban environment of the dominant culture in the capital as the focus of their struggle to affirm their "Costa Ricanness" and their blackness.

Elisabeth Guerrero's "Urban Legends: Tina Modotti and Angelina Beloff as *Flâneuses* in Elena Poniatowska's Mexico City" addresses the attempts of another group of outsiders, in this case foreign women artists, to make a place for themselves in the city they call home. Guerrero explains that Mexican writer Elena Poniatowska's work problematizes the attractions of the Mexican capital city, revealing that it can at times be brutal toward the popular classes as well as toward the women who attempt to conserve a space of their own within their cosmopolitan surroundings. Guerrero's essay explores Poniatowska's approach to the *flâneuse;* for the Mexican writer, the position of the *flâneuse* of our times is one of solidarity with the urban populace. Poniatowska writes with a social-justice awareness that is apparent in her journalistic chronicles as well as her fiction. Furthermore, the novelist writes with a feminist consciousness that celebrates the life and work of women artists, particularly those who are foreign born and therefore doubly outsiders; this essay focuses principally on the protagonists of her novels *Tinísima* (the Italian photographer Tina Modotti) and *Querido Diego, te abraza Quiela* (the Russian painter Angelina Beloff), figures who correspond with Poniatowska's prototype of the *flâneuse.*

Subtly or directly, all three of the essays in Part III suggest that creating geographies of inquiry and resistance sometimes entails migrating to a newly imagined space. In recognition of the phenomena of globalization, transnationalism, migration, and exile, the studies in Part IV, "Other Cities," address experiences of women living in exile or imagining a life in exile who look toward cities outside of Latin America as points of reference and objects of desire. Just as Parts I–III explore current writers' reconfigurations of the "lettered city," the first two essays in Part IV provide fresh reflections on earlier women writers' representations of urban space.

Ángel A. Rivera's study "Modernity, Flirting, Seduction, and Urban Social Landscape in Carmela Eulate Sanjurjo's *El asombroso doctor Jover*" notes that scholars have generally identified modernity as a male and urban phenomenon. However, a group of female writers at the threshold of the twentieth century were devising discursive and representational strategies that placed them in the midst of modernity. Puerto Rican intellectual Eulate Sanjurjo, whose novel *The Amazing Doctor Jover* represents a nineteenth-century Caribbean woman within the context of the European city of Barcelona, theorizes about the intellectual endeavors that would allow women writers to express or explore their subjectivities. Both the flirt and the frivolous woman are presented as part of a catalog of female counterparts that transgress accepted norms of behavior traditionally identified as feminine. Despite the apparent weak positioning of these roles, it is through them that Eulate Sanjurjo positions herself as a woman and as an urban intellectual at the close of the nineteenth century. For Rivera, this process allows us to render modernity as also feminine, rather than exclusively masculine.

Naomi Lindstrom's "Woman between Paris and Caracas: *Iphigenia* by Teresa de la Parra" investigates how the Venezuelan author wishes to replace expectations of the ladylike wife in Caracas with the model of the independent woman in Paris. Although the novel is set in Caracas, Paris is acutely present in the young female protagonist's consciousness, and only in part because of its mystique as the quintessence of European civilization. The protagonist's most recent visit to Paris—unlike her previous chaperoned stays in the same city—represents the one period in her life when, thanks to a liberal-minded host family, she was allowed to move about a city alone. Back in Caracas, her person, its proper location, and its chaperoning generate perennial tension among the protagonist, conventional relatives defending family interests, and characters associated with "free ideas." The novel's treatment of woman in the space of the city anticipates the concepts of feminist geography that would emerge in the late twentieth and early twenty-first centuries.

Jacqueline Loss's essay, "Amateurs and Professionals in Ena Lucía Portela's Lexicon of Crisis," links Rivera's study of Sanjurjo's literary renderings of a Caribbean/European modernity with contemporary Cuban writer Ena Lucía Portela's depiction of a Caribbean/European/U.S. postmodernity. Portela's novel traces a feminist geography of the post-lettered city in the late-twentieth- and early-twenty-first-century writing and publishing worlds of Havana, Barcelona, and New York. Loss explores how the Cuban novelist's "lexicon of crisis" must reinvent itself to better articulate the experiences of living in the current "Special Period in Times of Peace." For writers such as Portela, the downfall of the Soviet Union has left Cuba in an economic and ideological crisis that has translated into new literary partnerships—individual negotiations with foreign publishers in the cosmopolitan centers of France, Spain, and the United States. As Loss sees it, writers are now confronted with the dilemma of challenging readers' horizons of expectations for Cuba and Cuban literature. Portela's work mirrors a process of intellectual internationalization and debates the potential artistic and cultural concessions made for the sake of global marketing. In Portela's work, this quandary is mapped out on a Havana that both meets and defies the expectations of the international reading market.

Each of the studies in this volume, from Schwartz's essay on urban short stories to Loss's analysis of Portela's "lexicon of crisis," strives to bring attention to the important work of women writers who trace the contours of the cities of Latin America, responding to and representing creatively the transformations of their times. The literary production examined here is varied and the voices heard are often dissonant, questioning the validity for women of Rama's construction of the "lettered city." As we have seen with the 1985 earthquake in Mexico City and the 2001 attack on the Twin Towers in New York City, skyscrapers of steel and glass can collapse and shatter; future readers of de Certeau will not be able to re-create his optical perspective from atop the "gigantic rhetoric of excess in both expenditure and production" (91). And yet, as history has proven time and again, cities and their edifices can and will be rebuilt, as humanity reconstructs its urban centers after catastrophes, as if its continued existence depended on these structures. With the strength of steel and the clarity of glass, the writers addressed in this study have deconstructed and reconstructed the Latin American lettered city, confronted the "ideal" cities of the national "fathers," and proposed "possible" cities in their stead.

Notes

1. "La ciudad también tiene pliegues... Entonces tú trabajas los pliegues de esa ciudad. Trabajas políticamente, estéticamente, lingüísticamente, sintácticamente. Tú puedes apostar a una ciudad posible, esa ciudad que no está contenida en los discursos más oficiales, o más institucionales, o más dominantes,... y en la medida en que tú intentas reponer, restaurar, rehacer ciertos espacios, de manera gozosa o de manera híper dramática,... tú puedes de alguna manera ampliar el concepto de ciudad" (Spanish original of the epigraph at the beginning of this volume; quoted in Morales, 140).

2. Considering that it is the urban capital and other major cities that largely control the political, cultural, and economic life of Latin American countries, and the massive internal migrations from the country to the city that Latin American countries have experienced in the past half century, it would be appropriate to argue that even rural areas should be studied within the context of their relationship to urban zones. Noting that in the twentieth century urban residents in Latin America grew from roughly 10 percent of the population to 60 to 70 percent of the citizenry, Néstor García Canclini contends, "We have gone from societies dispersed in thousands of peasant communities with traditional, local, and homogeneous cultures—in some regions, with strong indigenous roots, with little communication with the rest of the nation—to a largely urban scheme with a heterogeneous

symbolic offering renewed by a constant interaction of the local with national and transnational networks of communication" (207–8).

3. See Domingo F. Sarmiento, *Facundo* (Madrid: Alianza Editorial, 1988; originally published in 1845).

4. "Pero, ¿cómo hablar de la ciudad moderna, que a veces está dejando de ser moderna y de ser ciudad? Lo que era un conjunto de barrios se derrama más allá de lo que podemos relacionar, nadie abarca todos los itinerarios, ni todas las ofertas materiales y simbólicas dehilvanadas que se presentan. Los migrantes atraviesan la ciudad en muchas direcciones, e instalan, precisamente en las cruces, sus puestos barrocos de dulces regionales y radios de contrabando, hierbas curativas y videocasetes. ¿Cómo estudiar las astucias con que la ciudad intenta conciliar todo lo que llega y prolifera, y trata de contener en el desorden?" (*Culturas*, 16).

5. "Más que una sustitución absoluta de la vida urbana por los medios audiovisuales, percibo un juego de ecos. La publicidad comercial y las consignas políticas que vemos en la televisión son las que reencontramos en las calles, y a la inversa; unas resuenan en las otras. A esta circularidad de lo comunicacional y lo urbano se subordinan los testimonios de la historia, el sentido público construido en experiencias de larga duración" (ibid., 221).

6. For a representative sampling of social-science research on women in urban areas of Latin America, see, for example, Mercedes González de la Rocha, *The Resources of Poverty: Women and Survival in Mexico City* (Cambridge: Blackwell, 1994); Helen Safa, *The Myth of the Male Breadwinner: Women and Industrialization in the Caribbean* (Boulder, Colo.: Westview Press, 1995); Elizabeth Hutchison, *Labors Appropriate to Their Sex: Gender, Labor, and Politics in Urban Chile, 1900–1930* (Durham, N.C.: Duke University Press, 2001); Félix Matos Rodríguez, *Women in San Juan, 1820–1868* (Princeton, N.J.: M. Weiner Publishers, 2001); Asunción Lavrín, *Women, Feminism, and Social Change in Argentina, Chile, and Uruguay, 1890–1940* (Lincoln: University of Nebraska Press, 1995); Donna Guy, *White Slavery and Mothers Alive and Dead: The Troubled Meeting of Sex, Gender, Public Health, and Progress in Latin America* (Lincoln: University of Nebraska Press, 2000) and *Sex and Danger in Buenos Aires: Prostitution, Family and Nation in Argentina* (Lincoln: University of Nebraska Press, 1992); Sarah LeVine, with Clara Sunderland Correa, *Dolor y alegría: Women and Social Change in Urban Mexico* (Madison: University of Wisconsin Press, 1993); Linda Seligmann, *Peruvian Street Lives: Culture, Power, and Economy among Market Women of Cuzco* (Urbana: University of Illinois Press, 2004); June Edith Hahner, *Emancipating the Female Sex: The Struggle for Women's Rights in Brazil, 1850–1940* (Durham, N.C.: Duke University Press, 1990) and *Poverty and Politics: The Urban Poor in Brazil, 1870–1920* (Albuquerque: University of New Mexico Press, 1986); Jula Tuñón, *Women in Mexico: A Past Unveiled* (Austin: University of Texas Press, 1999); Elizabeth Jelin, *Family, Household, and Gender Relations in Latin America* (New York: Routledge, 1991); Silvia Arrom, *The*

Women of Mexico City, 1790–1857 (Palo Alto, Calif.: Stanford University Press, 1985); and Susan K. Besse, *Restructuring Patriarchy: The Modernization of Gender Equality in Brazil, 1914–1940* (Chapel Hill: University of North Carolina Press, 1996).

7. "Mi sensibilidad literaria, política y estética está con los sectores, digamos, oprimidos por el sistema. Entonces ahí tengo yo puntos obsesivos, fijos, absortos. Yo creo que estoy apuntando siempre a esa parte de la ciudad. A esos cuerpos, a esas historias, a esa parte que está en cierto modo anulada por los discursos oficiales, o simplificada por los discursos oficiales" (Morales, 141).

8. "la *ciudad letrada,* porque su acción se cumplió en el prioritario orden de los signos… Obviamente se trataba de funciones culturales de las estructuras de poder, cuyas bases reales podríamos elucidar, pero así no fueron concebidas ni percibidas, ni así fueron vividas por sus integrantes" (*Ciudad,* 33). We are using John Charles Chasteen's English translation, which, while beautifully done, is somewhat liberal in its rendering.

9. "los múltiples encuentros y desencuentros entre la ciudad real y la ciudad letrada, entre la sociedad como un todo y su elenco intelectual dirigente" (ibid., 45).

10. "Sólo [la ciudad letrada] es capaz de concebir, como pura especulación, la ciudad ideal, proyectarla antes de su existencia, conservarla más allá de su ejecución material, hacerla pervivir aun en pugna con las modificaciones sensibles que introduce sin cesar el hombre común" (ibid., 46).

11. The essays included in this volume focus primarily on capital cities as the dominant national centers. We encourage future research on cultural production in midsized cities as well.

12. United Nations Publications, "InfoNation," online at http://www.un.org.

13. Although oral contraceptives are widely accepted, neither vasectomies nor condoms are commonly used in Latin America to prevent conception. Female sterilization is, remarkably, the predominant form of birth control, despite greater risks than a vasectomy. In Mexico and El Salvador, 30 percent of married women of reproductive age are sterilized, and in Brazil and the Dominican Republic the figure reaches more than 40 percent (see Brea).

14. We use the term "cartography" to refer to the act of mapping physical space in terms of social relations. For pertinent discussions on the concept of cartography, see, in particular, Steve Pile and Nigel Thrift, *Mapping the Subject,* and Kathleen Kirby, "ReMapping Subjectivity."

15. For an in-depth discussion of the topic of the construction of space as seen through the lens of feminist geography, see Doreen Massey's *Space, Place, and Gender,* in particular Part III, "Space Place and Gender" (175–272), and the collection of essays edited by geographer Nancy Duncan, *Body Space.*

16. Malinche, an indigenous woman who was the interpreter for the Spanish conqueror of Mexico, Hernán Cortés, was initially seen as a traitor. She has undergone reevaluation in recent decades by critics such as Cypess.

Works Cited

Brea, Jorge. "Population Dynamics in Latin America." *Population Bulletin* 58:1 (March 2003): 10–32.

Castro-Gómez, Santiago. "Los vecindarios de *La ciudad letrada*: Variaciones filosóficas sobre un tema de Ángel Rama." In Moraña, 123–33.

de Certeau, Michel. *The Practice of Everyday Life*. Trans. Steven Rendall. Berkeley: University of California Press, 1984.

Duncan, Nancy, ed. *Body Space*. London and New York: Routledge, 1996.

———. "Introduction: (Re)Placings." In Duncan, 1–10.

Fernández L'Hoeste, Héctor D. *Narrativas de representación urbana: un estudio de expresiones culturales de la modernidad latinoamericana*. New York: Peter Lang, 1998.

Franco, Jean. *The Decline and Fall of the Lettered City: Latin America in the Cold War*. Cambridge: Harvard University Press, 2002.

García Canclini, Néstor. *Culturas híbridas*. Mexico City: Grijalbo, 1989.

———. *Hybrid Cultures*. Trans. Christopher L. Chiappari and Silvia L. López. Minneapolis: University of Minnesota Press, 1995.

Harvey, David. *Urban Experience*. Baltimore: Johns Hopkins University Press, 1989.

Jones, Julie. *A Common Place: The Representation of Paris in Spanish American Fiction*. Lewisburg, Pa.: Bucknell University Press, 1998.

Joseph, Gilbert M., and Mark D. Szuchman, eds. *I Saw a City Invincible: Urban Portraits of Latin America*. Wilmington, Del.: Scholarly Resources, 1996.

Kirby, Kathleen. "ReMapping Subjectivity: Cartographic Vision and the Limits of Politics." In Duncan, 45–56.

Lefebvre, Henri. *Writings on the Cities*. Trans. and ed. Eleonore Kofman and Elizabeth Lebas. London: Blackwell, 1996.

Massey, Doreen. *Space, Place, and Gender*. Minneapolis: University of Minnesota Press, 1994.

Morales, Leonidas T. *Conversaciones con Diamela Eltit*. Santiago: Cuarto Propio, 1998.

Moraña, Mabel, ed. *Ángel Rama y los estudios latinoamericanos*. Pittsburgh: Instituto Internacional de Literatura Latinoamericana, 1997.

Nord, Deborah. *Walking the Victorian Streets: Women, Representation, and the City*. Ithaca, N.Y.: Cornell University Press, 1995.

Parsons, Deborah L. *Streetwalking the Metropolis: Women, the City, and Modernity*. Oxford: Oxford University Press, 2000.

Paz Soldán, Edmundo, and Debra Castillo, eds. *Beyond the Lettered City: Latin American Literature and Mass Media*. Ithaca, N.Y.: Cornell University Press, 2000.

Pile, Steve, and Nigel Thrift, eds. *Mapping the Subject: Geographies of Cultural Transformation*. London: Routledge, 1995.

Rama, Ángel. _La ciudad letrada_. Hanover, N.H.: Ediciones del Norte, 1984.

———. _The Lettered City_. Trans. and ed. John Charles Chasteen. Chapel Hill, N.C.: Duke University Press, 1996.

Remedi, Gustavo. "Ciudad letrada: Ángel Rama y la espacialización del análisis cultural." In Moraña, 97–122.

Resina, Joan Ramón, and Dieter Ingenschay, eds. _After-Images of the City_. Ithaca, N.Y.: Cornell University Press, 2003.

Rotker, Susana. _Citizens of Fear: Urban Violence in Latin America_. Trans. Katherine Goldman. New Brunswick, N.J.: Rutgers University Press, 2002.

Sassen, Saskia, ed. _Global Networks/Linked Cities_. New York and London: Routledge, 2002.

———. _Globalization and Its Discontents: Essays on the New Mobility of People and Money_. New York: New Press, 1998.

Schwartz, Marcy. _Writing Paris: Urban Topographies of Desire in Contemporary Latin American Fiction_. Albany: State University of New York Press, 1999.

Soja, Edward. _Postmodern Geographies: The Reassertion of Space in Critical Social Theory_. London: Verso, 1989.

Spitta, Silvia, and Boris Muñoz, eds. _Más allá de la ciudad letrada: crónicas y espacios urbanos_. Pittsburgh: Instituto Internacional de Literatura Iberoamericano, 2003.

Squier, Susan Merrill. _Women Writers and the City: Essays in Feminist Literary Criticism_. Knoxville: University of Tennessee Press, 1984.

Szuchman, Mark D. "The City as Vision—the Development of Urban Culture in Latin America." In Joseph and Szuchman, 1–31.

Williams, Raymond. _The Country and the City_. Oxford: Oxford University Press, 1973.

PART I
Mapping the City

1

Short Circuits

Gendered Itineraries in Recent
Urban Fiction Anthologies
from Latin America

MARCY SCHWARTZ

> ... what is poetry if not that desertion of the uses of the city?
> *Julio Cortázar on the dancer Rita Renoir*[1]

The Latin American city as a spatial, social, and cultural phenomenon has received much attention from the social sciences and cultural studies in recent years. Topics such as the patterns of urban violence, the emergence of the megalopolis, the city's environmental challenges, and public art confront earlier views that celebrate modernity and industrialization. Latin America's cities have earned a place in the study of globalization, particularly in current debates about neoliberalism. Latin American writing registers this reevaluation of urban space through revising generic categories that intersect with the city. Whereas the narrative "Boom" of the 1960s and 1970s launched the "nueva novela latinoamericana" as an urban genre that was almost entirely centered on male writers and masculine concerns, the resurgence of the *crónica* and the development of *testimonio* since the last part of the twentieth century occupy much of the urban writing scenario, featuring voices of subaltern and marginal sectors, often with a focus on popular culture.

Narrative fiction, however, has not abandoned the city, and women writers have contributed to refocusing the urban imagination since the Boom. Alongside the critical contestations of the cultural construct of the lettered city, recent anthologies of short fiction from Latin American cities offer new spatial imaginaries. In the following discussion I offer a reading of contemporary urban short-story collections in order to suggest some important revisionary strategies by women writing the city. This essay discusses short-story collections from and about Buenos Aires, Paris, San Juan, San José, São Paulo, and Rio de Janeiro where the contributions by women writers reconfigure the urban in Latin America.[2] The anthologies include *Buenos Aires: An Anthology of New Argentine Fiction* (*Buenos Aires: una antología de nueva ficción argentina*, Forn, 1992), *Seven Latin Americans in Paris* (*Siete latinoamericanos en París*, Ainsa, 2001), *The Infinite City: Versions of San Juan* (*La ciudad infinita: versiones de San Juan*, Fernández Zavala, 2000), *Stories of Secret San José* (*Cuentos del San José oculto*, Saraví, 2002), and *Urban Voices: Contemporary Short Stories from Brazil* (Ferreira-Pinto, 1999).[3] Although this does not pretend to be an exhaustive study, the appearance within some ten years of numerous anthologies of urban short fiction from an array of international publishers deserves attention as a symptom of urban "canonization" that calls for further examination.[4]

I have chosen to look at volumes that do not exclusively anthologize women writers as a means of uncovering the feminine and feminist voice within the intense production of urban writing over the last decade. The variety of spatial trajectories that these collections propose highlights the role of gender in the urban narrative imagination even more critically than anthologies of exclusively women writers. From belonging to displacement, nostalgic reflection to gritty alienation, these stories trace women's agency into the fictionalization of urban design. Their intercalation with fiction by men within these heterogeneous volumes, where they were chosen for their treatment of the city and not because they are women writers, gives their voice a more purposeful kind of agency. Although the scope of this essay does not permit an elaboration on canon formation and the role of anthologies in literary publishing and distribution, in the case of each of these anthologies the urban focus overrides considerations of gender. Reading the women's stories as a cross-cluster from a comparative angle reveals some particular common concerns. Three central topics among these stories form an interrelated network of feminist urban designs: a retreat into intimate, private space; a celebration of the body and sexuality; and a challenge to the concept of the lettered city. The discussion that follows offers examples of these central issues, an analysis of the narrative strategies these writers put to the service of these urban concerns, and the ways in which these issues interconnect with one another to reconfigure urban imaginaries.

INTIMATE SPACE: THE TORTUROUS REFUGE

Much of women's writing, and feminist thought, emphasizes breaking free of the interior spaces of the home and subjectivity. Luiza Lobo, in a discussion of Sonia Coutinho's fiction, takes note of "a new vein in women's writing which, while privileging the subjective, breaks out of the home both physically and stylistically, venturing into an epic mode and the tangled web of city streets" (163). Nevertheless, many of the stories by women in the urban anthologies under consideration here overturn the expectations of gendered spaces in contemporary fiction. They challenge sexist assumptions by (re)turning inward to domestic space. Writing often emanates from inside, off the streets, yet not necessarily to celebrate female subjectivity nor to denounce familial and societal sexist agendas. Instead, these narratives transform "home" into a voyeuristic scene or a charged metafictional zone. Rather than glorifying the internal subjective realm, these fictions reveal the torturous nature of urban interiors. Victims of split identities, of the informal immigrant economy, or of neighborhood terror and gossip, the protagonists of these stories struggle within domestic interior space.

The two stories that open Cristina Ferreira-Pinto's *Urban Voices* take the theme of urban alienation in new directions by maintaining the focus inside urban dwellings. "A Life Next Door" by Marina Colasanti and "Great Neighbors" by Tania Jamardo Faillace explore the paradox of intense identification and cold anonymity among urban neighbors. This first section of the anthology is subtitled "Walls," and clearly these stories render the walls permeable yet isolating. Colasanti's "A Life Next Door" in fact begins with an image of the fine line between one life and another in the urban realm: "[b]eyond the thin wall was the neighbor's life" (4). This very brief tale recounts the voyeuristic fascination of one neighbor with another. The protagonist becomes so familiar with the sounds of his neighbor's daily activities that he grows more and more "connected" to him, "absorbing his habits" (ibid.). He begins to pattern his own life after the neighbor's and eventually starts to spy on his coming and going. One day, watching him cross a busy street, he witnesses him being hit by a van. Quickly he sets to work building himself a coffin, so that it will be ready in time for the neighbor's wake next door.

The story that follows Colasanti's, Tania Jamardo Faillace's "Great Neighbors," also breaks down the walls between apartments for the reader, but simultaneously reveals the impenetrable boundaries between neighbors who do not communicate or reach out to each other, even in times of fear and crisis. This story is built of narrative fragments, separated by space on the page as well as by their alternating italicized and conventional type. Almost entirely told in dialogue, the irony of this story is the lack of communication screaming through the conversations. A brief reference, in dialogue, to "Little Red Riding Hood" introduces the story and the theme of vulnerability amid urban violence. While all the residents are watching television, doing needlework, or visiting with their families, they hear shooting outside in front of the building. A hung-over student, a military major and his family, a young couple, a grandmother reading right-wing Catholic articles, a teenager working on a school report on napalm, all engage in parallel but isolated discussions within their individual apartments about what the source of the gunshots might be: leftist insurgents, domestic violence, a police raid, or the result of a drunken fight. The conversations register the event as an interruption or intrusion, a mark against the decency of the neighborhood, a threat to the reputation of the building, or an impediment to the romantic mood between the young couple. Several think of calling the police, but no one does. Two residents mention that the major has a telephone and that he ought to call. Others comment that they expect to read about it in the papers the next day. One member of each conversation continually ignores the shooting, needing to be reminded that it just happened. The denial is confirmed by the building manager who toward the end of the story goes around to the various apartments and repeats, "It was really nothing . . . It won't even be in the papers tomorrow" (15). Several of the young people go out some time later, and find that "[a]ll over, staining the sidewalk, were dark, sticky footprints" (17).

The story begins and ends with ellipses, indicating the in medias res of the narration, giving the reader the sense of eavesdropping on ongoing conversations, turning the violence and its denial into a sinister, repetitive cycle. The narration converts the singular event of the shooting, reflected upon with banality and acceptance by the residents, into an episode of systematic political violence. Interior domestic space is neither safe nor intimate, but burdened by alienation and denial. One woman who had been waiting alone for her husband to return from his third job rushes over to him as he comes home to their apartment, asking what he had seen, whether the street was blockaded. He at first seems unaware of the shooting, but then answers as if he might have more to do with it than his wife thought: "'Now, now, honey, forget about that,' soothed her husband. 'One shot might not be such a bad thing anyway: empty the cuckoo's nest . . . You know, I really can't take it any more'" (15). The husband's casual attitude points to either denial or complicity, infantilizing his wife through fear and ignorance. The city's controls on information and communication silence the story such that the narration and its dialogue cover up the event rather than communicating it.

While outside the apartment walls occur events that residents may prefer to ignore, the close quarters inside often lead to controls that their occupants implement or to surprises for those who venture into them. The interior space of a San José luxury home in "Ejecución para dos manos derechas" (Performance for two right hands) by Myriam Bustos Arratia from the collection *Stories of Secret San José,* and a Parisian apartment in "La suplente" (The replacement) by Lira Campoamor Sánchez from *Seven Latin Americans in Paris,* form the basis of the plot in each story. In Campoamor Sánchez's story, when a Hispanic immigrant arrives to clean an apartment for the first time, replacing her Cuban colleague, she uncovers a surprise as she familiarizes herself with the interior of the apartment. Anxious about the job, she hopes that her presence will be "ephemeral, of no consequence," and continually calls this job "the first great change with order in my life."[5] She arrives punctually at midnight, wondering how her friend manages to find jobs at such strange hours, and recounts in the present tense and in halting detail her entrance into the apartment. She has been warned that she will be responsible for thirty-six Siamese cats that need to be kept inside. She does not find the small table she was told would be at the entrance, nor the piece of paper with instructions from the señora, nor the envelope with her pay. With the pacing of a suspenseful detective story, the woman moves tentatively through the apartment, turning on lights, hunting (unsuccessfully) for the paper with her instructions, until she comes upon a cadaver on the floor. The dark humor of the story catches up with the protagonist as her initial nervous hesitation about the job is legitimated when the apartment traps her in a crime scene.

In another story full of surprises, the owner of a spacious luxury home finds his retreat from the street in Myriam Bustos Arratia's "Ejecución para dos manos derechas." Certain that his newly purchased residence will be the solution to his writer's block, Belisario decides to dedicate each room to a kind of writing. He places a desk and bookshelves designated for specific genres in each of the rooms: one room is for personal letters, another for poetry, the next for journals of quotations and poetry, another for diaries, and the last for novels. He creates an internal lettered city within his home, and clearly considers writing a way to "flesh out ideas."[6] Writing is presented in this story as a material activity. Texts need the right kind of hands to shape and "turn them," poems need "rounding up" and "emergence."[7] Belisario strives to provide the "foundations" or the "other cloth" that will complete his compositions.[8] Nevertheless, his house arranged as writing laboratory still leaves him writing truncated, unfinished texts, stories with beginnings that are left undeveloped, poetic journeys initiated but left hanging.

Intercalated throughout Belisario's writing drama are fragments in italics that record the conversation of a patient with his psychiatrist, recounting a similar syndrome of unfinished texts. Slowly the story reveals that it is Belisario's twin brother Ernesto, living abroad, who suffers from the same writing disorder. The brothers are reunited when Belisario is diagnosed with cancer and asks his brother to come help care for him. During his recovery, he reveals to his brother that he has been unable to finish his creative texts, and Ernesto plunges in to complete them. What he reads astounds him, since he finds in Belisario's fragments the continuations of his own truncated works.

The trajectory of "Ejecución para dos manos derechas" is internal on several different levels; not only does the story take place inside the house but the plot also occupies the inner psyche of the characters, enters the connective bond between twin brothers, and emerges through the lonely activity of reading and writing. The house is a map for Belisario's writing fantasies, and when he sees it for the first time, he's convinced:

> seeing every space, every angle, every apex of the property, all visual windows and heart riled up from the emotion of finding himself not seeing it, but rather up to the depths of what seemed to be the exemplary den for his type of activity, determined with extreme urgency as the appropriate site to carry it out.[9]

The brothers go from writing texts marked by "hollows, continents stripped of contents," to recovering their collective voice.[10] The house serves as a vital zone of recuperation through writing. The male protagonists act in a passion play about writing and the space of literature. The romantic ideals of poetry in particular make this story more allegorical than metaphorical:

He destined for lyrical production the room next to the one for letters,
and he chose it because it had an atmosphere that he felt rosy and transparent, perfumed, even, with a sort of ancient and exotic aroma, perhaps
because behind the wide windows a tree, with a thick trunk and leaves of
an astonishing and extraordinarily satiny green, showed the splendidness
of its abundant clusters of flowers.[11]

The quest for identity, unity, and coherence of the self is guided simultaneously through language as space and space as language. That this story
is included in *Cuentos del San José oculto* is no accident; the only story by a
woman writer in this volume, it reveals a hidden, secret world of language
facilitated by architectural space.

CUERPO/CUENTO: FROM NARRATED BODIES TO CORPORAL TEXTS

Sara Castro-Klarén, in her introduction to a recent collection of essays
on feminist narrative, notes that one of the most promising movements
in feminist writing is "the return of the woman's body as a constitutive
part of the historical and with it the recuperation of the concept of lived
experience" (20). I choose to highlight three stories from these anthologies
that particularly feature the body as an urban topographical site: Márcia
Denser's "The Last Tango in Jacobina" from *Urban Voices,* and Ana María
Shua's "Cirugía menor" (Minor surgery) and Tununa Mercado's "Ver"
(Watching), both from *Buenos Aires.* Women's sexual expression adopts a
gritty tone in its urban contextualization in these stories. The city impacts
on physical encounters, frames and orients them, so that architectural confines and the urban design of roadways intersect with intimacy.

Diane Marting identifies the strong connection between sexuality and
the urban writing experience in a brief comment: "Indeed, writing about
sex has become almost obligatory in urban environments for many journalists and professional writers" (207). Although Marting's discussion
does not especially focus on the urban, as she traces the discourse of female
sexuality in Latin American fiction by women, she situates how the topic
of sexuality breaks through taboos beginning in the 1960s, coinciding
with the Boom in Latin American fiction and paralleling its urban concerns. The stories by Shua, Denser, and Mercado from urban anthologies
take on women's sexuality without falling into the generalizing, "gender-
transcending" trap that Marting eloquently exposes, nor do they adopt
sexuality's symbolic weight whereby the characters' sexuality determines

their relationship with society. Although women's writing on sexuality is "so frequently generalized to comment on gendered life experiences rather than the human qualities of a character" (Marting, 213), these stories distinguish themselves in their treatment of women's sexuality as a realm of experience that does not merely serve to limit and circumscribe their characters within gendered confines. Through the exploitation of urban space, the stories of Shua, Denser, and Mercado move beyond the equations of feminine sexuality with freedom and social-political critique to allow for narrative and subjective experimentation as well.

"Cirugía menor" by Ana María Shua, a writer well known for her treatment of women's sexuality, offers an effective narrative intersection of urban space and women's bodies. This story bridges this section to the previous topic, interior space, since the entire story takes place in a physician's office, an interior but alienating space for the protagonist. Shua's story concerns abortion, and presents the city as the site for reproductive freedom but exploitation of women through gendered medical services. Eventually a chapter in her novel *Los amores de Laurita* (1984), the story begins with a description of the illegal abortion clinic: "it's a house like the others on the block, a good house from the 1930s. It has two entrances and two stone gargoyle faces over each one."[12] Urban architecture structures the story, as the building's two entrances with stone gargoyle faces above them parallel Laura's bifurcating story about her decision to carry or abort the child she and Gerardo are expecting. Young and vulnerable, Laura suffers in the waiting room as she observes the assembly-line approach of this surgeon who operates on each of the women. Her second thoughts narratively occupy the rest of the story, imagining the continuation of the pregnancy with all of its physical transformations and her growing disaffection with Gerardo. The climax pulls the story back to the scene of the abortion, with graphic descriptions of Laura's position on the table, her feet in metal stirrups, her arms and legs strapped down. Her vulnerability, both emotionally and physically, wrenches the narrative back to the present reality, until she is led out of the office by her boyfriend into the taxi where they "begin to suspect that they don't love each other."[13] Devastating denial and contradiction disconnect Laura from her body, such that her story is encapsulated by the doctor's office as well as by her physical fantasy of a full-term pregnancy.

Denser's "The Last Tango in Jacobina" offers another view of sexuality in the city. This story exemplifies what I call urban grit, a rediscovery of the

city's seedy, greasy underside as a resistance to urban wealth and domination. Early on Denser's narrator pits the outside, fast-paced club life of
the young woman against dreary bourgeois boredom. She remembers her
mother sprawled on the red velvet couch, wearing a negligee, engaged in
continuous telephone calls,

> dragging the interminable telephone cord . . . a sort of Ariadne's thread
> that gradually winds around Chinese vases, statuettes, antique chests,
> bronze pedestals, Chippendale tables, disappearing under the drapes,
> under the heavy, perpetually closed curtains that filter a fine mist of
> hysterical particles, creating that gritty atmosphere of red and hot ashes
> of Pharaonic tombs. (179)

The story juxtaposes the family's upper-class São Paulo neighborhood with
lower-class outskirts, to underscore the material nature of the city. A few
initial descriptions characterize the city in tangible, concrete terms, introducing the physical attraction between the two unlikely partners: "It was a
hot, sunless Saturday, a sticky afternoon of sweat and steamy haze that
promised to drown the city at night as in a black barrel of asphalt" (182).

The "gritty atmosphere of red and hot ashes" foreshadows the tragic
ending of the story. Julia, the young protagonist, picks up her red Porsche
from Mingo, the mechanic, and decides to drive him around and then go
out drinking and dancing with him. He is clearly the "other" for her, a black
Northeasterner she is fascinated with for his difference. They go to a bar
where Julia as narrator remembers the sweat, grease, and heavy smoke in
the air. The Noches de Ronda bar "survived thanks to its clientele made
up of men with threadbare suits, young whores from the suburbs, police
investigators, trashy bohemians: the very best of the city mongrels" (187).
The place has "little greasy stools and minuscule tables . . . in that purplish
atmosphere saturated with smoke and lost illusions" (ibid.). Julia notes
the aroma of "sweat, booze and exhaustion" around the dancers (188), and
Mingo's scent of "sweat and gasoline" (189). At the end of the story, as she
leaves the bar and gets in her car to drive away, she traps Mingo between
the headlights and a post, "hot, sweet liquid running down my face, traces
of sweat, booze and dried up grease in the depths of my conscience, and
then the night blacked out" (190). Julia wakes up in a hospital bed, as the
story is narrated as a flashback during her recovery, the clean sheets contrasting with the grime of her urban adventure.

Tununa Mercado's voyeuristic narrative of female masturbation is
another tale of urban sexual adventure, one that converts the woman as

passive sexual object into an agent of autoerotic pleasure. The window of
an apartment on the top floor of a nineteenth-century building in Manhattan, on Tenth Street between Fifth and Sixth Avenues, serves as the stage
for a daily erotic performance. The third-person narrative voice is positioned with the unnamed male observer across the street who is captivated
for years by this repeated show of nudity, masturbation, and climax. Although the event is narrated only once, years after the observer has been
regularly enjoying the scene, the sequential indications make the event all
the more enticing. Every day a woman enters her apartment, undresses,
takes a bath, returns to the room naked, poses on the bed revealing her sex,
takes a phone call, and masturbates while talking on the phone. He would
sometimes resist the temptation to watch every day: "he compelled himself to not watch her, creating obligations for himself just at the time in
which she arrived or, even worse, he repressed his gaze, subjecting it to
a punishment that could be, according to the magnitude of the desire to
look that overtook him, the methodical reading of a book."[14] However,
the absence only enhanced the suspense and prolonged his desire: "If one
afternoon he had forced himself to elude contemplation, the mere idea
that the next day that omission would be amended had in him a cumula-
tive effect, as if the wait made him even more anxious to watch."[15] The
observer is aroused only through observation, and delays his climax until
hers, imagining the sounds of her breathing. At the end of the story, he
hangs up the receiver, suddenly revealing that he is the caller at the other
end of the line (87). Although the observer at the beginning of the story
is presented as an arbitrary, generic observer, by the end he has become
incorporated into the woman's pleasure either through the gradual narrative rapprochement and penetration, or through a fantastic move that
closes in on the denouement.

Mercado begins the story with the time and place, almost detectivesque
in its precision. The address of the building in the Greenwich Village neighborhood, where the bedroom window becomes a pornographic screen, is
repeated several times (81, 84, 86), providing an urban architectural frame
for the recurring scene. The woman's body itself, however, is the architecture that most clearly supports the story:

> The sex in the center of the scene, thus exposed, between two columns,
> like a hearth lit by the horde or like a bird's nest, or like a bramble of fire,
> or like a shrine, nearly obliges him to close his eyes, blinded by the flesh
> and by the body, by the girl and even by the feminine condition.[16]

The visual images here reveal an empowering presence. As Deborah Parsons demands in her study of urban modernist women writers in London and Paris, "[a] reanalysis of the historical depiction of the urban environment is . . . required for women to be recognized as observing subjects in the city" (224). Each of the stories in *Buenos Aires* includes a brief biographical note about the author and a personal statement by each writer about the story to follow. Mercado confesses here that she saw a scene like the one in "Ver" when she visited Juan Corradí in his apartment on Tenth Street in New York. She says the woman across the street "surrenders herself daily, always at the same time, for three nights straight, to a ceremony of love and passion."[17] She was captivated and watched every evening, while Corradí, having seen this many times already, took little interest. Her fascination engenders the story "that will manage to culminate in a dual, specular image of contradictory desires, and even of concerted desires."[18] That the story introduces a male observer, an urban voyeuristic convention, despite the author's revelation of the scene's origins, ironically offers the woman greater agency. The fictitious male observer is controlled by his desire for this repeated scene, while the anonymous woman takes pleasure in her autonomous role.[19] She sets the time and place, she determines the "encounter." The repeated mention of the street that separates them, "the street between them" or "the other side of the street," persistently imposes distance and anonymity that allow her the space for her sexual expression.[20] The voyeuristic scene told by the third-person narrator gives agency to the unnamed woman. She orchestrates the episode, night after night, starring in her own sexual show. Her desire is enacted although not voiced, because Mercado privileges the activity of her sexuality over the telling. The mute male observer, manipulated by her physical "discourse," comes under the spell(ing) of her repeated performance.

THE POST-LETTERED CITY FROM THE FEMININE IMAGINARY

I have contributed to collections whose titles refer to Latin American cultural production moving beyond the lettered city.[21] Although it was tempting to follow in this critical mode, my readings of these fiction anthologies point in some new directions with respect to Rama's overarching analysis of urban writing power in Latin America since colonialism. As Gustavo Remedi reminds readers in his contribution to a volume on Rama, *La ciudad letrada* only covers the urban cultural field in Latin America until the 1970s, and Rama's analyses need to be amended for more recent decades (Moraña, 112–15). Although Remedi considers the effect of mass-media communication ("the plugged-in city"), the corporatization of urban space ("the corporatized city"), the restrictions and compressions on public space, and the shifting roles of urban lettered institutions in Latin America at the end of the twentieth century, he leaves aside the impact of women rewriting the city (114).[22] The concept of a *post-lettered city*, a social space not just vaguely "beyond" but more critically *after* the earlier functioning of the written, stretches Rama's work on urban elite cultural space in the broadest contemporary perspective, where women's *writing*, not only their resistance, their orality, or their sexuality, can play a role. Susana Draper elaborates on Sandino Núñez's introduction of the term, and comments on how the post-lettered city seeks to "escape the useless distinction among the apocalyptic, the integrated (and other binarisms), and monumentalization ... The post-lettered city, as a current state of crisis and uncertainty, can also be a special moment to create another language, that is, to think in other ways."[23] The feminine and feminist voice is an essential avenue of this expansion, serving to reassess the power dynamic where earlier considerations of urban hegemony ignored women's experience and inscription. Moreover, women's written presence, as collections such as these demonstrate, does not merely fill in a previously empty category in a binary equation, but rather elaborates new and alternative visions for the city. Women's contributions to these recent anthologies help map some of its uncertain trajectories. These anthologies feature a great many stories— perhaps all of them—that contest, recast, or transcend aspects of Rama's lettered city, and some brief examples will trace how the women contributors question and offer alternative constructs through their engagement with urban writing.

Sylvia Iparraguirre's "Encontrando a Celina" (Finding Celina) from Forn's *Buenos Aires* revisits the categories of Rama's urban elite in a story that questions those very values and catches the reader in limbo with the protagonist between her Buenos Aires "lettered" life and the provincial town where she grew up. The gerund of the title indicates that this encounter is a process of recognition that the narrator/protagonist does not resolve. Iparraguirre comments in her brief introduction to this story that "in Médanos, as in nearly all similar towns in the world, the dilemma of adolescence (even at the end of the millenium, even at the end of history) will always be to stay or to go."[24] In the town resides Celina, the narrator's

old friend who married and had children instead of continuing her studies, while the narrator pursued her education in Buenos Aires. Celina only
wants to talk about books, hopes to finish her education, and pins all of her
expectations of cultured, lettered life on the capital city and on her recon-
nection to her old friend. Long, awkward dialogues make up most of the
story, during which the narrator begins to resent Celina's demands to help
her escape the confines of small-town family life through books and study
and her connections with the capital city. Celina's role in a community theater production cannot compare, she thinks, with her friend's urban experiences: "you must have seen so many good things in Buenos Aires, there
you can do everything."[25] Irritated with her simplistic idealization of the
city, the narrator blurts out: "in Buenos Aires nothing happens that's better
or worse than around here. Things aren't as they seem, people are bursting
with problems, people live badly, piled up in the trains . . . Look, the university, the theaters, all that means nothing, you understand?"[26] Driving
away from the visit, the narrator tears up a photograph of the two of them
that Celina had given her many years earlier. The story ends with an uncomfortable, unresolved tension. Each of the women resides in a different
urban conceptual moment, one in the "lettered" city and the other in a
"post-lettered" city. The two collide, but there is no room for compromise
or synthesis. Each of them has too much invested in either a private fantasy
(Celina) or an apologetic distance (the cosmopolitan, educated narrator)
to allow them to move out of their positions. The story registers the uneasy
transition of adulthood, of memory, of choices that seem to be simultaneously positions from which to move or change, and irrevocable determining stasis.

Another story from the *Buenos Aires* collection, Cecilia Absatz's "Rosenberg," more closely reconsiders the institutions of the "lettered" capital.
Absatz explores the world of urban journalism in all its corruption, tedium,
and sexism. Absatz's male, sexist narrator/protagonist writes for a newspaper and confronts the world from a defensive position. Having seen much
corruption and deception, he transfers the power dynamic of his profession and its pressures onto a gratuitously gendered imaginary world. He
calls his typewriter "a rough and noisy female that had to be raped with
every letter."[27] When his boss asks him to find out, secretly, the date that
the U.S. secretary of state will be meeting with a delegation from Chile, all
he can think about is escaping to the Caribbean. The "delicate" assignment
gives Rosenberg an unlimited expense account and as much time as he

needs. Like a gritty film noir, the city here functions as a concentration of communication, transportation, and diplomatic networks linked through writing (journalism). Rosenberg contemplates his fate from his office-building window, walks the city's streets, calls a travel agent, and finally heads to the airport. He calls his girlfriend to say good-bye from a tele-phone booth, and during the conversation he confirms the information his boss wanted, since she works for the U.S. embassy. He manipulates his married girlfriend, his boss, and his expense account in order to go to the Caribbean, where "You just have to lie in the sand and sleep. If you're hungry you can eat a papaya. You don't even have to climb the tree to look for it; when it's ripe it falls to the ground and opens, lascivious and red like a whore."[28]

"Rosenberg" dichotomizes the urban and nonurban according to his lettered profession as a journalist in Buenos Aires and his imagined vaca-tion on a Caribbean beach. The potential for infiltrating international intelligence, a compromising position of the investigative apparatus of the press, the secretive status of the U.S. and Chilean meeting resonant of the violent history of the Dirty Wars in the Southern Cone, all converge in the city through its lettered intelligentsia. The sexualized metaphors generated within the male narrator/protagonist's internal monologue have been scripted by a woman writer. "Rosenberg"'s detectivesque exploita-tion of the city turns on Absatz's ironic gender role transposition, whereby the narrator becomes the object of the reader's urban gaze. He uses and abuses the city from his position within the urban lettered class through the projection of his gendered, sexist imagination onto both urban and nonurban realms.

Several stories in *Urban Voices* design the urban via the cities' streets and movement through them. The Balzacian realist conventions of the urban grid collide with rather extreme experimental narratives in two stories by Helena Parente Cunha and Regina Célia Colônia from *Urban Voices*. Both situated in the section titled "Streets," these stories map the city onto the pages of the anthology and generate the urban noise, conges-tion, and bustle of early-morning encounters. Parente Cunha's "The Traffic Light" and Colônia's "Copacabana from 5 to 7" re-create place through a conjunction of time and space. Like a Bakhtinian chronotope, each of the stories enmeshes the moment, the scenario, and the space of reading.

Parente Cunha's story begins directly with its temporality and names the place: "8 in the morning. At the corner of Bento Lisboa Street and

Machado Plaza. The traffic light, the sun turned on, the sky turned off" (132). The short tale is told in one long paragraph of short, percussive, rhythmic, impressionistic phrases. The constriction of the discourse (some sentences are just one word) and consolidation of the prose (there are no paragraph or section breaks or pauses other than the fast-paced punctuation of periods) re-create the urban intersection, as the texture of the discourse imitates the confluence of noises, sensations, traffic, and people on this particular street corner one morning. The narration details the urban textures as a prostitute and her client are concluding their transaction. He pays her on the street corner and they are in the process of parting, but while she wants to get away, he continues to have a hold on her. During the seven minutes and nineteen seconds in which the story occurs, there is a car accident, a robbery, and dozens of other smaller urban occurrences. The text enumerates stark images of asphalt, blood, gravel along the curb, exhaust fumes, tires on the pavement, heels hitting the sidewalk, and the traffic light changing from red to green and back to red. The story captures the human drama of the couple parting in the midst of urban exchanges where the intersection and its activity surround the woman. As Parente Cunha reveals in the middle of the story, the woman's desire to be finished, to move away, to no longer be trapped at the corner, seems not strong enough to resist and escape "[t]he roaring of the gesture" (134).

Colônia's "Copacabana from 5 to 7" also exploits the narrative pacing and the space on the page in order to generate a morning map of its city. The facing left and right pages of the story offer parallel accounts. The left side offers a public, plural (tourists, school kids, grocers, domestic workers, pigeons), and mobile perspective, while the one on the right gives an individualized account of Rodrigo's last dream and waking. The breaks on the left-side pages coincide with the brief account of Rodrigo on the right. The choppy, fragmented structure of "Copacabana from 5 to 7" re-creates the movement of the workers and inhabitants of the story, as the narration introduces individuals with information about their family, where they live, and what time they must wake up in order to get to Copacabana. The center and the periphery intertwined, the beach resort functions thanks to its streets via which the workers in the economy of daily urban migration can come and go. The story demands that we, like the inhabitants, "stop seeing each street in its nocturnal depth, to perceive it stretching out: its previous connections and the ones up ahead, bridges that lead to other signs. The dynamic of the image being, at this hour, that of joining together moving parts, replaceable ones, whose combination produces meaning and a new object" (117).

In these two stories, the cultural city confronts the commercial city, unseating conventional hierarchies and classist conceptions in a literary challenge to yet another urban dichotomy. Colônia forces the lettered institutions—museums, libraries, galleries, schools, ministries, pharmacies—to interact with the institutions of other urban economies such as markets, transportation, restaurants, hotels, bars, health clubs, sanitation. Both this story and "The Traffic Light" represent the urban through concrete forms on the page, rhythmic composition, and experimentation with the city's materiality by uncovering informal and formal economies at work.

TEXTUAL BORDERS: WOMEN'S VOICING IN NARRATIVE CODAS

The organization and order of texts in these anthologies vary from a careful construction of architectural and spatial subsections in *Urban Voices* to seemingly more random arrangements in some of the others. However, two of the volumes stand out in their placement of women writers in positions that guide the reader's orientation to urban imaginaries. *Urban Voices* and *The Infinite City* begin and end with very short prose pieces by women. As portals into and out of these volumes, they highlight women as definitive urban voices.

The Infinite City: Versions of San Juan, a large-format art book with poetry alongside the reproductions of paintings, was sponsored by the San Juan Puerto Rican Commission for the Celebration of the Year 2000, a municipal and mayoral initiative. The collection was produced initially as a limited boxed edition of three hundred numbered folios signed by both artists and authors.[29] The introduction to the book by Margarita Fernández Zavala states:

> This gathering of creators represents a variety of generations and approaches whose production together gives an idea of the wide spectrum of experiences, possibilities, dreams, risks, myths, and fantasies that the city of San Juan tends to propose.[30]

The prologue is by well-known Puerto Rican writer Magali García Ramis and the penultimate piece is by Aurea María Sotomayor. These are in fact the only prose works included in the volume, and although they may not conform to conventional ideas of the short story, they narratively frame the book's varied visual and verbal gallery.

García Ramis's "...Del color de la ciudad" (On the color of the city) serves to introduce the volume, nearly telling the story of this visual/verbal celebration of San Juan. A verbal painting of the city's hues, from the walled Viejo San Juan to the university to the crowded buses on the streets, rather than attempting to describe the visual work in this project, it offers her own. Like a *modernista crónica* of urban impressions, she records the social, geographic, and material vibrancy of the city. Gulls, students, fishermen, food carts all watch, traverse, and occupy their perches.

This prologue incorporates a metafictional, almost documentary tone. Like Borges's games of *mise en abîme,* where a story about a map suggests including the map on the map, García Ramis introduces *The Infinite City* with a poetic narration of itself. The first paragraph hints at the visual reproductions included:

> The man is black, the city is multicolored. Its colonial homes are repeated in a hundred lithographs, in a million postcards, in the old memories of its many inhabitants.[31]

The visual, the verbal, and the social all dynamically write and paint and occupy the city. Even more specifically to this project, however, García Ramis episodically includes the gatherings that produced the collection:

> And in a neighboring street, in front of a pink Art Deco house and a food business covered with orange plastic, a row of stalled cars where the architects and poets go, the only ones that dream the city . . . In a curve, walking by appear the painters . . . The city between two waters has lights that don't deceive, hand to hand, verse by verse, light of the moon or brushstrokes.[32]

This introduction makes a story out of the project itself, includes its gathering of creative contributors (the introduction mentions that the writers and artists did have some encounters in the process of the book's production) as an urban happening in its own right.

Sotomayor's brief narrative appears before a print by Jorge Zeno of the sea, and is framed with verbal images of desiring the sea. Concluding with "But I have the sea," this prose poem surrounds the island from the sea's perspective, "to go over the land from the sea. To look at the island from the sea."[33] Sotomayor begins with an epigraph by Italo Calvino ("Lying is not in discourse, it is in things"), launching an exploration into the words that might be energized to describe a city. Evoking and synthesizing Foucault's *Les mots et les choses,* shy of declaring verbal language insufficient, Sotomayor situates the city bracketed by the sea, a floating consolidation of desires. "A meadow in the city provides escapes and occupations, offers the twenty facets of desire speculating about itself in twenty subtly creative surfaces . . . And as in the gaze characters are assigned, so in letters routes are made ghosts."[34] Although names and words may have limits, the sea is infinite, and the infinite city of this project relies on these verbal tracings, these itineraries of language.

The first and last brief stories in Ferreira-Pinto's *Urban Voices* are by Marina Colasanti, "A Life Next Door" (discussed earlier) and "A Shooting Star in the City Sky." The former introduces the book's first section, "Walls," while the latter provides the book's "Exit." The last fragment of *Urban Voices* includes the gritty ("dingy"), alienating patterns of urban life in bloody cement, arbitrary floor plans, and neighbors who do not address one another (245). The final image, however, shifts the mood by opening toward the sky and rethinking an acrobat's tragic fall: ". . . they perceive the wire stretched taut high up, an improbable route between two buildings, a knife stroke cutting the darkening sky" (ibid.). This surprise lifting out of the gloomy urban scene juxtaposes a (probably) fatal fall with a shooting star. These contradictory movements upward and down guide our image of the city, countering the horizontal movement of the *flâneur.* Depending on and *contributing to* the city's architectural structure and skyline, both the high wire and the buildings suggest alternative avenues. They fantastically question the maps of urban writing, and leave indeterminate the outcomes of the city's multiple trajectories.

In the introduction to *Urban Voices,* editor Ferreira-Pinto makes a special mention of Colasanti's position in both the opening and closing texts:

> Her story "A Shooting Star in the City's Sky," in the final section, "Exit,"
> offers the reader precisely this: a door that leads out of the Brazilian
> urban space, but that also takes us back, forming a complete circle.
> Colasanti's story has the diminutive quality of a small jewel; it is a bright
> star apparently destined to fade against the dull horizon of everyday
> urban life—a life that is frequently mechanical, often unfulfilling,
> sometimes repressive. Yes this star represents also the persistence of those
> visionaries who insist on going against the probabilities, and in so doing
> shake us out of our routines. Thus, if the stories in this anthology let us
> glimpse at a sometimes gloomy or melancholic portrait of Brazilian
> society, Colasanti's story is a final reminder that there *is* an exit. (xxv)

The editor's inspirational statement, more extensive than the piece it describes, contributes to this architectural framing by women's voices. Calling attention to her conscious use of Colasanti's texts as the anthology's "bookends" underscores the metadiscursivity of the individual texts as well as of the activity of composing such anthologies. The spatial design operating on multiple levels, textually and editorially, adds complexity to these collections precisely *because* they are urban.

CONCLUSION: ANTHOLOGIZING URBAN DESIGN

Although the concept "urban writing" in Latin America is almost a redundancy since Rama, the inscription of women's voices onto the city has emerged more recently with an assertiveness that these anthologies capture and celebrate. Whether contesting the lettered city, exploring the body and sexuality, or redefining interior spaces, these women write the city not to offer women a place in the urban experience (which none of them doubt she already has), but rather to reexamine her subjectivity and her agency within the urban experience. As Parsons reminds us:

> The urban writer is not only a figure within a city; he/she is also the producer of a city, one that is related to but distinct from the city of asphalt, brick, and stone, one that results from the interconnection of body, mind, and space, one that reveals the interplay of self/city identity. (Parsons, 1)

Parsons continues by reviewing how the city historically has been conceived as a male space, "in which women are either repressed or disobedient marginal presences" (2). The versions and visions of the city according to the writers anthologized in these Latin American collections of the past ten to fifteen years fictionally reposition both men and women in the urban power dynamics of class, education, and social geography. Frequently, the protagonists of these stories are men who occupy familiar roles as journalists, voyeurs, lovers, and writers. These are stories that largely avoid the autobiographical in exchange for the allegorical. When there are autobiographical elements, they are subsumed under a broader purpose, often substituting the gender of the characters involved, transposing the recalled event and recounting it in order to exploit its urban situatedness. Bodies, buildings, borders, and bureaucracy interact in urban writing, where contemporary women have veered away from the conventional concerns of the public and the private, or turn those dichotomies on end. These writers launch new itineraries for urban design, and their stories share an uneasy, indeterminate, gritty recovery of the city's possibilities.

NOTES

1. "...qué otra cosa será la poesía sino esa deserción de los usos de la ciudad" (17). See his essay "Homenaje a una joven bruja" (17–26). All translations are mine, except from the Brazilian anthology published in English translation.

2. I have decided not to focus on Mexico City in this study because other contributors to the volume discuss Mexican writing. However, I would like to mention the collections by Quirarte and Miklos on Mexico City that are contemporaneous with the anthologies I have included in my study.

3. Two of these collections, *La ciudad infinita* and *Cuentos del San José oculto*, incorporate visual art as well, the first sponsored by the mayor's office for the municipal celebration of San Juan in the year 2000, the second published by the San José art gallery Andrómeda, an organization that is active in multimedia projects among writers and artists.

4. Very few specifically *urban* anthologies have appeared in recent years, and the titles discussed here form a contemporaneously cohesive corpus. According to Daniel Balderston's annotated bibliography of Latin American short-fiction anthologies, only a handful of Brazilian collections in the 1960s and 1970s, and a small number of Mexican anthologies from the 1980s, rely on the urban as a thematic concept. The cluster of titles I touch on here confirms that the urban as an organizing principle for anthologies gains ground in the 1990s. Volumes such as those edited by Blunt and Rose, and by Higonnet and Templeton, attest to literary space in women's writing gaining more attention across national literary boundaries in the 1990s.

5. "efímera, y sin ninguna consecuencia" (49); "el primer gran cambio con orden en mi vida" (first mentioned on page 39; subsequently repeated on pages 43, 46, 50, 53).

6. "corporizar las ideas" (67).

7. "tornearlos," "redondeamiento," and "afloramiento" (70–71).

8. "cimientos" (87), "otra tela" (69).

9. "[V]iendo cada espacio, cada ángulo, cada vértice del inmueble, todo ventanas visuales y corazón encabritado por la emoción de hallarse no viéndola, sino metido hasta el fondo de la que aparecía como guarida ejemplar para el tipo de actividad suya, precisada con extrema urgencia de sitio adecuado para realizarla" (57).

10. "[H]ondonadas," "continentes despojados de contenidos" (81).

11. "A la producción lírica destinó la habitación que se hallaba a la par de la habilitada para las epístolas, y la escogió porque tenía una atmósfera que él sentía

rosada y transparente, perfumada, incluso, de un suerte de aroma antiguo y exótico, tal vez porque tras los vidrios del amplio ventanal mostraba la esplendidez de sus abundantes flores arracimadas, un árbol de grueso tronco y hojas de un verde insólito y extraordinariamente satinado" (62).

12. "Es una casa como las demás de la cuadra, una buena casa de los años treinta. Tiene dos entradas y dos caras gargoladas, de piedra, sobre cada una" (121).

13. "empiezan a sospechar que no se quieren" (128).

14. "[S]e obligaba a no verla creándose obligaciones justo a la hora en que la muchacha llegaba o, peor aún, reprimía su mirada sujetándola a un suplicio que podría ser, según la magnitud del deseo de ver que de él se apoderara, la lectura metódica de un libro" (84).

15. "Si una tarde se había forzado en eludir la contemplación, la sola idea de que al día siguiente esa omisión iba a ser reparada, tenía en él un efecto de acumulación, como si la espera del otro día lo cargara aún más de ganas de ver" (84).

16. "El sexo en el centro de la escena, así expuesto, entre dos columnas, como un hogar encendido por la horda o como un nido de pájaros, o como un zarza de fuego, o como un sagrario, lo obliga casi a cerrar los ojos, enceguecido de la carne y del cuerpo, de la muchacha y hasta de la condición femenina" (85).

17. "[S]e entrega cotidianamente, a la misma hora siempre, durante tres noches seguidas, a una ceremonia de amor y de pasión" (80).

18. "[que] logrará cerrarse en una imagen dual, especular, de deseos enfrentados, e incluso de deseos concertados" (ibid.).

19. See Judith Garber's article for a provocative sociological discussion of the politics of urban anonymity. She concludes that anonymity can limit representation and can work against political projects, and she signals identification as the counter side of anonymity. Her brief mention of sexual anonymity does not explore much beyond anonymity's protection of prostitutes, or gay and lesbian individuals who seek to avoid being recognized and exploited or persecuted (32).

20. The narrator refers to the "calle de por medio" (80) and "al otro lado de la calle" (87).

21. I refer to "Cortázar under Exposure" and "Del extrañamiento al exilio."

22. Remedi calls these "la ciudad enchufada" and "la ciudad corporativizada," respectively. Clearly, cultural critics such as Néstor García Canclini and Jesús Martín-Barbero have taken the analysis of urban institutional mechanisms in these directions, but they fall short when it comes to uncovering the gendered dimensions of those processes. Carlos Monsiváis and Beatriz Sarlo most aggressively address the role of women as agents and the images of urban writing and urban culture in the media, in education, and throughout the popular and historical development of the city.

23. "[E]scapar al inútil par de lo apocalíptico o lo integrado (y demás binarismos), y a la monumentalización... La ciudad posletrada, como estado actual de

crisis e incertidumbre, puede ser también un momento especial para crear otro lenguaje, esto es, para pensar de otros modos" (Draper, 46).

24. "[E]n Médanos, como en casi todos los pueblos similares del mundo, la disyuntiva de la adolescencia (aun en el fin del milenio, aun en el fin de la historia) será siempre irse o quedarse" (162).

25. "[V]os habrás visto tantas cosas buenas en Buenos Aires, allá se puede hacer de todo" (174).

26. "[E]n Buenos Aires no pasa nada ni mejor ni peor que acá. Las cosas no son como parecen, la gente revienta de problemas, la gente vive mal, amontonada en los trenes... Mirá, la facultad, los teatros, todo eso no significa nada, ¿entendés?" (174).

27. "una hembra tosca y ruidosa a la que había que violar en cada letra" (147).

28. "Sólo hay que acostarse en la arena y dormir. Si uno tiene hambre se come una papaya. Ni siquiera hay que subirse al árbol a buscarla; cuando está madura se cae al suelo y se abre, lasciva y roja como una puta" (151).

29. I am working with the printed catalog edition that also was published in 2000.

30. "Esta pléyada de creadores representaría una diversidad generacional y de enfoques cuyo producto conjunto habría de dar una idea del amplio espectro de experiencias, posibilidades, sueños, riesgos, mitos y fantasías que la ciudad de San Juan suele proponer" (4).

31. "El hombre es negro, la ciudad es multicolor. Sus casas coloniales se repiten en cien serigrafías, en un millón de postales, en la memoria de antaño de sus tantos habitantes" (7).

32. "Y en una calle vecinal, frente a una casa rosa Arte Deco y a un negocio de comida forrado de plástico anaranjado, una hilera de carros atascados donde van los arquitectos y los poetas, los únicos que sueñan la ciudad... En un recodo, caminando de frente aparecen los pintores... La ciudad entre dos aguas tiene luces que no engañan, mano a mano, verso a verso, luz de luna o pinceladas" (8).

33. "Mas tengo al mar... recorrer la tierra desde el mar. Mirar la isla desde el mar" (63).

34. "Un prado en la ciudad depara fugas y ocupaciones, obsequia las veinte facetas del deseo especulándose en veinte superficies sutilmente creativas... Y así como en la mirada se asignan caracteres, así en las letras se afantasman las rutas" (63).

Works Cited

Ainsa, Fernando. *Siete latinoamericanos en París.* Madrid: Popular, 2001.

Balderston, Daniel, comp. *The Latin American Short Story: An Annotated Guide to Anthologies and Criticism.* Westport, Conn.: Greenwood, 1992.

Blunt, Alison, and Gillian Rose, eds. *Writing Women and Space: Colonial and Post-colonial Geographies.* New York and London: Guilford, 1994.

Castro-Klarén, Sara, ed. *Narrativa femenina en América Latina: prácticas y perspectivas teóricas.* Frankfurt: Verveut and Madrid: Iberoamericana, 2003.

Cortázar, Julio. *Territorios.* Mexico City: Siglo XXI, 1978.

Draper, Susana. "Cartografías de una ciudad posletrada: *La república de Platón* (Uruguay, 1993–1995)." *Revista Iberoamericana* 69.202 (2003): 31–49.

Fernández Zavala, Margarita, ed. *La ciudad infinita: versiones de San Juan.* San Juan: Municipio de San Juan, 2000.

Ferreira-Pinto, Cristina, ed. *Urban Voices: Contemporary Short Stories from Brazil.* Lanham, Md.: University Press of America, 1999.

Forn, Juan, ed. *Buenos Aires: una antología de nueva ficción Argentina.* Barcelona: Anagrama, 1992.

Franco, Jean. *The Decline and Fall of the Lettered City: Latin America in the Cold War.* Cambridge: Harvard University Press, 2002.

Garber, Judith A. "'Not Named or Identified': Politics and the Search for Anonymity in the City." In *Gendering the City: Women, Boundaries and Visions of Urban Life,* ed. Kristine B. Miranne and Alma H. Young. Lanham, Md.: Rowman and Littlefield, 2000. 19–39.

Higonnet, Margaret, and Joan Templeton, eds. *Reconfigured Spheres: Feminist Explorations of Literary Space.* Amherst: University of Massachusetts Press, 1994.

Lobo, Luiza. "Sonia Coutinho Revisits the City." In *Latin American Women's Writing: Feminist Readings in Theory and Crisis,* ed. Anny Brooksbank Jones and Catherine Davies. Oxford: Clarendon, 1996. 163–78.

Marting, Diane E. "Dangerous (to) Women: Sexual Fiction in Spanish America." In *Narrativa femenina en América Latina, Prácticas y perspectivas teóricas,* ed. Sara Castro-Klarén. Frankfurt: Verveut and Madrid: Iberoamericana, 2003. 197–219.

Miklos, Daniel, comp. *Una ciudad mejor que ésta: antología de nuevos narradores mexicanos.* Polanco, Mexico: Tusquets, 1999.

Moraña, Mabel, ed. *Ángel Rama y los estudios latinoamericanos.* Pittsburgh: Instituto Internacional de la Literatura Iberoamericana, Serie Críticas, 1997.

Parsons, Deborah L. *Streetwalking the Metropolis: Women, the City, and Modernity.* Oxford: Oxford University Press, 2000.

Quirarte, Vicente. *Elogio de la calle: biografía literaria de la ciudad de México.* Mexico City: Cal y Arena, 2001.

Remedi, Gustavo. "Ciudad letrada: Ángel Rama y la espacialización del análisis cultural." In *Ángel Rama y los estudios latinoamericanos,* ed. Mabel Moraña. Pittsburgh: Instituto Internacional de la Literatura Iberoamericana, Serie Críticas, 1997. 97–122.

Saraví, Tomás, ed. *Cuentos del San José oculto.* San José: Andrómeda, 2002.

Schwartz, Marcy. "Cortázar under Exposure: Photography and Fiction in the City." In *Beyond the Lettered City: Latin American Literature and Mass Media,* ed. Debra Castillo and José Edmundo Paz-Soldán. Garland Press, 2000. 117–38.

———. "Del extrañamiento al exilio: el 'no-lugar' urbano en la ficción hispanoamericana de fin de siglo XX." In *Más allá de la ciudad letrada: crónicas y espacios urbanos,* ed. Silvia Spitta and Boris Muñoz. Pittsburgh: Instituto Internacional de Literatura Iberoamericana, 2003. 333–51.

2
What Happened to the Cool City?
Seventy Years of
Women's Narrative in Brazil

LIDIA SANTOS

O Arnesto [sic] nos convidou
Prum [sic] samba (ele mora no Brás).

Arnesto invited us
To a samba (he lives in Brás).

Adoniran Barbosa, "O Samba do Arnesto"

MAPPING THE CITY

It is not surprising that women writers in the last seven decades have changed the face of fiction in Brazil from the moment they began to include the urban environment in their narratives. The concept of the citizen solidified during the Enlightenment suffers a strong setback when the woman writer creates female characters in the city. Inevitably, such characters are forced to confront a concept of subject that does not correspond to themselves, since it implies an individual of the male sex, proprietor and patriarch (Serret, 104; Santos, 956). The first manifestations of the feminist movement are characterized by the demand that equal rights, as established during the Enlightenment, be extended to women. Thus, in its beginnings, the women's social movement was based on the same ethics that excluded them in the first place. In the last decades of the twentieth century, the very validity of a female subject's claims was questioned, since the notion of the moral subject, as established in the period of modernity, fell into crisis.

In response to this crisis of the subject, theorist Seyla Benhabib has initiated a new tendency in women's studies. The novelty in Benhabib's thought consists in recuperating the moral and political project of modernity from the gains obtained with postmodern feminist theory. With it,

Benhabib disregards the abstraction and individualism of the category of subject as formulated in the eighteenth century, and replaces this abstraction with the idea of a concrete human being, related to others, acting in a historical and cultural context where the life experiences of women cannot be excluded. Although I recognize that such a concept, as an internal critique of the philosophical project of the Enlightenment, maintains its liberal foundations, I will embrace here Benhabib's idea of an "interactive universalism," a proposition that substitutes the "legislative" universalism, that is, a normative one, with the constitution of a project based on "ethical relationships," which includes a "critical theory of society and culture." Stemming from this theoretical base, I will also investigate the relationship between the concept of citizenship established by the liberalism of the eighteenth century and women's new subjectivities, as defined in the twentieth century.

My intention in selecting writers for this study was to find unusual angles in cities, urban portraits indissolubly linked to the unconventional experiences of women who were reinventing the female role. From there emerges a certain interference of biography in the works read, a certain preference for the *muses of the city*.[1] I understand the role of muse not as an objectifying one created by the male gaze. Rather, I believe that the authors themselves forged such a role, both in life and in literature. Included in the seduction exercised by these women, the part of muse was the weapon they chose to guarantee their survival in the hostile environment of the cities in which they lived. The feminine perception works, in the majority of the chosen authors, through metonym or, more precisely, in the use of the detail (Schor). In contrast to the total city designed by Brazilian modernist male writers, the women focused on specific neighborhoods within the city.

Following their choice, I have transformed some of these zones into obligatory stops in the cognitive map of this essay. São Paulo emerges here through Brás, a working-class neighborhood mythicized through popular music, as in the lyric of the samba quoted in the epigraph. A song by Adoniran Barbosa (1910–82), one of the most prolific popular composers of São Paulo, is part of the collective memory of the Paulistano.[2] The identification of the rhythm of samba with Brás confirms its description by Patrícia Galvão in her 1930s novel *Industrial Park*, as a working-class neighborhood. This type of community in São Paulo reemerges at the end of this essay through the work of Teresa Caldeira, whose anthropological research has helped me to understand the writings of Patrícia Melo in the 1990s. The city of Rio de Janeiro, in turn, appears through Copacabana, the neighborhood where Clarice Lispector lived most of her life and where Sonia Coutinho places the stories I discuss here. Finally, a short note regarding the presence of a *no-neighborhood* in the female literature of the black diaspora, exemplified by the novel *Ponciá Vicêncio* (2003), by Conceição Evaristo, closes the essay. Through the hands of these authors, I travel ahead and invite the reader to follow.

PAGU, WHO LIVED IN THE BRÁS OF THE 1920S

The work of the Brazilian writer Patrícia Galvão, or Pagu (1910–62), can be taken as a starting point in the examination of a new conceptualizing of the female subject, especially with regard to the urban context. Rediscovered in the 1960s, Pagu's work was reedited in the 1970s and 1980s as that of an avant-garde writer.[3] In 1980, she was transformed into a cinematographic character (Andrade and Tassara; Benguell; Branco). Nevertheless, despite this homage, Patrícia Galvão has not yet earned deserved attention from Brazilian feminist critics. In a survey of literature written by women in Brazil, Nelly Novaes Coelho refers to the author as a "polemical figure" of an "extremely agitated" life, and says "it is still necessary to wait" before assessing Pagu's literary contributions.[4] Critics' reservations may be owing in part to Pagu's commitment to the Communist Party at the time she wrote *Industrial Park* (1933). Even in the 1930s, her conversion to communism may have been seen as a betrayal of the upper-class scene that surrounded the Cannibalism artistic movement, to which she was linked at a young age.[5] Until she joined the Communist Party, Pagu was a sort of enfant terrible among the golden youth of São Paulo, having participated in the hip bohemian circles of the then provincial city. In the center of the party, on the other hand, her petit bourgeois origin provoked special treatment and exacerbated discipline. This is shown by the party directors' demand that she publish *Parque Industrial* under a pseudonym; Pagu chose "Mara Lobo." After this followed other pseudonyms, under which she published poems and journalistic articles. In addition to her controversial political stance, this confusion of names further contributed to her work having to be rediscovered years later.

Obedient to the party rules, Patrícia Galvão subtitles *Industrial Park* as a "working-class novel." According to Coelho, the explicit political tone and propagandistic style of the text was responsible for the refusal on the part of her contemporary critics to consider her text a literary work. Afterwards, the emphasis of feminist critics on self-knowledge and the subsequent denunciation of the exclusion of women in the Marxist model of class oppression assured, once again, that Pagu's legacy would remain obscured. In my reading of *Industrial Park* I would like to rescue not only the anticipation with which the author traced the exclusion of women from citizenship in modern times, but also the ethical stance that she applied in dealing with these issues. This path attempts to be faithful to Pagu herself. Rejecting the straitjacket that the Communist Party had imposed on itself since Stalinism, she disassociated herself from the party in the 1940s. Nevertheless, in her journalistic and theatrical practice, to which she dedicated the last phase of her short life, Pagu continued to preach humanism. The ferocious criticism she applied to both her former comrades and literary circles in her last writings demonstrates how she remained attuned to the country's intellectual dynamics.

Pagu's role in literary circles began early; she was a beautiful woman and the muse of Brazilian modernism, which she became acquainted with while still in secondary school. The permanence of her image in Brazilian culture has been shown in the press brochure of the Brazilian visual art exhibition at New York City's Guggenheim Museum in 2001, *Brazil: Body and Soul,* which reproduced a famous painting, *Cinco Moças de Guaratinguetá* (1930) by the modernist Di Cavalcanti (1897–1976); Pagu's portrait occupies the foreground of the work (Di Cavalcanti, 2001). In another painting of the same period, *Moça de Guaratinguetá* (1929), Pagu's image dominates the entire plane of the picture, her figure encompassing the frame. This confirms the centrality of Pagu's beauty in the artistic avant-garde circles of Brazilian modernism. It is worth asking why Patrícia Galvão, whose times and politics were similar to those of Frida Kahlo, has not received from feminist critics the attention showered upon the Mexican painter. Apart from Kahlo's undeniable talent, I believe her persona is more useful to the discussion of biopolitics by the feminism of difference.[6] Rather than establishing Pagu as a figurehead of an interactive universalism, I am looking to her for the expression of a feminism that is able to unite the questioning of the single and immutable subject with issues of social inequality that do not disappear in impoverished countries like Brazil. On the contrary, economic inequality increases vertiginously with the implementation of the neoliberal model. In life, Galvão already paid the price of hero formation preached by the Communist Party. We shall then leave Galvão the muse and instead follow the literary work that she has crafted.

Industrial Park, if not a feminist tale, is, without a doubt, a novel about women. The narrative is centered on women of different classes, especially working-class women. Alfredo Rocha, the only male character fictionally developed, is a bourgeois figure consumed by his contradictions. The majority of critics dedicated to the work of Pagu recognize in the character traces of her first husband, the modernist writer Oswald de Andrade. Although qualified as an "industrial park" through the Marxist model, the São Paulo that makes up the environment of her novel is restricted to downtown and to Brás, the neighborhood where Galvão was born and raised. By introducing the issue of women's lives in the plot, Pagu gives an original accent to the modernist model of the city, characteristic of male intellectuals of her generation. For these men, velocity and machines were seductive, whereas for Pagu, the accelerated rhythm evokes the menacing dominance of the machine over women. For example, in the novel's description of the work at the factory, the women are "automatons" (16).

Industrial Park makes explicit another possible reason for the refusal on the part of feminist literary circles to consider Pagu's legacy. The novel takes it upon itself to explain, in the socialist model, the oppression of the bourgeoisie on São Paulo's working class during the 1920s and 1930s. One of her "scenes" (the narrative is a cubist montage and is characterized by "flashes" of urban life) includes the feminists of the time as part of the oppressing classes: "They are the emancipated, the intellectuals and feminists that the bourgeoisie of São Paulo produces" (68).[7] The scene, in an elegant bar, ends with a toast to the recently achieved female vote (1932). The question regarding the extension of the right to vote to working-class women is answered with the justification of its exclusion "by nature," since "they are illiterate" (70).[8] Galvão thus denounces the contradiction present at the beginning of the women's movement. Defending "natural rights" and the universal right to literacy, she shows that these same foundations are used in order to oppress and exclude working-class women from one of the most important rights of citizenship: the right to vote.

Galvão later recognizes her intention to *épater les bourgeois:* "At that time, to *épater,* I too wrote my social novel, the first in this city, and it was called *Industrial Park*" (*Industrial,* 124). The result, however, goes beyond the scandal. An aspect not yet discussed by the literary critics of this novel is the characteristically female vision of the city of the author. This is recognizable in Galvão's novel in her cinematographic style and fragmented prose. When reading in-depth the fragmentation of *Industrial Park,* the shock suffered by women in the city is noticeable, a different shock from the one described by Walter Benjamin when he referred to the trajectory of the *flâneur* in the city. For the German philosopher as well as for Galvão's male intellectual contemporaries from São Paulo, the *flâneur* refers to the male character who is perfectly at home in the city in which he circulates. In contrast, in Galvão's work, shock reveals the vulnerability of women within the urban landscape. Created by men and for men's enjoyment, the streets expose women to male aggression. Benjamin stated that the city hides the footprints of its criminals. Galvão makes us see how the city makes crimes against women less visible. From *garçonnières* to rape in the streets, from the seduction represented by the luxury cars to the subsequent invisibility of the bordellos, the city of *Industrial Park* is constructed as a trap for the humiliated and manipulated female body.

In this sense, Galvão predates the critique of biopolitics by contemporary feminism. The influence of cubism or, as correctly perceived by K. David Jackson, of expressionism, has the female body described metonymically, or hyperbolized in its aberrations. However, while stressing its use and destruction—not only by men but also by the "streets of the capitalist world" (29)—the *paulista* author is a precursor of the theory of woman as "cyborg" (Haraway), or of the "political body" of women (Butler). The compartmentalization of the city, on the other hand, marks women's places, which are assigned by class: the home, in the case of the bourgeoisie or middle-class women; and the factory, the street, or the bordello in the case of the working-class women. *Industrial Park* is, in fact, a list of these women's places, with a body that can be only "a belly" or "stockingless legs." Thus, the rejection of Pagu's work could be related to its permanent distancing from the mainstream theoretical precepts of her time. The inclusion of women in the supposed homogenization of the working class decenters the Marxist idea of social class, while the inclusion of working-class women in the feminist fight makes weaker the case for the supposed biological element that animated the feminist movement in the 1920s and 1930s. In both cases, however, there is a deep ethical sentiment in her treatment of women. Moreover, the universalism of Pagu's work, aligned with the communitarian thought that characterized the Marxism of her time, situates working-class women in the time and space that they lived, a posture that Benhabib is currently trying to recuperate.

Another innovation of this book can be seen in the chapter that describes carnival. The São Paulo there portrayed is a communitarian city. The Brás depicted by Galvão shows the daily interaction of white, black, mulatto, and European immigrants united through their mutual working-class origin. The novel paints a picture that is very different from what was later brought forth by the Vargas government (which twice arrested Pagu). The fixation on the national character of Brazilian society imposed by the fascist state during the dictatorship of Getúlio Vargas erased differences. However, the version of Brás and of greater Brazil in *Industrial Park* is different: "At Colombo's, white, black, or mulatto women, like runway girls, don't pay to get in" (36).[9] To this mixture are added the immigrant women, such as the "fat Italian women" (ibid.). This ethnic mix, although not clearly pointing out differences in the multiculturalist sense, makes clear the presence of ethnic diasporas in the melting pot that characterized Brazilian cities during the 1920s.

Finally, Patrícia Galvão has also anticipated the trail of women's literary writing that would be forged after her passing. In the chronicles written at the end of her life, she made known the presence of Clarice Lispector in Brazilian literature; this recognition suggests to me the metaphor of heritage elaborated by French feminism in the 1960s (Cixous). Pagu's support of Lispector's work is a transforming gift, naming the latter an heir and continuing her lifeline as a female writer in Brazil. Although the brand of feminism that defends aesthetic heritage might still be centered in the peculiarity of women's experience—thus attending to the female biological aspect—I accept Patrícia Galvão's judgment. I will now also go forward in the direction of Clarice Lispector, searching out Pagu's footsteps for her.

CLARICE, THE MUSE OF COPACABANA

Although the name Galvão is a point of reference when discussing the presence of the city in women's narrative in Brazil, it is only with Clarice Lispector that this theme becomes predominant.[10] The literary lineage between the two writers is undeniable, especially in their treatment of the city. In Galvão's work, the city is a scenario where working-class women, oppressed by social injustice, circulate. In Lispector's work, urban life is a theater where the female social actor unlearns the melodrama of domesticity. Both, however, share the attempt to erase the frontiers between art and life. Contesting through this trajectory the identity attributed to the women of their time, both writers possess—attached to the persona they have created—mythical beauty. They were sphinxes and muses of the cities where they lived. Furthermore, the journalistic practice that contributed to the iconic fixation of their images is common to both writers.

Galvão and Lispector also share a similarity in their literary treatment of urban women's issues. The Benjaminian shock, for instance, reappears in the work of Lispector as the strangeness that overcomes bourgeois women in contact with the street. Critics have pointed to the epiphanies that her characters experience. As destabilizing incidents, these epiphanies disrupt the middle-class lives of her protagonists, changing the course of their lives forever. In her 1979 collection of short stories, *A Bela e a Fera ou a Ferida Grande Demais* (Beauty and the beast or the biggest wound ever), this is the case, for example, of Ana, protagonist of "Amor" (Love), in which a blind man walking down the street and chewing gum is seen by Ana from the window of a streetcar in the high-class district of Jardim Botânico. This vision causes a transformation in the protagonist's life. A similar episode is seen in "Beauty and the Beast or the Biggest Wound Ever" when Carla, a bourgeois woman emerging from the hairdresser in Copacabana, is accosted by a beggar. Whereas Ana in "Amor," overwhelmed by the vision of the blind man, loses control of herself, causing the basket of eggs she was carrying to fall from her hands and break, the character in "Beauty and the Beast" similarly reacts to the shock of the beggar's proximity, uttering unexpected phrases such as asking the beggar if he speaks English.

Jean Franco does a feminist analysis of this short story, extracting from it the foundation of her interpretation of Lispector's work. According to Franco, the most salient characteristic of the Brazilian author's writing is its modernist aspect. The bourgeois female characters' encounters with the unusual as represented by other social classes, especially through monstrous figures such as the wounded beggar, are seen as the modernist desire to control the aberrant, the only way by which modernist writers can deal with social exclusion (Franco, 211). However, this reading seems reductive to me; taking into account the question of feminine citizenship, the novelty of these two stories by Lispector consists not merely in controlling the aberrant, but rather in describing the learning of individualization by women, a process that leads to different paths from those traveled by men.

Much has been written about the recurrence of these startling events in Lispector's writings, but there is little concern for the characters themselves.

A closer reading of the characteristics of these women can reveal very interesting facts about the destabilizing of conventional values. In the stories just cited, the fortuitous encounters of her feminine characters are with a blind man and a beggar, figures exalted by Christianity to evoke charity. But then, the blind man was chewing gum—that is, he was integrated into the budding consumer society and is behaving as a young rebel—while the beggar was making a living from his wound.[11] Therefore, the shock described in the narrative does not restrict itself to what Franco terms the unexpected encounter of a bourgeois woman with "the aberrant other." Instead, this shock is established principally through Lispector's overturning of certain categories that belong to bourgeois Christian moral codes, such as the essential goodness of the poor as a justification for charity.

The same occurs with the essentialism of the working class by Marxism. As I have pointed out in another study (Santos, *Tropical Kitsch*), in the novel *A hora da estrela* (*The Hour of the Star,* 1977), the protagonist, Macabéa, a poor immigrant from the Northeast, escapes her oppressed destiny by learning how to forge a good excuse not to go to work, so as to enjoy a free day for her own pleasure. Her boyfriend, Olímpico, can hardly be described as a working-class hero, since he is a dishonest social climber. On the other hand, both Macabéa and Janair, a character in the novel *A Paixão segundo G.H.* (*The Passion According to G.H.,* 1968), are presented as sensitive human beings, equal in the modern sense of equality to the bourgeois narrators of the two novels. Macabéa demonstrates her insight because she can enjoy the aria "Una furtiva lacrima" of the Donizetti opera *The Elixir of Love;* Janair, the servant, shows sensitivity because she can paint designs on the walls of a maid's room (a principal place for subordinate women). Janair's designs provoke in her ex-employer, the narrator, an emotion similar to that described by Adorno as the characteristic enjoyment of a work of art. This demonstrates that Janair is also an artist. The narrator's evocation of the Orient, provoked by the remembrance of the black skin of the ex-employee, does not only reveal the feeling of having been in touch with a "low and primitive" region, as stated by Jean Franco. On the contrary, by contextualizing the blackness of the maid within a millenary culture, Lispector practices the "interactive universalism" defended by Seyla Benhabib. The character's drawings add to the artistic work of the narrator—a sculptor—the artistic experience of an equal, particularly as the latter connects the black maid with the ancient art of Egyptian minarets, which function as metaphors of Janair's bedroom.[12]

In Lispector's work, the learning of citizenship among people of all social classes takes place principally in the city. The streets are capable of bringing together persons such as the blind man or the beggar with the closely guarded women in their elegant apartments. Moving around in the city of Rio de Janeiro, Lispector's female characters rehearse their positions as subjects in the world where they must live. As with Pagu, the city is never an abstract entity. It is mapped onto neighborhoods and streets. The stories that mark the beginning of Lispector's career take place in diverse neighborhoods, which, just as in the case of Pagu, mark social differences.

Carnival, which Pagu had used as an allegory of the coexistence of ethnic diasporas in the city, is a theme in the story "Mistério em São Cristóvão" (Mystery in São Cristóvão), from the collection 1965 *Laços de Família* (Family ties). This story narrates the strange experience of a girl who watches from the window as a group of three masked men invade the garden of her family home, located in the lower-middle-class neighborhood of São Cristóvão. In "Preciosidades" (Preciousness), the Largo da Lapa (an old part of the city, at that time a bus and trolley stop, but also a point for vagrants and outlaws) marks the difficult passage of the narrator through the streets. Her encounter with a group of young men who touched her— Marta Peixoto sees in this encounter an allegory of rape (Peixoto, 83)— brings, once again, the work of the two authors closer together. Again, it is in the streets that their women characters are most vulnerable to male seduction and aggression.

In the story "Feliz Aniversário" (Happy birthday), the different neighborhoods where the sons and daughters of the protagonists live serve to underline the differences between the siblings, making it clear that family ties had long ago been replaced by economic relationships external to the family. On the occasion of the eightieth birthday of the matriarch, the positions of the daughter who dwelled in Copacabana, at that time an upper-middle-class part of Rio, are clearly contrasted with those of "the daughter-in-law from Olaria," a lower-middle-class section of the city. The feelings of distance thus created between both sides closely reflect the basic question in Lispector's work: that gender inequalities will be intensified as social inequalities increase. In *The Hour of the Star*, the narrator declares that Macabéa, the poor protagonist, lives "in a hostile city" (Lispector, *Hour*, 29).[13] She dies on the street, hit by the enchanted Prince Charming who, as predicted by a Gypsy card reader, would save her. This "hour of the star" (which the narrator explains is the moment of someone's death) is also similar to Pagu's descriptions of the urban milieu. The luxury car of the rich driver who hits Macabéa has much in common with the elegant sedans that attract the poor girls in *Industrial Park.*

Is the real city where Clarice dwelled also built against her?[14] Judging by the newspaper chronicles she published in Rio's *Jornal do Brasil,* this does not seem to be the case. These chronicles, collected into a volume, reveal a constant dialogue between the writer and the city (Lispector, *Descoberta*). The themes she writes about in her stories—unusual encounters, strange persons seen on the streets—are also constant themes in her journalistic pieces. The differences lie in the tone, as these take the form of correspondence. Clarice uses the newspaper to respond to her readers, or perhaps, as Nádia Gotlib would insist, to seduce them. The writer's responses, also unsettling, form part, according to Gotlib, of a seduction game very similar to Pagu's half a century earlier. The difference lies in that, conscious of the dangers of victimization that underlie the role of muse, the historical figure Clarice uses all possible subterfuges to escape it. But she does not always manage this escape. Clarice lived most of the time in Leme, a hidden corner of Copacabana, ambiguous to the myths created about her.

Part of the myth of Lispector lies in the fact that she never lived up to any defined role. Like Pagu, she de-essentializes the role of woman. Even though her characters were in the majority of cases women, one cannot say that she was a feminist writer. Nor can social issues be taken as the essence of her work, as they do not have a prominent role in her writings. Nonetheless, her texts gave women a unique and enigmatic voice in Portuguese. The high quality of her writing, the unexpected twists of her narrations, the seduction she exercised in different realms of cultural expression can now be prized in spaces other than literature. Her life, for example, has also been scrutinized in recent critical approaches, revealing that she lived halfway between being a myth and an everyday woman; she enjoyed displaying her own beauty and reveled in her vanity.

BRÁS OF BRAZIL: COPACABANA IS NOT COOL ANYMORE

The encounter of the socialite of Lispector's short story "The Beauty and the Beast, or the Biggest Wound Ever," outside of the Copacabana Palace Hotel, directs the reader to a neighborhood replete with 1950s glamour.[15] The hotel lodged Hollywood stars at the time; for example, Orson Welles stayed there as Franklin D. Roosevelt's Good Neighbor policy representative. Until the 1960s, the nightclubs preferred by the city's elite were located in Copacabana. There they organized fashion shows, and chic heiresses, such as Carla, the protagonist of "The Beauty and the Beast," held their society debuts. Thus, the Copacabana of the short stories by Clarice Lispector was the *coolest* neighborhood of Rio de Janeiro and the sophisticated center of the South Zone of the city, and also its most segregated part. The conflict narrated in the short story "The Beauty and the Beast" is built upon the unusual and sudden appearance of a beggar showing an exposed wound, in just this zone of the city characterized by the elite's policy of exclusion.

However, upon considering the recent work of Sonia Coutinho, we find that Copacabana lost the title of a cool neighborhood long ago. The names of the American stars were all that remained of its glorious past, and Coutinho transfers these names to her characters. Thus, the first short story of her 1985 collection *O Último Verão em Copacabana* (The last summer of Copacabana, 1985) is titled "Every Lana Turner has her Johnny Stompanato." Another is "The Greta Garbo Enigma," and there is also "The Fortieth Birthday of Mary Batson." In other short stories within the book, Billie Holliday, Thelonius Monk, Ornette Coleman, and Miles Davis make appearances, adding the proper music to the cinematographic gallery. The central themes of the stories are quite uniform: the solitude of the middle-aged independent woman, a dweller of a small apartment in the transformed metropolis of 1980s Rio de Janeiro.[16] In contrast with Pagu and Lispector, who turned to journalism after careers as fiction writers, Sonia Coutinho turns to fiction writing after establishing her profession as a journalist. This is stressed in both the introduction and the prologue of the volume, as is the origin of the author, who "came from Bahia" (vii). The characters mix these biographical data—the profession as a journalist, the provincial origin—with the desire of the narrators to write stories about Copacabana, or "the South Zone of Rio de Janeiro."

In these stories are found a noticeable number of male characters who seek out the middle-aged women available on the beach, a sufficiently democratic place to promote the encounter of different social groups. In this way, there is an interaction between the solitude of the professionally and sexually active women liberated of domesticity by feminism, and the neighborhood composed of "one thousand windows" that "become small illuminated squares, more and more numerous" (17).[17] The tiny rooms where these women live neither offer protection to them nor liberate them from frustrated love relationships, even when they are paired with men supposedly equal to them. On the other hand, this literature is no longer occupied with national themes. Moreover, the women writers are not the city muses seen in Lispector and Galvão. The femme fatale is now a professional with time only for fortuitous love, and Copacabana myths become old fashionable American mass culture icons. Would this be a universal sentiment? In other words, would we, along with Sonia Coutinho, fall under the influence of postliberation feminism of the 1960s and 1970s, a kind of feminism that, instead of emphasizing equality, has moved toward difference? As an argument for an affirmative answer to this question, one can say that although the work of Coutinho can be aligned to postmodernism, her vision of the city is still modern, because she bases her fiction on the experience of the metropolis. To put it another way, Coutinho depicts a city that, despite its broadened grandeur, still maintains the special atmosphere of certain neighborhoods such as Copacabana which, though decadent, offer the citizen a sense of belonging and recognition.

During the 1990s, the Brazilian woman writer could discard the focus on feminine experience. This is the case of the writer Patrícia Melo, whose novels quote, in a postmodern manner, a narrative genre until then restricted in Brazil to male writers: the detective novel. The city described in her books is the megalopolis, this embroilment of tentacles where neighborhoods had already lost their difference and where human relationships had become more and more impersonal, impeded by the walls that concretely segregate urban life into fortified enclaves. In Melo's 1995 novel *O Matador* (*The Killer*), an omniscient narrator chronologically tells the story of a young criminal. Set in São Paulo, the plot reproduces what Teresa Caldeira calls the "speech of crime," meaning the endless repetition of violent crime narratives, which contributes to the growth of fear and the even tighter self-segregation of the enclave's populations.

The narratives of Patrícia Melo follow the model of some male writers such as Rubem Fonseca, who, since the 1970s, have urban violence as their primary theme. As a professional writer today, Melo can go beyond women's issues. The city described in her novels is a generic one, not mapped by neighborhoods or streets. Instead, the geographic spots are megastores, such as the Mappin of the novel *O Matador*. The coexistence of social exclusion among the segregated elite acquires a tone similar to a warlike conflict. A homicide committed by chance transforms the protagonist into a professional assassin when his neighbors choose him to be their avenger, paid by them to kill. In contrast with Patrícia Galvão's novel *Industrial Park*, where violence against women has very well-defined causes, *O Matador* describes the city of São Paulo as a senseless spiral of violence that feeds on itself. For this reason, the work of Patrícia Melo is aligned in the category of the "contemporary extreme."[18] Although they hurt the women more brutally, the men are also portrayed as mere toys, both perpetrators and victims of a force of violence without cause or goal. What is most harsh in Melo's depiction of the city seems to be the abandonment of ethics, which affects even the narrator of the novel. In *O Matador*, using a supposedly neutral perspective, the narrator limits himself to describing the trajectory of the protagonist and his initiation, gratuitous and casual, into the world of crime that he will not leave until the end of the novel.

Teresa Caldeira exposes very clearly how the "speech of crime" that *O Matador* reproduces indicates the "disjunctive character of Brazilian democracy" (321), especially visible in the big cities. According to Caldeira, it is possible to see in a Brazilian megalopolis such as São Paulo the political reappropriation of public spaces by their citizens, who have never had so much opportunity to organize themselves politically. In this case, the anthropologist has as a reference the consolidation of democratic transition, begun in the mid-1980s, after more than twenty years of military dictatorship. On the other hand, as a reaction to democratization, the deterioration of this same public space by danger and crime generates in the middle class the fear "that the poor can no longer be kept in their places" (322).[19]

This issue also concerns the literary critic, as one of the novelties of women's writing in Brazil is the recent appearance in the market, with critical recognition, of a literature of socially excluded women, especially that written by black women. The event today is entirely different from the emergence of Carolina Maria de Jesus, in the 1950s, whose success quickly was transformed into a reterritorialization of the writer. This was primarily because de Jesus could not count on the support of the black movement. At that time it was not nearly as extensive as it is today. This has now changed in the literary sphere; for example, among other initiatives, the *quilombhoje* social movement has been responsible since 1976 for the uninterrupted annual publication of *Cadernos Negros*, a collection of literary texts written by men and women of African descent.[20] Among the various writers brought to light by *Cadernos Negros*, the name of Conceição

Evaristo is notable for its staying power.[21] Both a poet and short-story writer, the author published her first novel, *Ponciá Vicêncio*, in 2003; this novel adds the treatment of "places of black people" (Gonzáles and Hasenbalg) to the discussion of women's places.

Like Clarice Lispector's character Macabéa in *The Hour of the Star*, Ponciá Vicêncio is a "voiceless" character: "She spoke little and when she did speak she sometimes said things that he [her husband] didn't understand" (16). Yet, the literary treatment that Conceição Evaristo gives this "voiceless" character differs radically from that adopted by Lispector. Whereas the latter assumes in *The Hour of the Star* the impossibility of representing a subaltern character, Evaristo, to the contrary, pacts with the reader that she will represent that portion of the Brazilian population that she belongs to by birth and with which she maintains family and cultural ties. Comparing the acknowledgments section of both books, one sees that instead of phrases like "it is my fault," or "I can't do anything about it," or even "let her be damned," with which Lispector prepares her reader for the distance from the issues concerning the character she proposed to create (Lispector, *Hour*), Evaristo lists her own family, beginning with one of her sisters, whose life and suffering seem to have been one of the models on which she bases her protagonist. Her daughter, mother, and sisters are prominently featured in the acknowledgments section of her book, thus indicating the establishment of a lineage that has for a long time characterized the foundation of women's writing.

The difference in treatment continues in the portrayal of the two characters: whereas Macabéa is seemingly a cyborg, without any origin or family ties, Ponciá, even though she is a migrant like Macabéa, clearly knows the rural roots to which she returns in moments of profound despair. From the perspective of rural tradition, the city appears as a place of loss and fragmentation. Just as in Macabéa's case, the city only offers "dirty places" to Ponciá. She sleeps with her husband in a filthy bed, and her hardship is stressed by having only empty tins of guava paste to use for plates. As in Lispector's novel *The Hour of the Star*, poverty becomes concrete as opposed to the abstraction of poverty found in socialist novels of Marxist origin. Also similar to the case of Lispector is this type of rejection of the literary tradition of the socialist novel. Even though the life of Ponciá Vicêncio may be paradigmatic as applied to the poor (and black) segments of the Brazilian population, the solution that the novel offers for the character's life is based in myth and not in historical materialism. The character's madness was already foretold by family destiny; it was predestined as an inheritance from her grandfather. The family meeting, which maintains the narrative suspense, is measured by mythical time, controlled by the spiritual leader of the community, the old shaman Nêngua Kainda. Through her prophecies, the family of migrants reintegrates itself into the rural world again, leaving behind its deterritorialization in the no-place of the *favela,* a word that defines an informal dwelling as opposed to formal neighborhoods. In this sense, Evaristo, like the other writers read here, occupies herself with detailed parts of the city. In her novel *Ponciá Vicêncio,* the *favela* portrays the *(no-) neighborhood* destined for black migrants. Their final meeting place is in the rural plantation where the whole family used to work as laborers. Regarding her daughter, the mother, Maria Vicêncio, concludes: "There was her girl—unique and multiple" (129).

The concept of feminine subjectivity contained in that phrase sums up the transformation achieved in written texts by the recent narrative of black Brazilian women. In place of a homogeneous feminine identity, their texts depict a multiplicity of options that characterize that identity. Through mythical ties, black Brazilian women are linked to a transcontinental tradition with diffuse African roots. Through historical ties, they also recognize one another, not only in the national trajectory of black Brazilians, with which they share a sense of community and cultural tradition, but also in the cosmopolitan tradition of struggle, which, during centuries, consolidated itself in the black Atlantic (Gilroy). Through ties of gender, they are women who share well-defined experiences of oppression, as demonstrated in Ponciá Vicêncio's relationship with her husband.

Thus, the publication of urban fiction written by black women in Brazil adds various divisions to the fragmentation of the unique subject of modernity, pointing out how this concept of modernity, even in Brazil, referred not only to males, but also exclusively to whites. Moreover, in building their characters through the concrete experience of social exclusion in the city, black women writers show the path to a broadening of citizenship. In this way, it will be possible to include a feminine category composed by different ethnicities and social locations in the literature written by women. Pagu, a precursor by seventy years, would certainly appreciate such an ethical posture.

NOTES

1. The literary criticism based on the reinvention of the modern subject seems to have brought back interest in the biography of writers. In the case of women, the biography often illuminates aesthetic options, highlighting the relationship between experimentation and the life experience of the writers.

2. "Adoniran Barbosa, the most original of the [*sic*] São Paulo's samba composers, has depicted that city through songs of naive melodies and lyrics of spaghetti style. The great originality of his works consists of mixing the ill-spoken Portuguese of the lower classes with a mispronounced popular language, product of the melting pot formed by immigrants from different countries, notably the Italians (hence his spaghetti style, in a certain measure comparable in literature to the pre-modernist poet Juó Bananére, also born in São Paulo). A mix of humor and melancholy marked the way he sang the dramas of popular, humble and suffering characters living through the violence brought by the urbanization process" (Rennó). It is interesting to note that Barbosa was a contemporary of Pagu, born in the same year as the writer.

3. Pagu was "rediscovered" by the Brazilian concrete poets. Augusto de Campos situates her "rebirth" in 1963 (one year after her death), when he was amazed about the true identity—Patrícia Galvão—of the unknown poet who, in 1948, signed a poem as Solange Sohl, to whom Campos himself dedicated a poem written between 1950 and 1951. In 1975, the *Álbum de Pagu/Pagu's Album,* discovered by José Luís Garaldi, was published in the journal *Código no. 2.* In 1978, Campos released, in *Através no. 2,* an anthology of her work titled by Décio Pignatari, another concrete poet, as *Patrícia Galvão—Cannibalistic Muse-Martyr* (*Patrícia Galvão—Musa-Mártir Antropófaga)* (Campos). In 1993, Elizabeth Jackson and K. David Jackson published their English translation of the novel *Parque Industrial,* with an introductory study that is an excellent presentation of Pagu to English speakers (Galvão, 1993). My quotations of this work follow, in Portuguese, a 1994 edition of the novel. For the English quotations, I use the translation by Jackson and Jackson.

4. Pagu makes contact with Brazilian modernism through the poet Guilherme de Almeida, who was secretary of the high school where she studied. From 1928 to 1930 she participated actively in the most radical wing of the literary movement, "Cannibalism" (Antropofagia). Treated as a doll by Tarsila do Amaral and Oswald de Andrade, the poet who led Cannibalism, Pagu ends up marrying the latter in 1929. The product of their union, Rudá, was born in 1930. In 1931, Patrícia Galvão enters the Communist Party. After being "proletarianized" and obligated to use a pseudonym to sign her writings, she travels around the world (1933), working as a correspondent for Brazilian newspapers. In 1935, in Paris, she is imprisoned and threatened with deportation to Nazi Germany. The ambassador, Souza Dantas, saves her and obtains her repatriation. Back in Brazil, she separates definitively from the poet Oswald de Andrade. That same year, she is imprisoned by the dictatorship of Getúlio Vargas for the first time. She flees from the hospital where she was

transferred. Two years later, she is again imprisoned and tortured. Finally freed in 1940, she marries the writer Geraldo Ferraz, her lifelong companion. In 1941 Geraldo Galvão Ferraz is born. Her trajectory also includes her (failed) candidacy for state deputy for the Socialist Party (1950) and two suicide attempts. Antonio Riserio reports that Pagu rode a bicycle with the last Chinese emperor, who gave her, as a present, soybean seeds. In that way, Pagu was responsible for the introduction of this industrial crop to Brazil (Galvão, *Pagu,* 22).

5. Although she had chosen the working-class area of Brás as the environment for her novel, a São Paulo neighborhood where she was born and raised, Pagu herself came from neither a working-class family nor a well-off family.

6. I refer to the theories that further the decentering of the feminine subject through the notion of a performative identity, transforming the female body into a political body (Butler).

7. "São as emancipadas, as intelectuais que a burguesia de São Paulo produz" (89).

8. "—Essas são analfabetas. Excluídas por natureza" (ibid.).

9. "No Colombo, as damas brancas, pretas ou mulatas como as meninas fugidas de casa, não pagam entrada" (42).

10. Clarice Lispector, considered the best woman writer of Brazil, was born in the 1920s in Lithuania. She arrived in Brazil as a child with her parents, a poor Jewish family. They settled in Recife, where Clarice grew up. In her first writings one can find references to the long illness of her mother. When the mother died, Lispector's father moved to Rio de Janeiro with his two daughters. There she studied law and met her husband, a diplomat, with whom she traveled abroad to his postings. After fifteen years of marriage and the birth of two sons, she divorced and settled with her sons in Rio de Janeiro, where she lived until her death. She was recognized as an unusual writer, particularly because she applied innovative literary forms to feminine issues. Lispector's international fame came about through the French feminist Hélène Cixous, who translated her work and theorized about feminism utilizing Lispector. It is said that the Brazilian writer's frequent use of the word *bliss* (in Portuguese, *felicidade*) was taken from the American writer Katherine Mansfield.

11. "o ganha-pão do mendigo era a redonda ferida aberta" (137).

12. Lucia Villares goes further in this issue. In an interesting analysis of the haunting drawings in this novel, Villares states that the drawings reveal the whiteness of the protagonist, contrasted with the invisible blackness of the maid; "The presence of the 'African queen' as an autonomous subject with an autonomous culture is crucial in this novel" (Villares, 2002).

13. "numa cidade toda feita contra ela" (Lispector, *A Hora da Estrela*).

14. Brazilians have become accustomed to calling our most beloved writer by her first name.

15. With the title of this section, I reproduce an expression created by Patrícia Galvão, trying to imitate her optimism about Brazil as well. The last words of the *Industrial Park* chapter "Brás do Mundo/Brás of the World," a definition aligned with the international proletarianism of the 1930s Left, are "Other men will remain. Other women will remain. Brás of Brazil. Brás of the world" (Galvão, *Industrial,* 88)/"Outros ficarão. Outras ficarão./Brás do Brasil. Brás de todo o mundo" (Galvão, *Parque,* 83).

16. I refer to the transformations of the city, as described by Jean Gottman in 1950. The French geographer is considered responsible for the definition of mega-lopolis, a term by which he describes the new urban entity that involved the economically city-tied, but politically separate suburbs, based on the use of the automobile. Gottman differentiates megalopolis from metropolis, in the sense that the latter still maintains a central nucleus, its largest municipal unit from which the growth started. The megalopolis starts when the center decreases in population while smaller towns in suburban areas surrounding the central part of the city start growing. In this last part of my essay, I describe how women writers offer an image of their cities that perfectly corresponds to these descriptions.

17. The author depicts another characteristic of the metropolis described by Gottman: its monotony in design (Gottman, 110). At the same time, the windows as metaphors of the isolation of human beings in the metropolis evidence the in-fluence of French existentialists in the work of Sonia Coutinho. The description of the "small squares" reminds one of monads, the philosophical concept of isolation and impenetrability reread by existentialists as one of the characteristics of urban life, responsible for the existential solitude and incommunicability among human beings.

18. The term, based on Maurice Blanchot's work, refers to "novels whose styles or themes engage a hyperreal, often apocalyptic, world progressively invaded by popular culture, permeated with technology, and dominated by destruction. In this world, violence—often the only stable element—operates as ethos" ("Con-temporary"). Patrícia Melo appears on the list of writers characterized by the term.

19. It is worth noting that a great part of the anthropological research by Caldeira was done in the Moóca neighborhood, actually an extension of Brás. As in this neighboring community, "the industrial workers who settled in Moóca around 1900 were European migrants: mostly Italians, but also Spanish, Portuguese, and Eastern Europeans" (Caldeira, 13).

20. It is worthy of note that the name of the social movement and publisher—*quilombhoje*—is a combination of the name of the resistance group of slaves that evaded plantations in colonial times (the *quilombos*) followed by the word *hoje* (today). The resulting meaning reaffirms the idea of resistance.

21. The publisher's biographical note goes on to point out that Evaristo has academic training in literature. She has a master's degree in Brazilian literature,

and is currently a doctoral candidate in Brazilian literature at a prestigious Brazilian university. Beginning in 1996, Evaristo has spent time in Austria and Puerto Rico, where she has given conference talks. Since then, it should be noted that, in 2003, she gave conference talks about Afro-Brazilian literature in the United States at both Columbia and Yale universities. Her works have been translated into German and English (in both British and U.S. editions).

WORKS CITED

Andrade, Rudá de, and Marcelo G. Tassara. *Pagu—Livre na imaginação no Tempo e no Espaço*. São Paulo. Documentary. Video Co, 21. 2001.

Barbosa, Adoniran. *O Samba do Arnesto*. Manaus: Sonopress/EMI Music Ltd. 2000.

Benguell, Norma. *Eternamente Pagu*. Rio de Janerio: Embrafilme e Riofilme, 1988.

Benhabib, Seyla. *Situating the Self: Gender, Community and Postmodernity in Contemporary Ethics*. Cambridge: Polity Press, 1992.

Benjamin, Walter. *Charles Baudelaire: A Lyric Poet in the Era of High Capitalism*. Trans. Harry Zohn. New York: Verso, 1997.

Branco, Ivo. *Eh, Pagu, Eh*. Documentary. 2003.

Butler, Judith. *Bodies That Matter: On the Discursive Limits of "Sex."* London: Routledge, 1993.

Caldeira, Teresa. *City of Walls: Crime, Segregation, and Citizenship in São Paulo*. Berkeley: University of California Press, 2000.

Campos, Augusto de. "Nota Introdutória." In *Pagu, Patrícia Galvão: Vida-Obra. Antologia*, ed. Augusto de Campos. São Paulo: Brasiliense, 1982. 9–10.

Cixous, Hélène. "Le rire de la méduse." *L'arc* 61 (1975): 39–54.

———. *Vivre l'Orange*. Paris: des femmes, 1979.

Coelho, Nelly Novaes. "A Literatura Feminina no Brasil—das Origens Medievais ao Século XX." In *Gênero e Representação: Teoria, História e Crítica*, ed. Eduardo de Assis Duarte Constância Lima Duarte and Kátia da Costa Bezerra, vol. 1, *Coleção Mulher e Literatura*. Belo Horizonte: Pós-Graduação em Letras: Estudos Literários, Universidad Federal de Minas Gerais, 2002. 89–107.

"Contemporary Extreme." *PMLA* 119.2 (2004): 364.

Coutinho, Sonia. *O Último Verão em Copacabana*. Rio de Janeiro: José Olympio, 1985.

Di Cavalcanti, Emiliano. *Five Girls from Guaratinguetá*. Solomon R. Guggenheim Museum. *Guggenheim: The Guide to the Guggenheim Museum* (October–November 2001): cover and 23.

Evaristo, Conceição. 2003. *Ponciá Vicêncio*. Belo Horizonte: Mazza.

Franco, Jean. *The Decline and Fall of the Lettered City*. Cambridge: Harvard University Press, 2002.

Galvão, Patrícia (Pagu). *Industrial Park.* Trans. Elizabeth Jackson and K. David Jackson. Lincoln: University of Nebraska Press, 1993.

———. (Lobo, Mara). *Parque Industrial.* 1933. São Paulo: Alternativa, 1981. Facsimile of the original edition.

———. *Pagu, Patrícia Galvão: Vida-Obra. Antologia.* Ed. Augusto de Campos. São Paulo: Brasiliense, 1982.

Gilroy, Paul. *The Black Atlantic: Modernity and Double Consciousness.* Cambridge: Harvard University Press, 1993.

Gonzáles, Lélia, and Carlos Hasenbalg. *Lugar de Negro.* Rio de Janeiro: Marco Zero, 1982.

Gotlib, Nádia Batella. "Readers of Clarice, Who Are You?" In *Closer to the Wild Heart: Essays on Clarice Lispector,* ed. Cláudia Passos Alonso and Claire Williams. Oxford: Legenda/European Humanities Research Center/Oxford University, 2002. 182–97.

Gottman, Jean. *Since Megalopolis: The Urban Writings of Jean Gottman.* Ed. Jean Gottman and Robert A. Horper. Baltimore: Johns Hopkins University Press, 1990.

Haraway, Donna. "Manifesto for the Cyborgs: Science and Technology and Socialist Feminism on the 1980s." In *Resistance Literature,* ed. Barbara Harlow. New York: Methuen, 1987. 65–107.

Jesus, Maria Carolina de. *Quarto de Despejo.* Rio de Janeiro: Livraria Francisco Alves, 1960. Published in English as *Child of the Dark,* trans. David St. Clair. New York: Penguin Books, 1963.

Lispector, Clarice. "A Bela e a Fera ou a Ferida Grande Demais." In *A Bela e a Fera.* Rio de Janeiro: Nova Fronteira, 1979. 131–46.

———. *A Descoberta do Mundo.* Rio de Janeiro: Nova Fronteira, 1984.

———. *Discovering the World.* Trans. G. Poteiro. Manchester: Carcanet, 1986.

———. *A Hora da Estrela.* 1977. 21st ed. Rio de Janeiro: Francisco Alves, 1993.

———. *The Hour of the Star.* Trans. Giovanni Pontiero. Manchester: Carcanet, 1986.

———. *Laços de Família.* 3d ed. Rio de Janeiro: Editora do Autor, 1965.

———. *The Passion According to G.H.* 1964. Trans. Ronald W. Sousa. Minneapolis: University of Minnesota Press, 1988.

Melo, Patrícia. *The Killer.* Trans. Clifford E. Landers. Hopewell, N.J.: Ecco Press, 1997.

———. *O Matador.* São Paulo: Companhia das Letras, 1995.

Peixoto, Marta. *Passionate Fictions: Gender, Narrative and Violence in Clarice Lispector.* Minneapolis: University of Minnesota Press, 1994.

Rennó, Carlos. *Homage to Adoniran Barbosa.* 2004. http://www.vivabrazil.com/adorian.htm.

Ribeiro, Esmeralda. *Malungos & Milongas. Conto.* São Paulo: Quilombhoje, 1988.

Risério, Antonio. "A Narrativa Feminina Publicada nos *Cadernos Negros,* Sai do Quarto de Despejo." In *Gênero e Representação na Literatura Brasileira,* ed.

Eduardo de Assis Duarte, Constância Lima Duarte, and Kátia da Costa Bezerra. Vol. 2. Belo Horizonte: Universidad Federal de Minas Gerais, 2002.

————. "Vida-Obra, Obra-Vida, Vida." In *Pagu, Patrícia Galvão: Vida-Obra. Antologia,* ed. Augusto de Campos. São Paulo: Brasiliense, 1982. 18–30.

Santos, Lidia. "Melodrama y nación en la narrativa feminina del Caribe contemporáneo." *Revista Iberoamericana. Representaciones de la nación: lengua, género, clase y raza en las sociedades caribeñas* 205 (October–December, 2003): 953–68.

————. *Tropical Kitsch: Media in Latin American Literature and Art.* Trans. E. Enenbach. Princeton, N.J.: Markus Weiner, 2005.

Schor, Naomi. *Reading in Detail: Aesthetics and the Feminine.* New York: Methuen, 1987.

Serret, Estela. "Ética y feminismo." *Debate Feminista* 21.11 (2000): 103–28.

Villares, Lucia. "The Black Maid as Ghost: Haunting in *A Paixão Segundo G.H.*" In *Closer to the Wild Heart: Essays on Clarice Lispector,* ed. Cláudia Pazos Alonso and Claire Williams. Oxford: Legenda/European Humanities Research Center/ Oxford University, 2002. 126–41.

3

On Being a Woman in the City of Kings

Women Writing (in)
Contemporary Lima

ANNE LAMBRIGHT

In the 1999 novel *Pista falsa* (False clue) by Peruvian writer Carmen Ollé (b. 1947), the female protagonist reflects briefly on a subtitle she notices on the cover of a popular magazine. It reads, "What does it mean to be an old *limeño?*" ([male] resident of Lima).[1] The question and subsequent reflections on the part of the protagonist would seem of negligible importance within the rest of the novel, which is a sort of mystery story. But in this essay I propose that the question, and indeed its silent and silenced counterquestion—"What does it mean to be a modern *limeña?*"— are ones that today are of central importance to women narrators in Lima, the City of Kings.[2] A survey of contemporary narrative fiction written by Peruvian women reveals a marked interest in the capital city, its current conditions, its rapid transformations, and its destiny, as well as a concern for the place of women within this space. As Deborah Parsons reminds us, the urban writer not only inhabits the city but also creates it; thereby, "the writer adds other maps to the city atlas; those of social interaction but also of myth, memory, fantasy, and desire" (1). Directly or obliquely, women writers are creating a new map, a new geography of Lima, through which they bring feminine voices to a well-recognized topic in the narrative of their male counterparts.

Indeed, the question that Ollé poses in the first pages of her novel echoes a similar interrogative, explored in various ways by such canonical Peruvian writers as Julio Ramón Ribeyro, Mario Vargas Llosa, Alfredo Bryce Echenique, and Jaime Bayly.[3] At the same time, by taking the question from a popular magazine and including it in a narrative about the life of a woman, Ollé is implicitly poking fun at those earlier explorations. By silencing the question of the female experience in Lima, the writer mirrors the masculine practice of silencing women and excluding them from national narratives, and yet Ollé also subtly yet concertedly converts her narrative into a counterhegemonic, subversive response. The geography of Lima developed in *Pista falsa,* like that in other narrative fiction written by Peruvian women writers in recent years, is a geography of resistance that confronts a complex hegemonic geography and cultural imaginary that endeavor to exclude women, silencing and relegating them to certain private and domestic spaces within which they are defined and controlled. For this reason, the topic of Lima in what we could call the Peruvian feminine imaginary deserves greater attention, as it not only reflects the intellectual concerns of Peruvian women but is also a product of real tensions lived by women writers today in Peru, where the predominance of masculine writers can be overwhelming.[4] This essay, then, will initiate a discussion of urban space in Peruvian women's narrative by considering the work of three of the country's most recognized women writers: Carmen Ollé, Irma del Águila (b. 1966), and Pilar Dughi (b. 1956).

Despite the attention given to the role of Lima in Peruvian national discourse and particularly in Peruvian literature, the place of Lima in women's writing has been neglected. Indeed, the most important work on Lima in Peruvian literature to date, Peter Elmore's 1993 *Los muros invisibles: Lima y la modernidad en la novela del siglo XX* (The invisible walls: Lima and modernity in the twentieth-century novel), overlooks women writers completely.[5] Julio Ortega's article examining discourse on Lima, "Para una arqueología del discurso sobre Lima" (Toward an archaeology of discourse on Lima), gives no mention of feminine views of Lima beyond a scant reference to *vals* composer Chabuca Granda.[6] And yet, Lima appears as a potent symbolic and political space in Peruvian women's writing as early as the nineteenth century. An obvious example is the role the coastal city plays in Clorinda Matto de Turner's (1852–1909) *indigenista* classic, *Aves sin nido* (*Birds without a Nest,* 1889). Here Lima is portrayed as the site of national modernization, progress, and redemption, contrasted with the backwardness, stagnation, and corruption of the Andean highland towns;

says one of the main characters, "Going to Lima is like reaching the ante-chamber of Heaven and viewing the throne of Glory and Fortune" (*Birds*, 89).[7] Other earlier women writers in whose work Lima figures prominently include María Wiesse (1894–1964), whose narrative takes a critical look at middle-class Lima, and Katia Saks, whose 1960 novel *Los títeres* (The puppets) paints an interesting portrait of a liberated bourgeois woman in Miraflores, an upper-class suburb of Lima.[8] The views of these earlier women, whether adoring or critical, point to the importance of the capital city as a site of cultural and national imagination and serve as literary antecedents to the contemporary narrative examined in this essay.

In order to understand better the new "geographies" of Lima proposed by today's women writers, it is important to comprehend their acts of mapping, their delineation of space, and their localizing of urban subjects. In the introduction to their edited volume *Place/Culture/Representation*, James Duncan and David Ley remind us that cartography is not only a science but also a sociopolitical practice: "Knowledge put to use, knowledge in the service of power that is deeply intertwined in the cultural, social and political webs of a society. . . . Topography is also therefore a science of domination—confirming boundaries, securing norms and treating ques-tionable social conventions as unquestioned social facts" (1). He who has the authority to create maps, to delineate a geography, has access to power. By suggesting other geographies, other types of knowledge, current women authors usurp power in order to weaken boundaries, question norms, and denaturalize certain social "facts." Indeed, contemporary Peru-vian women's narrative is not simply, or even explicitly, concerned with Lima as urban space; rather, the focus of their writing is specifically on women's experience within this space. In the words of these women, Lima is portrayed both as a site that the dominant culture constructs, controls, and manipulates and as a place where women search for ways to resist its authority over their lives.

Another aspect that we see depicted repeatedly in these women's nar-rative is Lima's precarious position between modernity and postmoder-nity. How do these women deal with a postmodern Lima that has not quite negotiated modernism and that at best is working within an accelerated and yet defective modernity?[9] The economic and social situation for women in Lima echoes that of most urban centers worldwide—more women are in the workforce, attending university, and marrying later. This state of affairs requires women to leave the private sphere and enter the public, to negotiate the streets. Yet, time and again Peruvian women's narrative shows that, rather than facilitating this seemingly liberating situation for women, Lima is still structured such that moving about the city is at best challenging, and at worst dangerous. As will be seen later in the discussion of a novel by Ollé, Lima's streets do not welcome women, but rather provoke them to seek the very isolation they had purportedly shed as women gained more rights and became more involved in the national economy.

In *Postmodernism, or, the Cultural Logic of Late Capitalism,* Frederic Jameson observes that in the postmodern world the subject finds himself in a state of crisis owing to a great extent to the very distribution of urban space. In the postmodern era we suffer from a breakdown of spatial limits and hierarchies—what Jameson calls a crisis of boundaries—that denotes a crisis of the subject. Jameson asks, "Does (postmodern space) not tend to demobilize us and surrender us to passivity and helplessness, by systematically obliterating possibilities of action under the impenetrable fog of historical inevitability?" (86). Kathleen Kirby comments that this "us" of which Jameson speaks is of markedly masculine character. Upon experiencing postmodern space, the subject described by Jameson is surprised to see himself lost, vulnerable because of the lack of recognizable and manageable limits, and, as a consequence, he suddenly understands himself as a corporeal being. Kirby argues that the luxury of moving freely in the public realm, of forgetting oneself as a body-subject, is a luxury a woman has never had. Therefore, Kirby suggests, "to become conscious of embodiment could only be a positive step for masculinity, as much as such consciousness is also a perpetually wearing aspect of femininity" (53). Kirby imagines the different ways in which a man and a woman would negotiate the same postmodern landscape:

> For the man, I imagine that the most prominent feature of the landscape would be pathways, along which he projects himself, making his world a space that returns to him a self-image of movement, command, self-assurance and self-satisfaction. For the woman—and as a woman— I imagine a world structured not by pathways but by obstacles: the people in it may be threats as much as impediments; rather than seeing how to get from 'point A' to 'point B' I often see what is keeping me from getting there. (Ibid.)

The lack of pathways and abundance of obstacles for *limeñas* negotiating their city-space is a consistent theme among these women writers.

One can immediately appreciate the barriers that make difficult the very existence of women in Lima in Irma del Águila's 2000 collection of short stories, *Tía, saca el pie del embrague* (Auntie, take your foot off the clutch). Together the stories demarcate a geography of Lima that promotes the isolation of women and prevents their understanding themselves as urban subjects. Like the other works studied here, these narratives emphasize the conflict between modernity and postmodernity in Lima and portray the city as a site of conflict rather than community. As Rocío Silva Santiesteban notes in her foreword to the collection, "Lima is the protagonist of this collection of short stories: a disseminated city that mistreats its inhabitants or takes them to extremes, pressing the accelerator to the floor, to push them into a head-on collision."[10] The opening story, "Tú y yo" (You and I), exemplifies these conflicts. It narrates the trip home of a young woman, Susana, from a billiard hall. During the trip the first-person narrator seems to be accompanied by her twin sister, Amanda, though at the end the reader learns the sister had been killed at age five in a car accident, while sitting in the seat normally occupied by the narrator.

From the billiard hall through the bus ride to Miraflores, the middle-upper-class suburb of Lima where the protagonist lives, Susana narrates her voyage as if accompanied by her sister, and she and the reader encounter Amanda's (rather than Susan's) reflection every time the protagonist passes a window or mirror.[11] If it was the danger of the streets that took her sister, it is the reflective glass of the city that returns her. The narrator uses this reencounter to relate her experience within the city. Although this story can certainly be read as an exploration of the guilt the protagonist feels at not having been killed along with her twin, what interests us here is the use of the city in the construction of the narrative.

In the billiard hall, an interior monologue/dialogue between the two, narrated in free indirect style, comments on the discomfort "they" feel in this masculine space. Noting that the men in the hall are eyeing "them," Susana comments to Amanda/herself, "it would have been better if you had worn jeans. Don't bother me, you protest, in the end it's all the same, because with jeans you know they still harass us, that they're too tight in the rear or too tight in the crotch; shorts are even worse. Look, even with our Hindu skirts because they are transparent in the light. Anyway, we always get defensive in this masculine territory."[12] Women either must put up with the aggressive looks of men, meant to emphasize both their sexual vulnerability and their exclusion from this masculine sphere—their lack of a "right" to occupy this space—or they must leave and give up an activity they otherwise enjoy. The scene highlights the way that geography serves to reflect and enforce social norms.

The protagonist does leave, and as she travels the streets on her way home she creates a sociocultural map of Lima. At the bus stop, Susana notes her surroundings:

> (it is decorated with photos of girls and guys in languid poses, packaged
> in their jeans). The language of advertising and what a contrast with
> the silence of the wait, our wait. A moment to look around at what
> imperceptibly changes, transforms. The streets, for example, have been
> recently patched, the trees on the side street are drying up, or rather, keep
> drying up, the two or three street kiosks that had been on the corner have
> gone or been driven off by the municipality. A pipe must have broken
> nearby because it smells like sewer water. One says Lima never changes
> but it's not true, it changes clothes constantly. And moods, yes, although
> we insist on saying that we have only summers and winters, with the
> same gray sky. It's a lie, what doesn't change is our atavistic perception of
> the city and its inhabitants.[13]

The decay of the city, patched over with glitzy advertisements or bits of fresh pavement, denotes a transformation that the city dwellers miss. This oblivion is at least in part due to the isolation that the production and utilization of common space promotes.[14]

The narrator describes the bus ride, in one of the many microbuses that transport commuters. Packed full at rush hour, passengers cannot avoid uncomfortable body contact with one another and "a free trade of breath and sweat."[15] Yet, the narrator notes, "curiously, however, the passengers seem to be lost in themselves, eyes nailed to a bag, faces resting against a window, or hypnotically counting the trees on the streets that sail past. The loneliness of crowds. The complicit anonymity."[16] The narrator counts herself among those isolated and alone. Furthermore, she experiences a lack of identity, an invisibility that is ironically both overcome by and reinforced through her identification with her spectral sister.

It is indeed only in the mirrors of the bar in the billiard hall or the windows of the bus or of commercial establishments that Susana is able to see herself in this city, and then she only recognizes Amanda. She makes explicit the need for city glass to prove her/their material existence: "in front of the display windows of the 'Época' bookstore, we are tangible again."[17] Once she leaves the commercial zone of Miraflores, Susana loses her sister, and the reader learns that Amanda is long dead. In the residential neighborhoods, it is the lack of city glass that interrupts the sisters' re-union: "running down Balta Street we leave behind the tall bank buildings with their thick polarized panes, and cafés, cinemas, pizza parlors, and other shops with wide display windows."[18] And yet, the reader knows that what Susana is finding in those windows is an illusion; the woman sees her reflection in the glass of the city but is unable to recognize herself. She even wonders if it had not been she, Susana, who had been killed in the accident rather than Amanda. The city, marked by the aggressive male gaze, the urban decay, the crowding yet silent bodies, allows the protagonist to see only a ghostlike mirroring that she cannot even recognize as herself. In del Águila's depiction, Lima impedes the realization of the female subject, allowing her to be but a deceptive reflection.

The urban isolation and the spatialized struggles of women are also articulated in Pilar Dughi's 1997 novel *Puñales escondidos* (Hidden dag-gers). The protagonist is Fina Artadi, who, like so many female characters in contemporary Peruvian women's fiction, is alone—a spinster without living family and with a married lover. "Miss Fina," as she is always called, is a lower-level administrator of a bank where she has been working for many years and from which she will soon retire. Miss Fina is negatively affected by the accelerated change in the urban space that surrounds her; she does not know how to confront these real (physical) and symbolic transformations, which contrast with her own personal stagnation. Where men may see pathways or possibilities within the new structuring of space (even if the possibilities are dishonest or criminal), Miss Fina finds barri-ers. This situation is reflected in the narrative reproduction of Miraflores, the Lima suburb where the story takes place. The protagonist moves through Miraflores and comments that "it was no longer that small, tranquil city of ample homes and large parks where in the afternoons people strolled along the levees above the cliffs. In the formerly quiet streets now there were traffic jams, because the narrow ways were no longer sufficient for the flow of the population. While the city changed, she had remained in the bank. . . ."[19] Beyond the bank, the novel reproduces other spaces in Mira-flores—a supermarket, a beauty salon, the woman's apartment. Even those spaces that could be considered "feminine" are alienating within the frame-work of the changing city. They are spaces of solitude, not community.

Perhaps Fina's solitude is most acutely displayed in her place of em-ployment. The narrator describes the bank, symbol of the national econ-omy, as "an entelechy that rose over the little black heads of the clients who swarmed around the tellers' windows, believing, with spontaneous faith, in the virtues of a solemn corporation. For this reason, the old building was imposing, as befitted an institution that should transmit an image of security, success, and solvency."[20] The protagonist notes the fallaciousness of the image of the building, a structure that in reality obscures the dishonest moves of its executives and some employees and conceals its ruthless disinterest for its regular clients. Miss Fina compares herself to her male colleagues, young subordinates who will soon pass her in the institutional hierarchy. The ease with which they move within the financial world (even the facility with which they commit fraud) is contrasted with the isolation Miss Fina feels in the same institution. The space does not correspond with the values that it supposedly houses, a fact that estranges Miss Fina and is simultaneously celebrated and exploited by her male colleagues.

The very alienation the protagonist experiences provokes a resistance to the system to which she is subject and an attempt to resignify the space that orders it; in this way, the text creates a geography of resistance. Michel de Certeau reminds us that "innumerable ways of playing and foiling the other's game, that is, the space instituted by others, characterize the subtle, stubborn, resistant activity of groups which, since they lack their own space, have to get along in a network of already established forces and representations" (18). Miss Fina, unsatisfied with her position in the space that defines her, begins to resist her designated role—that of a faithful yet unambitious employee, a hardworking, docile woman—and imposes her own values on the corporate space, originally created and defined by men. Steve Pile observes that "resistance does not just act on topographies imposed through the spatial technologies of domination, it moves across them under the noses of the enemy, seeking to create new meanings out of imposed meanings, to re-work and divert space to other ends" (16). Thus, Miss Fina lends her own money to a client who needs to cover a check written on insufficient funds and spends hours of her own time trying to prove that one of her male subordinates has embezzled funds from an elderly client. Through her actions, Miss Fina aims to recover the values that the institution proclaims. Nevertheless, the lack of connection between ideal space and real space eventually defeats the woman, who in the end commits a crime of her own, appropriating $250,000 from the account of a dead woman—another act of resistance, because in this case Miss Fina will use the funds for her own retirement, protecting her own interests before those of an institution that has exploited her and ignored her accomplishments.

(It must be noted, however, that Miss Fina's crime is somewhat less serious than those committed by the male characters. Because the deceased has no heirs, the loser in this transaction is the institution, not another person.) Thus, Dughi shows how even as the city seeks to constrict women, they are able to take advantage of certain institutional practices in acts of resistance against their own subjugation. Miss Fina creates her own geographies by redefining and renegotiating the power structure of those that surround her.

This restructuring of urban geography as a response to the solitude imposed by official geography is also present in *Pista falsa* by Carmen Ollé. As with Dughi's work, the protagonist of the novel is a single woman without family.[21] Irene, whose mother and two siblings live in Miami, spends Christmas with her boss and New Year's with a single Spanish girlfriend, and has a lover who is engaged to another woman. Although the pretext of the narrative is a mystery—Irene decides to investigate the suspicious death of Tessa, a friend who committed suicide at age twenty-one—one could understand the plot as a reflection of the title, a sort of false path; for the novel is, above all, a story of lonely women. Besides the protagonist, there is an insane ex-ballerina who, after living in the streets for many years, commits suicide; Melania Melitta, a distant relative of Tessa and former opera singer who lives alone in the provinces; and Tessa's mother, married for a third time but living without her husband in a retirement home. The multiple reflections on Lima reveal the complicity of the city with the women's solitude.

As in *Puñales escondidos,* the protagonist remarks on the changes suffered by the city:

> As a teenager she loved to stroll down the Jirón de la Unión, but after
> all that migration from the highlands to the city, it was invaded by street
> vendors. The beautiful colonial churches, the ficus-shaded atriums, and
> the passageways with ancient names: Merchants, Swordsmiths, Button-
> sellers, etc. . . . She saw herself walking there among the imaginary
> women from the illustrations.[22]

Irene dwells more comfortably in the world of fantasy because it provides her something her real surroundings do not: "really, her desires lay beyond real time. She was fed up with life offering her few opportunities to feel electrified inside."[23] She imagines herself among imaginary women, because urban space is not propitious to a community of women. In one of Melania Melitta's interior monologues, we read that "Lima was a city of melancholic sounds, and this melancholy came from the gray-green sea,

or from the hills colored like sphinxes. Lima herself, wasn't she a kind of
Thebes full of (female) enemies?"[24] The narration insists: "no other city
inspired such irrational fear in her as this one, but it wasn't a product of
her imagination. She detested opening the pages of a newspaper; there was
displayed all the reigning schizophrenia."[25] Lima, in this novel, is a place
of contradictions and contradictory juxtapositions. The work re-creates a
great variety of public spaces (parks, streets, cafés), as well as private spaces
(houses, hotel rooms), and the female protagonist moves rather freely
about the city, entering these different zones. Nevertheless, her movement
does not denote freedom or a sense of ownership of the urban space that
surrounds her; rather, the protagonist, like the other women in the novel,
is confused, decentered, misplaced. Much of her movement is, in fact, provoked by the commands or desires of the male characters, who do show an
agility and security in their movement about the city.

This question of movement through the city is highlighted in Ollé's *Una
muchacha bajo paraguas,* written in 1980 but not published until 2002. In
this novel, the protagonist, perhaps a literary projection of the author herself, narrates simultaneously her time in Paris, living a bohemian writer's
life along with other expatriate artists of various nationalities, and her return to Lima four years later. In the contemplations of the first-person narrator, the Peruvian and French capitals mesh, play, and contrast:

> My solitude in Lima was implacable. The cloudy, unreal morning. Like
> the voice of my mother at breakfast when I was single. On my return, the
> women from Malambito smiled at me in the bathroom of a *peña* and
> Lima was juxtaposed with Paris like in a dadaist landscape. The urine
> puddled on the bathroom tiles smelled desperately that night. . . .
>   A city in pieces remained faithful on my mental stage. The Eiffel
> Tower rose before me when the bus turned a corner in Pueblo Libre.
>   My friends prowling about the Latin Quarter. Four years without
> confronting Lima.[26]

The absolute solitude felt in Lima is opposed to the sense of community,
however fleeting or precarious, among the immigrant community in Paris.

Whereas Paris is a city that begs to be inhabited and explored, Lima
provokes isolation and enclosure. The narrator laments, "Lima is not a
place of encounters but of shocks."[27] In contrast, she imagines the freedom
of Paris: "it's a sunny morning in a faraway city. I get up and prepare tea.
Nevertheless, I am going to end up in the university dining hall in Paris, in
the Dauphine. That's how the city was. Wherever I walked I'd end up where

I wanted to be. If not, I'd lose myself among its incongruent city blocks and would lunch alone. Upon return, I'd write a page on my Underwood."[28] On the other hand, in Lima the protagonist has no desire to leave her apartment: "to get coffee in Lince you had to go to the center or to the locales dispersed throughout the streets of the Barrio. None of them excited me; they didn't inspire my vagabond soul. . . . In the café, alone, I contemplate the clients, listen to the murmur of the passersby and the scandal of the cyclists who are trying to alarm. I wrote letters that I never mailed, letters that have been lost. . . ."[29] The irony of these two passages is not lost on the reader: for the protagonist, "home" is alienating, while the "foreign" is liberating. Particularly in the protagonist's capacity as a writer, Paris inspires the writing of a page of her novel, whereas Lima allows only for letters that will never be read.

This concern for the state of a woman writer in Lima is acute in Ollé's narrative. In ¿*Por qué hacen tanto ruido?* (1997) (Why are they making so much noise?), the narrator-protagonist, a frustrated writer, experiences a solitude that is both sought—as she consistently escapes to her room to read or to try to write—and feared. Many of her experiences with the city take place in her trips to the pharmacy to buy tranquilizers, through the crimes and acts of violence she reads about in the newspapers, or from the vantage point of the window of her bedroom.[30] Regarding the latter, she says, "I am standing in front of the window saying this: poetry is lived. But I can't live it."[31] The connection between writing/poetry and the city is implicit throughout the novel, and it is repeatedly shown that, like poetry, the protagonist cannot "live" the city.

Its public spaces incite anguish in the narrator: "the yellow lights and the white bar provoked in me a sensation of terror that perhaps came from a provincial club or from the remains of Sunday halfway standing, drunk, surrounded by police."[32] As in del Águila's short story, the protagonist of this novel loses touch with herself in the city: "it's almost ten o'clock in the Chasqui alleyway . . . I begin to discover myself as a stranger in that T-intersection in which two new buildings are being erected."[33] The novel specifies the names of neighborhoods, plazas, streets, buildings, and establishments; it carefully creates a detailed map of Lima. Yet the map provided is one that insists on the exclusion, or at least provokes the extreme discomfort, of women, especially of women writers: "while I dragged myself to the pharmacy . . . I had thought about how my women poet friends didn't have anywhere to go in this city on such a beautiful windy night."[34]

Lima is shown as a place that is hostile to poetry, where one cannot make a living by writing, where the dangers of the city are immediate and omnipresent, and where solitude is both an imposition and a begrudgingly accepted escape.[35]

Specifically regarding the relationship between poetry and Lima, the protagonist laments that the city both drives her to write and impedes her literary endeavors: "something compelled me to leave by means of writing. Perhaps the city, this source of signs and threats; I didn't feel like deciphering them."[36] Like the protagonist of *Una muchacha bajo paraguas,* the woman remembers a much more productive stay in a European city, and asks herself why she is in Lima, "why precisely here where nothing is poetic?"[37] Part of what impedes the woman's progress as a writer, it becomes clear, is precisely her status as a woman. She is expected to work to support her writer husband and their daughter, to provide emotional support to her partner, whose literary endeavors are apparently more important than hers, and even to serve as his psychological "nurse" while he decides if he should leave her for another woman.

Faced with these impossible expectations, the woman sees writing as a potential escape: "A novel. It's impossible: the argument, the characters, the plot, anyway. Only anarchic prose, hybrid, oneiric, whatever. What am I trying to do? they ask. Philosophy? What I want is to change houses . . . Destroy any look that tries to judge me."[38] The novel, written as she wishes to write, provides a new space, an escape from the judging (masculine) eyes of the city. It is clear that the very novel we are reading is that novel described by the protagonist, and that in *¿Por qué hacen tanto ruido?,* as in her other novels, Ollé is theorizing how the city inspires women's writing while at the same time it endeavors to impede it. If urban geography provokes discomfort, isolation, and stagnation in women, through writing they are able to create other geographies, geographies of resistance.

Indeed, the Lima portrayed in these narratives is stifling and oppressive. And yet, ironically, it is also inspiring; for it is in the protagonists' very acts of moving in Lima, and in the authors' attempts to write the city, in their appropriation, however uncomfortable, of urban space, that we can appreciate their resistance. The women protagonists of these narratives mobilize—run, defraud, investigate, write—in order to rebel against their own stagnation and solitude (searching for "opportunities to feel electrified inside") and to uncover truths or options hidden within the city by the forces of authority. At the same time, the women writers of these narratives mobilize, taking over Lima as subject and literary space, in order to rebel against their secondary status as professional writers in Peru. Their narrative demands that the question "What does it mean to be a (contemporary) *limeña?*" must also form part of the Peruvian literary dialogue, while their writing simultaneously begins to provide their readers with answers.

NOTES

1. "¿Qué es ser antiguo limeño?" (13). Unless otherwise indicated, all translations are mine.

2. Lima was founded in 1535 on January 6, the Catholic Feast of the Kings; thus it is known as the "City of Kings."

3. It would be impossible within the limitations of this space to list all of the works that deal specifically with Lima by these and other male writers. I will, however, mention a few exemplary works with which I am implicitly dialoguing in this essay. Of course, the short stories of Ribeyro are indispensable documents of life in Lima from the mid- to late twentieth century. Many of Vargas Llosa's novels, such as *La ciudad y los perros* (1963), *Tía Julia y el escribidor* (1977), and, especially, *Conversación en la Catedral* (1969), contain seminal descriptions of the city as it struggles with modernity and postmodernity. And any discussion of Lima in twentieth-century Peruvian narrative would be incomplete without a contemplation of the title character's experience with the city in Bryce Echenique's *Un mundo para Julius* (1970). More recently, Jaime Bayly is presenting the world of the disenchanted, upper-middle class *limeño* youth in works such as *No se lo digas a nadie* (1994). There are many other interesting and valuable representations of this fascinating city. I choose to mention these as they are perhaps those most recognized internationally and, thus, are the visions of Lima that are most validated both inside and outside the country.

4. In several conversations and interviews I have had with women writers such as Ollé and the younger Carla Sagastegui, I have repeatedly heard their frustration at being marginalized from the official literary scene. Contemporary Peruvian women's writing is rarely translated for foreign markets, is not read in Peruvian schools, and is not given serious critical attention in or out of Peru. Prizes such as the Magda Portal prize for short narrative by women are scoffed at by male writers.

5. Elmore examines the narrative of Martín Adán, José Diez Canseco, José María Arguedas, Ciro Alegría, Julio Ramón Ribeyro, Alfredo Bryce Echenique, and Mario Vargas Llosa.

6. Ortega says Granda offers a "versión aseñorada" (a "lady-fied" version) of criollo discourse on Lima.

7. "Viajar a Lima es llegar a la antesala del cielo y ver de ahí el trono de la gloria y la fortuna" (*Aves*, 132). The discourse on Lima in the second two novels of Matto de Turner's national trilogy, *Índole* (Disposition, 1891) and *Herencia* (Inheritance, 1895), is decidedly less admiring. My thanks to Naomi Lindstrom for bringing this to my attention.

8. Little has been written on the literary production of women in Peru. One concise yet informative essay that gives an overview of twentieth-century women's narrative is Giovanna Minardi's introduction to the volume of short stories by Peruvian women writers that she edited in 2000.

9. Many theorists have discussed coexistence of multiple temporalites in Latin America, where the premodern continues and aspects of the postmodern may predate entrance into modernity. For Néstor García Canclini, cities are the spaces where this "multitemporal hybridity" is best appreciated.

10. "Lima es la protagonista de este conjunto de cuentos: una ciudad diseminada que maltrata a sus habitantes o los lleva hacia extremos, apretando el acelerador hasta el fondo, para obligarlos al choque frontal" (Presentación).

11. Miraflores is the principal setting of the narratives studied here and of many of the works by male writers such as Vargas Llosa, Bryce Echenique, and Bayly. Traditionally one of the most affluent areas of Lima, it is where many writers were raised and where many still live. Lately, as is narrated by Dughi, the area has somewhat declined as the most wealthy have moved on to other suburbs.

12. "hubiera sido mejor que vinieras en jeans. No molestes, protestas, en el fondo es la misma vaina, porque con los jeans sabemos que joden igual, que si te lo pones al cuete o que si el tiro está alto; los shorts menos, pues. Mira, también con nuestras faldas hindúes porque se transparentan a contraluz. De más, siempre nos ponemos a la defensiva en este territorio masculino" (14).

13. "(...está decorado con fotos de chicos y chicas en pose displicente, enfundados en sus jeans). El lenguaje de la publicidad y qué contraste con el silencio de la espera, nuestra espera. Un momento para mirar a nuestro alrededor que imperceptiblemente cambia, se transforma. Las pistas, por ejemplo, han sido parchadas últimamente, los árboles de la vía auxiliar se están secando, mejor dicho siguen secándose, las dos o tres carretillas de vendedores ambulantes que ocupaban la esquina se han marchado o deben haber sido desalojados por el municipio. Debe haberse roto alguna cañería por aquí cerca, porque huele a aguas servidas. Una dice, Lima nunca cambia pero no es cierto, se muda de ropa a cada rato. Y de humor, vaya que sí, aunque nos empecinemos en decir que aquí sólo hay veranos e inviernos, con el mismo cielo gris. Mentira, lo que no cambia es nuestra atávica percepción de la ciudad y de las personas que la habitan" (15).

14. The sense of isolation, or anomie, felt by urban dwellers has been oft treated in urban studies. What is clear from the narratives studied here, however, is that

these women writers portray the female subject as especially plagued by isolation in Lima. According to these works, in Lima men move about and occupy urban space much more freely, confidently, and collectively (in the good-ol'-boys-club sense) than do women.

15. "un libre comercio de alientos y sudores" (16).

16. "curiosamente, sin embargo, los pasajeros aparentan estar perdidos en sí mismos, los ojos clavados en un bolso, recostando la cara contra la ventana o contando hipnotizados los árboles de las calles que rebasan. La soledad de las multitudes. El anonimato cómplice" (16–17).

17. "frente a los escaparates de la librería 'Época', somos tangibles nuevamente" (20).

18. "en la bajada Balta van quedando atrás los altos edificios de bancos con gruesas lunas polarizados y cafés, cines, pizzerías y demás comercios con amplios escaparates" (21).

19. "ya no era esa pequeña ciudad tranquila de amplias residencias y grandes parques, donde la gente se paseaba por las tardes rodeando los malecones sobre acantilados. En las calles antiguamente silenciosas, ahora se producían embotellamientos de vehículos, porque las estrechas pistas ya no se abastecían para el flujo de la población. Mientras la ciudad cambiaba, ella había permanecido en el banco..." (21).

20. "una entelequia que estaba por sobre las cabecitas negras de los clientes que pululaban delante de las ventanillas, creyendo, con espontánea fe, en las virtudes de una corporación solemne. Por eso, el antiguo edificio era imponente, como correspondía a una institución que debía transmitir una imagen de seguridad, poder, éxito y solvencia" (19–20).

21. When asked why so many of the female protagonists in contemporary Peruvian women's narrative are middle-aged single women, Ollé replied that it is because that is the situation of so many of the writers themselves. Ollé argues that because of social expectations, it is very difficult for married women with children to find the time and support to be writers (personal conversation). This observation is reflected in the situation of the female protagonist of *¿Por qué hacen tanto ruido?*, discussed later.

22. "De adolescente le fascinaba deambular por el jirón de la Unión, pero después de toda esa migración de la sierra a la ciudad estaba invadido de ambulantes. La bellas iglesias coloniales, los atrios sombreados de ficus y los pasajes con nombres antiguos: Mercaderes, Espaderos, Botoneros, etc... Se figuraba caminando por ahí junto a las mujeres imaginarias de las ilustraciones" (13–14). The Jirón de la Unión is a street in the center of Lima.

23. "realmente, sus deseos se ubicaban más allá del tiempo real. Estaba harta de que la vida le ofreciera pocas oportunidades para sentirse electrizada por dentro" (14).

24. "Lima era una ciudad de sonidos melancólicos, y esa melancolía provenía del mar verde gris, o de los cerros del mismo color de las esfinges. Lima misma ¿no era una especie de Tebas llena de enemigas?" (36).

25. "ninguna ciudad como ésta le inspiraba tanto temor irracional, pero no todo era producto de su imaginación. Detestaba abrir las páginas de un periódico, ahí se mostraba toda la esquizofrenia reinante" (37).

26. "Mi soledad en Lima era implacable. La mañana nublada, irreal. Como la voz de mi madre en el desayuno de soltera. A mi vuelta, las mujeres de Malambito me sonreían en el WC de una peña y Lima se yuxtaponía a París como en un paisaje dadaísta. El orín encharcado en las baldosas del baño olía desesperadamente esa noche...

"Una ciudad en retazos permanecía fiel en mi tablero mental. La torre Eiffel se elevaba al voltear una cuadra de Pueblo Libre en el micro.

"Mis amigos merodeando el Barrio Latino. Cuatro años sin enfrentarme a Lima" (37).

Malambito is a lower-class, predominantly Afro-Peruvian neighborhood in Lima; a *peña* is a type of bar that plays typical Peruvian music. Pueblo Libre is a lower-middle-class neighborhood in Lima.

27. "Lima no es una ciudad de encuentros sino de sobresaltos" (81).

28. "es una mañana de sol en una ciudad lejana. Me levanto y preparo un té. Sin embargo, voy a recalar en el comedor universitario de París, en el mismo Dauphine. Así era la ciudad. Por donde caminara llegaría al punto deseado. Cuando no, me perdería entre sus incongruentes manzanas y almorzaría sola. Regresando escribiría una página en mi Underwood" (86).

29. "para tomar un café en Lince había que trasladarse al centro o a los locales desperdigados en las bocacalles del Barrio. Ninguno me entusiasmaba, no inspiraban mi alma de vagabunda. ...En el café, aislada, contemplo a los visitantes, oigo el murmullo de los pasajeros y el escándalo de los motociclistas que quieren alardear. Yo escribía cartas que nunca mandaba, cartas que se han traspapelado..." (91–92). A middle-/lower-middle-class area of Lima, Lince houses many embassies, a hospital, and a large city park.

30. The novel is set during the 1980s, the time of most extreme violence by the Shining Path and Tupac Amaru terrorist groups. This violence and the city residents' reactions to it are reported in the papers the protagonist reads. Regarding the role of media in the shaping of the city, Joan Ramón Resina writes, "architecture has become obsolete as the sole or even primary medium for visualizing the city. The image of the contemporary city is not only mediated by a variety of communications media but actually emerges from them" (5–6).

31. "estoy de pie ante la ventana diciendo esto: la poesía se vive. Pero no puedo vivirla" (12).

32. "las luces amarillas y el bar blanco me provocaban una sensación de terror

que tal vez provenía de un club provinciano o de los restos del domingo semier-guido, ebrio, rodeado de policías" (17).

33. "son casi las diez en el pasaje Chasqui... Empiezo a descubrirme como una desconocida en ese pasaje en T el que ahora se elevan dos nuevos edificios" (33).

34. "mientras me arrastraba hacia la farmacia... Había pensado en que mis amigas poetas no tenían adónde ir en esta ciudad en una noche tan hermosa de gran viento" (34).

35. Regarding the type of solitude offered by Lima, the narrator writes: "esta soledad no es romántica de Nerval ni el spleen baudelariano, no la locura nie-tscheana en Sils Marie... Es la de los vagos que caen más bajo hasta que la sorpresa que motivan parece humana. En un terreno baldío, un vago, un demente, cuyos cabellos erizados parecen enredaderas mugrosas: una imagen de Lima que digieres como si digirieras mierda, ¿me gusta la mierda?" (this loneliness is not romantic like Nerval's or like Baudelaire's spleen, or Nietschean madness in Sils Marie . . . It's one of vagabonds that have fallen so low that the very surprise they provoke seems human. It's an untilled land, a vagabond, a demented person, whose bristled hair looks like mossy, climbing vines: an image of Lima that you digest as if you were digesting shit, do I like shit?) (53).

36. "algo me impulsaba a salir fuera a través de lo que escribía. Tal vez la ciu-dad, esa fuente de signos y amenazas; descifrarlos me daba pereza" (28).

37. "¿por qué precisamente acá donde nada es poético?" (43).

38. "Una novela. Es imposible: el argumento, los personajes, la trama, en fin. Sólo la prosa anárquica, híbrida, onírica, lo que quieran. ¿Qué pretendo? pregun-tan. ¿Hacer filosofía? Lo que deseo es cambiar de casa,... Liquidar cualquier mirada que pretenda ser juez" (65).

WORKS CITED

de Certeau, Michel. *The Practice of Everyday Life*. Trans. Steven Rendall. Berkeley: University of California Press, 1984.

del Águila, Irma. *Tía, saca el pie del embrague*. Lima: San Marcos, 2000.

Dughi, Pilar. *Puñales escondidos*. Lima: Banco Central de Reserva del Perú, 1997.

Duncan, James, and David Ley. "Introduction: Representing the Place of Culture." In *Place/Culture/Representation,* ed. James Duncan and David Ley. London: Routledge, 1993. 1–21.

Elmore, Peter. *Los muros invisibles: Lima y la modernidad en la novela del siglo XX.* Lima: Mosca Azul, 1993.

García Canclini, Néstor. *Hybrid Cultures: Strategies for Entering and Leaving Mod-ernity*. Trans. Christopher L. Chiappari and Silvia L. López. Minneapolis: Uni-versity of Minnesota Press, 1995.

Jameson, Fredric. *Postmodernism, or, the Cultural Logic of Late Capitalism.* Durham, N.C.: Duke University Press, 1991.

Kirby, Kathleen. "Re:Mapping Subjectivity: Cartographic Vision and the Limits of Politics." In *Body Space: Destabilizing Geographies of Gender and Sexuality,* ed. Nancy Duncan. London: Routledge, 1996.

Matto de Turner, Clorinda. *Aves sin nido.* 1889. Oaxaca, Mexico: Oasis, 1981.

———. *Birds without a Nest: A Story of Indian Life and Priestly Oppression in Peru.* Trans. J. G. H. Lindstrom and Naomi Lindstrom. Austin: University of Texas Press, 1996.

Minardi, Giovanna. *Cuentas: narradoras peruanas del siglo XX.* Lima: Flora Tristán/ Santo Oficio, 2000.

Ollé, Carmen. Personal conversation. January 10, 2002.

———. *Pista falsa.* Lima: El Santo Oficio, 1999.

———. *¿Por qué hacen tanto ruido?.* Lima: San Marcos, 1997.

———. *Una muchacha bajo paraguas.* Lima: El Santo Oficio, 2002.

Ortega, Julio. "Para una arqueología del discurso sobre Lima." In *Cultura urbana latinoamericana,* ed. Richard Morse and Jorge Enrique Hardoy. Buenos Aires: Consejo Latinoamericano de Ciencias Sociales, 1985. 103–13.

Parsons, Deborah. *Streetwalking the Metropolis: Women, the City, and Modernity.* Oxford: Oxford University Press, 2000.

Pile, Steve. "Introduction: Opposition, Political Identities and Spaces of Resistance." In *Geographies of Resistance,* ed. Steve Pile and Michael Keith. London: Routledge, 1997.

Resina, Joan Ramón. *After-Image of the City.* Ithaca, N.Y.: Cornell University Press, 2003.

Silva Santiesteban, Rocío. "Presentación." In del Águila, no page.

4

Failed Modernity

San Juan at Night
in Mayra Santos Febres's
Cualquier miércoles soy tuya

GUILLERMO B. IRIZARRY

> I parked the car, or I should say, the piece of junk eaten up by the ocean
> salt with which I inconveniently move through the city.
>
> *Cualquier miércoles soy tuya, 11*[1]

> If what remains of a sacrifice can be called abject, in another connection
> consuming the leavings of a sacrifice can also be the cause of good
> rebirths and can even lead to finding salvation
>
> *Julia Kristeva, Powers of Horror, 76*

The opening sentence of Mayra Santos's *Cualquier miércoles soy tuya* (Any given Wednesday I'll be yours) succinctly locates the novel's action and underscores the symbolic value of movement and activity within the city.[2] The "worn-out, corroded vehicle" brings to mind the difficulty of movement and velocity within this tropical island.[3] Tropicality and Caribbeanness trump modernity, and the novelistic endeavor reproduces this literary and ideological proposal. Although *Cualquier miércoles* never declares the name of Puerto Rico, its capital, San Juan, marks the plot's central coordinates. As such, the text underscores the problematics of a twenty-first-century city within a global thrust for convergence in modernity and illuminates the realities of this improbable historical horizon.[4]

Santos's San Juan locates trans-island human and commercial interactions, recuperates long-standing regional interventions of colonial powers, and reflects upon the failure of modernity and modernization within Puerto Rico, the Caribbean, and, metonymically, the periphery of global capital. The cityscape signifies modernity as a cessation in an overpowering global project. Failure, then, marks a point of entry through which to expose alternative circuits of communicability within subalternity.[5] The

67

narration illustrates what Alberto Moreiras would call a "negative instance within cultural consumption itself . . . the preservation of a sort of residual subject sovereignty or local singularity" (64). The homogenizing thrust of globalization cannot domesticate the radical heterogeneity of the city (and the Caribbean) and, as such, new political subjectivities emerge eluding the mediation of the state and of supranational administrative structures.[6]

Cualquier miércoles soy tuya depicts what Steve Pile terms "spatialities that lie beyond 'power'" (5). It portrays a radically heterogeneous Caribbean subject, who comes into being through the cartography of a non-sovereign, stateless island nation. The protagonist, Julián Castrodad, an aspiring writer, narrates a nocturnal and subaltern cityscape, populated by undocumented workers, homosexual prostitutes, drug traffickers, Santería practitioners, frustrated writers, unfaithful husbands and wives, and a variety of characters scheming in "occult economies" (Comaroff and Comaroff, 26). The novelistic world brings to light the sociohistorical fragmentation of twenty-first-century Puerto Rico and its precarious civil society. The narrated city becomes both metonymy and metaphor of the nation while indexing the nation's discursive and ideological strategies, reflecting upon its act of "conceiving and constructing space" and its "differentiation and redistribution of parts and functions" (de Certeau, 94). All the while, the novel reminds the reader that the modern project implied in the city "generates a loss which, in the multiple forms of wretchedness and poverty outside the system and of waste inside it, constantly turns production into 'expenditure'" (ibid., 95).

This study of the novel underscores how the writer articulates new political subjectivities and constructs an ecology of power that redeploys the "residues" of the system to engage in possibilities of "rebirth" and "salvation" (as suggested by Kristeva in the second epigraph to this essay). Indeed, the novel's portrayal of the city supports Kristeva's notion of "radical otherness"—"tearing oneself away from any identity (including one's own)" (*Nations*, 22–24)—and Gayatri Chakravorty Spivak's "irretrievable heterogeneity" (290), which provide alternatives to nationalistic discourses grounded in essentialist visions of this "imagined political community" (Anderson, 6), and of its "fictive ethnicity" (Balibar, 96). By underscoring the zones of abjection and marginality, Santos calls attention to the residues implied in a twenty-first-century "global city" and the possibility of constructing an alternative political landscape.[7]

At the outset of the novel, Julián Castrodad loses his dead-end job as proofreader for *La Noticia,* a sensationalist, local newspaper, and finds employment at a motel in the outskirts of San Juan.[8] The aspiring writer makes the best out of the situation by starting to write a novel about the lives of people who visit the Motel Tulán. Tadeo Chamdeleu, a Haitian undocumented worker who was raised in the Dominican Republic's Baní region, mentors the frustrated novelist on how to work in this marginal landscape. At the Tulán, a diversity of social players meet, and their destinies intertwine. A mysterious "Dama Solitaria" (solitary lady) visits the motel on Wednesdays to escape domestic tensions and finds a quiet room there to write her familial and personal memoirs; she ends up having an affair with Julián. Chino Pereira, the head of a drug-smuggling gang, and some of his field soldiers repeatedly rent out the two most expensive cabins and, for a number of days, organize, weigh, and package new narcotics shipments before distributing them. Chino Pereira buys the silence of the motel employees, befriends Julián, and eventually hires Tadeo as a mule. Leaders of the labor union for the Power Authority's employees gather at the motel to strategize and meet secretly with their lawyer, Efraín Soreno, who happens to be the Dama Solitaria's husband. In time, the narrator discovers that Soreno had pilfered union funds and invested in Chino Pereira's drug trafficking and that Chino Pereira had hired the power company's employees to distribute and sell his product. At the end of the novel, Soreno is burned to death, Chino Pereira disappears, Tadeo is caught delivering a large quantity of cocaine, and Julián is rehired by the newspaper.

The Dama Solitaria's adulterous affair with Castrodad surreptitiously brings in this feminine character as an alternative narrative voice. With La Dama's bundle of papers, left in the trash can in her room, Mayra Santos deploys the well-traveled device of the found manuscript to establish an aesthetic discussion on the opposing values of masculine and feminine epistemologies. The intimate content and personalized style of her handwritten pages establish a counterpoint to the action-oriented plot and distant narrative style of masculine discourse in the novel. Julián not only finds the papers, but also sees fit to brazenly lift from them and to comment on the Dama's writing ability. The tension between narrative voices, seen as opposing social positions and discourses, reiterates the difference between dominant and subaltern epistemologies whereby the articulation of a woman's voice becomes a vehicle to present an alternative perspective on power relations within the city, the nation, and the globe. The epistemological and aesthetic scheme becomes more complex as we underscore representational dynamics that are made difficult because Mayra Santos, an Afro–Puerto Rican woman, embodies the narrative voice of a white male, who pilfers the narrative of an upper-class white woman. All the while, from a position of pseudo-anthropological authority, the narrator fashions a cartography of the city's outskirts and of a marginal (premodern) temporality.

It is important to understand the power dynamics behind the plot, which reveals the consequences of an imposed modernizing agenda in the Caribbean. During the twentieth century, the United States invested massively in this region and intervened aggressively in domestic matters to extract capital, to domesticate the means of production, to bolster its political and commercial hegemony in the region, and to fashion the Caribbean into "America's closed sea, the American Mediterranean" (E. Williams, 422).[9] Post–World War II, this broad intervention promoted massive migration to the major cities and broad support for modernizing projects and ideas. In Puerto Rico, Governor Luis Muñoz Marín (1898–1980, governor 1948–64) marshaled the modernization of the island, aided initially by U.S.-appointed governors, federally funded programs, and the overwhelming support of his Popular Democratic Party.[10] The international media celebrated the "Puerto Rican miracle" and, during the Cold War era, the island served as a paradigm of capitalist development, a showcase for Latin America.[11]

The particularities of Puerto Rico notwithstanding, the aesthetic and epistemological project involved in Mayra Santos's novel does not stand alone in the Spanish Caribbean's literary production. Within the region, a constellation of texts criticizes U.S. intervention in internal affairs, the lack of power to negotiate on an equal footing with powerful nations, and the individual countries' vulnerability. At the same time, the writers dramatize the ability of these countries to push through monumental difficulties and resist global capitalism and neocolonialism. The most interesting writings illuminate the zones of subalternity and abjection within the cities, pointing to a "multitude [that] affirms its singularity by inverting the ideological illusion that all humans on the global surfaces of the world market are interchangeable" and signify "the singular power of a *new city*" (Hardt and Negri, 395).[12] Indeed, these writings underscore the margins of the nation and index the problematics of globalization. This study is not directly concerned with how writers represent the city, or how they portray subalternity and marginality, per se, but with how the city and urban positionalities are constructed as residues of global processes, affecting specific local settings and social relations.

These narratives of globalization in late capitalism disregard nationhood and nationality as limits of their literary project and concomitantly disavow the state as the ultimate limit of subjectivity. In this regard, an assortment of fictional works in the Caribbean reflects upon the nature of governability, modernity, and subjectivity in contemporary times. Writers, and particularly women writers, engage in a symbolic castration of the state and an oblique critique of the nation's patriarchal symbolic structuring. Subalternity articulates a position of power from below, a claim to alternative historicity, and a transversal renegotiation with hegemony. As Jesús Martín-Barbero asserts, this type of narrative "comes into being in the double dehistoricizing and deterritorializing movement that breaks through cultural demarcations . . . [and that] tends to hybridicize itself as never before" (240).

Mayra Santos's work, in particular, articulates a critique of national discourse and engages a "process of naming, legitimization, and empowerment of the plurality which defines the historical and socio-cultural realities" of Puerto Rico and the Caribbean (Birmingham-Pokorny, 30). Her narrative project is in line with a broader critique of a "paternalistic" hegemonic discourse and cultural nationalism on her island, mostly associated with the values of the "Generación del 30" (Gelpí, 1).[13] Her poetry and fiction recover subaltern historicities, reinscribing epistemic violence upon the bodies of marginalized subjects and making difficult the codification of normative cultural identities. In her translocal novel *Sirena Selena vestida de pena* (Mondadori, 2000; published in English as *Sirena Selena* [Picador, 2000]), a drag queen transgresses normative performances of gender and "allows the self to manipulate and work narratives of identity to surpass the limits prescribed by dominant ideological culture" (Castillo, 16). The overarching aesthetic and epistemological project finds a postcolonial and postnational territoriality, and, as such, problematizes hegemonic discourse and rejects more traditional anticolonial and anti-imperialistic epistemologies.

CARTOGRAPHIES OF SUBALTERNITY

San Juan's urban cartography situates *Cualquier miércoles*'s ideological and epistemological proposal. Early on, the male narrative voice declares that the landscape for movement is "the city," and particularly "the uninhabited city" (11–12), and reflects upon the value and meaning of this territory: "It is said that cities are the site of anonymous accumulation but, in these islands lost in the middle of the Caribbean, only a few travel the nocturnal cities. . . . At dusk . . . the city remains . . . ready to embrace the nighttime marauders."[14] The narrative voice prefers to focus on a time–space intersection of marginal social, cultural, economic, and power interactions. The dominant settings are impoverished neighborhoods on the periphery of San Juan, cyclopean public housing projects, and a seedy motel in the outskirts of the city.

A diversity of characters, representing varied social situations, converges in the motel. Julián and Tadeo meet in its office. Chino Pereira and his soldiers organize the drug shipments. The leaders of the power company's workers' union meet with their lawyers, including Efraín Soreno, in its suites. Also, the Dama Solitaria becomes sexually involved there with Julián. These ephemeral human contacts connote the Tulán as a site that challenges legality and that lies beyond hegemony. The motel becomes an image that stands for the production of society, culture, and identity, because it privileges temporary interactions and marginal exchanges as the transactions that most accurately reveal the heterogeneous nature of these constructs.[15] As the novel depicts this dark side of society, it marks a zone of subalternity that points at a repressed level that produces capital, power, and meaning. Early in the novel, Castrodad asserts: "The motel Tulán brought closer the internal machinations of the wheel that made the city move. . . . And all the guests at this gorging . . . carry the weight of their guilt, their belief that they act in the margins of the city, when in truth they are the blood that makes it pulse."[16] Although daytime activity produces an organized vision of a social hierarchy, nocturnal pursuits orchestrate, in marginal locations, the circuits of communication that structure hegemony.

In addition to being a site of social encounters, political scheming, and the production of illegal commodities, the Tulán promotes the narrativization of subjectivities. Castrodad professes to be engaged in an investigation of ethnographic overtones. He accepts the night shift in the motel to access the underworld that would otherwise exclude him as a middle-class, college-educated, white Puerto Rican. From the beginning, his observations reiterate his distance and difference from his coworker and friend, Tadeo, and from the clientele he serves. His narrative object, however, mesmerizes and absorbs him. Finally, the narrator acknowledges that his previous image of Puerto Rico has disallowed countless subjectivities and negated scores of historicities. Through his encounters with these "nightly marauders,"[17] he discovers the personal histories of Chamdeleau, of a white descendant of a criollo grandmother (who acquired a high social status by engaging in adulterous exchanges with rich men), of a drug dealer and Santería practitioner (one of the most powerful men in San Juan's underworld), and of a Santería high priest (who had his religious gatherings in a two-million-dollar mansion in an exclusive access-controlled "*urbanización*"). The aspiring writer, additionally, finds the Dama Solitaria's confessional manuscript in the Tulán, which he in turn assimilates into his literary undertaking, reifying the social exchange that takes place in the novel.

The Tulán indexes numerous other spaces of marginality. Not surprisingly, some of these locations cohabit comfortably with hegemonic social landscapes, such as the home of the *santero*, Ojuani Jekún, or the law firms run by corrupt attorneys. These spaces point to sites of discursive repression and negativity more directly represented by marginal neighborhoods such as Las Parcelas Falú, Paralelo 37, and Los Lirios. Santos not only records these neighborhoods in her work, but makes them key sites of meaning. Castrodad marks them off as sites excluded from his own private, upper-class education. As he acknowledges, dominant pedagogies focus on white patrician figures and on elite historical programs, and dismiss unreservedly the eventuality of poor blacks and mulattoes and of marginal zones in which they reside. In various instances, Castrodad owns up to his own ignorance establishing that "anyone knew more than I about this island. Even drug traffickers knew more, even undocumented immigrants."[18]

His claim to ignorance highlights a cartography of knowledge previously inaccessible to him. These three neighborhoods are all located within the Carolina municipality, east of San Juan, which, since the nineteenth century, has been considered an area where blackness prevails culturally and demographically. Carolina has developed swiftly from a mostly agricultural zone to a densely populated urban area. The demographic and cultural specificity of this town indexes the attempt to include into the heterogeneous cartography of the nation and the region an area whose history has been forgotten but is of great value. The project of modernizing Puerto Rico, emanating from its center of political and economic power, San Juan, later sprawled into its periphery, transforming the bucolic countryside into a highly urbanized region. As the city advanced speedily, hastened by the promises of modernity, numerous marginal neighborhoods sprouted on the outskirts. Because these environs fell off the purview of this movement toward modernity, the city's (and the nation's) metanarrative negated their memory.

The Tulán lets Castrodad become aware of this blind spot in his cartography of knowledge. His desire to know, which shadows Santos's novelistic endeavor, directs his attention to studying and narrating these neighborhoods. Surprisingly, the undocumented immigrant becomes his guide, introducing him to the characters that roam the underbelly of legality and political power. With the enthusiasm of a young writer and the tools of a journalist, Castrodad begins researching the history of the Parcelas Falú and of "Paralelo 37." As per his research, the Parcelas Falú was formed when a rich, landowning family handed out small plots of land to its illegitimate mulatto children. These spurious descendants multiplied, fragmenting the land into smaller plots and sprawling beyond its borders, engendering an even more marginal neighborhood. Paralelo 37 "had sprouted out of nothing fifty years ago, behind the soda bottling factory. . . . Those who knew it, saw it as an abscess that had sprouted on . . . the Parcelas Falú."[19] Interestingly, the Falú's land had changed from a slaveholding plantation to a citrus farm in the early twentieth century, and, after World War II, had housed a bottling factory. The property's development thus insinuates the transformations of the island from an agricultural to an industrialized economy. Dominant metanarrative captures these transformations. Castrodad's literary project, on the other hand, depicts with intent the changes of a subaltern landscape, heterogeneous to the history of landowners and industrial capitalists, and to the memory of national elites.

Cualquier miércoles signifies the Parcelas Falú as detritus produced by the historical progression from premodern to modern economies. This environ illustrates what de Certeau would define as "wretchedness and poverty outside the system and waste inside it" (94): the negative by-products of the modern city. In Castrodad's research, the Los Lirios public housing project becomes modernity's prescription to remedy marginal territorialities. This *caserío* is represented as a product of state attempts to domesticate subalternity. Through this project, the state relocated subaltern subjects living in premodern locations, such as the Parcelas Falú and Paralelo 37, into a sort of factory of modern subjects. The intervention, nonetheless, fostered the splitting up of time and space. It fragmented the social landscape into avatars that may not be subsumed into the logic of the nation-state and the production of modern citizens. Subalternity, as such, ran rampant in a negative landscape that national discourse could not assimilate into its own logic.

The text, however, brings this heterogeneous zone into the discursive surface of the nation and the Caribbean region; it narrates the biographies of its subjects and historicizes their geography; it reveals the machinations of power within these marginal locations. Castrodad recognizes that "the most powerful people of the island . . . are not the legal rich, but those sheiks who from the inane countryside, the Caribbean coastline, and the gringo cities invent in the most real and raw manner what we call wealth."[20] He concerns himself with marginality and difference, all the while wanting to find social subjects different from him. He therefore resolutely moves toward understanding the heterogeneity inscribed in history and the problematics of national identity, memory, time, and geography.

As Castrodad begins to discover a territory excluded from his field of knowledge, he uncovers the interconnectedness of these spaces with his own geography. More than with distance and difference, Santos's concern with the cartography of the city has more to do with the unavoidable interconnectedness between diverse locations and subjectivities. Subalternity in and of itself is not the concern of this narrative project; nor is space, as sole object of narrative knowledge. Heterogeneity, as a product of interconnectivity between opposites, lies at the center of Santos's narrative project. Thus, interconnectedness advances an epistemological proposal that embraces a new standard for subjectivity in heterogeneity.

As has been proposed earlier, the motel stands as the geographic center of the novel. This locale stages the construction of knowledge, aided by the numerous paths that intersect there. The Tulán impedes supervision and domestication; it jams state control; it is a locus that denies repression and encourages movement and communication. Numerous images reiterate the importance of interconnectivity as a central theme. Cars and streets appear frequently in the novel: from the opening sentence that deals with Castrodad's rusty vehicle, to Chino's white BMW (one of his many cars) in which the narrator takes a ride, to numerous automobiles that enter and exit the Tulán. These vehicles hold polysemantic values as indexes of wealth, power, and virility, as synecdoches of movement and consumption in the modern city, and as metaphors for symbolic exchange. At another level, cars remind readers of the efficiency and speed of globalization, and of the capacity for producing and consuming commodities at a transnational level. Moreover, the different speeds of the various motorized vehicles point to the heterogeneity of time and space; for example, the contrast between Castrodad's old rusty vehicle and Chino's powerful Beemer suggests conflicting layers of modernity within the island and the Caribbean.

In the same way, streets emerge recurrently in the story with multiple semantic values. Highway 52 is mentioned as an important avenue that leads to the Motel Tulán. This is Puerto Rico's primary throughway, traversing the island from San Juan, in the north, to Ponce, in the south, through the Central Mountain Range. This highway signals the thrust of a project that aimed to minimize time and space, and synthesize productivity and power in the capital. A marker of historical value, Highway 52 was originally named Expreso Las Américas (Expressway of the Americas), ambitiously pointing toward a capacity to connect North and South America, thus making Puerto Rico a bridge between two continents—and two time–space zones. The expressway reiterates the desire for uninhibited communicability. In contrast with Highway 52, the story refers to many nameless city streets that allow multidirectional exchanges. Nonetheless, gates obstruct movement in some of these streets, at the entrances to some access-controlled neighborhoods, such as the impoverished *caserío* Los Lirios or the wealthy subdivisions. The contrast between the desire for greater speed and communicability, signaled by the expressway, and the obstruction of movement at the access points of gated communities, symbolizes heterogeneity within modernity, and denotes a failure inscribed within the same project. In this regard, the equalizing force of the modern project fails, fragmenting time and space, and allowing for a rampant proliferation of geographies and subjectivities. The gated communities, as such, signal a need to control movement and exchange of a certain type, a defense against contamination of the social hierarchy, and an obtrusive architecture that demarcates subjectivities. These explicit markers suggest that the naturalization of the social hierarchy has been disrupted and that artificial barriers are needed to maintain it.

Cualquier miércoles also reiterates exchange and connectivity by bringing up various media that facilitate communication, such as newspapers, cellular phones, and the Internet. The subplot of the power company employees' strike and a passing reference to the sale of the state-owned telephone company complete a broader concern with interconnectivity within modernity. It is of value to consider that in the text several of the media and utilities that foster communicability are the results of a modernizing plan. These innovations, understood broadly as technology, tolerate a variety of uses, some of which work against the intentions of modernity. In this regard, the drug traffickers employ cellular phones and other media to further their illegal business, and power company employees become the ideal distributors of narcotics. Thus, the narrative creates an image of technological advances that are intimately associated with a thrust toward modernity, but whose function and directionality have been contaminated. In this regard, a plethora of geographies and subjectivities occupy the modern city simultaneously.

From this vantage point, we could assert that Santos theorizes productivity as she depicts this labyrinthine cartography of the city. Although the city purportedly structures the production of subjects, knowledge, commodities, and ideologies akin to a modern program, the novel depicts a place that turns production into expenditure. *Cualquier miércoles* portrays an organization that possesses vast wealth and power, that supports an autocratic social structure, and whose sole raison d'être is to sell a commodity that the state forbids because it is an obstacle to productivity. Even though this commerce exists outside of the purview of the nation, it is portrayed as an unproductive other of the state. Although it exists within the territorial confines of the state, it establishes routes of exchange and communicability that reach outside of the nation, disavowing the epistemological limits of this territory. Surprisingly, the push toward modernity and modernization produced this landscape, heterogeneous to the nation and its program.

This alternative geography exists within the nation and, while negating its authority, makes use of its technologies. In addition to producing illegal drugs, wealth, and power, this complex alternative landscape produces subjects, culture, and knowledge that contradict those produced by hegemonic culture. But the novel does not create an image of parallel, autonomous existence of these two geographies. Quite to the contrary, it reveals a radically heterogeneous landscape of symbiotic coexistence of unproductivity and productivity, of illegality and legality, and of subalternity and hegemony.

This hydra-headed entity reifies itself in the commodities it distributes, but also, and more important for this study, in the aesthetic and epistemological constructs it spawns. Santos's narrative negates homogeneity of time and space. It denies an essential and simplified conception of culture and identity in her nation. Conversely, it embraces a radically hybridized version of San Juan and, by extension, Puerto Rico and the Caribbean. *Cualquier miércoles* depicts the unbridled cross-contamination of opposite subjectivities and geographies. It bares the marginal geographies of black and mulatto lower-class subjects and incorporates their expunged histories into the nation's metanarrative. As it recuperates these subaltern historicities, it uncovers the complexity of the present modern San Juan, which coexists with fragments of premodern historicities that have not been subsumed into the present. At an aesthetic level the problematics of time and space are evinced by the duality of narrative voices and their diverging concerns with different historical periods. While Castrodad concerns himself with present time, as would an ethnographer or a journalist, the Dama Solitaria focuses on the past, working within the confines of diary writing or confessional literature.

At the same time, the narration lacks an apparent bearing, an absence that Castrodad recognizes in several instances and that distinguishes him as a writer: "I want to narrate (to delirium). But I can not find the thread of a story."[21] Toward the end of the book, as numerous plotlines interlink, he cannot make sense of the situations surrounding him and starts to jot down all he can. He acknowledges his disorder: "Black ink surged from between my fingers. Like a spring, like a bloodletting, as if the pavement were flowing from my fingernails. . . . I continued writing, but now obeying another force that was taking hold like a frenzy. My notes took a different form in my hands . . . my hand and the ink and the paper. A way of losing myself in me."[22] Writing then becomes an endeavor that lacks organization and planning, pointing to a site of teleological dearth. In the same way that the city evinces numerous contaminations in its geographies and subjectivities, the narration reifies this radical hybridity in the narrative voice's confusion. Similarly, the effort to produce a metanarrative of the nation becomes unproductive. As such, Santos's work embraces confusion at an aesthetic level and concurrently functions within an epistemological lack of productivity.

More than any other, the chapter titled "Oró, Moyugba" reiterates the writer's aesthetic proposal. In this episode, Chino Pereira takes Castrodad to a Santería *tambor*. This Afro-Caribbean religious celebration honors the saint protector of *babalawo* Ojuani Jekún, Chino's godfather, a very wealthy man, and one of the most powerful Santería priests of the island. In preparation for the *tambor*, the unenthusiastic guest searches the Internet to find information on Afro-Caribbean religions and reflects upon the intractability of his identity as Puerto Rican:

> an islander up to a point, a denying black and white without being white. A hybrid, half of something, a duplicate of a duplicate. That is to say, one used to roaming through the labyrinth woven on the seas by the hunger of many monarchs: European monarchs, African monarchs, gringo monarchs. It is difficult to live in a labyrinth on the waters that promise an exit through Europe, another one through Africa, New York, Asia. Even harder when you no longer carry the lantern of nostalgia. . . . I never wanted to be Spanish, African, French, or Chinese. . . . I never wished to be a gringo. . . . However, the fact that I do not want to embrace the red, white, and blue and its emblem of modernity, productivity, and progress does not mean that I want to be "truly Caribbean." . . . It's too late for that. Too much hybridity, the labyrinth. I do not desire to be authentic.[23]

His conundrum, which surfaces as he decides what to wear for the *tambor*, insinuates an epistemological lack that does not wish to be resolved. But he keenly drapes this otherness onto himself, negating authenticity and homogeneity in the process toward self-definition.

The quote reproduces an aesthetic of confusion and heterogeneity, all the while mapping the rhizomatous history of colonialism, capitalist exploitation, immigration, and cultural exchange that molded Puerto Rico's present. As the speaker puts forth an image of radical hybridity, he sheds light on the history of this fragmentary present. If hegemonic metanarratives insist on a homogeneous Puerto Rican identity *rooted* in African, Amerindian, and Hispanic races and cultures (all the while erecting a hierarchy that favors Hispanic values), the chronicler adamantly maintains a fragmentary relation of identity and culture, a *present* that lacks historical synthesis. Moreover, the narrator asserts that the present situation of a globalized city like San Juan reproduces a deeper historical reality as a place created by multifarious encounters, themselves fostered by long-standing globalized projects; that is, the present structure of capital establishes San Juan as a globalized city, but its status is complicated by the long-lasting impact of transnational enterprises in the same location. This site of encounters (San Juan—metonymically reproduced in the motel) marks a locus of heterogeneity in identity and culture as much as it underscores heterogeneity in time.

To be tenacious about this matter, Santos opens the second half of the novel with an epigraph from Brazilian writer Clarice Lispector. These lines restate the idea of an unutterable heterogeneity that is brought to the fore through the failure of subsumption:

> To have within me the contrary of what I am becomes, in essence, indispensable: I do not dodge my struggle or my indecision, I, who am a failure. Failure allows me to exist. . . . I feed on what is left of me, and that is not much. There remains, nevertheless, a certain secret silence.[24]

This quote underscores the central theme of the work while at the same time foreshadowing Castrodad's visit to Ojuani Jekún's *tambor*. Both the episode and Lispector's quote contemplate the intractability of identity and culture within San Juan, and indict hegemony's claim to synthesis and homogeneity.[25] Castrodad faces the object of his narrative desire, the city's heterogeneity reveals itself, and the aspiring writer fails to synthesize the raw knowledge that he encounters.

To initiate this meeting, Chino Pereira picks his guest up and drives him to a well-to-do, enclosed suburb of San Juan. Surprisingly, the Santería celebration takes place in a neighborhood of million-dollar homes inhabited by the elites of the nation. The *babalawo*'s mansion, the largest in his subdivision, houses a wealth of exotic flora and fauna, and boasts ample rooms full of people of all social classes. The motel employee is in awe of this site of encounters where some of the practitioners speak Yoruba and engage in ritualistic performances previously unknown to him. Castrodad begins to shed dichotomous beliefs of geography and subjectivity. He acknowledges his mystification: "an amalgam of variegated things: cement, peacocks, altars, professionals, parrots, and cellular phones under a tropical sun? In what world am I? . . . by mere tension of opposites, all that was created should explode in thousands of pieces."[26] The Santería ritual stages his anagnorisis. The celebration completes his education as an aspiring writer because he forgoes homogeneous national metanarratives and dichotomous epistemologies. As he attempts to bring into literary language the scene he is witnessing, his erratic discursive stream of questions exposes his failure and, simultaneously, a renewed understanding of his position:

> I couldn't stop wondering what . . . my father's colleague was doing in this *tambor*. Was this not for initiates, for poor inhabitants of the slums, trapped in the thicket of primitiveness and superstition? How many other professionals were here, asking, like any other person, for a favor from their guardian angels, promising sheep, chickens, candles, raising prayers

to the African power of the beyond? How many others were neighbors of this access-controlled subdivision, members of the highest echelons of the country, into which Ojuani Jekún had infiltrated thanks to the favors of his godchildren? How many of his godchildren were doctors, professors, lawyers? And how many were drug traffickers? . . . One faith, one thousand paths, one thousand skin colors, one thousand social castes, all gathered, overflowing its banks. This *tambor* proved itself another labyrinth.[27]

Ojuani Jekún's affair uncovers a clandestine landscape of interconnectivity that reifies the novel's central epistemological proposal. Where hegemonic discourse asserts the separation of dominant and subaltern systems of meaning, *Cualquier miércoles* disavows these hierarchies. As Castrodad scrutinizes this heterotopical geography, new objects of knowledge appear heretofore absconded.

The narrator inserts several meaningful references to the creation of knowledge. He confesses to reading widely and having hardly learned from writers the stature of Shakespeare, Tabucchi, Thomas Mann, and Saramago. But he intently asserts that he was least touched by Puerto Rican writers: "'you have to read our great ones' . . . René Marqués, José Luis González, Emilio Díaz Valcárcel, Enrique Laguerre.' . . . I sat down diligently with these books in the studio. I took them to the beach. I took them for a stroll around the whole city. They did nothing for me."[28] His Puerto Rican list indirectly criticizes canonical values and positions. These important writers reproduce hegemonic values and concern themselves with the grand metanarrative of the nation. Not being touched by the oeuvres of these particular figures implies that dominant discourse has fossilized a particular way of plotting the nation. This canonical gaze cannot shed light on the reality that Castrodad witnesses or that is experienced by other inhabitants of the island. Moreover, the narrator dismisses an authority recognized in magisterial figures of the national community.

Cualquier miércoles also refers frequently to journalism as a problematic site for the production of knowledge. On numerous occasions, Castrodad refers to the sensationalist *La Noticia* as the most popular daily of the island. He condemns newspapers for making commodities out of the news, for not taking time to reflect on the status of human condition, and for establishing a hierarchy of truth that downplays or negates the stories of "real relevance" (*relevancia real*). He keenly proposes recording the current situation of the subaltern people of the world: "at the end, in the paragraph

that no one would read: 'Sixty-five black men also died in the uprising. Several Zulu women showed evidence of having been raped. Among the dead
there were eleven black children.'"[29] The narrator suggests that the tools
employed to circulate information reiterate the centrality of dominant
epistemologies. In the stories of those erased from discourse lies knowledge of greater relevance than elite subjects recognize. This reference similarly establishes a vision of global subalternity as a central, yet concealed
reality in globalization. The literary project articulated in *Cualquier miércoles* is occupied with narrating subalternity in globalization, regardless of
the explicit geography involved.

The narrator, interestingly, believes that fiction can penetrate reality and
uncover truth more aptly than newspapers, information media, and nonfiction. This idea is brought to the fore in the last chapter, when *La Noticia*
rehires Castrodad as a copy editor. Back in his old workplace, he unwor-
riedly edits "a bunch of half-true, half-false stories, that I had to revise for
accents and grammar so that they would appear like 'the truth.'"[30] At night,
he endeavors to complete his novel, which, by his own appraisal more
straightforwardly reflects the truth, despite its shortfalls. But he defines
this object of his narrative desire as a particular epistemological and aesthetic material: "the truth revealed by the raw ink, the one that remains
beyond the threshold of power games. I lend my fingers so that it may
flow."[31] His literary enterprise deals in ambiguity and in the failure of its
own desire. He succeeds by circumventing a need to control the outcome,
to codify truth, to reproduce authority, to construct homogeneous empty
narratives. The locus of his reflection is subalternity, which lies beyond
hegemony in a landscape heterogeneous to power.

This essay proposes that *Cualquier miércoles* problematizes culture
and identity in the context of globalization and calculatedly deals with the
city as a site of radical heterogeneity, produced by the violence of various
colonial and transnational capitalist endeavors, and, during the twentieth
century, by the imposed modernization of the island. San Juan, Santos's
globalized city, exhibits the impact of accelerated transnational exchanges,
the mediation of twenty-first-century technologies of interconnectivity,
the signs of long-lasting colonialism and capitalist exploitation, and the
effect of a forceful process of modernization and industrialization. Contemporary and historical processes molded present reality into a radically
heterogeneous landscape where fragments of variegated cultures and histories share a heterotopic geography. Santos asserts this proliferation of

geographies and subjectivities, and engages in depicting how a fictitious writer turns this complex reality into narrative.

The novel deploys geography as a vehicle to plot culture and identity; the narrative eye focuses on marginal spaces and on the routes employed to link up these settings to each other and to locations of hegemonic power. The Motel Tulán stands for interconnectivity between subaltern and hegemonic spaces, and, simultaneously, becomes a metaphor for the radically heterogeneous social space. The narrator historicizes subaltern locations and uncovers the biographies of the subjects inhabiting them. All the while, the novel attempts to bring into the nation's memory the stories occupying these marginal geographies, consistently excluded from hegemonic discourse.

The histories implied in these marginal locations negate the promises of modernity, suggested in the modernization project that the United States and the Popular Democratic Party asserted upon the island since the late 1940s and that have become hegemonic in the island. By this reading, *Cualquier miércoles* dwells on the geography of modernity's failure by dealing with the stories of subalternity. The novel suggests that the capacity for productivity, wealth, and power held in these zones of subalternity denotes that these spaces of negativity must be narrativized. Julia Kristeva, in the epigraph at the beginning of this essay, avows that "the leavings of a sacrifice can also be the cause of good rebirths." Santos focuses on the "leavings" (or the failures) of the modern city in order to retrieve negated knowledge and to underscore an irruptive force in subalternity. In reading heterogeneity from this perspective, we may assert that the novel puts forward a narrative that acknowledges a rampant fragmentation of time and space, and a radical contamination of dichotomous thinking that, in the novel, inscribes an epistemological failure. Castrodad articulates this problem by defining Puerto Ricanness as "a hybrid, half of something, a duplicate of a duplicate" (171), underscoring the intractability of national identity. The problematics of this construct notwithstanding, *Cualquier miércoles soy tuya* attempts to further a literary project that embraces an elevated standard of heterogeneity to understand the fragmentary landscape evinced by modern cities.

NOTES

1. "Estacioné el auto, o mejor dicho, la carcacha carcomida por el salitre con la que con tanto esfuerzo me muevo en la ciudad." All translations from the Spanish original are my own; page numbers refer to the original Spanish text.

2. Mayra Santos (Puerto Rico, b. 1966) is a professor of literature and culture at the Universidad de Puerto Rico, Río Piedras. She earned a Ph.D. in literature from Cornell University and has lectured and taught at various universities in her country of origin, in the United States, and abroad. Her literary career includes two collections of poetry, *Anamú y manigua* and *El orden escapado;* a collection of short stories, *Pez de vidrio* (that earned her the prestigious Premio Juan Rulfo Internacional); and two novels, *Sirena Selena vestida de pena* (Mondadori, 2000) and *Cualquier miércoles soy tuya.* She has also hosted a literature and culture program on Puerto Rico's public television.

3. "carcacha carcomida por el salitre" (11).

4. Numerous scholarly endeavors discuss the expectation of convergence in globalization and the failure of this global historical project. I must mention three that were of great value for this essay: Arjun Appadurai's *Modernity at Large* and the edited volume *Millennial Capitalism and the Culture of Neoliberalism,* by Jean Comaroff and John Comaroff; Julio Ramos's *Divergent Modernities* is invaluable for a discussion of modernity's mediation in literary and critical production in Latin America, even as it mainly focuses on nineteenth-century Latin America.

5. *The Other Side of the Popular,* by Gareth Williams, illuminates said alternate circuits of communicability by focusing on a variety of transnational transactions. Of particular note is his discussion of Salvadoran translocal crime organizations, located in Los Angeles and San Salvador. These symbolic exchanges become the phantom of globalization's networks of symbolic exchange and power transactions.

6. Michael Hardt and Antonio Negri's *Empire* discusses globalization as a phenomenon articulated via networks of influence and communicability. This theoretical framework grounds our understanding of culture produced "in globalization." Mayra Santos's novels fall perfectly within the purview of globalized cultural production as both were originally issued by transnational publishers and both appear to disseminate a particular epistomology of the Caribbean subject. A metropolitan consumer and the ideological correlative of a global culture encourage and justify the commodification of a racialized, exoticized, and translated Caribbean other. *Cualquier miércoles* portrays a heterogeneous subject, constructed *in the failure* of commodification. A subversive aftereffect of this process obstructs assimilation. Interestingly, the same networks of communicability that produce globalization facilitate this obstruction.

7. In *The Global City,* Saskia Sassen discusses how global cities became centers of control of internationalized production, and established themselves as part of a "global network of cities." Although this sociologist concerns herself mostly with New York, London, and Tokyo, she asserts that similar trends are evinced in "other major cities, though on a lower order of magnitude and based on regional- rather than global-level processes" (326).

8. The reference to *La Noticia* clearly alludes to *El Vocero,* a newspaper known for its graphic coverage of bloody murders and accidents. This publication has the widest circulation of any daily in Puerto Rico.

9. Military and political interventions, overt and covert, are well known and documented, particularly from the first years of the twentieth century. The U.S. military invaded Cuba, the Dominican Republic, Haiti, Puerto Rico, Venezuela, and Panama. The policies allowing for these interventions emanate from a reinterpretation of the Monroe Doctrine, expressed in the 1904 Roosevelt Corollary: "Chronic wrongdoing, or an impotence which results in a general loosening of the ties of civilised society, may in America, as elsewhere, ultimately require intervention by some civilised nation, and in the Western Hemisphere the adherence of the United States to the Monroe Doctrine may force the United States, however reluctantly . . . to the exercise of an international police power" (quoted in E. Williams, 422). The opposition established between "civilized" and noncivilized nations grounded this statement, and justifies military intervention as a noble, civilizing action. Militarized coercion guaranteed commercial intervention and influence, through absurd accords such as, but not limited to, the infamous "Platt Amendment" and the 1907 convention, signed with the Dominican Republic, that allowed the United States to assist said independent republic in the collection of customs revenues.

10. The most noteworthy of these programs is Operation Bootstrap, part of a broader post–World War II initiative for economic growth; it targeted impoverished zones by boosting industry and engaging in social engineering (internal migration to the city, and migration to metropolitan industrial zones in the colonial nation). Teodoro Moscoso (1920–92) designed and managed the island's program, even though Governor Muñoz Marín took most of the credit for the development of the island. For illuminating discussions of this modernizing project, see Maldonado's *Teodoro Moscoso and Puerto Rico's Operation Bootstrap* and Pantojas García's *Development Strategies as Ideology: Puerto Rico's Export-Led Industrialization Experience.*

11. Ronald Reagan's "Caribbean Basin Initiative" consolidates an ambitious neoliberal undertaking, which supports a coherent effort to guarantee a captive market for U.S. goods and a zone of diverse production of goods and services. The Caribbean, thus, appears as a coherent region with a participatory role in geopolitical matters. The incentives guaranteed in this initiative similarly impose provisions to assure a style of government and administration that secures U.S. hegemony in its periphery.

12. Some notable writers and texts are, from Cuba, Pedro Juan Gutiérrez's *El Rey de La Habana* (Anagrama, 1999) and *Trilogía sucia de La Habana* (Anagrama, 1998), and Anna Lidia Vega Serova's *Catálogo de mascotas* (Letras Cubana, 1999) and *Noche de ronda* (Baile del Sol, 2001); from the Dominican Republic, Pedro Antonio Valdez's *Bachata del ángel caído* (Isla Negra, 1999) and *Carnaval de Sodoma*

(Alfaguara, 2001); and from Puerto Rico, Luis Rafael Sánchez's *La guaracha del Macho Camacho* and Anna Lydia Vega's *Encancaranublado y otros cuentos* and *Falsas crónicas del sur.*

13. Gelpí's *Literatura y paternalismo en Puerto Rico* is fundamental in understanding the discursive apparatus deployed by an intellectual and literary cadre. The study underscores how the construction of a literary canon supports a particular hierarchy of values, disseminated through monumental tropes such as the family and the house, and by particular pedagogical narratives. Santos's literary project stands in clear opposition to these traditional values, and, similarly, challenges the structuring logic of "literary paternalism."

14. "Dicen que las ciudades son el lugar de la acumulación anónima pero, en estas islas perdidas en el medio del Caribe, sólo unos cuantos transitan las ciudades nocturnas... Una vez cae el sol... la ciudad queda... lista para acoger a los merodeadores de la noche" (12).

15. James Clifford's *Routes* fleshes out the idea of the chronotope of the motel as a location that marks ephemeral contacts and deracinated identities in the late twentieth century.

16. "El motel Tulán acercaba las maquinaciones internas de la rueda que echa a andar la ciudad... Y cada uno de los invitados a la carniza... carga con el peso de su culpa, el de creer que actúan en los márgenes de la ciudad, cuando en realidad son la sangre que la hace palpitar" (63).

17. "merodeadores de la noche" (12).

18. "cualquiera sabía más que yo de esta isla. Hasta los traficantes sabían más, hasta los inmigrantes indocumentados" (172).

19. "había surgido de la nada hacía ya cincuenta años, detrás de la fábrica embotelladora de sodas... Los que la conocían la veían como un absceso que le había salido a... las Parcelas Falú" (49).

20. "los más poderosos de la isla... para nada son los ricos legales, sino estos jeques que desde los campos anodinos, las costas caribeñas y las ciudades gringas se inventan de la manera más real y descarnada lo que es la riqueza" (58).

21. "Quiero narrar (hasta el delirio). Pero no logro encontrar el hilo de una historia" (21).

22. "Y manó de entre mis dedos tinta oscura. Como un manantial, como un desangre, como si la brea se estuviera colando por entre mis uñas... Seguí escribiendo, pero ya obedeciendo otra fuerza que se iba apoderando de mí como un frenesí. Las notas se me convertían en otra cosa entre las manos... mi mano y la tinta y el papel. Una manera de perderme de mí" (224).

23. "isleño hasta cierto punto, negro negado y blanco sin serlo. Un híbrido, la mitad de algo, el doble del doble. Es decir, un ser acostumbrado a deambular por el laberinto que tejió sobre los mares el hambre de los monarcas, monarcas europeos, monarcas africanos, monarcas gringos. Es difícil vivir en un laberinto

sobre el agua que promete una salida por Europa, otra por África, otra por Nueva York, otra por Asia. Más difícil aún cuando ya no cargas con la linterna de la nostalgia... Nunca quise ser ni español, ni africano, ni francés, ni chino... nunca quise ser gringo... Ahora bien, el hecho de que no quiero abrazar la red white and blue y su emblema de modernidad, productividad y progreso tampoco significa que quiero ser 'caribeño caribeño'... Es demasiado tarde para eso. Demasiada la hibridez, el laberinto. No quiero ser auténtico" (171).

24. "Tener dentro de mí al contrario de lo que soy me resulta en esencia imprescindible: no rehuyo mi lucha ni mi indecisión, yo, que soy un fracasado. El fracaso me da pie para existir... Me alimento de lo que queda de mí, y es poco. Queda, no obstante, cierto secreto silencio" (101).

25. Adorno's assertion that "the untruth of identity, the fact that the concept does not exhaust the thing conceived" guides my analysis. The philosopher asserts that "the objects do not go into their concepts without leaving a remainder" (5); later in *Negative Dialectics* he states that "the subject, understanding how much the cause is its own, should bow to what is heterogeneous to it" (148). Negativity conceptually brackets the inadequacy of homogeneous narratives to subsume residues; thereby, heterogeneity trumps identity in constructing a new epistemology.

26. "amalgama de cosas inconexas: cemento, pavos reales, altares, profesionales, cacatúas y teléfonos celulares bajo un sol tropical? ¿En qué mundo estoy?... por pura tensión de los opuestos, todo lo creado debería estallar en mil pedazos" (176).

27. "Yo no cesaba de preguntarme qué hacía... [el] colega de mi padre, en este tambor. ¿Acaso esto no era para iniciados, para pobres habitantes de barriadas, atrapados en las marañas de lo primitivo y la superstición? ¿Cuántos más profesionales habría aquí, pidiendo, como cualquier otro, un favor a sus ángeles de la guardia, prometiendo carneros, gallinas, velas, elevando plegarias a los africanos poderes del más allá? ¿Cuántos de los presentes serían vecinos de la misma urbanización cerrada, miembros de las capas más altas del país en donde Ojuani Jekún se había colado gracias a los favores de sus ahijados? ¿Cuántos de sus mismos ahijados serían doctores, profesores, licenciados? ¿Y cuántos serían traficantes?... Una fe mil caminos, mil colores de piel, mil castas sociales, todas congregadas, todas salidas fuera de sus márgenes. Este tambor se perfilaba como otro laberinto" (185).

28. "'tienes que leer a los grandes de aquí... René Marqués, José Luis González, Emilio Díaz Valcárcel, Enrique Laguerre'... Yo, diligente, me senté con los libracos en el estudio. Me los llevé a la playa. Los paseé por toda la ciudad. No me marcaron en nada" (134).

29. "al final, ya en el párrafo que nadie iba a leer: 'Sesenta y cinco hombres negros también murieron en la reyerta. Varias mujeres zulú evidenciaron muestras de haber sido violadas. Entre los muertos hubo once niños negros'" (128).

30. "un montón de historias medio ciertas, medio mentidas a las que debo revisarles los acentos y la gramatical para que parezcan 'la verdad'" (238).

31. "la verdad que deja ver la tinta viva, la que queda al otro lado de los juegos del poder. Yo presto mis dedos para dejarla correr" (ibid.).

WORKS CITED

Adorno, Theodor W. *Negative Dialectics*. Continuum: New York, 2000.

Anderson, Benedict. *Imagined Communities*. Rev. ed. 1983. London: Verso, 1991.

Appadurai, Arjun. *Modernity at Large: Cultural Dimensions of Globalization*. Minneapolis: University of Minnesota Press, 1996.

Balibar, Étienne. "The Nation Form: History and Ideology." In *Race, Nation, Class: Ambiguous Identities*. London: Verso, 1991.

Birmingham-Pokorny, Elba D. "Postcolonial Discourse and the Re-thinking of Gender, Identity, and Culture in Mayra Santos Febres's 'Broken Strand.'" *Diaspora* 10 (2000): 29–37.

Castillo, Debra. "She Sings Boleros: Santos-Febres' *Sirena Selena*." *Latin American Literary Review* 29 (2001): 13–25.

Comaroff, Jean, and John L. Comaroff. "Millennial Capitalism: First Thought on a Second Coming." In *Millennial Capitalism and the Culture of Neoliberalism*. Durham, N.C.: Duke University Press, 2001.

de Certeau, Michel. *The Practice of Everyday Life*. Trans. Steven Rendall. Berkeley: University of California Press, 1984.

Gelpí, Juan. *Literatura y paternalismo en Puerto Rico*. Río Piedras: Editorial de la Universidad de Puerto Rico, 1993.

Gutiérrez, Pedro Juan. *El Rey de La Habana*. Barcelona: Anagrama, 1999.

———. *Trilogía sucia de La Habana*. Barcelona: Anagrama, 1998.

Hardt, Michael, and Antonio Negri. *Empire*. Cambridge: Harvard University Press, 2000.

Kristeva, Julia. *Nations without Nationalism*. Trans. Leon S. Roudiez. 1990. New York: Columbia University Press, 1993.

———. *Powers of Horror: An Essay on Abjection*. New York: Columbia University Press, 1982.

Maldonado, A. W. *Teodoro Moscoso and Puerto Rico's Operation Bootstrap*. Gainesville: University Press of Florida, 1997.

Martín-Barbero, Jesús. *Al sur de la modernidad: Comunicación, globalización y multiculturalidad*. Pittsburgh: Intstituto Internacional de Literatura Iberoamericana, 2001.

Moreiras, Alberto. *The Exhaustion of Difference: The Politics of Latin American Cultural Studies*. Durham, N.C.: Duke University Press, 2001.

Pantojas García, Emilio. *Development Strategies as Ideology: Puerto Rico's Export-Led Industrialization Experience.* Boulder, Colo.: Lynne Rienner, 1990.

Pile, Steve. "Introduction: Opposition, Political Identities and Space Resistance." In *Geographies of Resistance.* Routledge: London, 1997. 1–32.

Ramos, Julio. *Divergent Modernities: Culture and Politics in Nineteenth-Century Latin America.* Trans. John D. Blanco. Durham, N.C.: Duke University Press, 2001.

Santos Febres, Mayra. *Cualquier miércoles soy tuya.* Barcelona: Mondadori, 2002.

———. *Pez de vidrio.* Río Piedras, Puerto Rico: Huracán, 1996.

———. *Sirena Selena.* Trans. Stephen A. Lytle. New York: Picador, 2000.

———. *Sirena Selena vestida de pena.* Barcelona: Mondadori, 2001.

Sassen, Saskia. *The Global City.* Princeton, N.J.: Princeton University Press, 1991.

Spivak, Gayatri Chakravorty. "Can the Subaltern Speak?" In *Marxism and the Interpretation of Culture.* Basinstoke, UK: Macmillan, 271–313.

Valdez, Pedro Antonio. *Bachata del ángel caído.* San Juan: Isla Negra, 1999.

———. *Carnaval de Sodoma.* Santo Domingo: Alfaguara, 2001.

Vega Serova, Anna Lidia. *Catálogo de mascotas.* Havana: Letras Cubanas, 1999.

———. *Noche de ronda.* Tenerife, Canary Islands: Baile del Sol, 2001.

Williams, Eric. *From Columbus to Castro: The History of the Caribbean: 1492–1969.* New York: Vintage, 1984.

Williams, Gareth. *The Other Side of the Popular.* Durham, N.C.: Duke University Press, 2002.

PART II

The Restless City

5

Anna's Extreme Makeover

Revisiting Tolstoy in
Karenina Express

DEBRA A. CASTILLO

"When cultures confront one another in this contested space of media interpretation and recontextualization, new opportunities arise for . . . 'reciprocal translation'" (18), says D. N. Rodowick hopefully, in an introduction to the topic "mobile citizens, media states" in the January 2002 issue of the *PMLA*. The objective of Rodowick's comments in this context is to bridge to an analysis of Guillermo Gómez-Peña's work from his discussion of Ian Chambers, whose enlarged concept of translation is decoupled from geographic considerations. Chambers works with translation in terms of the concepts of transit, transition, and the transitory, where language rather than geography defines a sense of home. For Rodowick, Gómez-Peña offers a superb exemplar of this concept in his performances and his theoretical commentaries, marked as they are by an always-estranged and defamiliarizing reading of identity against deterritorialization. Common to all these scholars—Rodowick, Chambers, and Gómez-Peña—is a speculation about a basic reorganization of critical axes from something like the cluster of meaning that adheres around the concept of space/identity/authenticity to one that emphasizes time/contingency/performance—perhaps even "larger-than-life" performance. Because Gómez-Peña's performances also include an element of linguistic undecidability (he uses Spanish, English, Spanglish, pseudo-Nahuatl, and nonsense, among other registers), they insist on an unsettling deterritorialization of language as well.

Three queries immediately present themselves: (1) What would happen if we were to imaginarily decouple language from place? (2) What do we mean when we talk about the concept of identity in highly performative texts? (3) What are the precise mechanisms for this conceptual/ geographic deterritorialization? The Mexican writer Margarita Mansilla, in her 1995 novel *Karenina Express*, reminds the reader of her work's nature as a critical practice or trope, always a (self-consciously, ironically) staged performance of a discursive fiction rather than the thing itself. Beginning with a riff on a highly familiar iconic figure/text, her work displaces itself from the presuppositions that give rise to it. In her novel, it is no longer the question of identity that is at stake in the narrative, but rather that of a postmodern agency unmoored from the grounding discourse of identity-speak, with all its concomitant associations to a national or geographic referent. Thus, for example, this Mexican novel with a Russian-referent, English-sounding title (calling to mind, among other referents, the Orient Express) first introduces our character's point of view by shifting the ground immediately, in the very first sentence: "Amalia was not located in the French Riviera."[1] France is evoked and dismissed; a counterfactual gesture. Even further, Amalia, and her alter ego, Ana, soon realize that "what was this vision if not a predetermined set and character from her next reading adventure [*lectu-aventura*]?"[2] Instead of a grounding in historical or geographic circumstance, Mansilla's fictional agency is conceived as a metaliterary performance—something constructed and staged. This performance is of an enlarged, but also fragmented, self/image, one that harks back to a narrative structure rather than any imagined authentic national self.

Where is the city in this novel? Like the fragmented meta-self, it is everywhere, and everywhere dispersed. Mansilla pays homage to the urban consciousness of her nineteenth-century literary-historical models, whose understanding was shaped by the industrial revolution and the rise of the bourgeoisie, and whose works define those peculiar literary sites: Paris, London, Moscow, Vienna. Her own novel offers both an ironic reflection on these earlier metaphors for a modern urban existence defined in its European particularity and a more contemporary, cosmopolitan, and American redefinition of the city. Her urban space is the multilingual, multicultural megalopolis that her European forebears never dreamed of or imagined:

Mexico City, New York City. At the same time, she never loses sight of this exploration as primarily that of a *lectu-aventura;* the urban spaces exist only in the literary imagination and only coincidentally overlap with known geography.

As is suggested in the title of her novel, Mansilla explores contemporary mores through a reexamination of one of the classic texts of nineteenth-century narrative, Tolstoy's *Anna Karenina.* Mansilla's narrator advises: "we need to reeducate the audience to believe in fiction once again."[3] Thus, following her own advice, her protagonist reimagines her own variations on the great nineteenth-century romance while bidding an ironic farewell to the pathetic texture of the earlier novel. Mansilla picks up on the powerful image of the train from Tolstoy's novel and plays with its metonymic condensation of the very idea of technology, modernity, and progress. In this sense, Mansilla is reinscribing a now-traditional paradox—that modernity (an imagined desirable state or even a kind of mathematical constant) itself is best defined in the onrush of continual movement, by velocity and blurred geographies: the shift of perception from the train itself to what a passenger might observe through the train's windows as it follows the rails from city to city. In this sense, *Karenina Express* can be imagined as a sort of tropic TGV in contrast with Tolstoy's steam locomotive; in each case, the train serves as a marker of modern high-speed movement for the masses. At the same time, the title suggests an understanding of "express" in its other sense, "un café express" or an expresso: a hypermodern caffeine rush. In contrast with Tolstoy's weighty (in both senses) tome, even before opening the book we already know that this is a lighter, faster, more streamlined Karenina, a Karenina for contemporary urban commuters who measure out time in nanoseconds.

This title is also unanchored from any particular spatial referent—it suggests a hurtling through rather than an anchoring in any particular geography—and is even to some degree ambiguous about the language of the text to follow: "Karenina" has obvious Russian associations; "express" sounds like English, but has been adopted into many languages. Of course, the author is not a nineteenth-century Russian man but a twentieth-century Mexican woman. Here too we experience a displacement of sorts, from the great male-imagined female characters of the nineteenth century—Galdós's Fortunata, Tolstoy's Anna Karenina, Flaubert's Madame Bovary—to a female author's take on her literary forefathers and fictional foremothers. We might argue that in this shift from male to female authorship, movement (of an intellectual sort) is privileged in another manner in her enterprise, through her focus on the female writer's literary progress.

Literary women have historically been eccentric to the great tradition of Western letters; thus, they have traditionally remained outside the canon defined and circumscribed by nation-oriented narratives and by male-centered practices of reading. The great sentimental novels distinguished by women's names on their covers to mark the presence of female protagonists are complemented in these national narratives by the adventure stories associated with masculine derring-do. The idea of a journey of self-discovery, like quest narrative in general, is firmly tied to the idea of a male quest (often an adolescent male quest); the female *Künstlerroman* is still inherently transgressive. Anna's most famous relation to the train, for instance, is not to take off on an adventure, but to throw herself under its wheels. Men journey across great geographic expanses, cross literary and literal borders, define the immigrant or exile experience; in contrast, literary women remain, like Jane Austen, imaginarily tied to a set of astonishingly interchangeable enclosed domestic spaces. Mansilla asks us to shift these perceptions. When we erase or defamiliarize the traditional travel referents and focus on a vectored now, something happens to these hoary literary expectations as well, and a femininized epistemological structure of movement offers up doubly transgressive potential. Mansilla in some sense spills together two literary subgenres; her project is both a rewriting of the romance novel and a rethinking of the encounter with modernity.

Mansilla's novel is the story of a literary journey—that is, the process of writing a novel—and it also includes other metajourneys through international literary history and modern theory, as well as references to trips by plane, train, and ship to places like New York City. One of the epigraphs to the novel—from Louise Bogan's "autobiographical mosaic" *Journey around My Room*—asks: "the initial mystery that attends any journey is: how did the traveler reach his starting point in the first place?" Mansilla's response is a long tangent from one ostensible starting point to another, constructing a cartography of a diverse body of writings by and about women, a trip that metaphorically goes back to Columbus. The prologue, which is placed at the end of novel, tells us: "This is a book about origins, about letters and stars and ships that navigate under a paper sky. . . . I have permitted myself to mark the earthly plane of the mathematical axes in red and the ordered chronometry of the heavens in blue, and have used purple paper for the *terra incognita* where writing grows. The meeting point for tracing the round trip is up to the reader, who can proceed in order or not, and interpret what is written in other languages."[4] (The cartographic projection is entirely imaginary; there is, unfortunately, no helpful color-coding in the black-on-white lettering of the actual novel.)

Here, at the very end of her text, the narrator duplicitously suggests that there are two stories in this novel, and provides a sketch of how to read them that cuts diachronically and synchronically, through the abscissa and the ordinate of the Cartesian plane. The first narrative, in Roman numerals, tells a love story; the second, in Arabic numerals, consists of the characters' appropriations of the story and their comments on and rewriting of it. Upon looking back to the text itself with this cartographic marking in mind, however, we will find that the divisions are not so clear-cut between stories, nor is the numbering itself consistent. The Arabic numbering begins the text and runs roughly in order from chapters 1 to 21, though there is a chapter 0 (a missing chapter or *capítulo faltante* [61]) inserted between 10 and 11, and two different chapter 13s (both literary biographies of different sorts) sequentially following each other. The Arabic-numbered chapters include the main line of the plot—the story of the writing of a novel— along with the narrator's comments on her ill-starred love life and her conversations with "AK." The chapters marked with Roman numerals are irregularly interspersed; the first (II) comes after chapter 4, followed by I after chapter 9, a different I after chapter 0, XIX between the second chapter 13 and chapter 14, a second II after chapter 14, followed by III, IV, V, and, after chapter 17, VI. There are no chapters corresponding to the Roman numerals between VII and XVIII. At the appropriately numbered chapter 0, the narrator notes that "the abscissas and the ordinates cross at this location. It is the axial point of the narration, and for that reason, characters, books, and the narrator have been excluded from this space."[5] Materials deployed in the Roman numeral sections, like the rest of the book, include household hints, recipes, and citations from the how-to book; they also include diary entries, letters, the transcription of a tape made during a visit to New York, a poem in prose, and a meditation on the narrator's love of chocolate. The book ends with a set of unnumbered materials that mimic a scholarly apparatus: translations of some of the long passages from English into Spanish (citations from other languages are generally not translated), a highly entertaining glossary (examples: "baroque, few save themselves from," "Cannes, see N.Y.," "desire, no comment," "Derrida, study him," "tears, no way around it," "New York, see vox

PARADOX," "Utopia, see N.Y."),[6] a section called "On the Museum's Ruins" in explicit homage to Douglas Crimp that consists of mock reviews of the novel, and, finally, on the last two pages of the novel, the prologue. Spanish is the dominant language of the text, followed by substantial portions in English, but the author plays constantly with languages in the body of her text, including at one point a translation of a German quote into French, but into neither English nor Spanish.

The novel opens in an unnamed Sanborns-type café/bookstore. Amalia has just lost her job and needs to come up with another, and, adding insult to injury, her most recent boyfriend (a married man) has just left her, taking the television with him. Her fellow classmates are entering professional life and the "publication frenzy," mostly for an infinitesimal and shrinking market of intellectual readers, and she's considering the "immediately finite horizon" of a potential career as a bi- or trilingual secretary. On her way out of the store after drinking her coffee, her eyes light on the how-to section, and she is immediately attracted to one of books in the display, *How to Write Romantic Novels*:

> She realized the book was already beginning to have an effect . . .
> period And comma finally comma open interrogation why not close
> interrogation She had a friend who had thrown herself into writing soap
> opera scripts comma tired of all her erudite baggage period[7]

Amalia takes the book home, but still wavers between the challenge of opting for a more intellectually acceptable academic project and the appeal of a descent into pop fiction. That unresolved wavering becomes the substance of the novel *Karenina Express*. In the pages of this text, she reads fragments of her how-to book while meditating alternately on the great male-authored romances of the last century, *Anna Karenina* and *Madame Bovary*, which combined best-sellerdom with highly desirable canonical status, and, (implicitly) the critically less well received contemporary woman-authored narratives such as Laura Esquivel's *Like Water for Chocolate*. In the latter's case, the popularly irresistible combination of romance and recipes made the Mexican novelist's book an international early-1990s best seller, which furthermore was parlayed into an equally phenomenally successful film, but unlike its nineteenth-century forefathers, which carry almost the aura of sacred texts, Esquivel's book was universally panned by the male-dominated literary establishment as "lite lit." What happened in the interim between Tolstoy and Esquivel so that we now read romance differently? And how can the author of a turn-of-the-twenty-first century romance rethink these changing mores, changing them again into an innovative form that nevertheless speaks to a contemporary audience?

The narrator of this novel asks: "How does the reader (Does the reader?) learn to enjoy a new narrative form?"[8] One answer is, of course, familiarity: formal reiteration makes the merely strange into an aesthetic form the reader can appreciate. But is the reader enjoying the newness of the form itself? Or does it become enjoyable precisely at the point that it is no longer new? Is the reader's pleasure perhaps related to a reshuffling of the old narrative structures in unexpected ways? À la Esquivel, Mansilla's narrator begins to record household tips ranging from banal to obscure, an homage to the successful formula of the earlier novel, but always a bit skewed from Esquivel's sumptuous celebrations of culinary genius. Thus, for example, she reprises Esquivel's famous opening with a note on how to cut onions without crying (133), but hers is a throwaway one-liner, and she matches Esquivel's phenomenal and exotic rose-petal sauce with a footnote recipe for to how to make violet ice (59). Other household advice ranges from how to keep feet warm in winter by wrapping them in newspaper before putting on socks (18) to how to blend an exotic perfume called "houri extract" (*extracto de huríes*).

Like Esquivel, the narrator of this book wants to make a parallel between writing and other forms of creativity associated with the feminine; unlike her antecedent, however, she never, ever takes herself seriously. Perhaps her clearest parallel between cooking and writing comes in a footnote late in the text that, typically for Mansilla, uses the culinary metaphor to make a point related to high culture and to the theoretical continuity between work and life (the text is in English in the original, so the kinds of awkward pronominal references that vanish in Spanish are highlighted instead): "NOTE: it is a matter of culinary expertise that if a writer is left alone too much he/she will inevitably spoil not only his/her current work but all future work, that is, he/she will spoil all his/her unwritten life" (103).

At the same time as she sprinkles her text with these ironic Martha Stewartisms, the narrator takes, and reproduces in the text, erudite notes on her project, sprinkled with quotations from such thinkers as Henry James, Fredric Jameson, Marx, Lyotard, Duras, Proust, and Derrida. She records quotes from these authors on note cards along with her commentaries: for example, "it is perhaps not until modernism that the difference between LITERATURE and BEST SELLERS begins to be noted. That is, the difference between Literature and literature"; or "fantasy: a book to teach desire. Warning. It is necessary to learn toreadinanotherway to read it."[9] Whereas the recipes and the household advice correspond to the type of how-to publications at the very top of every nonfiction best-seller list, the extracts from high-theory thinkers and writers propose a different point of entry into the writing process. In this latter respect, the narrator switches between questioning how to write and how to read, a concern that remains unresolved in the text, perhaps because she is unable to settle on whether her narrative is best captured by the metaphor of the abandoned stations where no train stops, or the entirely opposite idea of the landscape as perceived through the window of a moving train (179).

This too is a function of speed and the angle of perception. Unlike Tolstoy's nineteenth-century romance, in contemporary understandings, a romance novel has second-class status as a woman's text (both authors and readers): too obviously gendered, too quickly written, and too easily read. Like the abandoned station, it is eccentric to literature and excluded from the canon so paradoxically shaped by male romantic masterpieces such as *Anna Karenina* and *Madame Bovary*. At the same time, the author of this novel, like the passenger on the TGV, has an interrupted and blurred sense of a (literary) landscape passing by at high speed on her way to the city, the mecca of publishing, her sensibility capturing something akin to the "fractal history" described by Paul Virilio: "A landscape has no fixed meaning, no privileged vantage point. It is oriented only by the itinerary of the passerby. . . . Here, the landscape is a passage—the data transfer accident of the present to the most recent past" (xi). In this sense, the author-passenger is making a much more radical proposition about literary history, by which the seemingly solid academic discriminations of the previous scale of values are plunged into discontinuity.

When Mansilla's narrator asks herself the related question of for whom she is writing, her response is equally vexed. On the one hand, "we suppose that with modernism the reading public turned into a *publique introuvable* [unlocatable public],"[10] and somewhat later in the text, her "almost-sister" and alter ego offers her own perspective: "reading, Ana used to say, is fickle, because it is harder to do on Tuesdays than Thursdays, and on Sundays no one can understand a thing."[11] The narrator also shapes her text in specific ways out of her supposed regard for her alternately frivolous and hyperintellectual unlocatable reader, as, for example, expressed by this Englishlanguage footnote early in the novel: "*N. de narrador* Talking about the

19th century, Marx, Freud and Nietzsche, Anna all met, but about them it was almost impossible for her to say anything, the three having the same kind of beard. As for her friend, these three chapters constituted such serious reading that her notes take up several chapters which have been left out in regard to the reader's patience" (57). In passages like this, Mansilla breaks down distinctions of fact and fiction, allowing historical and invented figures to speak together, memorializing the circulation of ideas, but privileging movement over content, and favoring above all the veleities of her inconstant and easily distractible public, who, like her, are jangling along an urban public transportation system, unsatisfied with their life, jittery with caffeine, pretending to read in order to avoid the eyes of the fellow passengers.

Says the narrator, condensing these urban desires: "she wanted to read a novel about ships and trains, and baskets of fruit and passionate women with long hair and dark eyes. Suddenly she wanted an espresso, three sips of aroma and foam of an exquisite vital bitterness."[12] Here Mansilla's textualized woman author overlaps two structures of desire—"wanting to read" and "wanting an espresso"—with very different temporalities. In the first case, her longing is associated with the dilated time of nineteenth-century narrative, an expanded dialogue with a text experienced through the long and leisurely engagement with triple-decker novels that feature sloe-eyed women whose sensual daring is expressed in letting down their abundant waist-length hair. This first-articulated desire, interestingly enough, prompts a second, not for leisure, but for temporal contraction, not for a social *cafecito* with friends, but the three quick sips and instant jolt of an espresso. In her constant playing off of nineteenth-century European modernity and contemporary American cosmopolitanism, the narrator is, of course, marking intellectual as well as temporal distances. This expansion and condensation of temporality reminds me again of Virilio: "The beyond is no longer the beyond of a territory . . . ; it is the beyond of real time . . . from which we are progressively exiling ourselves" (91). Mansilla's narrative terrain, if we can still call it that, likewise moves beyond a spatial orientation; it is temporal and vectored, the moving target of a present that contemporary life attempts to exceed. Her dislocation of the charms of narrative through the desire for an espresso recalls her analogously jarring juxtapositions of academia and pulp fiction, canonical romance and sentimental shlock. In some sense the novel defines the unresolved tension between these two longings: nostalgia for an idealized, picturesque past, desire for the immediate gratifications of a postmodern urban present.

Given these tensions, it is no wonder that the novel we are offered is presented as a work-in-progress: "this tale, barely an outline, will remain forever inconclusive."[13] At the same time, progress, in a novel of this sort, is to be preferred over closure, and furthermore progress suggests a movement toward some perhaps as yet undefined goal, if only, as Virilio has it, the goal imagined in the beyond of real time. Indeed, Mansilla's is a project that has a clear vector: "this tale, barely an outline, will remain forever inconclusive . . . but certainly, just like my letters, notes, and postcards, it carries a direction [play on the word for 'address,' *lleva una dirección*]."[14] Here the Spanish word *dirección* hints at both a movement toward (direction) and a specific goal (address of arrival).

Anchoring this sense of direction/address in a more literal sense, the book includes reproductions of various letters and cards, both sent and received, as part of the body of the text. The postcard's text and its image irremediably blur, both projections of desire onto an imaginary and fervently desired space: "One day I gave him a postcard with the Umpirstatebildin in New York, which was one of my magic words when I was a child."[15] Here the word to conjure with, the magic word, is stripped of a concrete referent and becomes a mere collection of syllables—a kind of abracadabra—that vaguely presages wonders. When one character gives the postcard to another, it is not a trip to the United States, nor a visit to the Empire State Building in midtown Manhattan, New York City, that is represented in the transfer, but rather the symbolic access to the marvelous word of childhood magic uncoupled from any strict relation to geographic spaces.

Given the author's and the narrator's very wide range of high-culture references, it is not surprising to find in this self-consciousness about postcards and their direction an echo of Derrida's 1980 *The Post Card*, a reading of Freud that is similarly, if more densely than Mansilla's novel, organized around the concept of a love letter, still in transit, indecipherable and at the same time fully available on the reverse side of a postcard. Like Mansilla's text, in Derrida's project there is simultaneously an invitation to participate and a warning of a primary exclusion—the postcard epitomizes the letter that is not directed at us, but comes through our hands nevertheless, read or unread, on its way to another destination. At one point, more than halfway through his long book, Derrida announces: "once more the possibility of progress is announced, and finally as a kind of promise. But this progress will not belong to the order of that which one might acquire" (338). Earlier, at the very beginning of the text, he writes: "you might read these *envois* as the preface to a book that I have not written. . . . You might consider them, if you wish to, as the remainders of a recently destroyed correspondence" (3). For Derrida, one sort of theoretical conundrum is posed in the relation between the unwritten and the already destroyed, the book and its fragmentary remainder. In thinking of the postcard that serves as his primary referent, however, the concept of traversal is key. The postcard is not for us, he emphasizes, but passes by us on its way to another destination, one that lies outside the purview of the text, not "here," but ambiguously in transit between one "there" and another "there." In passing, it interpellates the reader into its mysterious decorum. Furthermore, the postcard has two sides: image and text, and, says Derrida, if the text is legible but ultimately indecipherable, the image at some level deciphers us, putting us into its space, its path.

Mansilla's text has a very similar function to Derrida's. This love letter between Tolstoy and Mansilla, or AK and Amalia, or the textualized reader and the narrator, puts us into that multiply traversed path: a book in progress, not yet written but moving in time and space between two addresses. Sometimes she uses the epistolary style; in one of her letters, for instance, the narrator writes, referring to the love affair: "I wish I could traverse it, share it, and give away little pieces of I love you. Time does not contain it, my writing does not contain it, my body, poor thing, is in a serious quandary."[16] More often, as can be expected, Mansilla's metaphor for this literary transmission is the train. Earlier in the text, the narrator has explained to her reader: "it is useful to make a stop and explain what is style. Style has its tracks and its stations. . . . In this tale, the reader should be ready for the inconveniences of frequent transfers without any guarantee of arrival."[17] Again, as with the letters or postcards, it is the movement in the direction of an as-yet undefined "there" that marks the narrative rather than the content of the text: "you are reading a somewhat retro love letter," says Derrida in his cover copy to *The Post Card,* "but you have not yet received it."

From still another perspective, Mansilla's narrative also wants us to be attentive to the crossings of languages in an abstract plane of literary intersections. Tolstoy's text derives from a Russian "there" and in Mansilla's is headed toward a Spanish "there." At the same time, while these referents are important as abstract sites marking an intellectual map of departure and not-yet arrival, the highly educated Mexican writer of this author's late-twentieth-century American continent is almost obligatorily cosmopolitan and polyglot. Thus, for example, the narrator directs one of her letters to her "very dear reader," who she presumes "knows all thirty-three natural languages that are indispensable to speak in order to survive this end of the millennium. . . . For this reason the translations that appear at the end of this little book are solely for you to verify the inconsistencies, the losses, the permutations, and form changes that literary works suffer when they are forced to pass through the funnels of translation."[18] The reader is not only polyglot, then, but fussily academic, worrying over the transit between languages and focused precisely on the process of this permutation of text into another text.

The choice of one language over another, or the inclusion of a translation in the text for sections written in languages other than Spanish, is never innocent. For instance, when one of the early sections of the novel includes a love letter written in English, the reader is quite rightly taken aback, for this long text violates our expectations about a novel published in Mexico, by a Mexican author, and up to this point written in Spanish, albeit with some French chapter titles. And yet, in addition to the suggestion of an international element to this epistolary play, at least one structural reason immediately suggests itself. Unlike Spanish, in English the writer's gender is completely unclear, because this language does not have grammatical gender that would mark the adjectives associated with the writer in the Romance languages (23–25). Helpfully, playfully, the unsigned letter ends with a parenthetical note—"(see p. 157)"—that refers the reader to the Spanish translation. The second version of the letter makes it obvious that a woman is the letter writer (e.g., in phrases such as "I am very fortunate"/"soy muy afortunada" [24, 158]), and thus main text and supplementary text offer their own instantiation of transfer and traversal.

In the main text, the English-language letter is followed with a comment on it by "Ana," this narrative's transposed voice of Tolstoy's tragic character: "there is no doubt that what hurts can be better swallowed in another tongue, which is the only good reason to learn languages."[19] In this manner, an ambiguously "Russian" character called Ana speaks in Spanish about a letter in English, which reflects, perhaps, a Mexican version of Anna Karenina's sentiments on being abandoned by Vronsky. She does so, moreover, in terms that clearly foreground the body—the hurt that rolls over the tongue and is consumed. Here, finally, is the clue to what I have called, in the title of this essay, "Anna's extreme makeover." Like the hapless or eager participants in a television reality show, Mansilla's characters radically reshape their bodies, remake their identities, passing through languages, cultural structures, academic presuppositions. Like a TV makeover, this is a public and performative event. In the novel's version, it articulates a shifting transformation that proposes at the same time to uncover a preexisting narrative shape and to give it a new, better—if invariably provisional, transitory, and permutable—form.

At one point in the novel, the character Ana comments, reflecting back on her namesake's famous suicide: "in my day, passion was carried to the wheels of a train."[20] For the Tolstoyan heroine, thus, closure is definitive and the symbol of modernity becomes the instrument of her death. Even more—the train represents the death of passion, that is, the romantic novel. In Mansilla's work, the question is how to innovate style and subject matter at the turn of the twenty-first century, rethinking at once death, romance, and the train. Here too the train, as a symbol of modernity and progress, is a constant presence, but rather than a mere prop in the background, it moves to the foreground of the narrative and takes on a certain autonomous quality as a plot device: "Ana said something, but the noise of the train as it invaded the farm/living room [*estancia*] did not allow her to be heard."[21] In this later novel, the train defines conditions of transmission, what is heard and by whom, and even where, for the noun *estancia* can be used both for the presumably male domain of the Russian farm and the domestic space of a living room.

Even the title of the novel refers to a specific train, one that appears in the novel with Mansilla's rewriting of Tolstoy's tragic ending:

> But this time Ana Karenina did not push her head forward in the direction of her lucid discourse in order to be carried off by the train's dark stain; this time she hurried her step in a flurry of silk skirts and hooped cotton petticoats with strips of lace that made the heads of various gentlemen turn, and she headed toward the platform where the K. Express awaited her.[22]

Here the fatal train of Tolstoy's novel becomes transformed into a metropolitan subway line (the "K" line, to be exact), a quotidian commuter ride that is also an homage to the twentieth-century fabulist of urban angst Franz Kafka. Likewise, Anna Karenina skips her tragic suicide scene, and instead Mansilla's Ana flirtatiously turns her back on that so-called lucid discourse, heading toward the subway platform, where she (improbably) sings something like a Russian version of a traditional Spanish *copla,* and then fades into the air. The narrator sits back, satisfied for the moment. Then she asks herself if Ana's happy determination will last, if she will find another Mr. Wrong (one more "count Wrong-sky") and another train platform: "but perhaps that would be the motivation, tomorrow, for another espresso."[23] The narrative goal, nevertheless, is less important than the direction of travel; the fact of being in transit is more intriguing than the ending of the story, the performance of Ana's makeover more interesting than either the before or the after.

"The story ends here," says the narrator in one of the first paragraphs of the next chapter.[24] Yet here, near the end of the novel proper, we find the narrator planning a new trip and packing up her trunks for an unknown destination. Letters, those "little paper ships for watercolors," "paper trains of dove gray," continue to sail back and forth between the lovers, but "Today is April on *Karenina Express* and in all its A-B-Cissas it is always the first season of the year."[25] Each narrative setting forth offers a new direction, new loves and new adventures, new discursive and artistic possibilities: "In her story love had been turned to paper, and not the other way around, thereby losing one time and gaining another. If once both of these times coincide, you will cry tears in the form of letters and will see once again the color of my eyes" (144; English in the original). Each new iteration of the story offers a reshuffling of the elements: how to write romance and how to read it, how to perform it so that it is always the same and always new, how to transfer agency to the female protagonist, making her the actor rather than acted upon, how to avoid the traps of nineteenth-century realist aesthetics and twentieth-century postmodern academic jargon.

At one point near the end of the novel, Mansilla's narrator follows a quote from her how-to-write a romance book with several stanzas of a famous Oscar Wilde poem. In her citation of Wilde's text, Mansilla's English has a punning error—she titles the poem "Ballad of Reading Goal"[26]—which entirely changes the context of the poem and leads the narrator into the meditation on her own setting of goals for conducting her reading/life. Wilde's poem, written from jail, includes a variation of the tag line "each man kills the thing he loves / Yet each man does not die." Mansilla implicitly rejects the nineteenth-century options of love or death, love and death, in favor of the freedom to remake the story at each subway stop or train station or cappuccino bar in the city, to reshape the reading goals so they are less jail-like, less restrictive, more vectored to the needs of a modern age. Mansilla's mode is that of ironic nostalgia, ambiguous fascination, a metaromance of the present moment, continuously displaced: "she also now knew that he would spend his life seeking a direction [*dirección*, address], in another country, in another language, in the skin of other women. . . . And console yourself, because there is nothing worse than a happy ending."[27] Luckily, the makeover is always to do again.

Notes

1. "Amalia no se encontraba en la Riviera francesa" (11).

2. "¿qué era esta visión sino escenario y personaje predicho en su próxima lectu-aventura?" (13).

3. "hubo que reeducar al público para que creyera nuevamente en la ficción" (85).

4. "Éste es un libro sobre los orígenes, sobre cartas y estrellas y barcos que navegan bajo un cielo de papel... Me he permitido marcar con rojo el plano terrestre de las abscisas y con azul la cronometría ordenada de lo celeste; con hojas violeta la *terra incognita* donde crece la escritura. La unión de los puntos para trazar la figura de un recorrido es cosa del lector, quien podrá ir o no en orden, e interpretar lo que se ha escrito en otras lenguas" (178–79).

5. "en este punto cruzan las abscisas y las ordenadas. Es el lugar del eje de la narración, por lo tanto, personajes, libros y narrador quedan excluidos de este espacio" (61).

6. "barroquismo, pocos se salvan," "Cannes, ver N.Y.," "deseo, no comments," "Derrida, estudiarlo," "lágrimas, ni remedio," Nueva York, ver vox paradox," "Utopía, ver N.Y.!"

7. "Se dio cuenta que el libro ya empezaba a hacerle efecto... punto Y coma finalmente coma se abre interrogación por qué no se cierra interrogación Tenía una amiga que se había lanzado a escribir guiones de telenovelas coma cansada de todo su bagaje de erudición punto" (12–13).

8. "¿cómo aprende (aprende?) el lector a gozar de una nueva forma narrativa?" (57).

9. "no es tal vez hasta el modernismo cuando se da la diferencia entre 'literatura' y 'best-sellers'. O sea, Literatura y literatura" (53); "la fantasía: libro para enseñar a desear. Advertencia. Necesario aprender a leerdeotramanera para leerlo" (55).

10. "se supone que con el modernismo el público lector se convirtió en un *publique introuvable*" (53).

11. "la lectura, solía decir Ana, es veleidosa, pues se deja hacer peor los martes que los jueves y los domingos no hay quien entienda nada" (130).

12. "tenía ganas de leer una novela que tuviera que ver con barcos y trenes, y macedonias de fruta, y mujeres apasionadas de cabellos largos y oscuras pupilas. Por lo pronto deseaba un express, tres sorbos de aroma y espuma de exquisita amargura vital" (154).

13. "este relato, apenas un bosquejo, quedará para siempre inconcluso" (117).

14. "...pero segura que al igual que mis cartas, notas y postales lleva una dirección" (117).

15. "Un día le di un postal con el Empayersteitbilding de Nueva York que de niña era una de mis palabras mágicas" (113).

16. "quisiera trasvasarlo, compartirlo y regalar trocitos de te quiero. El tiempo no lo contiene, mi escritura no lo contiene, mi cuerpo, el pobre, se ve en aprietos serios" (106).

17. "es conveniente hacer un alto y explicar qué es el estilo. El estilo tiene sus estaciones y sus vías... En este relato, el lector debe estar dispuesto a los inconvenientes de frecuentes trasbordos sin garantía de arribo" (36).

18. "[conoce] las treinta y tres lenguas naturales que es imprescindible manejar para sobrevivir este fin de milenio... De manera que las traducciones que aparecen al final de esta obrita son únicamente para que verifiques las inconsistencias, pérdidas, permutas y cambios de forma que sufren las letras cuando se las fuerza a pasar por los embudos de la traducción" (29).

19. "no cabe duda que lo que duele se puede mascar mejor en otra lengua, que es la única buena razón para aprender idiomas" (25).

20. "en mis tiempos la pasión se llevaba hasta las ruedas del tren" (17).

21. "Ana dijo algo, pero el ruido del tren que invadió la estancia no dejó que la escuchara" (80).

22. "Pero esta vez Ana Karenina no empujó la cabeza hacia adelante en dirección de su lúcido discurso para ser arrebatada por la mancha negra del tren; esta vez apuró el paso en un revuelo de faldas de seda y polleras de algodón con vueltas de encaje que hizo voltear la cabeza a varios caballeros y se dirigió al anden donde esperaba el *K. Express*" (139–40).

23. "pero eso sería tal vez motivo, mañana, de otro expresso" (140).

24. "El cuento termina aquí" (141).

25. "barquitos de papel para acuarela," "trenes de papel couché paloma" (143); "Hoy es abril en *Karenina Express* y en todas sus a-b-scisas siempre es la primera estación del año" (ibid.).

26. Although the pun *goal* for *gaol* seems particularly astute and fitting, I cannot be certain that this is not simply a serendipitous error in the text. Despite the narrator's warning about the slipperiness of her translations, in the Spanish version of this poem she cites the original title—"Balada de la cárcel de Reading"—giving some plausibility to the theory that it might be a simple metastasis of the two vowels (161). It is necessary to admit, though, that this is, of course, exactly

the kind of pedantic aside that Mansilla spoofs in so much of her text. The referentiality is, finally, inescapable.

27. "ella también sabía ahora que él se pasaría la vida buscando una dirección, en otro país, en otra lengua, en la piel de otras mujeres... Y consuélate, porque no hay cosa peor que un final feliz" (132–33).

WORKS CITED

Bogan, Louise. *Journey around My Room*. New York: Viking Press, 1980.

Derrida, Jacques. *The Post Card: From Socrates to Freud and Beyond*. Trans. Alan Bass. Chicago: University of Chicago Press, 1987.

Mansilla, Margarita. *Karenina Express*. Mexico City: UNAM, 1995.

Rodowick, D. N. "Introduction: Mobile Citizens, Media States." *PMLA* 117.1 (January 2002): 13–23.

Virilio, Paul. *A Landscape of Events*. Trans. Julie Rose. Cambridge: MIT Press, 2000.

6

The "Uchronic" City

Writing (after) the Catastrophe

> ... the acceleration of a dromological history and its rush not towards
> utopia, but the uchronia, of human time.
>
> *Paul Virilio*

In postmodernity, the notions of time and space used to refer to the city in Latin America are no longer valid. There are no pasts, no futures, and no presents. All that remains is the nostalgia for an Arcadia *illo tempore*. The city has ceased to be a place. Indeed, the concept of utopia now becomes the impossibility of and simultaneous desire for time. The city has moved from a fixed territorial entity to a deterritorialized geo-body looking for a time, the uchronic city.

In this essay I show a possible route, a constellation of texts that allow us to read and to perceive this new city. I will focus on Chilean women writers who deal with fictional representations of Santiago de Chile. However, I establish connections and links with other texts and cities—for example, Guayaquil, Ecuador—in an attempt to illustrate how the modern city's interruption and disappearance is a spreading phenomenon. I divide my itinerary into parts. First, I trace some of the main changes that the idea of the city has experienced through time. Then I refer to a variety of texts that re-create this constellation. Finally, I analyze more in detail a novel I consider paradigmatic of the uchronic city, *Mapocho* (Mapocho river) by Nona Fernández. Thus, I aim to explain one of the ways in which the (after)catastrophe of historical progress is being written.[1] Catastrophe is understood here as history itself, as the result of dictatorships and neoliberal democracies in the Southern Cone of Latin America. In one sense, to talk about "after catastrophe" is an oxymoron, because it is an ongoing event, therefore without an "after." But at the same time it has continuously already happened. In other words, it is precisely the oxymoronic disappearance of time, history, and memory that allows us to maintain the possibility of the "after" of something that has not ended. These writings are dealing precisely with that possible impossibility.

Cities have changed through time. They have taken various shapes and sizes. They have been funded, built, destroyed, and rebuilt; they have been praised and scorned. The city is not just a mirror of human endeavor, or of human life at large; it produces spaces and times, ever-changing lines in fugue. In the city we suspend beliefs and certainties: in a dialectical relation we are continuously created by the city and we, wandering and gazing, contribute to creating it. Today we have reached a point where the human connection with the city has been dramatically altered. The fragmented postmodern subject does not belong to the city anymore, nor does the cracked city belong to her or him. The absolute speed forged by the system's logic—late-capitalist, postfordist, empire—has overthrown the modern city's way of life, its pace.

Richard Lehan establishes three stages in the development of the modern city before reaching this postmodern phase: "commercial, industrial and 'world stage' city" (3). In a similar classification, Burton Pike makes the historical divisions ancient city, medieval city, Renaissance city, industrial city, and postindustrial city (xii). Pike characterizes the postindustrial city as "diffused and decentralized, a 'nowhere city'" (ibid.). My aim here is to show how in the fiction of several Latin American women writers we visualize the "otherness" of the postindustrial stage: the consequences and effects of late capitalism and the opposition and resistance to them. This literary response is tied to a traumatic political experience; dictatorships in Latin America during the 1970s and 1980s paved the way for neoliberalism, particularly in the case of Chile. The "new democracies" from the 1980s and 1990s are the best examples of this "transition" to economic neoliberalism. The new democracy in Chile does not oppose a dictatorial regime; on the contrary, this new democracy fulfills "the promise" implicit during the dictatorships, the hegemony of neoliberalism.[2] Like the *desaparecidos,* people kidnapped, tortured, murdered, and erased from the public record during the dictatorships, these writers represent a pattern of erasure in today's neoliberal climate. Memory, space, and time disappear as the alienated protagonists wander through the simulated cities of postmodernism.

The "nowhereness" of the city functions in the texts we are considering as the first step toward the no-when-city. The continuous destruction of the possibility of a city in which time and a space are plausible shows the recurrent strategy adopted by the hegemonic ideology. Memory and even history tend to vanish; there won't be another time, as there was none before. Thus, the city itself loses its potentiality of constituting a defined time and space. Those who dwell in it are either lacking agency or brutally repressed; they will be literally and literarily dead or disappeared, and will become the debris of a disappearing time and space. If there was a time when "the city [was once] a place of liberation for women" (Wilson, 7), those "liberations" were just another masquerade of the neoliberal catastrophe. Now the presence and reign of capitalism, its empire, needs no justification, no excuses, no possible unveiling, no discoveries to be made.

The city is a useful idea for reading "the past and present" (Pike, 4). As such, the possibilities to recover an individual and collective memory are put into question through the city as text, even as these memories are unfolded.[3] This link, city equals book, has been a recurrent one and presupposes a hermeneutical capacity of the reader/walker/(post-)*flâneur*: to walk, as well as to read, creates a machine and a dynamic of knowledge. In Gilda Holst's (Ecuador, b. 1952) brief short story "El libro" (The book, 1989) we read a new version of this relationship in the story of a passionate reader who loves to walk in the city: "She liked to stroll down the downtown streets; she felt that it was the only thing compatible with or comparable to the reading of a book, to traverse crossed, parallel lines, with potholes, illuminated by the six o'clock sun that made them so beautiful, wrapped in life, yet outside of it."[4] The city, with its "crossed, parallel lines, with potholes," is a text that will be deciphered by the reader through the reading of and walking through the short story. The dialogical relationship becomes evident: while the book writes the city, the city is the writing of a book. This connection, however, is never direct or transparent. Both writings are palimpsestic: no matter how hard we keep on trying to erase what was there before, phantasmagoric traces remain, and those traces are paradoxically the only ones that allow us to create the epistemological possibility for the construction of a future. In other words, only those leftovers that cannot be destroyed might constitute the beginning of a history that takes into account its past and does not attempt to erase and deny it.

Through the parallel we have established between the city and the written text, we are able to understand and visualize the radical modification in their structures: as the city deterritorializes and "detemporalizes," the text "de-autonomizes" and "de-literalizes." Both city and text are bodies in perpetual transformation, and in this process a third body has a central role. This is the body of what I call the post-*flâneur:*[5] someone who feels at home walking in the impossibility of the new Latin American City. Here the "practice of space," as de Certeau would put it, turns, first, into a practice of mere time and, second, into the catastrophe's practice itself, where time disappears:

> In Santiago it never rains, but today the opposite happens: the screen adorned with peacocks is steamed up, home's dark, a little bit cold. I go out. I walk through certain streets that have no direct exit but go in circles, end in small squares, and then continue. I like to get lost and wander aimlessly under this rain. I choose this street and not another. Despite it being Monday I see no people; it doesn't worry me; on the contrary, I like it that way.[6]

So begins "La Elegida" (The chosen one) by Chilean writer Lilian Elphick (b. 1959). This short story has usually been read as the self-discovery of the female body framed by an unreal or etherized Santiago.[7] The story tells of a woman who takes a stroll in Santiago, but everything has changed, there are no people on the streets and time has stopped, so the story can easily be read as a narrative of self-discovery, where the city is the woman itself. However, another reading is more suggestive in this context. Only the de-realization of the city ("In Santiago it never rains, but today the opposite happens") allows the main character a brief moment of happiness. This moment, a temporary lapse, will be soon forgotten once the city recovers and returns to its "reality": "It hasn't rained in Santiago . . . I feel a huge nostalgia for you . . . my chosen one without memory . . . then, there I forget you" (94).[8]

The text is seen not only as a city but also as the body of the nameless protagonist. The knowledge of the city, already fragmented by the text itself, can be sustained only as a nostalgic operation: what remains for a while is a past in an inexistent space and time. Unreality becomes thus the haven from a "real" city/body/text. Reality's omnivorous power has ironically erased the reality of affections and memory. But it is not possible to truly escape: the traces of the catastrophe are always there, even in the purest of the unrealities. Written in the late 1980s, "La Elegida" deals at another level with the destruction of the social body and social text, and their memory, as a result of seventeen years of dictatorship. The mourning for another city implies the destruction and disappearance of a previous reality that never really existed. When memory ceases, time itself vanishes: the doors for the reign of neoliberalism are fully open.

The alienation resulting from such a system is notable in Andrea Jeftanovic's (Santiago de Chile, b. 1970) short story "Crónica urbana" (Urban chronicle, 2000). Here, the two main characters, the narrator and the one he addresses, have a relationship from "apartment to apartment" without ever talking or having any kind of physical contact, the only kind that remains possible:

> We've never invaded each other by asking questions from the balcony.
> I don't know your name, nor your age, what you do or how do you smell.
> I know we pay the same amount in utilities . . . that we had a nightmare
> about the woman who committed suicide last month. I also know that I
> possess you, that you exist once a month, to be more exact, once every
> twenty-eight days; and that it's that or nothing at all. That if one day I
> wait for you outside your apartment, or I give you a call although I don't
> know your number and I would end up listening to the dial tone, or
> I write you something not knowing to whom I should address the letter;
> you are capable of abandoning the scene and withdrawing forever from
> the stage.[9]

This monthly routine blurs everything else. Its unreality becomes so powerful that all that surrounds the trajectory, a time-space relation, between the two apartments seems as if it had disappeared: "I miss the noise of the street's traffic. I ask myself if everybody died, if we are the survivors of some catastrophe."[10] Jeftanovic's text thus places together spectacle and disappearance. And the city struggles between them: "I was an unreal image in the middle of the city," states the protagonist.[11] The city turns into what "fills" it: spectacle, simulation. Like the bodies of the story—"your body like a movie screen"[12]—the city itself becomes a specter that is and is not there. Intangible but desired, simulation represents the collective consciousness of the city, a radical emptiness of space and time where love is an ephemeral parody. Indeed, the relation between these lovers becomes a possibility only on a flat screen that never changes, thus lacking a third and a fourth dimension. And, as we are told, this "unreal image" exists "in the middle of the city," in the city's core; the city is no longer capable of sustaining "real" relations because the city itself is becoming an impossibility, a lack of time and a lack of space that leads not only to the destruction of the attempted relation in the short story, but also to the vanishing of any connection with the city. In other words, there's a process of reification where affections are continuously being erased.

However, this erasure does not occur without traces of resistance. In fact, on several occasions, love attempts to constitute the only realm where simulation is overcome; love becomes the only space and time that the city would allow, and, while doing so, creates its own topos and chronos. This is seen in Andrea Maturana's (Santiago de Chile, b. 1969) "Roce 1" and "Roce 2" (Brush 1 and Brush 2, 1992), a simple story in which a woman and a man are walking in opposite directions and, because they are paying attention only to their thoughts, cannot avoid brushing into each other.[13] Then each one continues on his or her way: "Both have escaped . . . from their lives in order to meet in a corner and believe that they can create a common space. Such that everything that is not that corner and that common space does not exist."[14] But again there is no possible "common space." Memory cannot be established: "He crosses the street without looking back and she starts her car, not being able to remember, already, that which doesn't happen yet."[15] In fact, the future cannot be remembered. But in order to have the possibility of a future there is a need to create at least a capacity of memory. This scene indicates that everyday practices of late capitalism have managed to destroy our very sense of belonging to history.

In Nona Fernández's (b. 1971) *Mapocho* (2002), her first novel, Santiago can be read as the paradigm of the uchronic city. The title refers to the Mapocho River that runs across the city of Santiago. The protagonist, la Rucia, returns to Santiago for two reasons: first, to look for her brother, Indio, after her mother dies in a car accident in Spain, and, second, to deliver her mother's ashes into the river.[16] So, the blond European comes—again—to Latin America to meet the native, *el indio*.[17] But she will not find him easily. The novel's first sentence immediately alerts us to the fact that not only the protagonist but also the city is cursed: "I was born cursed. From my mother's cunt to the coffin where now I rest."[18] In a mode that reminds us of María Luisa Bombal's *La amortajada*, or Juan Rulfo's *Pedro Páramo*, the protagonist is dead and alive simultaneously.

La Rucia's perspective is twofold: she is the woman who walks the city and bears witness to its changes, and she is the corpse that looks at herself from the coffin floating in the Mapocho River. To this we must add the spectral presence of her father, Fausto, who is believed to have died in a fire in the first years of the dictatorship. We learn, however, that Fausto is another dead person who is alive. Through the novel and her revisit of the city, la Rucia re-creates a particular history of both Chile and herself, which includes a previous incestuous relationship with her brother. So la Rucia's return to Santiago becomes a journey where memory and history are filled with a multiplicity of (lost) times and spaces. In the end, no time is possible any longer: la Rucia is dead and alive; she lies between the absence of future and the (im)possibility of a past that haunts her and haunts the whole city.

In the novel, la Rucia's story develops parallel to the city's formation and later growth and expansion. The most evident link between them consists of the writing of history, a task being done by la Rucia's father, Fausto, whom she believes is dead. In his *Historia de Chile*, excerpts of which are visualized in the novel, the official version transmutes itself into a phantasmagoric retelling, where even the Devil plays a central part. Fernández attempts to create a history whose telos disappears, and it is in and through the city that we face the inevitability and the oxymoronic construction of this disappearance. The only present is this permanent destruction:

> More than hundred years have passed since Cal y Canto Bridge's
> inauguration, but now the bridge shivers with the river's force. . . .
> At 5:15, according to the clock at la Recoleta, a tremendous crack agitates
> the air. The bridge shakes. Its knees bend. It happens. After more than a
> hundred years of life, the colossus falls into the Mapocho. The bridge
> sinks. Tired, it gives up before the waters. It goes with the current.
> It disappears. It dies.[19]

Here, history is permanent destruction; the city takes part in history accordingly: by showing and exhibiting the constant catastrophe, the city is both exhibitionist and voyeur. Thus the protagonist, a post-*flâneur* in a city that is disappearing, becomes a part of this game of seeing and being seen. In the novel, we perceive the absent presence of a new velocity that has overcome and destroyed our previous conceptions of time and space that allowed us to write history and walk the city.

La Rucia's return to the city allows no recovery of a possible past, because there is nothing to be recovered. La Rucia's story and history have vanished. The only thing that persists is the continuous catastrophe. It reestablishes itself again and again through different landmarks: the fire in which a whole neighborhood dies, including, supposedly, Fausto; the car accident in which la Rucia's mother dies; the construction and destruction of the Puente de Cal y Canto, a bridge that connected the northern and southern parts of the city; and, of course, the guiding scene, la Rucia's coffin traveling to the sea. These events in the novel each have a connection to a political-historical episode related to the dictatorship. For example, we remember the bodies of the *desaparecidos* thrown into the Mapocho in the first days following September 11, 1973.

Because of this omnipresence of death, there's a ghostly atmosphere all over the remains of Santiago. Absence and presence are simultaneously there and then. The image of a gigantic building where Fausto lives is symptomatic of this empty presence:

> Some blocks away, the glass tower stands solid and firm. On the top
> floor the light of an apartment is on. It is the only apartment in that
> office building. The other floors in the tower are empty, dark, ready to
> activate themselves early tomorrow morning. The light that can be seen is
> dim, a standing lamp turned on some hours ago. Inside, next to the light,
> sitting on a sofa, is Fausto.[20]

Unreality, again, is the epicenter of the narrative machine. Even the fact that we are told that this is Santiago de Chile does not provide the slightest sense of reality. On the contrary, in Fernández's account the naming of the city, rather than recovering its familiarity, provokes defamiliarization.[21]

At one point in the novel, la Rucia finds out that Fausto is alive and tries to contact him. She finds a spot where she can, in another voyeuristic act, watch the apartment where Fausto lives. Suddenly, while she is observing him, Fausto tries to jump from the terrace but is stopped by the sudden appearance ex nihilo of his son, Indio. After this failed attempt, la Rucia tries to get into the building but "There's no answer. The tower's doors are closed and there are no bells or intercoms."[22] When they finally meet, the encounter significantly takes place at a graveyard. At first Fausto doesn't recognize his daughter; as he discovers her real identity, he realizes that the only possible presence is the presence of what surrounds them, an apparent death, an ambiguous and timeless state. Thus, the city's identity becomes a spectral one. All possible certainty has vanished, even the protagonists' dearest and deepest beliefs:

> Death is a lie. From the D to the H. All is a lie. Fausto knows it. For
> many years he has had the opportunity to prove it. It is not paranoia
> as the doctors say, nor a hallucination that can be cured with pills or
> treatments. The dead are alive. They are a reality. They resurrect daily and
> wander through the neighborhood's streets. They walk around; at nights

they gather next to his building; they wait for him sitting on nearby roofs and make signs or shout to him. The dead are alive.[23]

So if death is "nothing but a lie," the reader is confronted with a phantasmagoric conclusion: existence, which is based on the certainty of death, is a lie. Hence the importance of Fausto's writing; it constitutes the last chance to recover the reality of death and to recover time. Fausto's history, however, fails to achieve its goal. His solution is to put an end to his life: "The last thing could be one word: end . . . Why didn't he think of that before?"[24] In fact, it becomes for Fausto the "end of history": "He knows what he's doing. He approaches the edge of the desk with his belt around his neck. A satisfied smirk lines his mouth under his moustache. He breathes deeply, he contracts his lips, and with an almost imperceptible whisper, says the spell while his feet jump into the emptiness. 'End,' is heard."[25]

In the postdictatorship city, Fausto tells us, history has come to its conclusion. Time has ceased and the cities and their walkers are grieving for this lost chronos. In Mapocho the reader is confronted with a deeply nihilist gesture: even the capacity to desire is destroyed, and the reader too becomes the catastrophe that is history, a coffin sailing in the dirty waters of the river. Nevertheless, the end of history, as well as the end of the story, is not absolutely possible; the debris that is produced by progress remains there, creating a spectral residual accumulation that ends with la Rucia's coffin leaving the city and entering the Pacific Ocean, death's metaphor. Here the emergence of another death overwhelms the reader. The death of the dead; another time from where and when it will be possible to subvert the uchronicity of the city, and to build through the recuperation of memory a posthegemonic future and past.[26] But there is also another possible reading. The death of the dead may function as the recognition of final defeat, as the loss of hope. As Indio watches la Rucia's coffin in its way to the river of death, his perspective ends the novel, another ending of story/history:

> The same dead, the same shot-up bodies in the riverbank. The same woman looking for her daughter. We are in ground zero, he says, in the carrousel's axis. As you see, Rucia, there's no way to get out of here. I'm screwed. I let the sea take you, and you know nothing. You are seaweed, a grain of sand. One more salty drop in this huge ocean. I am just a coward, there's nothing left for me except to keep spying on you from behind the bushes.[27]

As the narrative concludes, then, nothing remains, only a meaningless voy-euristic act toward death. Death, its no-time and no-space, becomes para-doxically the only good (with all its economic connotations) that still has some meaning. Mapocho, the river, functions as a scar that marks the city, while *Mapocho*, the novel, aims to reveal the scars in Chilean society and history. Filled with hundreds of human corpses, Mapocho's clear and crys-talline waters get dirtier and dirtier on the way to the Pacific Ocean. Debris of the city, debris of the bodies that dwell in the city, debris of history, pieces of memory, the possibility of time, the river carries everything. As a silent witness of destruction and disappearance in the novel, the foul-smelling Mapocho is an open wound that won't heal.

This is the (permanent) catastrophe the writers are facing, not only a political and economic catastrophe, but also a human catastrophe. The writer deals with the ruins of history, and the cities and the bodies that circulate through them constitute a testimony, traces of that history. These texts become the possibility of memory, while at the same time they visu-alize how memory is being erased over and over again. Confronted with a new chrono-geo-body where space and time are first blurred and then erased, these narratives imply that we must persist in bringing flashes of the past into the present, to take time back to us and thus create new spaces of hope, or, from another perspective, give back to politics its previous vis-ibility, attacking and dismantling the prevalent idea of politics as the art of suppressing the political. This is the only potential way to reveal hege-mony's fissures and thus resist.

NOTES

I am deeply in debt to Zoë O'Reilly. Her comments and suggestions, during won-derful days in Dublin, created the speed of these lines.

1. Catastrophe as the way in which progress must be understood, following Walter Benjamin's famous ninth thesis: "This is how one pictures the angel of his-tory. His face is turned toward the past. Where we perceive a chain of events, he sees one single catastrophe which keeps piling wreckage and hurls it in front of his feet. The angel would like to stay, awaken the dead, and make whole what has been smashed. But a storm is blowing in from Paradise; it has got caught in his wings with such a violence that the angel can no longer close them. The storm irresistibly propels him into the future to which his back is turned, while the pile of debris before him grows skyward" (257–58).

2. Certainly, this statement should be made carefully. The situation is different from one country to another. But, I do believe it applies in general: the consequence of dictatorships is the implementation of neoliberalism, regardless of the intention of the respective de facto government. Also, today, the situations in Venezuela, Brazil, Ecuador, and Bolivia may indicate a different development.

3. As Scott and Simpson-Housley state: "we may say that writing the city represents an effort to awaken the possibility of ideological critique in imaginative fiction by ironizing, and hence problematizing, the dialectic between fictional realism and implicit ideology" (340).

4. "Le gustaba peatonear por las calles del centro, sentía que era lo único compatible o comparable con la lectura de un libro, recorrer líneas cruzadas, paralelas, con baches, iluminadas por el sol de las seis que las hacía tan hermosas, envuelta en vida, y al mismo tiempo afuera de ella" (89).

5. If in Benjamin the *flâneur,* who moves nonchalantly through the kaleidoscopic world of the modern city, is represented in the figure of Charles Baudelaire—"The crowd is his element, as the air is that of birds and water of fishes" once wrote the French poet—who will be the one to take Baudelaire's place, the hypocrite *lecteur?*

6. "En Santiago no llueve nunca, pero hoy sucede lo contrario: la mampara de pavos reales está empañada, la casa oscura, un poco fría. Salgo. Camino por ciertas calles que no tienen salida directa sino que dan vueltas y vueltas, terminan en plazoletas y luego continúan. Me gusta perderme y caminar sin rumbo bajo esta lluvia. Elijo esta calle y no otra. A pesar de ser lunes no veo gente; no me inquieta, es más, me gusta que sea así."

7. The few critics referring to her work remark on the "presence of the woman," "the feminine," "the female problematic," and so on in her work. As Roberto Rivera points out: "In the center [of Elphick's narrative] habits the woman, the woman's voice, turning around herself, talking to herself, knowing herself again and again."

8. "No ha llovido en Santiago... Siento mucha nostalgia por usted... mi elegida sin memoria... Entonces, ahí la olvido."

9. "Nunca nos hemos invadido preguntándonos cosas desde el balcón. No sé tu nombre, ni tu edad, lo que haces o cómo hueles. Sé que pagamos la misma cifra de gastos comunes... que tuvimos una pesadilla con la mujer que se suicidó el mes pasado. También sé que te tengo, que existes una vez al mes, para ser más exacto cada veintiocho días; y que es eso o nada. Que si un día te espero afuera de tu departamento, o te llamo aunque no sé el número y me quedaría escuchando el tono muerto, o te escribo algo sin saber qué nombre poner como destinatario del sobre; eres capaz de abandonar la escena y retirarte para siempre de los tablones" (107–8).

10. "Extraño el ruido del tráfico de la calle, me pregunto si todos murieron, si somos los sobrevivientes de alguna catástrofe" (106).

11. "Yo era una imagen irreal en medio de la ciudad" (109).

12. "tu cuerpo de pantalla de cine" (108).

13. "Roce 1" and "Roce 2," rather than short stories, are sketches of simple situations.

14. "Los dos han escapado... de sus vidas para encontrarse en una esquina y creer que pueden construir un espacio en común. Que todo lo que no sea esa esquina y ese espacio en común no existe" (22).

15. "Él cruza la calle sin volver la cabeza y ella hace partir su auto, sin poder recordar ya aquello que todavía no sucede" (25).

16. The mother had escaped to Spain because of the Pinochet dictatorship, which is never mentioned but whose presence is unavoidable.

17. The novel could be read as a rewriting of the "encounter of the two worlds." But the blond woman will not succeed this time. She is already dead.

18. "Nací maldita. Desde la concha de mi madre hasta el cajón en el que ahora descanso" (13).

19. "Ya han pasado más de cien años de la inauguración del Cal y Canto, pero ahora el puente tiembla con una nueva crecida del río... Cuando son las 17:15 horas en el reloj de la Recoleta, un crujido tremendo estremece el aire. El puente se sacude. Las rodillas se le doblan. Ocurre. Después de más de cien años de vida, el gigante se desmorona en el Mapocho. El puente se hunde. Se rinde cansado a las aguas. Se va por la corriente. Desaparece. Muere" (119–20).

20. "A unas cuadras, la torre de vidrio se eleva sólida y firme. Arriba, en el último piso, la luz de un departamento se intuye encendida. Es el único departamento en ese edificio de oficinas. Los otros pisos de la torre están vacíos, oscuros, listos para activarse en la mañana temprano. La luz que se divisa es baja, una lámpara de pie encendida hace unas horas. Adentro, junto a una luz, sentado en un sillón, está Fausto" (67).

21. It is interesting to note that in Isabel Allende's novels, written fifteen years earlier, we observe the reverse phenomenon. As Emily Gilbert points out in relation to *The House of Spirits*, "the un-naming of the city, which on the one hand universalizes the particular, also suggests its primacy and familiarity" (311). The shift toward the uchronic becomes clearer: even the "sense of hope" for the future that "emerges from Allende's novels" had disappeared.

22. "No hay respuesta. Las puertas de la torre están cerradas y no hay timbres ni citófonos a los que acudir" (73).

23. "La muerte es mentira. Desde la M hasta la E. Todo mentira. Fausto lo sabe. Durante mucho tiempo ha tenido oportunidad de comprobarlo. No es paranoia como diagnostican los médicos, tampoco es una alucinación que se pueda curar con pastillas o tratamientos. Los muertos viven. Son una realidad. Resucitan a diario y vagan por las calles del barrio. Se pasean, se instalan por las noches bajo su edificio, lo esperan sobre los techos cercanos y le hacen señas o le gritan. Los muertos viven" (115).

24. "Lo último podría ser una palabra: fin... ¿Cómo no se le ocurrió antes?" (215).

25. "Él sabe lo que hace. Se acerca a la orilla del escritorio con el cinturón al cuello. Una mueca satisfecha marca su boca bajo el bigote. Respira profundo, contrae sus labios y en un susurro casi imperceptible, enuncia el conjuro mientras sus pies saltan al vacío. Fin, se escucha" (222).

26. I follow Gareth Williams in the use of this term: "my appropriation of the term, together with Laclau's notion of recalcitrant negativity, permits us to give a name to hegemony's subaltern residues, negative languages, fragmentary responses, cultural leftovers, and fissured experiences. Post-hegemony, in this sense, is no longer a name for the hegemony of transnational capital, but the name of those 'places in which hegemony ceases to make sense' ([Jean] Franco)" (327). Previously, he points out: "I forward the term 'posthegemony' as the promising articulation of an *other* (subaltern) telos for reflection and for the critical evaluation of postnational commonalities" (15).

27. "Los mismos muertos, los mismos cuerpos baleados en la ribera del río, la misma mujer preguntando por su hija. Estamos en el punto cero, dice, en el eje del carrusel. Como ves, Rucia, de aquí no hay forma de salir. Estoy cagado. Dejo que el mar te lleve a ti que no sabes de nada. Eres un alga, un grano de arena. Una gota salada más en este océano inmenso. Yo sólo soy un cobarde. No me queda más que seguir espiándote detrás de los matorrales" (239–40).

WORKS CITED

Benjamin, Walter. *Illuminations.* Trans. Harry Zohn. New York: Shocken, 1969.

Elphick, Lilian. "La Elegida." http://www.letras.s5.com/elphick15043.htm.

Fernández, Nona. *Mapocho.* Santiago: Planeta, 2002.

Gilbert, Emily. "Transgressing Boundaries: Isabel Allende's Santiago de Chile." In *Writing the City: Eden, Babylon, and the New Jerusalem,* ed. Peter Preston and Paul Simpson-Housley. London: Routledge, 1994. 306–30.

Holst, Gilda. "El libro." In *Más sin nombre que nunca.* N.p.: Casa de la Cultura Ecuatoriana, 1989.

Jeftanovic, Andrea. "Crónica urbana." *Ecos Urbanos.* Santiago: Alfaguara, 2000. 101–10.

Lehan, Richard. *The City in Literature: An Intellectual and Cultural History.* Berkeley: University of California Press, 1998.

Maturana, Andrea. "Roce 1" and "Roce 2." In *(Des)encuentros (des)esperados.* Santiago: Los Andes, 1992.

Pike, Burton. *The Image of the City in Modern Literature.* Princeton, N.J.: Princeton University Press, 1981.

Rivera, Robert. http://www.letras.s5.com/elphick160403.htm.

Scott, Jamie S., and Paul Simpson-Housley. "Eden, Babylon, New Jerusalem: A Taxonomy for Writing the City." In *Writing the City: Eden, Babylon, and the New Jerusalem,* ed. Peter Preston and Paul Simpson-Housley. London: Routledge, 1994. 331–41.

Virilio, Paul. *Ground Zero.* London: Verso, 2002.

Williams, Gareth. *The Other Side of the Popular: Neoliberalism and Subalternity in Latin America.* Durham, N.C.: Duke University Press, 2002.

Wilson, Elizabeth. *The Sphinx in the City: Urban Life, the Control of Disorder, and Women.* Berkeley: University of California Press, 1992.

7
The Fourth World and the Birth of Sudaca Stigma

GARETH WILLIAMS

It is not difficult to see that ours is a birth-time and a period of
transition to a new era . . . But just as the first breath drawn by a child
after its long, quiet nourishment breaks the gradualness of merely
quantitative growth—there is a qualitative leap, and the child is
born—so likewise the Spirit in its formation matures slowly and
quietly into its new shape, dissolving bit by bit the structure of its
previous world, whose tottering state is only hinted at by isolated
symptoms.

G. W. F. Hegel, *The Phenomenology of Spirit, 6*

Force is the midwife of every old society that is pregnant with a new
one. It is itself an economic power.

Karl Marx, Capital, vol. 1, 916

In Diamela Eltit's nightmarish yet premonitory novel *El cuarto mundo*
(The fourth world) urban space is not a place for either anthropological or location-based subjectivities of any kind. Although the city
slowly becomes a forceful presence in the narrative's development, there
are no specific urban forms or landscapes to be found, and no city-based
interactions between what one might consider "real" people and the multi-
leveled negotiations of the public sphere. The novel thus refuses to present
the city as an organized, rationally administered, or governmental terrain
for the biopolitical production of "real" individual or collective identities.[1]
As such, it appears that the city is no longer the modern human environment necessary for extending or affirming the relation between collective
subjectivity and the historical discourses of economic development, progress, and civilization in Latin America.

However, this is not to suggest that the novel simply erases or ignores the
long-standing question of the relation between the city and subjectivity in

Latin America. After all, from the outset the novel is also deeply invested in thinking through the process of subject formation, and of inscribing a process of female empowerment in particular. The question, though, is how this relation between collective subjectivity and the city plays itself out in the novel.

Published in 1988 (that is, on the eve of Chile's transition from neo-liberal authoritarianism to neoliberal democracy), the novel's nameless and therefore geographically and culturally indistinct city is an abstraction that is under continuous and unmediated bombardment from another abstract system: the money that spews forth from the most "powerful nation in the world" as a result of the intensified dematerialization of cap-ital in recent years.

This essay focuses on the implications of the closing sections of the novel, which refer explicitly to the relation between subjectivity, the vio-lence of global economic power, the expropriation of collective urban and physiological life, and birth. Within this final section, Eltit portrays "the city" as the site of individual and collective humiliations, failures, and dismay. Modern life's rationalizing administrative and organizational im-peratives are torn asunder by the contemporary world's astounding drive toward generalized commodification and the intensified quest for surplus value.

Language in this context encounters its point of exhaustion and break-down. The city's inhabitants—the "*sudaca* race"—experience newly inten-sified forms of societal and corporeal exploitation. In the midst of this apocalyptic portrayal of life in the contemporary polis, a woman named *diamela eltit* gives birth to a female *sudaca* baby whom she has engen-dered with her now transvestite twin brother, María Chipia. The book ends merely by announcing that the female *sudaca* baby, like everything else in the city, will be put up for sale. As the final section of the narrative is the primary focus of this essay, allow me to quote at length from this dystopic final portrayal of contemporary collective life:

> Outside, the devastated city emits grunts and useless chatter. All kinds of
> rhetoric are rehearsed as it awaits the money fallen from the sky that
> burns like a firefly. The blinded, avid city hands over the destinies of its
> *sudaca* inhabitants. Terribly exhausted and grumpy, aged and greedy, the
> city trembles with Parkinson's disease. The voices tremble, the aged and
> grumpy voices tremble as they dispute the money fallen from the sky that
> burns like a firefly. The wheat, corn, and willow plantations are up for

sale at a ridiculous price, along with the *sudaca* youth who cultivated
them. The fields of the *sudaca* city are up for sale. Sweat is for sale.
A hysterical seller shrieks at the buyers, who astutely lower their prices
and even buy the sellers. The money fallen from the sky returns to the
sky and the sellers sell even that which does not belong to them. The
collapsed city is already a nominal fiction. Only the name of the city
remains, because everything else has already been sold on the open
market. In the anarchy of this supply and demand the final movements
are executed out loud, voicing the sale of nothingness. The money that
falls from the sky craves the emptiness of the city, together with every one
of the rhetorics of nothingness, in order to sow a vacuum over the already
sold fields that definitively belong to others. The money fallen from the
sky enters the genitals directly and the aged voices hand themselves over
to frenzied adultery. Adultery has adulterated the nominal city, which is
up for sale, for sale to bidders at any price. The transaction is about to
end, and on the money fallen from the sky there is clearly printed a smile
of contempt for the *sudaca* race. Far away, in a house abandoned to
fraternity, between April 7 and 8, diamela eltit, aided by her twin brother,
gives birth to a girl. The *sudaca* girl will be put up for sale.[2]

In a narrative register in which economic power, (de)territoriality, collective political existence, private (domestic) life, violence, uprootedness, sexuality, and commodification are thoroughly entwined, the fundamental
conditions of massive collective expropriation appear: "the complete separation of the labourers from all property in the means by which they
can realise their labour" (Marx, 786).[3] Indeed, the language of the novel
seems to present itself as a threshold of indistinction between formerly dif-
ferentiated public and private spheres, as the exploitative world of global
finance and the intimate zones of physiological existence—genitals, adultery, birth—become conjoined in a relation of absolute immanence between
economic rule (the intensified penetration power of capitalism's abstract
economy) and biological life.

As a result, notions such as "identity" and "difference" or "inside" and
"outside" are destabilized by a relation of absolute immediacy between the
free-floating circulation of money, the forceful expropriation and enslavement of labor by the violent conditions of contemporary accumulation,
and the frenzied bodies of the exploited. Distinctions between private
domestic life and collective economic existence in the city—distinctions
between biology, economics, and politics, in other words—are ungrounded.
They tremble as they are conjoined through a common relation of immediacy to absolute commodification and generalized enslavement.

Within this context the word *city* appears to denote little more than the exhaustion of historically received ideas regarding the relation between subject formation and concepts such as place, space, location, or environment. However, this is an extremely curious end to a novel that has, from its very first page, centered on the idea of subject formation. After all, the novel is grounded in the narrativization of a double process of subject formation. Its first narrative is that of a male twin and its second that of his female partner and counterpart. Both tell the story of their increasingly sexualized relationality. Therefore, it behooves us to consider the dialectical relation in the novel between subject formation and the novel's final gesture of handing everything over to global market forces. In other words, we need to consider the relation in the novel between empowerment and enslavement, as well as between identity production and capture.

It would not be difficult to read *The Fourth World* as an allegorical affirmation of collective female subject formation and liberation. There is a clear movement in the novel away from the male authoritarianism of father and son, away from the abjection of the twins' mother, and toward an open-ended performative femininity in which the prohibition of incest is overcome, the male twin slowly emerges as transvestite, a second sister (María Alava) enters the scene as collective guide and protector for the twins, and the twins' progeny is finally born female. As such, the novel's female narrator slowly transcends the limits of her enforced domesticity, breaks the shackles placed on her by the male figures who dominated both her life and that of her mother (through a mixture of corporeal violence and instrumental reason), and ultimately intervenes in the public sphere by giving birth to a *sudaca* baby.[4] The novel in this reading narrates the collective female struggle to become a social actor in the face of male dictatorial power structures and rationalities.

However, such a reading is predicated on our not dealing too closely with the novel's final dialectical twist toward intensified abjection and a collective condition of wretchedness never before seen. It is predicated, that is, on overlooking the question of capital's abstract economy that emerges in the novel's final pages. Although one can certainly say that in the end "a girl is born because, as symbol of a woman writer's production, her gender influences the value and success ultimately registered at the marketplace" (Norat, 148), this does little to account for the following sense of discomfort: "As a female reader, I ask myself at the conclusion of the novel: Isn't Eltit's baby girl destined for failure?" (ibid.). The discomfort underlying this question bears witness to the ways in which the novel's unquestionable devolution into femininity and female empowerment end as just one more relation to the universality of the market as the new Absolute of our times.

Criticism of Eltit's work has considered the final pages of *The Fourth World* as a comment on the inevitable fate of the powerless. Francine Masiello affirms that in this novel "Eltit concludes dramatically that all bodies have a destiny in common" (215). Janet Lüttecke, however, questions the political grounds of fate or destiny in the novel (perhaps in terms that Eltit might not necessarily want to recognize): "There is no apparent revolutionary action carried out either by the '*sudacas*' or by the main characters of the novel. They are all apparently resigned to their fate. Finally, almost all the action in the book takes place in an enclosed space, the twins' family home" (1088). Randolph Pope, on the other hand, takes things a step further. In his reading of the novel as resistance writing, he approaches the final pages of the book with understandable caution, as he brings attention to the question of the economy and the capturing of the narrative in the universal equivalence of money:

> If the novel began with the description of a feverous genetic act, it ends
> up giving birth in a vacuum, in a vacuum in which the word is no longer
> creative but, on the contrary, reductive, transforming everything into
> gold like King Midas, but into a gold that has an unstable price and that
> circulates infinitely. . . . It seems to be impossible to intervene in this cycle
> with destabilizing words when there is nothing left to undermine. (48–49)

As such, Pope's approach to the novel as resistance writing obliges us to account for the complete exhaustion of all resistance in the end, for in the *sudaca* baby's sale there is, quite literally, nothing left to resist. This is because the novel's obvious inscription of freedom and empowerment— its clear devolution into collective female presence—is actually equivalent to the lack of freedom of capital. Obviously, this refers in part to the birth of the book itself as a commodity. However, this commodification of the text is also something we need to think about in more detail.

In *The Political Unconscious* Fredric Jameson notes that once the semantic horizon of the literary is grasped as a *symbolic act* it immediately undergoes a dialectical transformation:

> It is no longer construed as an individual "text" or work in the narrow
> sense, but has been reconstituted in the form of the great collective and

class discourses of which a text is little more than an individual *parole* or
utterance. Within this new horizon, then, our object of study will prove
to be the *ideologeme,* that is, the smallest intelligible unit of the essentially
antagonistic collective discourses of social classes. (76)

This observation clearly suggests that as a body without organs the text is
an instance of and a constitutive threshold for surveying or mapping the
antagonistic historical workings of capital. Literature does not merely
describe, with anthropological care for "real" people in "real" locations,
the ways people live and think in, for example, a particular city in Latin
America. It does not have to be a faithful sociological repository for the
meaning of individual or collective life in a particular social context at a
particular historical juncture. As the ontological terrain that inscribes the
multiplicity of society's languages at any one time (that is, as "the coexistence of various sign systems which are themselves traces or anticipa-
tions of modes of production" [Jameson, 76]), literature is quite literally
the inscription of the signs of our capital times.

With this in mind, I would like to raise the question of whether there
is a politics in *The Fourth World* that is specific to, or thinkable through,
the birth and sale of a female *sudaca* baby in the heart of Eltit's nameless
and locationless city. As previously mentioned, this novel traces a gradual
devolution into female empowerment. However, it also exhausts this same
process within its final unfolding. As such, the novel's devolution into collective female empowerment coincides fully with the restrictiveness of the
global market, thereby presenting us with an affirmation of female empowerment and of capital's capture of individual and collective subjectivity simultaneously.

I would like to consider this challenging narrative as a portrait of the
Hegelian notion of "Unhappy Consciousness," which is to be understood
not merely as "the consciousness of self as a dual-natured, merely contradictory being" (126), but more problematically as the dialectical resolution of freedom into self-enslavement. As Hegel warns in a phrase that
could be considered curiously emblematic of the contradictions inherent
in Eltit's premonitory work:

> Point out likeness or identity to [the consciousness of self], and it will
> point out unlikeness or non-identity; and when it is now confronted
> with what it has just asserted, it turns round and points out likeness or
> identity. Its talk is in fact like the squabbling of self-willed children, one
> of whom says *A* if the other says *B,* and in turn says *B* if the other says *A,*

and who by contradicting *themselves* buy for themselves the pleasure of
continually *contradicting* one another. (125–26)

In this analysis, the dialectical "squabbling of self-willed children" is as
fettered and as fettering as it is free, as contradictory as it pleasurable.
However, before approaching the dialectic between subject formation,
enslavement, and abjection in the novel, we should first account for the
particularities of the work itself.

The Fourth World is not a novel in the sense of a single representational
narrative. It is not an explicit imitation of a world or of a particular way of
life in a specific space or environment. It is not a mimetic response to the
world, in other words. Rather, it portrays itself as the taking place—the
feverish embodiment in language—of two distinct and yet intimately
related (and often antagonistic) processes of narrativization. The novel is
structured around the divide, the fissure, or cut that conjoins these two
narrative bodies. As already mentioned, the first narrative is that of a male
twin and the second is that of his female counterpart. Both twins, and
therefore both narratives, are engendered as a result of a relation of indistinction between physiological life and power as violence. They are both
the effect of, and a response to, that relation, as well as to the corporeal
aggression that it generates.[5]

The novel's corporeal violence is also seen in the novel's delirious language and fragmented structures, which engender the novel itself as a
world. As such, *The Fourth World* strives to be the performance of its own
process of coming-into-being. In this regard, it is vaguely reminiscent of,
for example, *Finnegans Wake*'s well-known "riverrun of language." However, here the riverrun is a brutal bloodrun of words originating with the
birth of a delirious community of twins. After this double birth, the novel
continues with their distinct yet intimately conjoined processes of social-
ization, ending with the quest for the inception of an incestuous *sudaca*
progeny and its immediate surrender to the market forces of the city.

The novel, in other words, begins and ends with birth and therefore
takes place within the space opened up by these births. As such, the language of the novel is produced directly in the passage from one birth that
is two (the twins), to two births that are three (the passage from the birth
of the twins to that of their *sudaca* offspring). Therefore, the novel's explicit process of self-realization is, as Hegel puts it, its own "birth-time":
a process of transition, or the realization in language of a new ground for

itself that is nevertheless drawn from within its own unfolding. From its very inception the novel performs itself as a parturient, uterine, and almost insurrectional "bloodrun of language" in which being-in-common is born through the active generation of bodily contagions. As the repressed, rational male twin indicates in the novel's opening pages:

> We had our first limit experience. We remained immobile surrounded by the waters. My sister suffered all my weight and strived desperately to endure me. In turn, I was compressed by the walls, which pushed me onto her even more.
>
> An inflamed feeling of survival was awakened within us. Instinctively my sister initiated the escape by placing her head in the tunnel entrance. There was an organic tempest, a cellular revolt. All of my mother's physiological walls went into a state of alert before the trickle of blood that lubricated the exit. . . . My sister's animality began to startle me. I thought that both bodies were going to destroy each other in the struggle. They were anguish-filled hours. I felt my sister separate herself from me and get lost in all that blood. I didn't make the slightest effort, I wanted to skip the protocol of the blood but I was dragged along on my journey. Almost asphyxiated, I crossed the threshold . . . My semiconscious state sowed fragmentary stories capped by screams and bleeding thighs. Redness, protagonist of those visions, dripped thickly, spreading images of death. Something was once again muting my organism but also alerting my brain and generating defenses.[6]

The novel presents itself as the narrativization of a common space and of the active *spacing between* narrative bodies. It therefore strives to project itself as the violent sharing of blood, language, corporeal violence, fear, and frenzy. The narrative does not represent sharing as a potentially peaceful communion between gendered subjects. It does not represent the sharing of commonality as a resolution, a higher unity, or as a point at which community comes into being and defines itself finally, *as such,* as a particular subjectivity. Rather, the only higher unity or point of transcendence in the novel emerges at the end in the absolute guise of the market. During the course of the fiction, however, language works toward the dialectical ineffectiveness of all investments in completion and transcendence by portraying sharing as a constant, violent, and often spontaneous process of division; it exposes sharing as a highly contested limit or membrane between singular beings that are different, and yet that are profoundly and irrevocably tied together as each other's limit.

As previously suggested, then, we are not dealing with a foundational and essentially romantic language of individual or collective subject formation. Nor are we unearthing a derivative language of mere identitarian difference. Rather, the text appears to lean toward the possibility of a writing of commonality in which being-in-common is the agonistic limit that both joins and separates identity to, and from, difference. As such, it appears that the novel seeks to inscribe the limit at which the contemporary world's overly familiar languages of cultural identity/difference become de-grounded.

Within the novel the male twin strives desperately to shield himself from the liminal middle ground, and he does this by recurring to the authority of Oedipal family structures, "masculinity," individualism, privacy, discipline, and reason:

> I exercised the strict dimension of thought . . . I chose to impose my masculinity . . . She had a marked devotion for touch. She would cede to the passion of any unknown hand, of any damp lip able to gratify her in her recognition of her own skin. From me she had begun to learn to give herself over to any other other, when previously I had been her only other.[7]

However, the male twin is forced to confront the imminent erosion of identity/difference and to confront the trembling of this binary structure's social and philosophical grounds as a result of his sister's unrelenting desire for liminality:

> At night her small, convulsed body would stick to mine while her mouth, obsessed by panic, sucked on me. During the nights of that first year I learned much about the delicate and complex bodies of young girls. Rubbing against each other in the dark and also captivated by fear, I developed the idea that for me there was not really a place, that I was not even one, unique, just the half of an unnaturally complementary female other who pushed me toward hybridity.[8]

The twin is threatened, then, not by the active production of an identity/difference dialectic within the novel, but by the shadowy orgiastics of "indifferent identity" (Nancy, *Birth,* 9–35), in which the dialectic supposedly ungrounds singularity and difference simultaneously. The point of transformation for the male twin within his traumatic and increasing exposure to "indifferent identity"—the point, in other words, at which the in-difference of his *sudaca*-being is first engendered—comes with his first sexual encounter in the public sphere. In this section he seeks out and is accosted (at a crossroads no less) by, of all things, a shadow:

> At age twelve I had my first genital encounter . . . It was a street encounter
> on a heavily foggy day . . . It seemed to me to be extraordinarily fixed and
> crucial weather, which made me abandon known terrains and enter a
> hieroglyph of citizenship in which similitude and difference became
> blurred . . . I felt myself pushed against the stone wall, breathing in
> unison with the figure that was brushing up against me. Its hands began
> to caress me softly and with expertise, pressing to get rid of my bother-
> some clothes. I was gone over again and again by those hands that found
> in me the most beautiful thing about public exchange . . . something in
> me had become irretrievably perverted, and, deep down, I had opened
> myself up to a cynical yet sincere way of life . . . I could not determine
> who or what seduced me that evening . . . though I am sure of having
> encountered the plenitude of youth embodied in a mendicant girl or a
> vagabond boy who, as night fell, became my alms.[9]

This episode marks a sexualized rite of passage into the shadowy underworld of the *sudaca* city's "indifferent identities": into that reticent, suspended space in which "similitude and difference became blurred," in which
identity and difference become ungrounded and give way to the limit that
grounds their relation. Indeed, this violent exposure to in-different commonality is later intensified when the male twin is assaulted in the street
by the *sudaca* hordes:

> At age thirteen I was attacked brutally by a horde of furious young
> *sudacas* . . . They were all alike in the way they carried the lines of their
> faces . . . they looked like the architecture of the city, which disoriented
> the passers-by who could see the ways in which their differences very
> soon entered into mimetic relations with each other. Something
> similar happened to the faces of those young people. Their lowly
> roots formed a single body disseminated through distinct individual
> movements. Something else they had in common was the efficiency of
> their movements, which were very accentuated and on the limit of
> provocation . . . I found myself surrounded by an indeterminate number
> of figures coming down on me . . . The boys laughed and spoke in a
> dialect that I could not decipher . . . As night fell I felt the first shiver
> crossing my jaw. The deep wound took hold of my opened, mordant
> flesh. I had just experienced the formation of my first scar, which sat on
> the lower side of my face.[10]

These profoundly indifferent *sudacas* recall the architecture of the city.
They open up intelligibility to an incomprehensible negative language, and
thereby produce disorientation and confusion between opposites.

However, their presence within the novel—indeed, the whole of the argument thus far—does not actually unsettle the representational language of the male twin in the first half of the novel. The *sudacas* do not produce or actively affirm the disorientation and confusion of the male twin's authoritative language. In other words, they do not promise the possibility of a qualitative shift in register from active representation to representation's outer limits. As such, the *sudacas* in the male's narrative uphold no particular relation to a new ground or, for that matter, to the realization of new potentiality in the novel's language. After all, these *sudacas* are captured within the novel merely as the inferior and subordinate (and subordinated) determinants for male-dominated representation. They are the instrumental bondsmen who provide for the discursive conditions of sustained male rationality and authority (the Lord's language of self-reflection) in the novel.

There is, however, a qualitative distinction in the novel in the relation between lordship and bondage in the male narrator's language, and the transition to unhappy consciousness in the female twin's narrative. In other words, in the second half of the novel, the *sudacas* exist as indicators of a new ground that is synonymous with the female twin's will to create a *sudaca* baby filled with hatred. A will for *sudaca* language—a language that actively interrupts and destabilizes the order, system, and transparency of the first half of the novel—seems to emerge as an affirmation of sorts in the novel's second narrative, in which the twin sister takes over and quickly announces that her twin brother is now a transvestite who goes by the name of María Chipia. The male-dominated language of instrumental reason and representation becomes increasingly tenuous, and perhaps even abandoned for good. In contrast, the second half of the narrative becomes the enactment, predominantly in the present tense, of the feverish limit between mutually contaminating bodies. Indeed, it is with the increasing exhaustion of all vestiges of male-dominated reason and social hierarchy that the possibility of the *sudaca* birth emerges, as the twin sister announces: "I want to create a terrible and unpleasant *sudaca* work."[11]

In this final section of the novel the twin sister strives at all times to perform herself as a membrane: as *sudaca* liminality itself. She strives to become the creative embodiment of the limit between inside and outside beings. Her body becomes the site, the frontier, upon which identity and difference are suspended, and upon which in-different identities take place, perform, and unleash the violence of their creative in-difference:

I am lying on my side and my stomach falls entirely to the ground.
I am scared by its size. Behind me María Chipia is seeking pleasure
desperately. I do not mind his rhythmic assaults and his tangible
movements are already beyond my recollection. I do not find pleasure
in him nor feel sorry for myself . . . I let him attack me from behind . . .
Even though I know we are carrying out the *sudaca* stigma I continue
undaunted, looking for a way out . . . I should have attended to the
request of my *sudaca* blood. As a result of that urgent request I needed
that pleasure more than anything else in my life.

On the limit and always astraddle, I began to lose the notion of time,
for the frontier between outside and inside dissolved and María Chipia
became integrated into my neuronal structures.[12]

Indeed, this violent and creative enactment of contamination—this quest
for a specifically *sudaca* eroticism that ungrounds the inside/outside, iden-
tity/difference dialectic—is explicitly political in its intentions: "It was an
homage to the *sudaca* species. It was a manifesto. It was a dynastic celebration for the imminent arrival of the child who, on that day, would get to
know the immense force of its parents. The hatred of its parents."[13] As such,
it is here, on the female twin's body and in her process of narrativization,
in this eroticized quest for the pleasurable suspension of both identity
and difference, that "the communionless communism of singular beings"
(Nancy, *Inoperative Community,* 72) is announced (or at least promised).
Presumably, on her body the *sudaca* being-in-common takes place. As such,
her body realizes community's joyful incompletion and perpetual *sudaca*
(that is, negative) potentiality.

But such pleasure in potentiality is extremely short-lived (if not to say
illusory); for just a couple of pages later the twin sister—who now goes by
the name of *diamela eltit*—is said to give birth, in the present tense, to the
direct offspring of the twin's performative political manifesto, which will
immediately be captured by, surrendered to, or sacrificed for the extension
of the violent force of contemporary capital. Needless to say, this passage
from potentiality to actualization in the second half of the novel invites
us to wonder about what meaning, if any, can be assigned to such a *sudaca*
unfettering, in which unleashing and realization simultaneously signify
not only renunciation and sacrifice, but also the subject's unmediated (and
therefore immediate) exposure to the violent circuits of contemporary accumulation and expropriation.

As Giorgio Agamben has observed, the political organization of the modern nation-state was founded on the articulation of a functional trinity: that is, the nexus between a determinate localization (a particular extension of *land*), a determinate *order* (a state), and the forging of specific automatic rules (techniques and rationales for governing and guiding the conduct of whole populations from cradle to grave). The relations between the constitutive parts of this functional trinity were designed and implemented over time in order to lend institutional structure and cultural consistency to the relation between *birth* and collective political existence (174–75).[14]

As Agamben notes, the emergence and consolidation of the nation-state is predicated on, and is to a large extent conditioned by, the three elements *land, order,* and *birth,* which, through the notion of *citizenship,* together forge the essential "natural" ground of the social and juridical—that is, sovereign—subject. Within this modern horizon of social organization the birth–nation link has a fundamental legitimating function within the nation-state, for it establishes the imaginary or fictive relation that constitutes individuals or groups of human beings as particular, represented populations who are *naturally* inserted into the specific mechanisms and calculations of constituted power. In other words, the birth–nation link constitutes diverse agents as *one* imaginary body with equal rights within the national space:

> The fact that . . . the "subject" is . . . transformed into a citizen means
> that birth—which is to say, bare natural life as such . . . becomes . . .
> the immediate bearer of sovereignty. The principle of nativity and the
> principle of sovereignty . . . are now irrevocably united in the body of the
> "sovereign subject" so that the foundation of the new nation-state may
> be constituted . . . The fiction implicit here is that *birth* immediately
> becomes *nation* such that there can be no interval of separation between
> the two terms. Rights are attributed to man (or originate in him) solely
> to the extent that man is the immediately vanishing ground (who must
> never come to light as such) of the citizen. (128)

That is to say, the birth–nation link is designed to provide the image of a natural foundation for the immediate relation between human life, the nation-state as a legal-territorial entity, and "the nation" as a political-cultural hegemony. This absolute suturing of the nation-state to "the nation," through the birth and immediate recognition of supposedly sovereign subjects, is designed to render the nation an idealistically holistic cultural entity that is grounded in the law of nature as well as in the immanence of "the people." Needless to say, this suturing—the juridical constitution of a birth–nation (human–citizen) link in which national space is guaranteed as a fully legitimate legal-territorial entity, as a fully embodied political hegemony, and as a fully coherent national culture—also creates the conditions not just for historical forms of progressive or conservative processes of subject formation, but also for the often violent fantasies of cultural nationalism and of its concomitant identity-based discourses. However, the immediate link between nativity and "nationness," the immediate relation of continuity between man and citizen, or between "the people" and "the nation" (as upheld, for example, in Gramsci's evocation of the "people-nation" [418]), is the originary fiction of modern sovereignty, the origin of the national "imagined community," and the initial threshold for the consequent fabrication of national fictive ethnicity and "the nation" as a fictitious universality.[15]

What we encounter in the second half of Diamela Eltit's *The Fourth World*, however, are the historical conditions of modern freedom—that is, the relation between birth, citizenship, subject formation, work, community, the city, identity, the nation-state—resolved dialectically into absolute and immediate self-enslavement thanks to the violent and humiliating laws of the global market. The novel's devolution into collective female empowerment coincides fully with the emergence of a new chapter in the gendered history of capital's most naked forms of enslavement.[16]

The second half of the novel is characterized by a frantic yet pleasurable political/corporeal/sexual will and imperative: to craft "a terrible and unpleasant *sudaca* work" capable of breaking with everything that came before it. This labor of love/hate seeks to transcend and overcome the false duality of mind and body that lies at the heart of the male twin's narrative. It seems to do this by engendering a body (the female *sudaca* baby) that is itself the contamination of, and the hatred for, the historical relation between male instrumental reason and authoritarian forms of subject formation and social hierarchy.

However, there is also a definite will for grandeur through self-absorption, self-debasement, and penitence in the second half of the novel. As she strives desperately to engender the *sudaca* baby as a means of willing into existence the purity of absolute contamination (a new ontological ground that undermines the separation between private life and the spatial architecture of the *sudaca* city), the female twin, encouraged by the priest-like mediating figure of her younger sister, María de Alava, also embraces self-abnegation as she pays homage to "the most powerful nation in the world" by offering up ritualistic dance as a form of staving off the penetration power of the outside. But this is an enterprise and a political, performative manifesto that is doomed to failure because the actuality of the female twin's *sudaca* will—the labored materialization of the baby (the promise of a *completely new* ontological ground for life conceived from within the novel's own process of coming-into-being)—coincides fully with the surrender and sacrifice of all the fruits of her work and pleasure to the expropriating power of capital.

The female twin's *sudaca* will is negative and potentially transformational in the sense that it is directed against the (male) history that initially determined her being and that of those around her. However, it is also a positive force because her negative will—her political drive—coincides fully with the emergence of the universal will of an "other." This universal will is that of "the most powerful nation in the world," whose dominance now offers up *sudaca* bodies for sale and consumption with a velocity and intensity that bring the city to its knees, thereby reminding us that the novel's devolution into the labor of female empowerment is never enough, because it is potentially as restrictive as any other commodity or commodified language in the transnational marketplace. In the meantime, we are left either with a novel that can provide no political vision of either the present or the future, or with a cautionary and premonitory Hegelian tale regarding not only the limits of history's transformational political visions (the question and experience of freedom and its immanent relation to servitude), but also regarding the materialization or nonmaterialization of the new and distinct in contemporary times.

The question of the relation between the limits of history's transformational political visions and the birth of the new is immanent to the conditions of what Hegel and Diamela Eltit would call our current "birth-time." However, the terms of debate on the relation between freedom and servitude are still to be fully redefined after the collapse of history's orthodox communitarian forms, the increasing illegitimacy of liberalism, and the intensified dematerialization of capital's circuits in recent years. This is not to say, of course, that we cannot strive to grapple with the political and philosophical demands of what Diamela Eltit might call *sudaca* revolution against "the most powerful nation in the world" and its increasingly unmediated forms of accumulation and exploitation. However, in order to do so one would have to be able to account for, and to build on, the historical and conceptual passage of the modern polis from the image of an ordered and prosperous capitalist utopia to the transnational post-industrial trash heap for the dreams of millions.

This is, after all, the painful dialectical relation that ultimately allows Diamela Eltit to recognize that it is always Hegel (perhaps more than any-one else) who receives, time and time again, the keys to the abject realities of the contemporary *sudaca* city. However, what a novel such as *The Fourth World* shows—intentionally or otherwise—is that perhaps he should not. Because it is no longer clear what the possibility and form of a strictly Hegelian thinking of history is actually good for, other than for the con-tinual reinscription of enslavement as the dialectical destiny or fate (the *sudaca* stigma) of the powerless, perhaps the time has arrived for a think-ing of history and difference that is capable of rendering itself independent of Hegelian notions of negation. Now that might be a polis worth think-ing about. It might even be a good place to live.

NOTES

1. For the biopolitical production of individual or collective identities, see Foucault (1997, 2003). Also see Butler (83–105).

2. "Afuera la ciudad devastada emite gruñidos y parloteos inútiles. Se ensayan todas las retóricas esperando el dinero caído del cielo, quemándose como una mariposa de luz. La ciudad cegatona y ávida regala los destinos de los habitantes sudacas. Terriblemente desvencijada y gruñona, anciana y codiciosa, la ciudad, enferma de Parkinson, tiembla. Tiemblan las voces, tiemblan las voces ancianas y codiciosas disputándose el dinero caído del cielo pero que se quema como mari-posa de luz. Se vende el trigo, el maíz, los sauzales, a un precio irrisorio, junto a los jóvenes sudacas que han sembrado. En venta los campos de la ciudad sudaca. En venta el sudor. Un comercio histérico chilla a los compradores, quienes astuta-mente bajan los precios y compran hasta a los vendedores. El dinero caído del cielo vuelve al cielo y los vendedores venden incluso aquello que no les pertenece. La ciu-dad colapsada es ya una ficción nominal. Sólo el nombre de la ciudad permanece, porque todo lo demás ya se ha vendido en el amplio mercado. En la anarquía de la costumbre por la venta se ejecutan los últimos movimientos a viva voz, voceando la venta del vacío. El dinero que cae del cielo apetece el vacío de la ciudad y cada una de las retóricas del vacío para sembrar el vacío sobre los campos, ya vendidos y definitivamente ajenos. El dinero caído del cielo entra directo por los genitales y las voces ancianas se entregan a un adulterio desenfrenado. El adulterio ha adul-terado a la ciudad nominal, que se vende, se vende a los postores a cualquier costo.

La transacción está a punto de concluir, y en el dinero caído del cielo está impresa, nítidamente, una sonrisa de menosprecio a la raza sudaca. Lejos, en una casa abandonada a la fraternidad, entre un 7 y un 8 de abril, diamela eltit, asistida por su hermano mellizo, da a luz una niña. La niña sudaca irá a la venta" (158–59). All translations are mine.

3. In this sense, we encounter in the final pages of *The Fourth World* the realities and conditions of what Marx called "primitive accumulation" (873–940).

4. The use of the pejorative term *sudaca* is of particular significance in this passage and, indeed, throughout the novel. The *sudacas* are the subordinated surplus peoples, the obsolete subalterns or the postindustrial reserve army. They do not represent Gramsci's "people-nation" (418); that is, the *demos*, the organized ground of political community. The "*sudaca* race" in Eltit's formulation (as *sudaca*, rather than Chilean, Argentine, Colombian, etc., and as a race rather than a culturally specific group) passes beyond the "nation-people," beyond national boundaries, and beyond national interpellations. They evoke a transnational sphere of subordination: the sphere of a negative universality that exists on the painful receiving end of postmodern discourses of global superiority, progress, piety, rationality, and order. As a result, *The Fourth World* does not have to be read purely as a *Chilean* narrative. Rather, it can also be read as a postnational (post-Chilean; post-locational; posturban) narrative in which the biopolitical interpellations of "the Nation" (including the idea of the subject) are called into question by the unleashing and violent extension of unfettered capital.

5. As the novel's opening paragraphs demonstrate, this singular community comes into being as a result of a dictatorial, neocolonial relation of violence between male and female bodies (11–13). From the outset, the "fourth world" refers to a physiological or biological spacing in which the production and reproduction of commonality, of being-in-common, originates. The "fourth world" is not the sign of a world that follows previous forms of collective existence. It is a world that indicates a threshold of indistinction between the biological body and the collective political body that exists at the origin of all modern politics in the West, including both authoritarian and liberal-democratic forms of capitalism.

6. "Tuvimos nuestra primera experiencia límite. Quedamos inmóviles rodeados por las aguas. Mi hermana sufría todo mi peso y hacía desesperados esfuerzos por soportarme. Yo, a mi vez, estaba comprimido por las paredes que me empujaban, más aun, sobre ella.

"Se despertó en nosotros un enconado sentimiento de sobrevivencia. Instintivamente mi hermana inició la huida ubicando su cabeza en la entrada del túnel. Hubo una tormenta orgánica, una revuelta celular. Todas las paredes fisiológicas de mi madre entraron en estado de alerta ante el hilo de sangre que corría lubricando la salida... La animalidad de mi hermana llegó a sobrecogerme. Creí que ambos cuerpos iban a destrozarse en la lucha. Fueron horas angustiosas. Sentí a mi hermana separarse de mí y perderse en medio de la sangre. Yo no hice el menor esfuerzo, quería saltarme el protocolo de la sangre, pero me arrastraron en el viaje. Casi asfixiado crucé la salida... Mis entresueños tejían fragmentarias historias taponadas de gritos y muslos sangrantes. El rojo, protagonista de esas visiones, escurría líquidamente espeso, derramando imágenes de muerte. Algo estaba, una vez más, apagando mi organismo, pero también alertando mi cerebro y generando defensas" (26–27, 54).

7. "Ejercí la estricta dimensión del pensar... opté por imponer mi masculinidad... Ella tenía una marcada devoción por el tacto. Cedía a la pasión de cualquier mano extraña, de todo labio que, húmedo, la gratificara en el reconocimiento de lo propio de su piel. Desde mí había iniciado el aprendizaje de entregarse a otro, yo antaño su único otro" (17, 27–28).

8. "En las noches su pequeño cuerpo convulso se apegaba al mío mientras su boca me succionaba, obsesionada por el pánico. Durante esas noches del primer año aprendí mucho del delicado y complejo cuerpo de las niñas. Rozándonos a oscuras y también prendado del miedo desarrollé el pensamiento de que, para mí, no había verdaderamente un lugar, que ni siquiera era uno, único, sólo la mitad de otra innaturalmente complementaria y que me empujaba a la hibridez" (30–31).

9. "A los doce años tuve mi primer encuentro genital... Fue un encuentro callejero en un día pesadamente nublado... Me pareció un tiempo extraordinariamente fijo y crucial, que me hizo salir de los terrenos conocidos e internarme por el jeroglífico ciudadano en donde la similitud y la diferencia se desdibujaban... Me sentí empujado contra la pared de piedra, respirando al unísono con la figura que se acercaba rozándome. Sus manos empezaron a recorrerme en forma suave y experta, presionándome con los dedos para apartarme las molestas ropas. Fui recorrido una y otra vez por esas manos que encontraban en mí lo más bello del intercambio público... algo se había pervertido irremediablemente en mí y, en el fondo, me había abierto hacia una forma de vida cínica a la vez que sincera... No pude precisar quién ni qué me sedujo ese anochecer... aunque estoy seguro de haberme encontrado con la plenitud de la juventud encarnada en una muchacha mendicante o en un muchacho vagabundo que, cerca de la noche, se convirtió en una limosna para mí" (58–63).

10. "A los trece años fui atacado brutalmente por una horda de jóvenes sudacas furibundos... Todos ellos tenían algo en común por el modo en que manejaban las líneas de sus caras... el parecido era como la arquitectura de la ciudad, que desorientaba al paseante; éste veía cómo las diferencias muy pronto se mimetizaban entre sí. Algo similar pasaba en la cara de esos jóvenes. Su raíz popular formaba un cuerpo único, diseminado en distintos movimientos individuales. También era común en ellos, precisamente, la eficacia de sus movimientos, muy acentuados y en el límite de la provocación... Me vi rodeado de un número indeterminado de figuras que se me venían encima... Los muchachos se reían y hablaban en un

dialecto que no pude descrifrar... Al anochecer sentí el primer escalofrío reco-
rriendo mi mandíbula. La profunda herida arrebataba la carne abierta y mordaz.
Debí asistir a la formación de mi primer cicatriz, que se acomodó al costado inferior de mi faz" (89–92).

11. "Quiero hacer una obra sudaca terrible y molesta" (114).

12. "Estoy tendida de costado y mi estómago cae enteramente sobre el suelo.
Me asusto por su dimensión. María Chipia, a mi espalda, busca desesperadamente
el placer. No me importan sus rítmicas embestidas y sus movimientos tangibles ya
están perdidos para mi memoria. No lo complazco ni me compadezco... Lo dejo
atacarme por la espalda... Aunque sé que estamos cumpliendo el estigma sudaca,
continúo impávida, buscando yo misma una salida... debí atender el pedido de mi
sangre sudaca. Por el pedido urgente necesité ese placer más que cualquier otra
necesidad de mi vida. En el límite, llegué, siempre a horcajadas, a perder la noción
del tiempo, pues se disolvió la frontera entre exterior e interior y María Chipia se
integró a mis estructuras neuronales" (144–52).

13. "Fue un homenaje a la especie sudaca. Fue un manifiesto. Fue una celebra-
ción dinástica, celebrando la pronta llegada del niño, quien ese día pudo conocer
la inmensa fuerza de sus padres. El odio de sus padres" (152).

14. The final term of this trinity—the forging of techniques and rationales for
governing and guiding the conduct of populations—refers to the relation between
life (birth) and what Althusser called the ideological state apparatus; what Foucault
called the rationalizing technologies of government; or what in Marxian terminol-
ogy could be called "the nation" transformed into a material force.

15. I take the term "imagined community" from Benedict Anderson. I take the
terms "fictive ethnicity" and "fictitious universality" from two closely related essays
by Étienne Balibar (1991, 1995). In Balibar's formulations fictive ethnicity (1991)—
the institutional fabrication of a national "peoplehood"—is the effect of the nation-
state's constant and ongoing drive toward "fictitious universality" (1995). As Balibar notes, fictitious universality is the desired effect of the constructed realities
and imagined communities of modern nation-state formation. It is based on the
expansion of state institutions and is directly involved in the constitution of
national and predominantly (though by no means exclusively) secular social hege-
monies and forms of *citizenship*. The nationalization—the fictitious universaliza-
tion—of societies (which, of course, came hand in hand with capitalist expansion
and the increasing power of modern rationalization) relied for the most part on the
state's manufacturing of normative and normalized patterns of human behavior.
The establishment of such patterns is designed to guarantee both state hegemony
and internal forms of exclusion; the fabrication of minority and majority populations and identities; the suppression of unacceptable individual and/or collective
desires; as well as the state's invention and control of particular deviant behaviors
and forms of group organization (1995, 71). In this sense, fictitious universality

and fictive ethnicity are the underlying ground of what Foucault called the disciplinary societies, or the societies of enclosure, which characterized the eighteenth and nineteenth centuries and that reached their height at the outset of the twentieth century in the metropolitan industrial centers.

16. My reading in this final section owes much to Judith Butler's excellent analysis of Hegel's Unhappy Consciousness in *The Psychic Life of Power: Theories in Subjection* (31–62).

Works Cited

Agamben, Giorgio. *Homo Sacer: Sovereign Power and Bare Life*. Trans. Daniel Heller-Roazen. Stanford, Calif.: Stanford University Press, 1998.

Althusser, Louis. "Ideology and Ideological State Apparatuses (Notes towards an Investigation)." In *Mapping Ideology*, ed. Slavoj Žižek. New York: Verso, 1994. 100–140.

Anderson, Benedict. *Imagined Communities: Reflections on the Origin and Spread of Nationalism*. New York: Verso, 1983.

Balibar, Étienne. "Ambiguous Universality." *Differences: A Journal of Feminist Cultural Studies* 7.1 (1995): 48–74.

———. "The Nation Form: History and Ideology." In *Race, Nation, Class: Ambiguous Identities*, by Étienne Balibar and Immanuel Wallerstein, trans. Chris Turner. New York: Verso, 1991. 86–106.

Butler, Judith. *The Psychic Life of Power: Theories in Subjection*. Stanford, Calif.: Stanford University Press, 1997.

Eltit, Diamela. *El cuarto mundo*. Santiago de Chile: Planeta, 1988.

Foucault, Michel. "The Birth of Biopolitics." In *Essential Works of Foucault (1954–1984)*, vol. 1, *Ethics*, ed. Paul Rabinow, trans. Robert Hurley. New York: New Press, 1997. 73–79.

———. *"Society Must Be Defended": Lectures at the Collège de France 1975–1976*. New York: Picador, 2003.

———. "Subjectivity and Truth." In *Essential Works of Foucault (1954–1984)*, vol. 1, *Ethics*, ed. Paul Rabinow, trans. Robert Hurley. New York: New Press, 1997. 87–92.

Gramsci, Antonio. *Selections from the Prison Notebooks*. Trans. Quintin Hoare and Geoffrey Nowell Smith. New York: International Publishers, 1985.

Hegel, G. W. F. *The Phenomenology of Spirit*. Trans. A. V. Miller. Oxford: Oxford University Press, 1977.

Jameson, Fredric. *The Political Unconscious: Narrative as a Socially Symbolic Act*. Ithaca, N.Y.: Cornell University Press, 1981.

Lüttecke, Janet. *"El cuarto mundo* de Diamela Eltit." *Revista iberoamericana* 15. 168–69 (1994): 1081–88.

Marx, Karl. *Capital.* Vol. 1. Trans. Ben Fowkes. London: Penguin Books, 1976.

Masiello, Francine. *The Art of Transition: Latin American Culture and Neoliberal Crisis.* Durham, N.C.: Duke University Press, 2001.

Nancy, Jean-Luc. *The Birth to Presence.* Trans. Brian Holmes et al. Stanford, Calif.: Stanford University Press, 1993.

———. *The Inoperative Community.* Ed. Peter Connor. Trans. Peter Connor, Lisa Garbus, Michael Holland, and Simona Sawhney. Minneapolis: University of Minnesota Press, 1991.

Norat, Gisela. *Marginalities: Diamela Eltit and the Subversion of Mainstream Literature in Chile.* Newark: University of Delaware Press, 2002.

Pope, Randolph. "La resistencia en *El cuarto mundo* de Diamela Eltit." In *Creación y resistencia: La narrativa de Diamela Eltit, 1983–1998,* ed. María Inés Lagos. Santiago de Chile: Universidad de Chile/Editorial Cuarto Propio, 2000. 35–53.

PART III
Cities of Difference

8

The Cultural Memory of Malinche in Mexico City

Stories by Elena Garro
and Cristina Pacheco

SANDRA MESSINGER CYPESS

Even we who have seen these things with our own eyes, are yet so amazed as to be unable to comprehend their reality.

from Hernán Cortés, Letters

It's a dangerous city, it's an angry city.

Elena Poniatowska

Whether as Tenochtitlán or today's Distrito Federal, Mexico City has always been a special place, the first city of the New World for which we have ample written documentation. When Cortés reached Tenochtitlán, it was the most populated city in the Western Hemisphere, and it has maintained that reputation to this day. Once considered almost indescribable for the Spanish chroniclers, today's writers have filled pages and pages of stories about the many people who walk its neighborhoods and carry on their daily lives in this stimulating and often frustrating metropolis. As large as a small country, perhaps the largest city in the world today, Mexico City was once comparable to the Garden of Eden, where the air was clear and the land fertile and lush, whereas now it is smog-infested, unhealthy, and crime-ridden.

Just as the Aztecs envisioned their time within space in the form of a circular calendar stone, some of the same figures who populated Tenochtitlán at the time of the Conquest still revolve around the city today; that is, avatars of conquest and colonial-period figures come alive in stories by contemporary writers. In this essay, I shall focus on the presentation of avatars of La Malinche, or doña Marina, another of the names by which she is known, in stories that use Mexico City as a setting. In particular, I shall examine the representations and treatment of these contemporary Malinches by two women writers who situate their characters in Mexico City, Elena Garro (1917–98) and Cristina Pacheco (b. 1941).

Part of the reason for the perdurability of figures like La Malinche has to do with cultural memory, the phenomenon whereby "a social group consciously and unconsciously passes along value-laden memories" (Rodríguez, *Stories,* 10). For Jeanette Rodríguez, the Malinche motif is as much a part of Mexican cultural memory as is the Virgin of Guadalupe. As has been documented elsewhere, Guadalupe and Malinche exist at opposite poles in the Mexican cultural imaginary.[1] Whereas the Guadalupe story deals with "identity, salvation, hope and resistance to annihilation" (ibid., 13), the Malinche story has often meant that a series of negative attributes are considered inherent in feminine behavior; Mexican women are described within the Malinche paradigm as being unfaithful, untrustworthy, sexually promiscuous, easily dominated by the male in his role as "conquistador" (Cypess, 7). The emphasis of the disapproving perspective on La Malinche is rooted in a combination of nationalist and *machista* ideologies, so any positive aspects or extenuating justifications for La Malinche's behavior had been eliminated from the cultural memory until feminist rereadings of La Malinche surfaced. Women writers in particular have reexamined cultural memories in the form of their stories, for "like all memories, cultural memory changes over time" and the forging of new versions of memories can help to redefine a given culture (Rodríguez, *Stories,* 12). By seeing how La Malinche is represented in stories set in contemporary Mexico, we can observe the dynamics of the cultural memory at work.

It is possible, moreover, to relate the development of Mexico City, from its splendor in the pre-Hispanic era to its deterioration and possible reconstruction now, to the evolution of the Malinche motif, with its changes through time. Like La Malinche, Mexico City has also always inspired its writers, because Mexico City stands alone as the leading economic, cultural, intellectual, and political center of the country. If we believe the chroniclers, it was always an exciting place, even as the ancient Aztec capital of Tenochtitlán.[2] The Aztecs had arrived there around 1345 and established their stone-built city on an island in the middle of Lake Texcoco.

As the chronicles depict it, México-Tenochtitlán, as it was called in the pre-Conquest period, was a six-square-mile area filled with magnificent and well-built palaces and gardens, with wide market areas that were bustling with activity. When the Spaniards arrived, only four European cities had more than a hundred thousand inhabitants, and Seville, which was the largest in Spain at that time, had but forty-five thousand inhabitants, while México-Tenochtitlán encompassed more than five hundred thousand inhabitants. As Bernal Díaz's famous account reminds us, the sight of the city for the newly arriving Spanish soldiers "seemed like an enchanted vision from the tale of Amadís. Indeed some of our soldiers asked whether it was not all a dream" (178). Alfonso Reyes (1889–1959), continuing the metaphor of the dream, titled his description of the city "Visión de Anáhuac" (Vision of Anáhuac), using the Nahuatl name of the valley in which the city is located.[3] Although the sixteenth-century writer Bernardo de Balbuena could speak about the majestic and grand buildings of the city in his poem "Grandeza mexicana" (Mexican greatness), today's writers, in contrast, see the ruin and the disparity between the past and the present, between the cleanliness of the pre-Conquest period and the grime of contemporary Mexico City.

After the siege and destruction of the capital city by the conquistadors, the Spaniards began to rebuild it in 1525, and Mexicans have continued to renovate and reconstruct its buildings and sites, often because of natural disasters such as the 1985 earthquake, but more often because of human-provoked damage. The majestic mountains and the region of clear skies that surround the city are no longer visible because of the pollution spewed out by industry and aggravated by the countless cars and buses. On a BBC Web site on Mexico City, Elena Poniatowska comments that for her "It's a dangerous city, it's an angry city. You see people on the streets begging, you see children between cars, people running, not very well fed, without sweaters, you see things that make you shiver."[4] Juan Villoro, on the other hand, quoted in that same Web site, reminds us that "it is a very interesting scenario for a writer, an extraordinary mixture of cultures. You have the ancient city of the Aztecs, you have the colonial backdrop, and downtown, you have the postmodern city." Both Villoro and Poniatowska point to the contradictions inherent in Mexico City—its palimpsestic nature as a multilayered locale that accommodates, perhaps uneasily, various chronological periods, social classes, and ethnicities. On the one hand, there are constant reminders of the splendor of the past, with imposing colonial buildings in the historic center, but also homeless people sleeping in the doorways, stagnant water, garbage, and human waste.

The foulness of the air and streets of Mexico City, or "DF," as the capital is called to distinguish it from the name of the country, serves as a metaphor for critiques of Mexico. Carlos Fuentes also played with the image in his novel *La región más transparente* (1958; *Where the Air Is Clear*) by his use of the ironic title. As so many of his narratives attest, Fuentes admits to being fascinated by the literature of the city and he has often focused on the transformations that have taken place in Mexico City in his texts.[5] Perhaps no street in the DF was more famous than Calle de Donceles, the location of Fuentes's novella *Aura*. But that feminine character of the short novel was more symbol than realistic portrait and had little to do with the existence of the many women whose lives are marked by a struggle for survival.

The stories of these poor women have been largely ignored or marginalized until recently. Their desolation and mistreatment in a *machista* society have been the focus of a number of women writers, yet in a recent anthology of the cultural history of Mexico City these voices were omitted. A contemporary chronicler of the DF, Vicente Quirarte, in his book *Elogio de la calle. Biografía literaria de la Ciudad de México 1850–1992* (In praise of the street: A literary biography of Mexico City 1850–1992), presents the development of Mexico City as a character in literary texts. Although he maintains that the chroniclers of city life have been varied, and their depictions also very diverse, he does not mention the contributions of Garro or Cristina Pacheco as chroniclers of Mexico City's residents.[6]

Although Garro most often deals with other settings, her most famous story, "La culpa es de los tlaxcaltecas" (It's the fault of the Tlaxcaltecas), is intimately related to the capital in its dual nature as México-Tenochtitlán, whereas Cristina Pacheco is perhaps the most assiduous contemporary chronicler of the daily lives of the diverse citizens of the DF, the ones tourists might ignore—the washerwomen, the recent immigrants from the rural areas, the harried mothers desperate to feed their children, the submissive women in dysfunctional relationships. What I find noteworthy is that both Garro and Pacheco, generations apart and from different literary backgrounds, together use the Malinche subtext in their representation of the female inhabitants of Mexico City. As a review of their stories will show, they both acknowledge the presence of the cultural memory of La Malinche as an influence on interpersonal relations. Furthermore, the lives of these avatars seem to be following the same downward trajectory as the city itself, from splendor and fulfillment to decay and frustration.

Although I have chosen to compare the images and ideology of Elena Garro and Cristina Pacheco, at first thought the two writers do not appear to share thematics or ideology. As Fabienne Bradu notes, Garro's narratives often focused on her own private world, and offered her readers the perspective of her social class (19). In contrast, Cristina Pacheco has been called one of the most prominent writers of (feminist) testimonial literature today (De Valdés, 125; Peña, 769). If one had to compare Pacheco with writers of previous generations, one would think of Rosario Castellanos and Elena Poniatowska, both of whom have published stories that reveal their social conscience in relation to gender, race, and class issues. Castellanos focuses on a more rural world than that of Poniatowska, whose depiction of servants and lower-class urban women can be found, for example, in *La noche de Tlatelolco* (1971; *Massacre in Mexico*), *Flor de lis*, (1988; *Fleur de lis*), and in her most famous creation of Jesusa Palancares in *Hasta no verte, Jesús mío* (1969; *Here's to You, Jesusa!*). Whereas Garro was essentially a private person, especially after the Tlatelolco massacre in 1968 and her very difficult divorce from Octavio Paz, Cristina Pacheco is a very public woman, in the positive sense of the word.[7] A chronicler of contemporary Mexican culture, for almost thirty years she has published a story a week in the various journals of Mexico City, including *el día* y *Unomásuno*, and from 1986, *La Jornada*. In addition, each week, since 1979, she has hosted the highly rated television program *Aquí nos tocó vivir* (Here is where we live). Her work attempts to re-create personal testimonies by many of the poorest residents of Mexico City, those who live in the worst slums or in garbage dumps. Like Poniatowska, she uses popular dialects in her work, so that the voices of the marginalized are re-created for the bourgeois audience she reaches.

Despite these clear differences in both lifestyle and writing style, both Garro and Pacheco do reveal a concern "for the poor and the oppressed, particularly the indigenous Mexican" (Jehenson, on Garro, 127). Their characters, too, have often been identified with real people; that is, Garro's later texts, such as *Testimonios sobre Mariana* (1991; Testimonies about Mariana), or *Mi hermanita Magdalena* (1998; My little sister Magdalena), have been considered romans à clef, or autobiographical pieces disguised as novels, whereas Cristina Pacheco is thought to be literally transcribing the vignettes of actual Mexican inhabitants of the city. As Pacheco informs us, however,

> My goal with my stories is that they should appear completely real; this
> I must say has caused me problems, because there are people who
> believe they are stories that someone has told me and that I go and

write up at home. All the elements of my stories are completely fictitious, but I'm enthused by the idea that someone would believe they are completely real.[8]

Although their stories are fiction, what is *real* is that the two writers have created tales that serve as vehicles for a deeply rooted cultural memory of La Malinche.

Garro has always been associated with the evocation of a particular town, that of the Ixtepec of *Los recuerdos del porvenir* (1963; *Recollections of Things to Come*), more than with the city of Mexico.[9] Yet her celebrated text "La culpa es de los tlaxcaltecas," published in 1964, takes us into the heart of Mexico City's paradoxes—a place that exists in multiple temporal zones. Garro reminds us through character as well as through place that Mexico City is a palimpsest in which past events remain vividly alive because the artifacts of the past have never disappeared. In a way, Garro shows how the entire city itself is a public reminder of the Conquest period and its effect on contemporary Mexico. I have associated the story with the Malinche paradigm, calling its protagonist, Laura Aldama, an avatar of La Malinche; through the interactions between the husband and wife, Garro shows the impact of the Malinche–Cortés relationship and how it still affects Mexican patterns of behavior (Cypess). Its richly layered text offers, however, many readings and provides many possibilities for additional commentary.

A story of love and betrayal, Laura, as the Malinche avatar, her present husband, Pablo, and her first husband, an unnamed Indian from the Conquest period, appear to play out roles dictated by cultural memory relating to the Malinche myth, only to have them subverted at the end. As I have described elsewhere, Laura rejects Pablo and his hegemonic ideology in favor of returning to her first love, and to a Mexico that is faithful to the indigenous past (Cypess). It is by means of her journey through the city and through other parts of Mexico that Laura is able to make her decision to leave the center, leave the metropolis, and return to aspects of Mexican culture that had been placed on the periphery. Let us review how Garro suggests this reading.

As noted by Cynthia Duncan, Garro often presents a specific fictive character who acts as the recipient, or narratee of the story. In this case, Laura relates the events of her experiences to her maid Nacha. Duncan states that for most of her narratives, Garro creates a narratee who "plays the part of a skeptical listener or reader who questions the information he receives from the narrator before it is passed on to the real reader" (11).

In this story, however, Nacha is the only one to believe in Laura and verify her claims. It is Nacha, also on the periphery—the cook in the kitchen, the servant, possibly indigenous or certainly mestiza—who confirms the story of the Malinche avatar.

As the narrative begins, Laura apparently had been away from home, out in the world alone, defying patriarchal norms. In a disheveled dress, with blood stains, she shows up at the kitchen door. The reader sees Laura from Nacha's perspective and it is Nacha's observations that are recorded, after which she serves as Laura's narratee. Laura tells her how she had left their house on a journey with her mother-in-law in twentieth-century Mexico City, only to wind up in sixteenth-century Tenochtitlán, in the midst of the battles of the Conquest, finally returning again to twentieth-century Mexico: "As night was falling we arrived in Mexico City. How it had changed, Nachita, I almost couldn't believe it! At noon the warriors were still there and now, not a trace of their path. Nor were any remains left. We passed by the Zocalo, silent and sad; of the other plaza, nothing remained!"[10] According to Laura, at noon she had witnessed the battles of the Conquest, but by nightfall, all the remnants of the war had disappeared before her eyes. Along with the battle scenes, she also saw and spoke with a man she calls "primo marido," her first husband, an Indian of the Conquest period. Throughout the story, Laura describes going back in time to the events of the Conquest period as if these moments existed on the same plane as her life in the "present." Unlike what is expected of a woman of her social class, Laura disappears for days and cannot account for her behavior in rational terms; she admits to having seen the mysterious Indian in a café in Tacuba (one of the older regions of the city that existed in ancient Mexico).[11] Pablo, as might be expected, is suspicious of this Indian with whom his wife seems to be having a relationship. After all, they live in the patriarchal world of contemporary Mexico, and women of Laura's class are not supposed to have anything to do with Indian men; the only Indians allowed are the maids.

Pablo does not believe whatever Laura tells him, nor does he trust her, and her mother-in-law acts as if she had lost her mind. Only Nacha seems to accept Laura's confession as truth, because she has been listening to Laura describe her feelings about Pablo, and they also seem to ring true. Laura informs Nacha that she had married Pablo because he reminded her of someone she had known, but that she soon realized he was not like that "other" man (whom the reader soon learns is the Indian husband of the

Conquest period). As Laura tells it, Pablo "merely repeated the gestures of all the men of Mexico City."[12] As further explanation of what that means, Laura elaborates that Pablo often had rages of jealousy, would not let her leave her home, and when they were out together at the theater or in a restaurant, he would "arma[r] pleitos" (20) (start arguments). Pablo also would beat her, especially when he let himself think that her strange behavior meant that she was seeing another man—and possibly the Indian (ibid.).

Clearly, as Laura describes him, Pablo is showing the behavior of an irrationally jealous man who wants to control his wife at the same time he feels she is betraying him with other men. For Laura, this pattern of behavior is the manner of the "men of Mexico City" and fits the way they react to women: as if they were "Malinche" figures—women incapable of trust, sexually promiscuous, and in need of domination. When Laura describes her penultimate meeting with the Indian in the Café de Tacuba, she mentions that he left her to go off to combat, the details of which remind the reader of the battles of the Conquest (31–32); she describes to her narratee, Nacha, how the canals of the city were filled with bodies, an event that describes what took place during the siege of Tenochtitlán. Laura also recalls how frightened she became and how she left Tacuba to go back to the Aldama residence, taking a taxi that brought her by means of the *periférico,* the road that circles Mexico City, recalling the way canals had surrounded the Aztec central zone. Laura herself makes the association: "And you know, Nachita? The beltways were the canals infested with cadavers."[13] The fact that Laura takes the *periférico* functions on various levels. For one, the reference serves to remind the reader of the remnants of the Conquest period that still mark the geography of contemporary Mexico City. Moreover, the geographic allusion also reminds us of the journey made by Laura-Malinche, from the periphery as a slave in the Conquest period, to the consort of an elite (Pablo-Cortés).

But the journey from the margins to the center of power is part of the reason La Malinche was labeled a traitor, and for Laura, too, her journey from the periphery to the center marked one kind of betrayal—that of the original Malinche in terms of cultural memory—her disdain of the indigenous population in favor of the Spanish peoples. But Laura, unlike La Malinche, has a second opportunity to review the trajectory of her actions, both geographically and emotionally. With the help of Nacha, she leaves the Aldama home, she leaves the center, and disappears with the Indian, her first husband. Garro sets up this dual polarity, between Laura and

Pablo, and then between the Malinche paradigm and Laura's behavior, so she can show its fallacies.

In the particular terms of the story, Garro's narrative technique is so constructed that she disassembles the negative stereotypes about Mexican women that Pablo's behavior demonstrates. At first, it appears that Laura agrees with Pablo, for she calls herself a *traidora* (traitor), unfaithful (10), and she then elicits the cook's admission that she, like Laura (and all women), is also disloyal: "Yes, I too am a traitor, Señora Laura."[14] Throughout the story, a strong bond of female complicity is created between Laura and Nacha. Nacha's feeling of solidarity with Laura goes beyond merely agreeing with her as if she were humoring her. She attempts to protect her mistress from Pablo, and agrees that he is unworthy of Laura: "Very true! It is very true that the Master is a real pain! said Nacha with displeasure."[15] When the Indian returns to the house one night, it is Nacha who knows it first and informs Laura (33). The omniscient narrator discloses that there was an *intimidad,* an intimacy that had been established between them (ibid.). Finally, when her mistress manages to escape from her home and her unhappy marriage to Pablo Aldama, Nacha too leaves, even before collecting her salary. "Nacha's failure to collect her salary before leaving underlines the personal—against the economic—nature of her involvement in the mistress-servant relationship," says Cynthia Steele (307). Steele ends her reading of the story with a rather pessimistic comment, observing that while Laura has successfully made a break with patriarchy, "her servant unquestioningly moves on to another mistress, to her own, decidedly less romantic 'destiny'" (ibid.). For Steele, Garro has created a "semifeudal fictional world in which the maid's complicity with her mistress is primarily a function of her loyalty as a servant" (ibid.). I would like to suggest, however, that there is a more sympathetic way to analyze their relationship that has its basis in the Malinche paradigm.

The statement by Laura, "I'm like them, a traitor," and Nacha's response, "Yes, I too am a traitor," is a way of equating the two of them on the basis of their gender. Yet the very acts of the two women in relation to each other belie the assertion of their disloyalty, so that ironically, neither woman is fundamentally as treacherous as the stereotype would have us believe. The stereotype of the betraying woman is derived from masculinist ideology, and has to do in Mexico with the influences of the Catholic reading of Eve and the nationalists' view of La Malinche's role in Mexican history. According to the traditional discourse, then, women are not loyal, and servants are ungrateful and spiteful. This negative attitude toward servants may be an underlying motif in Garro's "El árbol" ("The Tree"), in which the servant Luisa attacks her mistress. In that story, there is a psychotic aspect to the dynamics of the mistress–servant relationship, and Garro does seem to discount their gender as a link of solidarity and instead to focus on the effects of ethnic and class differences between the two women. In "El árbol," Garro underlines the social and psychological consequences when lower-class women live in oppressive circumstances. Luisa's need to live in a prison, a real one, is also a metaphor for the way indigenous peoples endure in Mexico. But in "La culpa," Garro appears to be offering a positive view of the servant–mistress relationship in the way she reads them both through the prism of La Malinche. Whatever her socioeconomic status, the Mexican woman of today is labeled Malinche, betrayer of the *patria* (Cypess, 163). Yet Garro shows that judgment to be false, because Laura, ultimately, returns to her first husband, the indigenous man of the story, whom she had abandoned earlier for the white man. Laura has the opportunity that Malinche did not, to exercise her own agency by abandoning her bourgeois, patriarchal home and reuniting with the Indian husband.

Similarly, and here Garro does not show class differences, Nacha is also a loyal and supportive figure. It is her testimony about the surreal events that take place in the story that enables the reader to accept the events as reliable. Nacha, too, bears more than the burden of discourse; she shows that the new Malinche of the lower class can also exercise her agency, and she too leaves the patriarchal home: "I'm uncomfortable in the Aldama household. I am going to find myself another destiny, she confided to Josefina . . . And . . . Nacha left without even waiting to receive her salary."[16] Steele reads this ending—that Nacha left without her salary—as a romanticized semifeudal act, but it shows us that Nacha's body is not for sale. Nacha is not fired; she makes her own decision, and takes destiny into her own hands. Why should we consider that to be any less powerful an action than that of Laura? I would say that Nacha's act, as well as Laura's, should be read as a subversion of patriarchal stereotypes that classify all women as disloyal and unfaithful. The final gesture of the story is that of the servant Nacha, and it shows her in a dignified light, proud, and loyal—not to patriarchal principles, but to values elaborated by the female power in the story.

I may be charged with reading the destiny of Nacha in too optimistic a framework, for on one practical level, what was in store for Nacha once she left the Aldama home? My previous reading focused on the subject pronouns—the *Yo* (I) that expresses a strong subject position, in which the destiny Nacha follows is hers to choose, but it is also true that Nacha as a servant had far fewer choices than an educated woman of the bourgeois or upper classes. Garro does not chronicle that part of the story. On the other hand, Cristina Pacheco's stories, in the practical sense, show us much more of the gritty reality of the poverty, squalor, and lack of agency suffered by the servants and other workers in the urban Mexican environment. Empowerment, career, stable family would be untranslatable words to the women Pacheco chronicles, for their lives revolve around these issues in ways that are so distinct and distant from the bourgeois configuration of the concepts.

Many of Pacheco's stories show one of the messages of "La culpa," that for Mexican women, gender is the link of solidarity more than class, for even the poor men of their families oppress the female members, as in "Esposa y mártir" (Wife and martyr) or "Los trabajos perdidos" (Lost work) of *Cuarto de azotea* (1986; Maid's quarters). History is not being privatized in the stories of Cristina Pacheco, because she is not showing just one or two oppressed women within the generic family, but rather the full panoply of diverse women in the vast urban sprawl of Mexico City.[17] Her characters may be identified mostly as poverty-stricken proletarians, but she also depicts the bourgeois members of this society, and occasionally the upper-middle-class (as in "La dicha conyugal" [Marital happiness]).

The stories of Cristina Pacheco make us aware of the suffering of the lives of everyday poor Mexican women who are usually the most ignored figures in their society.[18] Pacheco's many collections of stories provide an entrée into a form of existence that most Mexicans would prefer to ignore and most tourists would prefer to avoid. Perhaps most telling of the attitude of past decades of Latin Americans about city life is found in her story "Valle de pecadores" (Valley of sinners), from the collection *Felicidades, abuelito* (1998; Congratulations, Grandpa). On the anecdotal level, it relates the events in a small town in which every year, the townsfolk put on a Passion Play for Holy Week. The most beautiful and accomplished young woman, Elena, is chosen to play the part of the Virgin Mary, a choice that changes her life. The title, however, should provide a clue that the story deals not only with the religious theme of sinners and saints, but with another traditional theme, the debate over country versus city life, a motif that dates back to at least the nineteenth century in Latin America.

The use of *valle,* then, is not only a reference to the "vale of tears that is life," but it also suggests "Valle de Anáhuac," the ancient term for the area of Mexico City, and may remind us of Reyes's *Vision of Anáhuac.* Indeed, the story's geographic trajectory goes from a rural village to the big city of Mexico, from an innocent world where saintly conversions may occur, to the decadence that has become synonymous with the urban environment. The attribution of moral value to physical spaces has a long history in many cultures, and certainly, the city as a place of sin is a common association. What Pacheco works out in this story through dislocations in space also alludes to Mexican cultural memory and the images of the Virgin of Guadalupe and La Malinche as indicators of feminine behavior.

The story is recounted by a young male narrator who is a witness to the events that mark the transformation of his friend Elena: "At fifteen [the year celebrated in Mexican culture as a liminal moment] Elena was the symbol of beauty and temptation. Perhaps for that reason we were surprised that Father Cornejo had chosen her to play the part of the Virgin Mary."[19] Elena plays the part every year, becoming more and more like a saint in her behavior and less like the gay coquette she had been at fifteen. After eight years of being overwhelmed by the role, Elena finally escapes from her small town and heads for Mexico City, never to return to the virginal life she was forced to live. There she is seen by one of the townsmen, who reports back how much she has changed in the city: "I met up with Elena. She seems very strange. Remember how she was very religious, a little saint; well, now she walks around all exposed, with short skirts. I think she's become a slut."[20] Although the news first makes the narrator sad, he soon realizes that Elena could not keep up with the burden that the role of the Virgin had placed upon her: "At first the news made me sad, but then I thought that perhaps Elena would be feeling as relaxed as us when, after Easter Sunday, we were free once again to be just ordinary sinners."[21] As an allegory, Pacheco's little vignette tells a great deal about the difficulties for women when the paradigm of the Virgin is held up to them as an ideal. By locating her story first in a small town, then placing her character in Mexico City, she is also emphasizing that the city is the place of decadence and immorality. Elena had to leave the town physically in order to rid herself of the restrictive role of the saintly mother. She leaves the village and the paradigm of the Virgin Mary and relocates to the city only to enact the stereotyped role of the Malinche figure, the sexually promiscuous icon on the opposite pole to the Mary figure.

The male narrator had first thought that Elena had accepted with plea-sure the role of the saint, but he learns only after her disappearance that she had been "so weighed down and unhappy with her new lifestyle."[22] The young man had no idea how difficult it could be for women to carry the burden of the Virgin's influence, how powerful a force it would be to liber-ate oneself from its burdens that a young woman like Elena was willing to risk abandoning her family and friends to be free from its strictures. Did she really turn into a "slut," as the narrator's younger brother recounts? Or is it, as is so common in Pacheco's narrative technique, that we have to read beyond what the character wants us to think? Rather than taking at face value what the men say, since they seem to be unreliable narrators in the way they are unable to understand the true feelings of the female pro-tagonist, I would suggest another way to read the ending, as a commentary on the Malinche paradigm.

Malinche, too, according to historical memory, was supposed to have said that she was happy to have left her family and become one of the "warriors" in the conquest of México-Tenochtitlán.[23] Just as there is no way to verify what Malinche might have thought, her actions have been transformed to promote at times a nationalist agenda regarding indige-nous peoples, and/or a patriarchal agenda about female behavior. In either of these two hegemonic discourses, the woman is disloyal and sexually promiscuous, characteristics falsely attributed to Garro's Laura, as we have seen, and now to Pacheco's Elena. Elena may have been exercising her free-dom to dress and act as she pleased, without having to conform to the burdens of the Guadalupe paradigm; in exiting from that set of demands, however, she is immediately read as its opposite, La Malinche. While it is the narrator's brother who presents the judgment against Elena, the nar-rator provides Elena, and the reader, with an alternative: perhaps all she wanted was to be "free once again to be just an ordinary sinner" (19). He attempts, with Pacheco's help, to wrest her and all women from the con-straints of paradigms enforced by cultural memory.

In another story, "El Papa en Santa Fe" (The pope in Santa Fe), also from the collection *Felicidades, abuelito*, Pacheco again presents the Malin-che subtext, only to subvert the patriarchal prescriptions of the paradigm. Instead of focusing on a young woman on the verge of womanhood at fifteen, she recounts the experiences of an old woman in a poor section of Mexico City who suffers great disappointments in the face of an indifferent church hierarchy. The story offers the reader an ironic view of the church's relationship with its parishioners, and, by extension, with the contributions of the church to the American inhabitants.

Pacheco's old woman is called Marina, a significant name that suggests to the reader the comparison between this woman and her indigenous precursor. Within the religious frame of the story, the name enables us to recall that Marina was the first documented, baptized woman in Mexico, and often she is described as declaiming the faith and helping to baptize and convert other indigenous peoples. Manuel Aceves, in *Antilaberinto,* declares, "she was the first religious teacher of the Americas."[24] In addition, José Emilio Pacheco informed me (conversation, March 9, 2002), that the name of her neighborhood, "Santa Fe," refers to a region in Mexico that was purposely begun after the Conquest period, in recognition of the Spanish religious fervor to bring their faith to the New World. However, at the time in which Cristina Pacheco's story is set, Santa Fe was famous as the area of the *pepenadores,* the poor who live off the garbage dumps.[25]

This contemporary Marina awaits the projected arrival of the pope, preparing herself in body and spirit for his arrival. But the priest of the parish finally admits to her that the pope will not visit their church, because they are too poor to merit his presence:

> But the priest admitted to her one day that the pope would not
> visit them. "The organizers thought that Santa Fe is too poor a
> neighborhood, it's dirty, there are many crooks and lawbreakers.
> It can be dangerous for the pope . . . Don't lose faith. The spirit of
> the church is everywhere and his blessing will reach you all."[26]

The inhabitants of Marina's neighborhood are described as "children, old-timers, crazy people, alcoholics, drug addicts."[27] She can survive in this world, but ironically, the pope cannot. Thus, the story questions in a subtle way the nature of the gift of the Catholic faith in the New World. As the simple Marina asks, "If God, who was the King of Kings, went to the home of a leper, how is it that he isn't going to come see those who have nothing?"[28]

Just as the traditional Marina in the chronicles of Bernal Díaz del Castillo accepted the Catholic faith and remained faithful despite all the problems that it brought, this Marina also stands fast to her church and the pope. Pacheco describes her so that Marina's dignity catches our attention and overshadows her simplicity of character. Moreover, what really stands out is not just the picture of a submissive and patient woman, who may at first recall more the Virgin of Guadalupe than her namesake. In the final words of the story, which are Marina's, she shows herself to be more combative and questioning than the priest or the church hierarchy might like. Her question is one that Pacheco might well be asking readers to contemplate: "Why should the poor be blamed for the ugliness of their lives?"[29] The message appears clear. First, Cristina Pacheco shows the kindness and integrity of this simple woman who works without pay, dedicating herself to the glory of the church. Nevertheless, the organizers, the patriarchy, do not take into consideration the plight of the poor, the common folk. Pacheco suggests that the upper classes blame the poor for living so badly without trying to help them or understand their plight. This Marina, however, asks the appropriate question, "Why should the poor be blamed for their wretched existence?" The answer is left for us to consider.

Pacheco shows many poor women who appear to others as defenseless and marginalized, as in the aptly titled story "La esclavitud" (Slavery) of *Cuarto de azotea*. This vignette deals with the plight of Alicia, a twelve-year-old Oaxaca Indian girl who is a virtual slave serving in the household of a Mexico City couple who beat her, mistreat her, and starve her after her father has sold her to them in exchange for two thousand pesos. La Malinche was a slave, too, given to the Spaniards as a gift, without the exchange of money. She turned out to be a very valuable gift, but she has been mistreated and inaccurately represented in history. Pacheco shows how this young Indian girl is also badly represented by her masters. When another poor working woman appears sympathetic to her, Alicia confesses why she is so distressed: "'Now she says that I'm lazy and stupid and not worth anything.' Alicia bows her head; she looks at her bare feet, dirty legs, torn dress. 'Well, as little as I may be worth, I'm still a person.'"[30] Ultimately, this is the message of Cristina Pacheco, that the poor people whose lives she chronicles in her stories are humans with a dignity and value that have been too long ignored. She follows in the narrative trail of writers such as Garro, Castellanos, and Poniatowska in trying to bring to light the voices of the marginalized and forgotten.

Although both Pacheco and Garro make use of the Malinche paradigm as a prism through which to view disadvantaged women, they do not imply that the paradigm is a stable and inviolable pattern. They show changes in the characteristics of their women protagonists, so that the female figures are cut from a mold that is later subverted. The women characters whose lives have been represented in the texts by Garro and Pacheco may initially remind us of the Malinche paradigm, yet in each case, the repetitive actions and responses embedded in cultural memory have been stripped of the concretions of reflexive responses so that the authentic individual (*gente* in Alicia's terms), can be noticed. Garro, true to her belief that literature can correct reality (Bradu, 13), restores to La Malinche her indigenous existence and an appropriate companion.[31] Pacheco's Malinches, on the other hand, seem to exist without companionship, and find themselves still marginalized from the dominant power structures. But if they do not gain access to centers of power, nevertheless they seem to be reevaluating their own life patterns and refuse to exist in the shadows of the periphery. Their small gestures of questioning the dominant powers are a step in the right direction, a way of reaffirming the possibility of their own agency and a refusal to live according to the dictates of an outdated cultural memory.

These characters' struggles just to survive in the labyrinth of the big city, of Mexico City, have not been carried out in vain, for both Elena Garro and Cristina Pacheco prove that these marginalized women merit a space in the cultural discourse. Both writers highlight social problems in which the burdens of a cultural memory based on sexual oppression, and ethnic and class exploitation, are reiterated. Despite existing within a patriarchy that considers them disloyal, inferior, and promiscuous, these Malinche avatars are attempting to redefine themselves in the literal and figurative journeys they undertake, a journey away from the fixed notions of what it means to be a woman in Mexico. Their neighborhoods in Mexico City may no longer befit a pope's presence, but at least the Malinche-like figures who wander its streets no longer function with passive acceptance. Garro and Pacheco resist the constraints of cultural memory and imply that patriarchal cultural norms can be modified, La Malinche can find redress by reclaiming her indigenous past, and maybe even Mexico City can be restored to its previous splendor as a city of shared aims and ethnic liberation.

NOTES

1. The bibliography on this topic is vast, but numerous references can be found in Cypess, *Malinche*; Rodríguez, *Our Lady of Guadalupe*; Leal. For further discussion of the Malinche paradigm, see Cypess, *Malinche*.

2. For an indigenous depiction of the pre-Conquest city, consult "Fundación de México Tenochtitlán" in the Codex Mendocino.

3. Quirarte calls "Visión de Anáhuac" "una de las mejores lecturas que se hayan hecho sobre las ciudades que forman la Ciudad de México" (16; "one of the best readings that have been done about the cities that comprise Mexico City").

4. http://www.bbc.co.uk/worldservice/arts/features/latinamericanwords/mexico/index.shtml.

5. Here is the exchange between Debra Castillo and Fuentes on the theme of the city, as reproduced on the Web site noted in bibliography under Fuentes:

DC: You talk in Christopher about the problems of the city of thirty million, a city the size of a country, and you mention *Where the Air Is Clear,* which nicely focuses the kinds of changes that have taken place in the city. How could you associate particularly those two novels, but also your fiction in general, with a kind of contemporary ideology of the city?

CF: I was always a reader fascinated by the literature of the city. I think that for me literature became a reality the moment I read Balzac, the moment I read Dickens, the moment I read Dostoevsky, Gogol; the writers who introduced us to the modern city, in a word, and later Dos Passos, Doblin, Joyce, who have dealt with the modern city. But before that were those four writers: Gogol, Dostoevsky, Balzac, and Dickens, because they made me realize, my God! here I am surrounded by a Paris, a London, a St. Petersburg of my own and nobody has dealt with it.

6. It is not that Quirarte ignores the changing view of female characters. As one example, from the period of Porfirio Díaz, Quirarte contrasts the depressing depictions of brutalized young women in the text of Heriberto Frías, *Los piratas del boulevard* (1905), in contrast with the delicate feminine portraits of Amado Nervo in "Almas blancas." Nervo's young women bring flowers to the Virgin, while Frías describes girls who at the age of five are beggars, pickpockets, and prostitutes (25). Quirarte's selection of writers, however, rarely includes women.

7. For further discussion about the relations between Garro and Paz, see Rhina Toruño.

8. All translations are mine, unless otherwise noted. "Mi pretensión con mis cuentos es que parezcan completamente reales; eso debo decir que me ha causado problemas, porque hay personas que creen que son historias que alguien me cuenta y que voy y escribo en mi casa. Todos los elementos de mis cuentos son completamente ficticios, pero me entusiasma la idea de que alguien pueda creer que son completamente reales" (http://oncetv-ipn.net/cristina_pacheco/cristina/cristina/entrevista_022.htm).

9. For a study of space in *Recuerdos,* see Patricia Rosas Lopátegui, "Los espacios poéticos y apoéticos en *Los recuerdos del porvenir* de Elena Garro," *Hispanic Journal* 16.1 (1995): 95–108.

10. "Al anochecer llegamos a la ciudad de México. ¡Cómo había cambiado, Nachita, casi no pude creerlo! A las doce del día todavía estaban los guerreros y

ahora ya ni huella de su paso. Tampoco quedaban escombros. Pasamos por el
Zócalo silencioso y triste; de la otra plaza, no quedaba ¡nada!" (15).

11. Laura says she went to Café de Tacuba, which still exists today; it is also the
name chosen by a contemporary new-rock band from Mexico. The pre-Hispanic
region was founded by Tepaneca Indians and later formed part of the Mexican
confederacy. During the wars of the Conquest, it was occupied by the Spanish and
partly destroyed (1521); Laura makes reference presumably to the fighting.

12. "sólo repetía los gestos de todos los hombres de la ciudad de México" (20).

13. "¿Y sabes Nachita? Los periféricos eran los canales infestados de cadáveres"
(32).

14. "Sí, yo también soy traicionera, Señora Laurita" (10).

15. "¡Muy cierto! ¡Muy cierto que el señor es fregón!—dijo Nacha con disgusto"
(17).

16. "Yo no me hallo en casa de los Aldama. Voy a buscarme otro destino, le
confió a Josefina... Y... Nacha se fue hasta sin cobrar su sueldo" (33).

17. It seems pertinent to recall that Cristina Pacheco's spouse, José Emilio
Pacheco, the distinguished writer, poet, and critic, wrote one of the very first stories about the metro in Mexico City—"La fiesta brava" in *Los principios del placer*
(The beginnings of pleasure). A number of his pieces also re-create life in Mexico
City, with *Las batallas en el desierto* (1981; *The Battles in the Desert*) being the most
renowned. In addition, José Emilio supplied the afterword for a book of black-and-
white photographs showing daily life—and the contrast between the ancient and the
modern—in Mexico City. Consult Pablo Ortiz Monasterio, *The Last City: Cultural
Portrait*, afterword by José Emilio Pacheco (Santa Fe, N.M.: Twin Palms, 1996). It first
appeared in Spanish as *La última ciudad* (Mexico City: Casa de las imágenes, 1996).

18. I have chosen to call her work "stories" rather than to become involved in
questions of genre—whether the texts are *testimonios, crónicas,* or simply fiction.
Pacheco calls them *cuentos* that are based on real life but are fictions reflecting her
own artistry.

19. "A los quince años, Elena era el símbolo de la belleza y de la tentación.
Quizás por eso nos sorprendió que el padre Cornejo la eligiera para representar el
papel de la Virgen María" (16–17).

20. "Me encontré a Elena. Está rarísima. Ya ves que era muy persignada y muy
santita, pues ahora anda toda zancona. Yo creo que se volvió güila" (19). The use of
an idiomatic vocabulary—words such as *zancona* and *güila*—is more common
among country folk and reflects the careful characterization through dialogue that
is part of Pacheco's style.

21. "Al principio, la noticia me llenó de tristeza pero luego pensé que tal vez
Elena se sentiría tan relajada como nosotros cuando, después del Domingo de
Ramos, quedábamos en libertad de ser otra vez pecadores comunes y corrientes"
(ibid.).

22. "tan agobiada y descontenta de su nuevo estilo de vida" (18).

23. See Bernal Díaz's version of Malinche's reencounter with her family and his narration of her words. My commentary (Cypess, 30–31) suggests that we may not be able to trust Bernal Díaz completely because he did have a particular message he tries to convey—that his doña Marina is a model Spanish colonial.

24. "Fue la primera catequizadora de América" (16). Mariano G. Somonte also categorically states, "¿Quién sino doña Marina pudo llevar a cabo tal catequización?" (Who except for doña Marina, could have carried out such religious teachings?; quoted in Aceves, 26).

25. We should recall that Cristina Pacheco calls herself as a writer a *pepenadora*, or one who collects the leftovers of others to make use of them. She recognizes at once the reality and humanity of these real figures who exist in poverty and her own use of the details of their lives.

26. "Pero el cura le admite un día que el Papa no les va a visitar: 'los organizadores han pensado que Santa Fe es una colonia demasiado pobre, está sucia, hay muchos ladrones y maleantes. Puede ser peligroso para el Papa... Tú no pierdas la fe. El espíritu de la Iglesia está en todas partes y su bendición les llegará a todos ustedes'" (56).

27. "Niños, ancianos, dementes, alcohólicos, drogadictos" (55).

28. "Si Dios, qu'era Rey de Reyes fue a la casa de un leproso, ¿Cómo no ha d'ir a ver a los que no tienen nada?" (59).

29. "¿Qué culpa tienen los pobres de vivir feo?" (ibid.).

30. "Per'ora dice que soy floja y soy tonta y que no valgo nieso —Alicia inclina la cabeza: se mira los pies descalzos, las piernas sucias, el vestido roto— Ora que, por menos que yo valga, pos soy gente" (64).

31. Bradú comments: "la creación literaria es, para ella, una suerte de compensación o de corrección de una realidad —muchas veces la del poder— que no acaba nunca de aceptar y que repudia a través de o gracias a sus ficciones" (13) (literary creation is, for her, a kind of compensation or correction of a reality—many times that of power—that she never winds up accepting or that she repudiates through or thanks to her fictions).

Works Cited

Aceves, Manuel. *Antilaberinto*. Mexico City: Distribuciones Fontamara, 1997.

Bradu, Fabienne. *Señas particulares: Escritora*. Mexico City: Fondo de Cultura Económica, 1987.

Cortés, Hernán. *Letters from Mexico*. Trans. Anthony Pagden. New Haven: Yale University Press, 1986.

Cypess, Sandra Messinger. *La Malinche in Mexican Literature: From History to Myth*. Austin: University of Texas Press, 1991.

De Valdés, María Elena. "Feminist Testimonial Literature: Cristina Pacheco, Witness to Women." *Monographic Review/Revista Monográfica* 4 (1988): 150–62.

Díaz del Castillo, Bernal. *The Conquest of New Spain.* Trans. J. M. Cohen. New York: Penguin Books, 1963.

Duncan, Cynthia. "Narrative Tension and Perceptual Subversion in Elena Garro's Short Fiction." *Letras Femeninas* 15.1–2 (1989): 11–21.

Fuentes, Carlos. "Travails with Time: An Interview with Carlos Fuentes by Debra A. Castillo." *Review of Contemporary Fiction* 8.2 (summer 1988); http://www.centerforbookculture.org/interviews/interview_fuentes.html.

Garro, Elena. "La culpa es de los tlaxcaltecas." In *La semana de colores.* Xalapa: Universidad Veracruzana, 1964. 9–33.

———. *Los recuerdos del porvenir.* Mexico City: Joaquín Mortiz, 1963.

Jehenson, Myriam Ivonne. *Latin American Women Writers: Class Race, and Gender.* Albany: State University of New York Press, 1995.

Leal, Luis. "Female Archetypes in Mexican Literature." In *Women in Hispanic Literature: Icons and Fallen Idols,* ed. Beth Miller. Berkeley: University of California Press, 1983. 227–42.

Mexico City. http://www.mexicocity.com.mx/view.html.

Pacheco, Cristina. *Cuarto de azotea.* Mexico City: Ediciones Gernika, 1986.

———. *Felicidades, Abuelito.* Mexico City: ISSSTE, 1998.

Pacheco, José Emilio. Personal conversation. March, 9, 2002. http://oncetv-ipn.net/cristina_pacheco/cristina/cristina/entrevista_022.htm.

Peña, Margarita. "Literatura femenina en México en la antesala del año 2000 (Antecedentes: siglos XIX y XX)." *Revista Iberoamericana* 55.148–49 (1989): 761–69.

Quirarte, Vicente. *La ciudad como cuerpo.* Mexico City: Biblioteca del ISSSTE, 1999.

———. *Elogio de la calle. Biografía literaria de la Ciudad de México 1850–1992.* Mexico City: Cal y Arena, 2001.

Rodríguez, Jeanette. *Our Lady of Guadalupe: Faith and Empowerment among Mexican-American Women.* Austin: University of Texas Press, 1994.

———. *Stories We Live. Cuentos que vivimos.* Mahwah, N.J.: Paulist Press, 1996.

Steele, Cynthia. "The Other Within: Class and Ethnicity as Difference in Mexican Women's Literature." In *Cultural and Historical Grounding for Hispanic and Luso-Brazilian Feminist Literary Criticism,* ed. Hernán Vidal. Minneapolis: Ideologies and Literatures, 1989. 297–328.

Toruño, Rhina. *Cita con la memoria: Elena Garro cuenta su vida a Rhina Toruño.* Buenos Aires: Prueba de Galera, 2004.

9

Writing Home

Afro–Costa Rican Women Poets
Negotiating Limón and San José

DOROTHY E. MOSBY

> Perhaps to lose a sense of where you are implies the danger of losing a
> sense of who you are.
>
> *Ralph Ellison*

In the contemporary literature by blacks of West Indian descent in
Costa Rica, the cities of Puerto Limón and San José are significant
sites of exploration because of the historic and cultural importance of
these two locations. Women writers in particular have addressed the often
difficult relationship between Afro–Costa Rican identity and these two
centers. Through the act of memory and the motif of the journey, Eulalia
Bernard (b. 1935), Shirley Campbell (b. 1965), and Delia McDonald (b.
1965) articulate cultural and ethnolinguistic tensions in their poetry as
memories and bodies shift between the provincial port city, Puerto Limón,
as the "black capital," and the nation's political center, San José, as the "white
capital." Limón and San José represent the transformation in black identity in Costa Rica, and the generational relationships to these two cities
by the poets reflect the process of "becoming" Afro–Costa Rican. With the
dislocation of West Indians from their points of origin in the Caribbean,
there arises a need to establish a home even if home is a "site fixed in the
geography of the imagination" (Mosby, 96). The three writers signal that
Limón is a space vital to the expression of Afro–Costa Rican cultural identity, and often there is an implicit bond between the port city and this
identity. To be black in Costa Rica, particularly according to the poetics
of second-generation Eulalia Bernard, means also a profound cultural link

with Limón and with West Indian cultural heritage. In turn, in the work of the younger poets, Campbell and McDonald, Limón is sometimes an "unhomely" or ephemeral home that nevertheless merits homage because of its cultural significance or as a place inhabited by memories. In contrast, San José, specifically in the work of McDonald, is a site of "unbelonging."

Located on the Caribbean (Atlantic) coast of Costa Rica, Puerto Limón has special cultural and historical meaning in the contemporary history of blacks in the Central American nation. Puerto Limón is a port city that served as the point of debarkation for thousands of Afro-Caribbean laborers from the latter part of the nineteenth century through the first three decades of the twentieth century.[1] It is in Limón that black workers, contracted by the Northern Railway Company beginning in 1872 and the United Fruit Company from 1899 to 1934, constructed an enclave that reflected their condition as British subjects and their dreams to fulfill the terms of their labor contracts and triumphantly return to their island homes.

The national capital, located in the Central Valley, forms the geographic, political, and cultural center of Costa Rican identity. San José is often viewed as developed and metropolitan whereas Puerto Limón is regarded as a site of neglect and provincialism. The multicultural and multiethnic history of Puerto Limón and the peoples who lay a cultural claim to the port city is characterized by the dominant culture emanating from San José as "folkloric," "dangerous," and "foreign." In particular, the laboring, dark West Indian body associated with Puerto Limón contrasts with the image of the national self radiating from San José, the *leyenda blanca,* a national myth of whiteness and cultural homogeneity.[2] To be Costa Rican, or "Tico," and to participate in the national culture and political life—in effect, to be considered a citizen—is to be "white," Spanish-speaking, and Catholic.

From 1872 to 1948, San José sought to maintain its perceived homogeneity by excluding the new arrivals from the national culture and the city's geography through a de facto segregation that discouraged large-scale West Indian settlement in the capital.[3] Reform movements emerging after the 1948 civil war changed the status of blacks in Limón. Citizenship was extended to blacks born in Costa Rica, launching a wave of internal migration as *afrolimonenses* began seeking opportunities in the capital. However, even with the increased migration of Limón blacks to the Central Valley (called *meseta central* or *valle central*), and conversely of *meseta*-dwellers to the Caribbean coast, Puerto Limón and the citizens of Afro–West Indian descent who are historically linked to the city still signify marginalization.

As pertains to these two urban centers, rooted in the poetry of the three Afro–Costa Rican women are expressions of cultural and national identity and the resulting sentiment of a double-consciousness of being black and Costa Rican. In the work of second-generation Bernard and fourth-generation Campbell and McDonald, Limón is constructed as a real and imagined space of "cultural authenticity" that represents the stable "home" for a subject that is continually in the process of "becoming," as Stuart Hall observes. Hall claims that "Cultural identity . . . is a matter of 'becoming' as well as of 'being.' It belongs to the future as much as the past. It is not something that already exists transcending place, time, history, and culture. Cultural identities come from somewhere, have histories. But like everything else which is historical, they undergo constant transformation" (70).

The relationship of the Afro–Costa Rican subject to San José and Limón is the product of a continual process whereby historical forces shape how identity is constructed and represented. San José, as it appears explicitly in the work of McDonald, is configured as a city that is replete with opportunity, but also as a hostile space that has yet to fully embrace Afro-Costa Ricans as citizens of the nation. Limón appears as a site central to the expression of Afro–Costa Rican identity where there is a homologous association between the port city and black identity. Although Bernard's second-generation perspective often elevates Puerto Limón to mythic proportions, she also conveys nostalgia for the port city's past in the midst of its urban decay and neglect. Owing to generational differences, Campbell and McDonald recognize the cultural importance of Limón, but reflect on their struggle to affirm their "Costa Ricanness" and their blackness. In all three poets, Limón appears as a place of deterioration and mistreatment as well as a place for restoration and recovery. The symbolic renewal through poetry revitalizes Puerto Limón and vindicates Afro–Costa Rican identity in the process.

Born to Jamaican parents in the port city before the 1948 civil war, Eulalia Bernard expresses the perspective of the second generation. She examines ethnic and cultural identity, often with Puerto Limón at the center of her poetry. She is the author of four collections of poetry written in Spanish, English, and Limonese Creole: *Ritmohéroe* (Rhythmhero, 1982), *My Black King* (1991), *Griot* (1996), *Ciénaga/Marsh* (2001). Although the publication dates of her work are quite recent, she began her literary career earlier with the release of a spoken-word album, *Negritud,* in 1976, which served as a catalyst in locating an audience for her work. Much of her poetry accentuates the connection of the Afro–Costa Rican population with the African diaspora and the West Indies (especially Jamaica), but also the tensions between the desire to be at home in Costa Rica and the difficulty in achieving that desire.

Bernard's generation was the first following legislation guaranteeing black enfranchisement to leave Puerto Limón and the Caribbean province to pursue educational and economic opportunities in the capital. Hers is called the "wounded generation" because before the civil war the "native-born" black children of West Indian immigrants were stateless—neither Costa Ricans nor Jamaicans. According to Carlos Meléndez and Quince Duncan in *El negro en Costa Rica*, "Great Britain [did] not recognize them because they were born in a foreign country. Costa Rica [did] not recognize them because they are black, children of Jamaicans" (134). For a few generations, the condition of black West Indians in the country was one of "unbelonging," marked by their exclusion by the white-identified mestizo national population and eventually by Great Britain because they were black subjects situated outside of the political limits of empire.

Even after the extension of Costa Rican citizenship to the black population, the racial marker of difference and "foreignness" remains, as does the exclusion of the new citizens. Renato Rosaldo reminds us in "Cultural Citizenship, Inequality, and Multiculturalism" that "one needs to distinguish the formal level of theoretical universality from the substantive level of exclusionary and marginalizing practices" (252). To address the need to belong, Bernard's poetry constructs Puerto Limón as the historical and imagined home for Afro–Costa Rican identity. For Bernard, a connection with Limón is an important link that gives a once "nomadic" West Indian identity in Costa Rica a secure home. In this configuration, Limón is presented as a place to fix an otherwise unstable identity that is unwelcome by the nation-state and unable to return to the ancestral home. It is constructed as a deteriorated but "safe home" because of the history of West Indian settlement in the enclave; nevertheless, for this very same reason, this home is rejected by the prevailing ideology of the nation-state.

The city sometimes assumes mythic qualities as her poetic voice expresses nostalgic yearnings for a more certain past. Some of those sentiments are voiced in "Carbunclo" (Carbuncle), a poem from Bernard's first published collection, *Ritmohéroe*, where the poetic voice laments some of the changes to Limón initiated by the nation-state without the consensus of the West Indian population. A "carbuncle" is a mythical gem that is purported to give off light in the dark. The city is a carbuncle that glows and emits light in the poet-narrator's memory of the past like the firefly that serves as a catalyst for remembering. Through memory and the opening image of the now scarce firefly, Bernard expresses concern for the contemporary and historical Limón that is linked to the poetic subject's understanding of self, place, and change. "Carbunclo" articulates the disquietude resulting from the disjuncture between childhood memories and present conditions in the port city.

The presence of a firefly reminds the subject of an earlier period when the creatures used to light up the active city's sky, glowing like a carbuncle. The rare and darkened firefly "symbolizes the once vibrant culture that shaped the port city. The small insect that once brought 'great light' to the nights of the town no longer has a home there and has disappeared like some of the Afro–West Indian cultural practices in the region" (Mosby, 98). The carbuncle that once characterized the port city has lost its luster, just as the glowing firefly that dotted its landscape in abundance has disappeared. A transformation has taken place in the city, marking a change in the habitat of the firefly as well as for the cultural habitat for the people of West Indian descent in Puerto Limón.

In "Carbunclo," the parcels of the city territory have also lost their nostalgic glow. The space that belonged to the West Indian blacks and their descendants as their home has been reinterpreted for them from the outside by the national government rather than from within. The two neighborhoods mentioned in the poem—Jamaica Town and Cieneguita—hold special meaning to earlier generations of black Costa Ricans. The neighborhoods, like the people who inhabited them in the past, were transformed by external cultural forces. The former West Indian neighborhoods of Jamaica Town and Cieneguita were named by the residents who inhabited these areas to the north and south of the city, respectively. Jamaica Town was renamed "Barrio Roosevelt" to honor a visit by the American president Theodore Roosevelt and Cieneguita became "Barrio Cristóbal Colón" to commemorate the brief arrival of the explorer Columbus in 1502—also reflecting the authority of the Central Valley in Puerto Limón. While expressing sorrow for how the city's landscape has changed through the years, the poem also reveals a sense of resignation—accepting the transformation that came with the change in the names of the neighborhoods. There is loss of the authentic and the local, which have been replaced by the naming practices of the national without the consent of the local population.

In "Carbunclo," there is no explicit mention of resistance or suggestion to take back the original names, as in Toni Morrison's *Song of Solomon* when the residents of locally named Doctor Street refuse to accept the official name of white municipal authorities by renaming it "Not Doctor Street." Names given by the immigrant community to the locations they occupied were changed by national authorities as if to erase the impact of West Indian culture. Nevertheless, the memory of the West Indian enclave passes on the symbolic weight of the city beyond nostalgic yearning and expresses hope that the city will glow again, just as the poetic voice hopes to see the firefly of her childhood once more.

There is a considerable identification with the body and Limón in the poetic expression of Eulalia Bernard. Afro–Costa Rican identity personified as the human body is tied closely with the city. There is a desire to save the city and to renew oneself in the process—in effect, a way toward self-salvation and self-preservation. Instead of conveying existential malaise about the city's neglect and degradation, the poetic subject becomes an engendered and embodied agent that signals the condition of the city or takes action for the benefit of her *pueblo* (meaning both people and town). The city is also presented as a body in which a double discourse is invoked, wherein the immediate image of the poem presents one discursive level that simultaneously serves as a metaphor for a second level. The double discourse in Bernard's poetry presents the "body as city." The engendered body operates as a metaphor for the political, social, or cultural condition of Limón, for the relationship between the Afro–Costa Rican population and the nation-state, or for the connection between the black residents of Puerto Limón and the city itself. In "Metamorfosis de tu recuerdo" (Metamorphosis of your memory), from *Ritmohéroe*, the image of the male body becomes a metaphor for the city. The first stanza of the two-stanza poem begins with the verse "I remember you," followed by a series of adjectives in the masculine form indicating male energy, beauty, strength, and potency. The second stanza opens with "I [now] see you," followed by adjectives in the masculine form indicating feebleness, disintegration, defeat, and misery.

The poem can be read as a commentary on the deterioration of the male body, but this body also represents the West Indian culture of the port city, as well as the city itself. Like the poetic voice's memory in "Carbunclo," the "body as city" dynamic is also situated between memory of the past and its accompanying nostalgia and its current condition, which in "Metamorfosis de tu recuerdo" is a body in decay. The male body, once admired, is now weak and broken. Although the word *city* (*la ciudad*) is a feminine noun in Spanish, the word for *port* (*el puerto*) is masculine, as in Puerto Limón. By associating the masculine gender of the adjectives in the poem with the labor history of the port city, the male body becomes an appropriate symbol for the city because it was constructed and sustained through the labor of the black male body. Kitzie McKinney observes: "Unlike many black women writers, particularly of the Caribbean, who represent the male as an absent or negative figure, Eulalia Bernard remembers the experience of her community as Antillean male immigrants founded settlements, sent for families, and supported their communities" (15). Puerto Limón, in the past a powerful black male body, is now reduced and impotent.

In contrast to the image of the broken male body in "Metamorfosis de tu recuerdo," it is the female body in "Deseo" (Desire), also from *Ritmohéroe,* that becomes an agent for change. Bernard places the black female body at the center of the poetic discourse to call for the rebirth of Puerto Limón. The engendered body becomes the site from which emerges the desire for social, political, and economic progress in the city. From the site of her body, the poetic subject contemplates the larger goal of the battle for her *pueblo* and the relative frailty of her body to conduct such an endeavor. The female body experiences a "tormented womb" that is likened to a frustrated longing to produce a sustainable future for her city in the place of children. The poetic voice expresses her dissatisfaction and anguish for the condition of her *pueblo,* as well as her need to effect change. In spite of her physical weakness, the black female subject is motivated to transform the city and converts herself into the salvation of her *pueblo.* She is at once the sacrifice with her fragile body positioned on a bed and the savior with her desire to garner strength "to continue the construction of the temple of redemption for my people and town: Limón" (*Ritmohéroe,* 37). The salvation of the city and its culture will be achieved through the female body that becomes an agent of change as she produces, reproduces, and transforms her *pueblo.*

"Ahora que soy tuya Limón" (Now that I am yours, Limón) from *Ciénaga/Marsh* (2001), a multilingual collection, continues with the placement of the female subject at the center of the poetic discourse and extends the "body as city" dynamic. Through the repetition of the title verse, the female subject becomes possessed by the city and the two become inextricably linked. The engendered body is connected to the city like a lover— gazing upon the city, dancing with it, sympathizing with its anguish. The poetic voice has witnessed a trajectory of time in the city where the old buildings, like the Marcus Garvey–era Black Star Line, become historical landmarks and are seen as something to be valued and preserved. The houses of prostitution are replaced by the places where culture is a desired commodity to be exchanged instead of human flesh. There is an acknowledgment of the port city's variegated social history (and by association the poetic voice's history) as a site where cultures come together and mix—a truly hybrid and multicultural site in a nation where the last vestiges of the *leyenda blanca* remain. In this place transformed by time, the poetic subject is able to examine Limón and see herself as a part of the city. She has internalized the "map" of the city's painful past and she observes the lines in her hands as traces of that history on her own body. Her womb carries the Jacobinesque revolutions like that which touched off Haitian independence two hundred years ago—marking a watershed moment in the history of people of African descent in the Americas.

Unlike the portrayal of the city in some of the earlier Limón-themed poems that appear in *Ritmohéroe,* there is positive regard for the changes that have taken place in the city. The signification of certain buildings has changed. Their meanings have become valued and in turn validate and reflect the history of the city. The culture that is housed in museums mirrors the multiethnic and multicultural history of the people, who also have been changed by the passage of time. The men are no longer "roll-on-roll-off" and the women are no longer pleasure objects of "uncultured sailors," denoting a transformation of the sexual mores of the port city away from the exchange of sex to the understanding of cultural history. The trajectory of Limón is even inscribed on the body and the psyche of the poetic voice, "I have in my feet your rambles of yesteryear," through the paths and roads. The city is also in her eyes one with the flow of the rivers that eventually end in the Caribbean Sea, the body of water that separates Limón from the islands of the West Indies. It is through this flow that the poetic subject becomes reborn or renewed in these waters, marking acceptance of the transition.

Bernard's poetry fits within a tradition of black Latin American women poets such as Virginia Brindis de Salas, Nancy Morejón, and Mayra Santos Febres who also draw on the relationship of the racialized female body and urban spaces. Bernard takes the additional aesthetic move to express a dynamic where the engendered body represents the city or forms a symbiotic relationship where the body and the city depend on one another in her deployment of the double discourse. She places the female voice at the center of her poetry in roles as savior, agent, and lover, as well as the voice of social and cultural consciousness. There is an overwhelming concern for the well-being of the *pueblo,* in the sense of both people and town.

Bernard does not deal explicitly with San José as a site in her poetry in the same manner that she explores Limón. Instead of addressing life of Afro–Costa Ricans in contemporary San José, she prefers to tackle larger issues of social justice, human rights, and the myths of democracy, equality, and ethnolinguistic homogeneity that form the national discourse of the country. In Bernard's poetic negotiation of home and Afro–Costa Rican identity, Limón occupies a space of critical importance for a people shaped by exile and multiple migrations. Her Limón-themed poems form a link between the city and its black residents. The real and imagined Limón is a place where the poet can examine the effects of historical changes on the constantly evolving identity of blacks in Costa Rica, how the linguistic and cultural influences from the national Hispanic culture have shaped Afro–Costa Rican identity and Limón as a city, and the creation of a home place for that community.

Afro–Costa Rican roots are given a home in Limón that culturally straddles the Hispanic culture of Costa Rica and the "Afro-Saxon" culture of the British West Indies. In spite of unequal distribution of state resources and cultural exclusion that has created the neglected condition of the port city, Puerto Limón carries great symbolic importance. The city is considered by blacks of West Indian descent and by the national government as the locus of Afro–Costa Rican culture. Claiming Limón as home "fixes" a transforming and unstable subject by giving it visible and accessible roots (as opposed to Jamaica or other West Indian nations). The "fixing" of Afro-Costa Ricans to Limón is an effort by Bernard to stabilize an identity that is continually in the process of becoming—a way to establish a cultural home for Costa Rican blacks, if not a real one for those who live in the capital.

The younger poets Shirley Campbell and Delia McDonald, both born in 1965, express a different relationship with Limón, and many of their preoccupations on cultural, ethnic, national, and gender issues come from the experience of life in the "white capital," San José. The capital is home and it is the place their post-1948 generation knows most intimately. It is, however, an "unhomely" place where a sentiment of unbelonging remains. Limón, on the other hand, is the ancestral home, but it can also be an alien

and alienating site for those who grew up in the heart of the dominant culture in the capital. The poetry of Shirley Campbell in particular displays
an ambivalent bond with the port city and the coastal province. It is a place
where her poetic subjects desire to find a cultural home, but are outsiders.
San José has a more explicit presence in the work of Delia McDonald and
displays similar tensions of desire and unbelonging as Shirley Campbell's
work. In her poems about the port city, McDonald attempts to locate
her poetic subjects within the cultural home of Limón, similar to Eulalia
Bernard's poetic discourse, but an outsider dynamic remains.

San José and Limón are not intentionally set up as antagonists in the
works of Campbell and McDonald, but the cultural symbolism of Puerto
Limón does carry great weight. Limón represents cultural authenticity
and ancestral history, but it also represents neglect and unbelonging from
the perspective of the dominant culture. In turn, San José, particularly in
McDonald's poetry, embodies democracy and progress, but it also signifies
a frustrated desire to belong, alienation, difference, and provincialism in
the cosmopolitan center. Like their parents and grandparents, they discover
that San José is not the promised land. The experience of the two cities
voiced by Campbell and McDonald discloses how these two critical landscapes frame an identity that is in a continual process of "becoming," as
they negotiate these two locations and their histories.

Campbell has produced two collections of poetry, *Naciendo* (Being
born, 1988) and *Rotundamente negra* (Absolutely black, 1994). *Naciendo* in
particular is a poetic exploration and vindication of a people's history. Her
first collection presents a youthful voice that wants to connect with her past
through a "return to origins," where she struggles to look to Limón as the
cultural center for Afro-Costa Ricans. It is an effort of a third-generation
Afro-Costa Rican, born in San José, to understand her relationship with
her native land through the cultural legacy left by previous generations and
the significance of Puerto Limón. She attempts "to connect her nationality
with her 'nation' and to the place venerated as the center of her Afro–Costa
Rican culture" (Mosby, 174). In the presentation of *Naciendo,* Campbell
declares:

> [the poetry] is for my people, who look at me with strange eyes asking
> me what right do I have to write about that which I have not lived, to
> which I respond that my poetry is only born of this urgent need to
> continue forward; of this necessity that history be justified before our
> untiring battle. (5)

Several of the poems in *Naciendo* confront the difficult position of reclaiming the past and reconciling the Costa Rican national identity with blackness. This double consciousness reveals the rejection by the dominant Hispanic culture and the exclusive sense of cultural authenticity of Afro–West Indian influences in Limón, which is distant and alienating for a younger generation that is much more Hispanized than its predecessors. In Campbell's poetic journey to Limón, "there is an incomplete fit in both cultural spaces and an uneven, slippery effort to straddle the two cultures. She is not clearly at home in either culture and truly negotiates the 'third space' not only for her poetic subject, but also for her generation's struggle with place, history and identity" (Mosby, 175). The tensions present are between the desire to understand her cultural identity by connecting her subject-self with the past, with Limón as the *patria chica*, or "little nation," of her people, and with her blackness, which marks her difference and "unbelongingness" in the national discourse.

In the "return to origins" poems in *Naciendo*, Limón is not always explicitly mentioned, but is understood symbolically as the poet-narrator makes a journey to the cultural center of her *pueblo* to understand her cultural legacy and her identity. In the opening poem, "De frente" (Facing forward), the poetic voice speaks of her quest to immerse herself in history. She announces, "I have returned / ready to scrub myself / of caresses with time / to reveal a life / soaked in kisses / and covered in misery" (9).[4] This return to the cultural home forces an encounter with the past and ultimately drives the poet-narrator to her own rebirth: "Today I return / to wipe clean the knees / of the past / to give myself cleansed / as if being born / facing my own entrails" (9).[5] The return to Puerto Limón as the home of Afro–Costa Rican culture is also a vindication of a history ignored by official accounts. The poet-narrator returns to symbolically deliver this history in the act of wiping clean the knees that represent its subjugation. In the process of remembrance and rebirth, the poet-narrator is able to cleanse herself of the negatives of the past and face herself and her heritage, "as if being born facing my own entrails." Instead of creating a "body as city" dynamic, the city remains in the background of the examination of the past, and history itself becomes embodied.

"Nosotros creemos en la humanidad" (We believe in humanity) continues the concern for history of the *pueblo* (people and town). The poetic voice powerfully states, "we will be heroes / without blood / with children / and with a country / we believe in the humanity / of this town / ours / that straddles the sea / and falls in love / with hope" (12).[6] The poet-narrator, through the use of the pronoun *we,* incorporates herself in the history of West Indian settlement in Limón and its role as part of the Costa Rican nation, "con hijos y con patria." She claims the city for her people, "este pueblo / el nuestro," which not only straddles the sea, but is also personified for its unyielding hope for the future.

There is a preoccupation for the condition and care of Limón as the symbolic center of Afro–Costa Rican culture. When Limón is degraded, there is a rally to protect the city and by extension Afro–Costa Rican cultural identity. Similar to the expression of the physical deterioration of Limón in Bernard's "Metamorfosis de tu recuerdo," Campbell expresses concern for the decay of the city in an untitled poem from *Naciendo:*

> We know
> your eyes sparkle more
> than the lights
> of all the railroads put together
> We know that your voice is higher
> than the summit of any mountain
> that your hand is greater
> than all hands together
> we know you are eternal
> and for that
> we will not allow them
> to continue
> sullying your face. (14)[7]

As in Bernard's poem, Limón is approached as a human entity with the use of *you* and *your.* The city is granted some larger-than-life qualities: "your eyes sparkle more / than the lights / of all the railroads put together." The motif of the train is a familiar one in Afro–Costa Rican literature, referring to the ever-present railroad that initially attracted West Indian laborers for its construction and later carried blacks to and from San José. The train represents the impact of West Indians on their new land and the process of nation building. The city is great, strong, and eternal because of its cultural importance, but it has been soiled and the poetic voice of the people will not allow this to continue. Like Bernard's "Deseo," there is a sense of agency to work for the salvation of the city because of its significance and its veneration as symbolic home. The repetition of the collective "we know" marks the passing of history and identity through the generations and stimulates the need to reconcile the proud past and the city's present.

In other poems about Limón there is also an important city-body connection. The city again is animated and given human characteristics in another untitled poem from *Naciendo*. The poetic subject forms a bond with the city through contact with her body:

In this town
even the stones vibrate
I have felt them
dance beneath my feet
I have felt them shout
in anger
and in happiness
opening furrows
in the earth
stirring beneath history
beneath firm skin
beating. (21)[8]

Contact with the city establishes a connection between the self and home as the point to claim one's origins. The land takes on the qualities of a living entity—the stones "vibrate" and "dance" and experience the human emotions of anger and happiness. The personification of the land reinforces the link connecting the subject-self to the town and its history. The land bears witness to history and is the storehouse of memory. Janet Jones Hampton observes that in this poem the "stones convey, through touch, sight, and sound, the dynamism of the community. Both the pain and joy of the community are expressed through this element of nature" (35). Once again, the land and identity are united in a homologous association where Limón is equated with Afro–Costa Rican identity.

There are again echoes of the "city as body" relationship in another untitled piece from *Naciendo*. The city is portrayed as a dilapidated and failing body that is in need of healing and salvation:

In the mornings
I suffer for being unable
to restore you
I twist and turn
over the same silence
and I suffer for being unable
to rebuild you
In the afternoons
I discover anew your canals

I return to measure your blood
and your borders
and again
I cannot protect you
In the evenings,
I kneel upon your roads
and I ask God
to see with his pain
and ours
if we can straighten anew
the backs of men. (50)[9]

The poet-narrator as agent admits that she cannot restore Limón, much like the weak and frail female body in Bernard's "Deseo." In Campbell's poetry, the poetic voice suffers along with her city in a cyclical pattern of suffering as the day progresses into night. The canals, borders, and roads mark the landscape of the city. The poetic voice hopes that she will be able to give it new life by straightening the stooped and burdened backs of the inhabitants of the city who labor for their mutual survival. *Naciendo* is a poetic connection with Afro–Costa Rican identity, a collective past, and the *pueblo* through Puerto Limón. The poetic return to origins produces not only a poetry that searches for a bond with the port city, but also one that clamors for the vindication of history and hopes for brotherhood and sisterhood among Costa Ricans of all colors in the fight for social justice.

Like her compatriot Shirley Campbell, Delia McDonald was born in 1965 and raised in San José. In her three collections of poetry, *El séptimo círculo del obelisco* (The seventh circle of the obelisk, 1994), *Sangre de madera* (Blood wood, 1995), and *La lluvia es una piel* (Rain is a skin, 1999), both Limón and San José appear as significant sites in the understanding of both an individual and a collective past. McDonald also makes a poetic "return to origins" in the three-part collection *La lluvia es una piel,* and her verse reflects a poetic tension between the two cities: one the physical home and the other the imagined—representative of her poetic subjects' relationship to the two sites. The first part features introspective poems on spirituality, which are continued in the third section, but it also contains several poignant poems that portray the social isolation of the black child in San José. The second part of *La lluvia es una piel* presents fragments of memories of travel to the coast and vignettes of daily life suspended in memory and in the written word. Images of the sea and of the train that used to run from San José to Limón dominate the poems with the smells, sounds, and sights of the landscape.

In the introduction to *Memory, Narrative, and Identity,* Amritjit Singh, Joseph Skerrett Jr., and Robert E. Hogan assert, "we 'remember' not only things that have actually happened to us personally, but also ... we 'remember' events, language, actions, attitudes and values that are aspects of our membership in groups" (17). In poem 13 from *La lluvia es una piel,* the remembrance of her family's migration to the capital is the central theme of the poem, but there is also the subtext of exclusion and difference. The poetic voice charts her position in the geography of Costa Rica, launched from the memory of her family's arrival in San José and her effort to claim place:

> We arrived in San José
> burdened with ceremonies and silences
> and we went to live in a neighborhood.
> My neighborhood is called México.
> Barrio México.
> And it is an avenue
> with plazas and whispers
> and with a great "X"
> that crosses the Paso de la Vaca
> and the area of the market, "El Líbano"
> and a row of equally silent multicolored houses equally silent.
> My house is in the center.
> It is the house of the
> "colored folk," the neighbors say,
> at the end of Sixteenth Street,
> and Eighth Avenue,
> diagonally across from Abonos Agro
> and 25 meters
> from Don Chalo's corner store. (29)[10]

The poet-narrator reconstructs her individual and family's memory through the creation of a map of San José and then plots the details: neighborhood (Barrio México) and its borders and landmarks (plazas, Paso de la Vaca, the market, Abonos Agro, Don Chalo's store). The poet-narrator carefully stakes her location in Barrio México, San José—signaling the physical location of her street and her house in the row of houses, which is the culminating point in her poetic cartography. In plotting the location of her home, she is also faced with being left out because of her family's ethnic and cultural difference. The poetic voice observes that for her white and mestizo neighbors, who define the ethnic "norm" of Costa Rican national identity, it is the house of the "colored folk."

In this cleverly designed poem, the poet-narrator addresses her small part of the capital by naming her place, situating her location within it at the center. Although she claims her home space and pinpoints it as the nucleus of her counterdiscursive map, she also remains on the periphery of the nation within this cartographic portrait. The subject, through this very personal memory, shares the collective experience of blacks in San José who are noted for their racially marked bodies in the heart of the dominant culture and are not fully embraced as true "Ticos." As she names her place within the core of the dominant culture, the poet-narrator also calls attention to her marginalization and isolation. She and her family are marked for their difference within the heart of the capital city.

Poem 25 in the same collection also follows the family's arrival in San José and further touches on the awareness of the sense of difference in San José. The poetic voice announces: "At home, / we are blacks / of paper and hallelujahs, and we hold on to voodoo and *makeatelyu* / in a basket with a top, / scared to listen / to the calls of the rest" (43).[11] In contrast to the neighbors who call her family "morenos de raza," or "colored folks," at home they call themselves black. However, instead of proudly displaying this ethnolinguistic difference, English and *makeatelyu*, the local Afro–Costa Rican expression for the Limonese Creole language ("make I tell you"), the family hides and guards it out of fear for what "they"—the members of the dominant culture—will say.

Memories of growing up and living in the capital are sometimes depicted with much pain, particularly the experience of being the only black child in a majority school with a staff that holds stereotyped ideas of the country's black citizenry. Poem 17 recalls the poet-narrator's memory of comments by school officials when her mother brought her to primary school for the first time:

> The girl's mother
> is a black woman
> with skin like a nocturnal rain
> of firewater and cinnamon.
> She came today and left her
> As if there weren't places for those people! (33)[12]

These verses serve as testimony to the treatment of difference in the capital and the devaluation of blackness. The teacher affirms the need for a separate space for "those people"; there is no place for them in the capital, in the school, or perhaps anywhere in the nation—another expression of collective and individual unbelonging.

The notion of unbelonging continues in the recollection of memories associated with school in San José. The additional memories of school are not positive ones, but experiences that provide fodder for a young poet's creativity:

> At six,
> I found myself in school.
> A howling prison,
> white and blue,
> blue and gray,
> stairs and mosaics of colors.
> My teacher,
> —is a sugar bowl—
> round and white,
> dressed always in green
> and red flowers above her ears,
> She,
> sat me in a corner
> and has a cat with golden suns
> on her back,
> —since then I hate them—
> And in my corner
> far from the white daughters
> always in rebellion
> and of course, I was already good
> collecting words. (30)[13]

In school in the capital city, the racially marked poetic subject learns that in the schools where the future citizens of the nation are educated, there is no place for her. The isolation the poetic voice experiences in the classroom populated by the students of the dominant culture reflects the exclusionary practices of the nation-state that marginalizes the racial other. The cultural and national authority in the form of the large teacher separates the Afro–Costa Rican subject from the white students in the class, enforcing the dominant discourse that favors whiteness. The colors of the poem, white, blue, and gray, are cold colors symbolizing the poetic subject's isolation, while the colors of the mosaic tile in contrast represent the multiple cultures and colors that actually form the nation. These circumstances of segregation and inequality produce rebellion in the poetic subject as she collects words to talk about herself and resist the dynamic established by the teacher enforcing the ideology of the dominant culture. The poetic voice is determined to make a space for herself in the classroom, in the city, and in the nation by empowering herself with the word to challenge the dominant culture from the inside.

The poems in *La lluvia es una piel* that specifically depict Limón are largely based on memory. McDonald links the collective memory of Afro-Costa Ricans with the place that is associated with efforts to unify black identity in Costa Rica with Puerto Limón and the Caribbean province. The poet invokes memories through childhood and adult recollections of the sea, the train, the geography of the coast, the city of Puerto Limón, and small towns that dot the shoreline. There is a clear effort to link her generation with its cultural roots: "On vacation we would go to Limón / in the middle, a rabble of colors; / and the sun, / with a hat of coconut palm, would reach us on the low curves" (49).[14] In another untitled poem, McDonald paints a lighthearted, folkloric portrayal of the festive journey of blacks who live in the capital (black *chepines*) to Limón on the train: "Each stop is a calypso dance, the black *chepines* / we are happy with our / celebration of smiles, / and the vendors board the train / barking their wares" (58).[15] In a poem titled "Limón," the poetic voice engages in an effort to build the city, not with blocks of cement and mortar, but "with fragments of sand." The poetic voice proclaims: "I build you slowly / with fragments of sand. / Sea within / the architecture / of coral I build you" (61).[16]

The tone in the verses about Limón does not engage with the city on the same level as Bernard or Campbell, or as profoundly as in McDonald's poems about San José. Her treatment of Limón is not a voice of protest or agency, but a collection of individual and collective memories, a journey to cultural origins of the imagination that are retained and pieced together like fragments of cloth in a quilt. The act of remembering validates a marginalized experience. According to Terry DeHay, "remembering is the process of reclaiming and protecting a past often suppressed by the dominant culture, and in this sense, as re-visioning, it is essential in the process of gaining control over one's life" (44). By turning her focus to a memory framed within the port city, McDonald performs a "double act" that destabilizes the position of the dominant discourse on ethnic and gender difference. She conducts what Stuart Hall describes as "an act of cultural recovery," deploying memory against a national rhetoric that negates the significance of a minority culture. Memory is a considerable part of her quest to discover self, community, and identity.

In the poetry by Afro–Costa Rican women, Limón is presented as a real site, as an ideal place, and as an imaginary space. Limón resonates with a certain attachment to cultural "authenticity" or legitimacy, marking the "black capital" as symbolic home for Afro–Costa Rican identity. Blackness in Costa Rica is necessarily located in Limón and this relationship between place and subject produces and reinforces identity through an understanding of history and what the city signifies. The "white capital," San José, finds the construction of its national identity challenged from within by the two younger poets, especially in the work of Delia McDonald. The veracity of the carefully constructed *leyenda blanca* is weakened by the counterdiscursive project that claims its place in San José and centers the Afro–Costa Rican historical experience. Bernard, Campbell, and McDonald validate this cultural specificity through memories, both individual and collective, in a poetic return to origins. Eulalia Bernard conserves the Afro-Caribbean cultural past of Limón in her poetry, while the younger poets display a greater tension between their efforts to reclaim the historical "old home" of Limón and their place in the "new home," San José. The poetic representation of these two urban centers by two different generations of writers illustrates the negotiation of Afro–Costa Rican cultural identity as subjects respond to the transformation of place and engage with the past of West Indian migration.

NOTES

1. West Indian migration was continuous from 1872 to the 1930s, with a decline thereafter until it appears to eventually stop altogether in the 1950s owing to greater West Indian immigration to Panama, England, Canada, and the United States. There is little data that provides accurate figures on the numbers of West Indians who migrated to Costa Rica. See Ronald Harpelle, *The West Indians of Costa Rica: Race, Class, and the Integration of an Ethnic Minority* (Quebec: McGill-Queen's University Press, 2001), and Trevor Purcell, *Banana Fallout: Class, Color, and Culture among West Indians in Costa Rica* (Los Angeles: UCLA Center for Afro-American Studies, 1993) for information on the collection of immigration data and the inaccuracy of the official records. Currently, there is a new emigration trend as Afro-Costa Ricans leave for the United States, Canada, and Europe for better economic and professional opportunities.

2. The term *leyenda blanca* comes from the *Historical Dictionary of Costa Rica* by Theodore S. Creedman (x).

3. Although no written law has been found in the country's statutes, Afro–West Indian residents of Limón could travel to San José for business, to purchase goods, and for medical treatment, but were "prohibited" from remaining in the city for more than seventy-two hours. This appears to be more of a practice of convention because of affinities with Limón. This is documented by several sources, including *El negro en Costa Rica* by Carlos Meléndez and Quince Duncan, and it is also in the historical record that a few families of West Indian descent settled in San José and the Central Valley in the late nineteenth and early twentieth centuries because they were in the employ of British families.

4. "He vuelto / dispuesta a restregarme / de caricias con el tiempo / a descalzarla vida / empapada en besos / y calzada en miseria."

5. "Hoy regreso / para limpiar las rodillas / al pasado / para entregarme limpia / como naciendo / frente a mis entrañas."

6. "seremos héroes / sin sangre / con hijos / y con patria / creemos en la humanidad / en este pueblo / el nuestro / que cabalga sobre el mar / y se enamora / de la esperanza."

7. "Nosotros lo sabemos / tus ojos brillan más / que las luces / de todos los ferrocarriles juntos / Sabemos que tu voz es más alta / que la cumbre de cualquier montaña / que tu mano es más grande / que todas las manos juntas / te sabemos eterno / y por eso / no vamos a permitir / que te sigan / ensuciando el rostro."

8. "En este pueblo / hasta las piedras vibran / las he sentido / danzar bajo mis pies / las he sentido gritar / de ira / y de felicidad / abriendo surcos / en la tierra / hurgando bajo la historia / bajo la piel firme / latiendo."

9. "Por las mañanas / sufro por no poder / restaurarte / me retuerzo y doy vueltas / sobre el mismo silencio / y sufro por no poder / reconstruirte / Por las tardes / averiguo de nuevo tus canales / vuelvo a medir tu sangre / y tus fronteras / y otra vez / no puedo armarte / Por las noches / me arrodillo sobre tus caminos / y le consulto a Dios / a ver si con su dolor / y el nuestro / podemos erguir de nuevo / las espaldas de los hombres."

10. "Nosotros llegamos a San José / cargados de ceremonias y silencios / y nos fuimos a vivir a un barrio. / Mi barrio se llama México. / Barrio México. / Y es una avenida / con plazas y murmullos / y con una gran equis / que atraviesa el Paso de la Vaca / y los alrededores del mercado, el Líbano / y una fila de casitas multicolores igualmente silenciosas. / Mi casa está en el centro. / Es la casa de los / "morenos de raza," dicen los vecinos, / a la salida de la calle 16, / avenida ocho, / diagonal a Abonos Agro / y a 25 metros / de la pulpería de don Chalo."

11. "En casa / los negros somos / de papel y aleluyas y guardamos el vudú y el makeatelyu / en una canasta con sombrero / con miedo de escuchar / los llamados de los demás."

12. "La madre de la niña / es una negra / con la piel como una lluvia nocturna

/ de aguardiente y canela. / Vino hoy y la dejó / ¡Como si no existieran lugares /
para esa gente!"

13. "A los seis años, / me encontró la escuela. / Una galera aullante, / blanca y
azul, / azul y gris, / escaleras y mosaicos de colores. / Mi maestra, / —es una azu-
carera— / redonda y blanca, / vestida siempre de verde / y florecitas rojas sobre las
orejas, / Ella, / me sentaba en una esquina / y tiene un gato con soles dorados /
sobre el lomo, / —desde entonces los odio— / Y en mi rincón / lejos de sus hijas
blancas / yo siempre en rebeldía / y por supuesto, ya era buena / coleccionando
palabras."

14. "En vacaciones íbamos a Limón / en medio, una algarabía de colores; / y el
sol, / con un sombrero de cocoteros, nos alcanzaba en las curvas bajas."

15. "Cada parada es un baile de calipsos, los negros chepines / estamos alegres
con nuestra / fiesta de sonrisas, / y al tren suben los vendedores / atropellando los
anuncios."

16. "te construyo lentamente / con fragmentos de arena. / Mar adentro / la
arquitectura / del coral te construyo."

WORKS CITED

Bernard, Eulalia. *Ciénaga/Marsh.* San José: Asesores Editoriales, 2001.

———. *Griot.* San José: Seventh-Day Adventist Youth Society, 1996.

———. *My Black King.* Eugene, Ore.: Peace Press, 1991.

———. *Negritud.* Sound recording. INDICA, 1976.

———. *Ritmohéroe.* 2d ed. San José: Editorial Costa Rica, 1996.

Campbell Barr, Shirley. *Naciendo.* San José: Editorial Universidad Estatal a Distancia, 1988.

———. *Rotundamente Negra.* San José: Arado, 1994.

Creedman, Theodore S. *Historical Dictionary of Costa Rica.* Metuchen, N.J.: Scare-
crow, 1977.

DeHay, Terry. "Rereading Photographs and Narratives in Ethnic Autobiography:
Memory and Subjectivity in Mary Antin's *The Promised Land.*" In Singh, Skerrett, and Hogan, 26–44.

Hall, Stuart. "Cultural Identity and Cinematic Representation." *Framework* 36
(1989): 68–81.

Hampton, Janet Jones. "Portraits of a Diasporan People: The Poetry of a Shirley
Campbell and Rita Dove." *Afro-Hispanic Review* 14 (spring 1995): 33–39.

McDonald Woolery, Delia. *El séptimo círculo el obelisco.* San José: Ediciones del
Café, 1994.

———. *La lluvia es una piel.* San José: Ministerio de Cultura, Juventud y Deportes,
1999.

———. *Sangre de Madera.* San José: Ediciones del Café, 1995.

McKinney, Kitzie. "Costa Rica's Black Body: The Politics and Poetics of Difference in Eulalia Bernard's Poetics." *Afro-Hispanic Review* 15.2 (fall 1996): 11–20.

Meléndez Chaverri, Carlos, and Quince Duncan Moodie. 10th ed. *El negro en Costa Rica.* San José: Editorial Costa Rica, 1993.

Mosby, Dorothy E. *Place, Language, and Identity in Afro–Costa Rican Literature.* Columbia: University of Missouri Press, 2003.

Rosaldo, Renato. "Cultural Citizenship, Inequality, and Multiculturalism." In *Race, Identity, and Citizenship: A Reader,* ed. Rodolfo Torres, Louis F. Mirón, and Jonathan Xavier Inda. Malden, Mass.: Blackwell, 1999. 253–61.

Singh, Amritjit, Joseph Skerrett Jr., and Robert E. Hogan, eds. Introduction. In *Memory, Narrative, and Identity: New Essays in Ethnic American Literature.* Boston: Northeastern University Press, 1994. 3–25.

10
Urban Legends

Tina Modotti and Angelina Beloff
as *Flâneuses* in Elena Poniatowska's
Mexico City

ELISABETH GUERRERO

A city is a spiritual value, a collective physiognomy, a persistent and creative character. . . . To form "cities," cities with complete awareness of themselves, and color of customs, and seal of culture, should be one of the terms of our development.

José Enrique Rodó[1]

For half a century, Elena Poniatowska's urban chronicles, fiction, and testimonial collages have documented the tremendous transformations of Mexico City into what is today a megalopolis with 25 million inhabitants. In Poniatowska's writings, the capital city beckons prospective residents with its cultural richness and potential work opportunities. Nevertheless, the Mexican writer problematizes the city's allure, exposing the urban center as one that can be brutal to those who attempt to reserve a space for themselves within the cosmopolitan milieu.[2] This essay explores how the prominent Mexican intellectual turns a gaze both benevolent and critical upon the metropolitan heart of Mexico, pointing out its flaws even as she celebrates the courage of its inhabitants, particularly that of the socially marginal and of the artistic elite.

To theorize the work of Poniatowska, I turn to the figure of the *flâneur,* one who ambles through the city and then turns home to pick up the pen or paintbrush to represent what he has surveyed. This essay explores Poniatowska's approach to the *flâneuse,* or woman urban stroller-artist; for the writer, the *flâneuse* of the twentieth and twenty-first centuries takes a position of solidarity with the populace. This ethic of social justice is apparent in both Poniatowska's chronicles and her novels. Furthermore, the novelist and essayist writes with a feminist awareness that celebrates the lives of women artists and particularly explores the status of fellow foreign-born women in Mexico; the Italian protagonist of the novel *Tinísima* (1992) and the Russian main character of *Querido Diego, te abraza Quiela* (*Dear Diego,* 1978), correspond to Poniatowska's prototype of the *flâneuse.*

The concept of the *flâneur* and the leitmotif of the ragpicker provide critical tools for theorizing Poniatowska's urban chronicles as well as her novels *Querido Diego* and *Tinísima.* Walter Benjamin gathered the term *flâneur* to discuss the oeuvre of Charles Baudelaire, a poet of modernity who wandered through nineteenth-century Parisian avenues and wrote about the spectacle of urban life. Baudelaire sketched a portrait of the *flâneur* in his essay on the etchings of Constantin Guys. For the poet, Guys was the prototype of the *flâneur,* a painter of the transitory nature of modern city life. Various critics have described Baudelaire's *flâneur* as a privileged masculine figure who stands apart from the happenings that he surveys. For example, in his study *Divergent Modernities: Culture and Politics in Nineteenth-Century Latin America,* Julio Ramos describes the Latin American nineteenth-century rambler as a cosmopolitan subject resembling the Baudelairean artist, a *flâneur* who scrutinizes his environs from a distant elitist gaze: "In strolling, the urban, privatized subject approximates the city with a gaze from which s/he sees an object on exhibit."[3] Nevertheless, Baudelaire's verses also represent the female waifs and strays that Benjamin gathers in his analysis as well, figures such as the prostitute, the widow, the elderly woman, and the ragpicker, vagabonds who amble through the urban landscape. The ragpicker, gathering the detritus of the city, offers a particularly adequate metaphor for transforming the *flâneur* into Poniatowska's version of the *flâneuse.* Whereas Benjamin makes use of the Baudelairean *flâneur* in order to interpret urban modernity, we will see how the cosmopolitan writer Poniatowska's placement in the modern city of the *flâneuses* Tina Modotti and Angelina Beloff entails a social and feminist awareness.

Several feminist theorists have argued that Baudelaire's and Benjamin's *flâneur* is exclusively a masculine figure. According to Janet Wolff and Griselda Pollock, the life of a *flâneuse* was not possible during the nineteenth and twentieth centuries; limited to private space, the woman artist could not enjoy the freedom and privilege of leisurely exploring the city streets to observe and portray modern life. Thus their works tended to be more intimate and less public, as are, for example, Frida Kahlo's self-portraits in contrast to Diego Rivera's murals. Nevertheless, Deborah Parsons maintains that the allegorical figure of the ragpicker opens the door to the *flâneuse* in critical theory. Like the *pepenadores* (trash pickers) who gather rubbish in Mexico City's garbage dumps, the ragpicker is a marginal figure who empathizes with the populace while he gathers stories from the dispersed fragments amid the urban space. Although his movement through the city is neither as leisurely nor as secure as that of the traditional *flâneur,* the flexibility of the Benjaminian figure of the ragpicker as *flâneur* permits its use as a critical metaphor for a woman or a man who beholds and writes about the fragmentary nature of modernity or even of the global cities of advanced capitalism.

With this in mind, the trope of the *flâneur* of modernity continues to be a useful critical tool for examining urban postmodernity. Following his study of Baudelaire, Benjamin continues his exploration of *flânerie* in his Arcades Project, a literary collage of observations about modernity taken from his strolls through the streets of Paris and Berlin. Although Benjamin predicted the demise of *flânerie* with the disappearance of the Parisian arcades, for many critics the *flâneur* remains a relevant metaphor for the urban artist who transits the city today. As Keith Tester explains, "the figure and the activity [of the *flâneur*] appear regularly in the attempts of social and cultural commentators to get some grip on the nature and implications of modernity and postmodernity" (1). The Benjaminian *flâneur* has become the stroller of our times; rather than ambling down the avenue, today's *flâneur* rambles through the postmodern spaces of the shopping mall and the Internet, spaces of the simulacrum that Jean Baudrillard has described (*Simulacra and Simulation*).

The challenge that the postmodern *flâneur* confronts is to not become lost in this simulacrum. Néstor García Canclini remarks: "To narrate is to know that the orderly experience that the *flâneur* expected upon strolling through the city at the turn of the century is no longer possible. Now the city is like a video clip: effervescent montage of discontinuous images."[4] In this age of globalization and communicative technology, urban cartography extends beyond its limits. For Baudrillard, the postmodern experience is a simulation that weakens the possibility of any real political action on the part of civil society. However, Poniatowska does not appear to be in agreement. Instead, the critical pedagogy theorist Peter McLaren offers a more apt vision for Poniatowska's work: a vision of the city stroller with a social conscience. McLaren imagines today's *flâneur* as an urban ethnographer who must respond to global consumerism with a critical awareness:

"for me the figure of the *flâneur/flâneuse* embodies an attempt in urban settings to live within the blurred and vertiginous strategies of representation and the shifting discourses of capitalism's marketing strategies and mechanisms and merge [yet not fuse] with them" (144). Drawing from McLaren, I propose that in her chronicles and urban novels, Poniatowska responds to the challenges of advanced capitalism with the critical perspective that the theorist describes, a social justice stance and, I would add, a feminist stance. The Mexican writer's new paradigm of the walking artist is one who does not distance herself from the common public, nor is lost in the crowd, but rather who seeks to join with the populace in a gesture of solidarity.

Drawing from this feminist awareness, Poniatowska's work focuses on two principal groups: people of limited economic resources and women artists. In fact, for Poniatowska, these two groups are fundamentally linked. As literary critic Anadeli Bencomo notes, "On repeated occasions, the Mexican writer links the feminist character of her work with the conditions of thousands of Mexicans who lack power."[5] Poniatowska proposes a utopic vision in which the work of writers and artists with a social conscience can annul the silence of the poor:

> Women's literature today must come as part of the great flow of literature of the oppressed, of the landless, of the poor, those who have no voice, those who do not know how to read or write. . . . Now, in that great silence, in that powerful Latin American silence, there is dawning not a literature of intimate confession or "love is tears" but rather a literature of existence and denunciation. (Cited in Bencomo, 95)[6]

For this reason, Poniatowska is interested principally in subaltern groups and in women writers, painters, and photographers, and she narrates the challenges that these populations face upon seeking a safe home in the megalopolis that is Mexico City today.

The writer began her career as a journalist with a series of interviews and columns in the society section of *Excélsior* in 1953. Further along in her career, as a response to the events of 1968 when the Gustavo Díaz Ordaz government ordered the shooting of hundreds of students who were protesting in the Plaza de Tlatelolco, Poniatowska initiated a wave of New Journalism in Mexico.[7] Her groundbreaking *La noche de Tlatelolco* (1971) is a collage of testimonies of the event. This polyphonic and fragmented work reflects the tragedy of 1968 amid urban chaos; in this manner the work corresponds with the Benjaminian leitmotif of the ragpicker who gathers the detritus of society. Following *La noche de Tlatelolco,* Poniatowska's chronicles have continued to collect the voices of those who are socially scorned, such as domestic workers, seamstresses, and characters like Jesusa Palancares, a woman who labors to survive in the social underworld in the testimonial novel *Hasta no verte, Jesús mío* (*Here's to You, Jesusa!* 1969).

It is important to recognize that although Poniatowska's writings signal the social injustices of the Mexican polis, she does not present her characters as victims; rather, she focuses on their capacity to defend their interests against the odds. Jean Franco points out that Poniatowska utilizes the testimonial genre to emphasize the power of the individual in civil society, or what Franco calls popular agency:

> Poniatowska has consistently amplified the testimonial genre by converting it into fiction and by incorporating many testimonials into a chronicle of a single event. This corresponds to a recurrent theme of "popular agency," that is, the potentiality of ordinary people (the young people of *La noche de Tlatelolco,* the earthquake survivors of *Nada, nadie*) to act on their own behalf. (72)

In fact, to underscore the possibilities for the popular classes to transform Mexico City, Poniatowska constantly dialogues in her work with the voices of individuals from diverse social sectors. For the literary critic Beth Jörgensen, dialogue is the element that stands out most in Poniatowska's writing; this is "the dialogue that she has actively sought, first from a position of cultural outsider, and then from a position of increased cultural rootedness and authority within Mexico" (xix).

Following the publication of *La noche de Tlatelolco* Poniatowska continued to incorporate the multiple voices and social solidarity that Jörgensen describes, first with another testimonial volume, *Fuerte es el silencio* (1980), which addresses the hunger strike of the mothers of disappeared youth, and with *Nada, nadie. Las voces del temblor* (1987), which documents the 1985 earthquake that devastated Mexico City. As a number of critics have observed, among them Franco and Carlos Monsiváis, Poniatowska celebrates the promise of civil society in her chronicles; in *Nada, nadie (Nothing, Nobody),* for example, she notes that when the state interferes with both human rescue efforts and the contributed funds designated for recovery, the citizens themselves take charge. As García Canclini has observed, small social groups within the urban space today replace greater entities such as social class or even the nation. The testimonial voice of a physician in Poniatowska's *Nada, nadie* makes this distinction between the state and the people, declaring that although the national government falters, the people of Mexico do not: "I would think that the old inferiority complex that Mexicans have should be completely questioned. We are not incompetent. What is incompetent is the system that we live in. The earthquake proved to us that when we work together, we do a good job" (172).[8] In this manner, Poniatowska's writings indicate dissatisfaction with the Mexican government even as they express respect for the citizens of Mexico.

Following *Nada, nadie,* Poniatowska has published several additional collections of prose with a social and feminist bent; for example, in her collection *Luz y luna, las lunitas* (1994), the essay on domestic workers, "Se necesita muchacha," laments illiteracy and describes scenes of poverty. Also of interest is the recent chronicle *Las mil y una... (la herida de Paulina)* (2000), which documents the case of Paulina, a fifteen-year-old girl who became pregnant after being raped by an intruder. Although the ministry of health authorized an abortion, hospital staff in Mexicali refused to carry out the procedure and Paulina had the baby. In the text, Poniatowska expresses her concern for the tenuous civil state under the strengthened presence of the staunchly Catholic PAN (the National Action Party), and commends the child's bravery for publicly denouncing her rapist. Poniatowska explains in the book that she writes works such as these because she identifies with the less powerful, adding that although she does not lay claim to any absolute truths, the process of writing assists her in reckoning difficult social questions: "If I became a journalist it's because I've only had questions, never certainties. What I am sure of are my intentions. . . . I quickly discovered minorities and identified with them. They are my legion."[9] Faithful to the Poniatowskanian tradition, her chronicle seeks to indicate solidarity with the subaltern. In this sense, her writings comply with McLaren's suggestions for the postmodern *flâneur,* a figure who responds with a critical awareness to the consumerism that burdens urban centers today.

In addition to her urban chronicles, Poniatowska scrutinizes the urban environment and questions social inequalities in her novels as well. I can't fail to mention the acclaimed testimonial novel *Hasta no verte, Jesús mío,* based on her interviews with a tough-talking elderly woman who had survived abuse, poverty, and the tumult of the revolution of 1910–17. The Jesusa Palancares who narrates the text has many trades: *soldadera* (woman soldier or companion of the revolutionaries), waitress, washerwoman, healer, and also oral historian, as she regales the listener with her thoughts and experiences. Poniatowska draws together these monologues in *Hasta no verte, Jesús mío.*

In the text, the character Jesusa recognizes the difficulty for a woman to move freely through the city: "It'd be better for all women to be men, for sure, because it's more fun, you're freer, and no one makes fun of you" (191).[10] The narrator explains that whether young or old, a poor woman alone must struggle for respect; a young woman is at risk of sexual harassment, while an elderly woman faces mockery. Furthermore, she recalls that, when younger, if she were to go out dancing and it grew late, she was obliged to avoid the police, who saw her not as one to save from harm but rather one from whom to protect society: "A woman couldn't be out at all hours back then. I don't remember who was president—I think it was Obregón—and he decreed that any woman who was on the street at nine o'clock at night would be taken to jail" (194).[11] In the testimonial novel, Jesusa, a poor woman alone, pays a price for daring to survive and to move freely in the Mexican capital city.

The combination of social consciousness and urban focus found in *Hasta no verte, Jesús mío* is incorporated throughout Poniatowksa's fiction. More recent novels worth mentioning include, for example, the winner of the 2001 Premio Alfaguara *La piel del cielo,* which addresses the life of a Mexican astronomer, and *Paseo de la Reforma* (1996), which takes place in the Distrito Federal in the mid-twentieth century. For the purposes of this essay, I focus on two novels about woman artists; the first wife of Diego Rivera, the Russian painter Angelina Beloff, narrates the epistolary novel *Querido Diego, te abraza Quiela,* and the Italian photographer and activist Tina Modotti protagonizes the biographical novel *Tinísima.* The two live their most productive years as artists during the 1920s. Poniatowska's narratives indicate that in this moment of social transition after the First World War and the Mexican Revolution, Modotti and Beloff face their new roles as *flâneuses* or urban artists with ambivalence. As feminist geographer Doreen Massey points out, the modern city-space of the nineteenth and twentieth centuries is gendered; unlike a man, a woman cannot be lost in the anonymity of a crowd. However, Poniatowska does not interpret this difference as defeat; instead, she constructs a *flâneuse* who identifies with the crowd. The gaze of Poniatowska's *flâneuses* is one of solidarity, not distance. Furthermore, although the main characters depend on the approval of their husbands and mentors, and the vicissitudes of life create many lapses in their artistic careers, in both novels there are moments of inspiration, passion, and perseverance. In fact, Poniatowska represents Mexico City as the place of greatest artistic inspiration for the two protagonists.

The historical figure Angelina Beloff, or Quiela, lived for ten years with Rivera in Paris during the trying postwar period; there the talented Russian painter suffered hunger, isolation, the death of her infant son, and Rivera's desertion. In the novel *Querido Diego,* Quiela responds with ambivalence to these troubles; a figure who bridges two eras, Quiela alternates between activity and passivity. In part she is a self-abnegating woman devoted to Rivera, who tolerates his infidelities and awaits him patiently. On the other hand, Beloff boasts of her ability to take care of herself alone and to have a trade, and there are luminous moments in the novel when she demonstrates her own passion for art. This spark ignites during her early studies in Saint Petersburg; she recalls with delight her walks home alone in the evenings after painting class, her father's pride in her scholarship at the academy, and her intense enjoyment in learning her trade: mixing the colors, sketching day and night. Even as the character yearns for her two lost Diegos, the deceased baby and the distant Rivera, her artistic spark ignites again in Paris when she visits museums, strolls down the boulevard, and returns home to paint:

> When I got home I began to paint passionately . . . I sat down in front of your easel and removed the canvas you left half done . . . and I took out a clean canvas and began. It is impossible to be devoid of talent when you have the kind of revelations I had yesterday. I eagerly painted the head of a woman I saw in the street when I was returning from the Louvre, a woman with splendid eyes, and now that the light is gone I am writing to you about the commotion and my happiness. (18)[12]

In this manner, Poniatowska represents Beloff as a *flâneuse,* making transit through the urban geography and creating works of art to represent the people of the metropolis.

Poniatowska's Beloff is a product of her times, a talented artist who alternates between ability and passion, on the one hand, and fragility and humiliation, on the other. To give an example, Beloff accepts the pesos that Rivera sends (with no letters) and writes that she could come live with him in Mexico, reminding him that she never interfered with his work and even sent their severely ill infant out of the apartment so that he would not distract Rivera with his cries. Yet on the very next page, she takes pride in her autonomy: "The greatest source of satisfaction in my life has been the fact that I achieved economic independence, and I am proud of being one of the most advanced women of my time. Even when I was expelled from the Academy of Fine Arts for participating in the student strike, my parents did not lose faith in me" (80).[13] Her passion for art and social justice continues despite the obstacles that she has faced, and the city that she most wants to know and paint is now Mexico City. "I feel Mexican (64),"[14] she declares to Rivera in one of her unanswered letters, and when she finally comprehends that the great muralist will not return for her. Poniatowska's postscript in the novel explains that the Russian painter decides to make Mexico her homeland without Rivera, and that she travels there to live and to paint alone.

The Italian photographer Tina Modotti also figures in Poniatowska's writings, in the biographical novel *Tinísima*. In contrast with the more intimate work of Beloff, Modotti's photographs incorporate a social awareness, celebrating *la mexicanidad* (mexicanness) even as they deplore injustices against indigenous people, the poor, and the working class. In this sense, Poniatowska makes good use of Modotti as a *flâneuse* with a social conscience. In the novel, Modotti adores Mexico City, but Mexico will betray her. The challenge that Modotti faces as an artist is to extend her gaze, walk freely through the city streets, and capture on film what she sees without interference because of her gender, her foreignness, or her evident sensuality. Whereas Baudelaire's *flâneur*'s gaze is often erotic, looking upon the women of the brothels or *folies* with desire or disgust, Modotti as *flâneuse* must struggle to see rather than be seen. The character loses the battle to become more than the object of the public's eye; her sensualized and sensationalized role as an artist's model and an exotic and politically suspicious foreigner makes it impossible for her to disappear from society's gaze until it is too late.

It is crucial to point out the illustrations that Poniatowska includes in *Tinísima*, because they celebrate the Italian artist's sexuality even as they indicate her indisputable talent. Alongside journalistic images that document the sociopolitical surroundings of the 1920s and 1930s, there are works of her husband, the photographer Edward Weston, and of her comrade, the muralist Diego Rivera, works that portray Tina as a sensuous nude with luminous skin. Simultaneously, Modotti's own photographic works show her particular vision of Mexico, a contradictory place filled with beauty and yet with social injustice. In "Elegance and Poverty," Modotti's lens contrasts the region's extremes of wealth and penury, capturing a moment of irony when a weary worker sits to rest in the street. Behind him stands a billboard displaying a gentleman dressed in a tuxedo; the advertisement reads, "We have everything a gentleman needs to dress elegantly from head to toe" (112).[15] Other photographs by Modotti combine technical and aesthetic efforts together with the tenderness of her gaze; they capture, for example, the face of her murdered lover, the calloused hands of a manual laborer, and several photos of the curved and illuminated silhouette of a plant or a flower, images that recall the paintings of her contemporary Georgia O'Keeffe.

In the novel, Poniatowska indicates that for a time Modotti lives happily in Mexico. The photographer finds herself inspired by the people, the artisans' wares, and the vivid colors; she is supported by her mentor and husband Weston and her work is celebrated by enthusiasts. When Weston teaches her the art of taking and developing a shot, she experiences a rush of creative energy: "Edward had placed within her grasp the elements of discovery: the silver plates, the celluloid, the emulsion, and the light, elements that could be turned upon herself or that she could turn upon the world" (89).[16] The young Modotti feels fully realized as an artist when she is surrounded by the graces of the capital city: "Did you notice, Eduardito, that the girls sweep and wash down the sidewalk before the sun rises? Each person cleans his own little piece of the city. Isn't this a fair distribution of beauty? In Mexico every stone is alive, it speaks. I am going to make a place for myself in this land" (70).[17] Modotti enthuses that Mexico has called her to realize her highest potential as an artist and as a human being: "Edward, I feel as if I have been reborn" (72).[18] When a friend warns her to curb her enthusiasm, she denies that Mexico could betray her: "Mexico belongs to whoever conquers it. I was born for Mexico. Mexico is mine; I am from Mexico" (72).[19]

Nevertheless, some time after Weston, now her ex-husband, has left for California, tragedy comes upon her when her lover, the Cuban activist Julio Antonio Mella, is assassinated, and in the novel Mexico does indeed betray her. Stemming from the murder of her companion and from her association with the socialist movement, the Italian photographer is attacked by the press and the government. Poniatowska expresses in the novel the evidence that she found in the historical archives; amid the nationalism and masculinism of the postrevolutionary period, the newspapers and the court not only suspected Modotti's politics and her foreign status but also assailed her for her sensuality and her liberty as a woman artist. In the court, "Suddenly, Tina is not a photographer. She is nobody except a family name that is spelled out with disgust, every letter underlining the fact that she is a for-eign-er and therefore prohibited from getting involved in Mexican politics" (16).[20] The headlines call her "Mata Hari" and take pains to describe her clothing, her body, her "licentious" lifestyle, her "artist's den." Although Diego Rivera comes to her aid, Modotti is judged as a conspirator and is expelled from Mexico. Tragically, in Europe she abandons art and sets her sights on militancy; nevertheless, her life does not cease to be remarkable. *Tinísima* traces Modotti's trajectory in Germany and the Soviet Union, where she turns to espionage; later, in Spain during the civil war, she works as a nurse.

Aged by her experiences, Poniatowska's character Modotti returns to Mexico and this time, like Angelina Beloff, she goes unrecognized. The Italian photographer opines that Mexico has changed for the worse; the great muralists no longer predominate, and now there are more cars than people in the streets. Furthermore, she recalls how Mexican society had disparaged her in the court and in the newspapers in 1929, and is horrified by the degradation of women: "In Mexico, women are held in contempt; they are consumed, ripped apart, stigmatized, hung by their necks on the patriarchal tree and left to swing, their tongues hanging out and their sex in the air" (322).[21] For this reason, Modotti welcomes getting old, as with this change she escapes from detection and vindictive judgments: "Blessed, then, blessed voyage nearing its end" (ibid.).[22] Shortly following her return to Mexico, the photographer and activist dies of a heart attack.

In this manner, Poniatowska's narratives present a certain disillusionment with the possibilities open for women artists, particularly for foreign-born women in the Mexico of Beloff and Modotti. Just as rural citizens are seduced by the image of a consumerist utopia and the promised land of urbanism, the women artists in Poniatowska's work also seek paradise in the capital city, and they too learn that the urban utopia does not exist. Poniatowska explains:

> Though a rural shack, however humble, may seem better to us than a
> proletarian slum, those who come from the countryside still believe
> in the benevolence of the great city that one day will give them what
> the land hasn't: the lottery, radio and TV prizes, songs dedicated to
> *mamacita* because today's her birthday, the domestic appliances
> that Pelayo hands out, the photo-illustrated dime novels of crime and
> romance.[23]

While rural residents seek a better life in the city, Angelina Beloff and Tina Modotti travel to Mexico City in hopes of discovering the charms of Mexico and the sophistication of the city, an intellectually stimulating life, inspiration for their art, and perhaps even critical acclaim and economic security. In contrast to these aspirations, *Querido Diego* portrays the abandonment, the isolation, and the abnegation of Beloff, while *Tinísima* narrates vehement attacks by the press and the early death of Modotti. In this fashion, Poniatowska signals the obstacles that have impeded women artists (particularly openly sensual ones such as Modotti) from fully achieving liberty to survey the streets and record their particular versions of urban history. Nevertheless, Poniatowska also honors the opportunities that her characters benefit from as *flâneuses*. We have seen that in the two novels there are moments of individual and artistic liberty when the Italian photographer and the Russian painter transit through the city and achieve transcendent works of art. Through the narratives of Poniatowska, their works and lives endure.

The protagonists of *Querido Diego* and *Tinísima* are beings who navigate the urban space as women and as artists, who not only wish to observe but rather who aim to transform their vision into a work of art. For this reason, it has been of special interest how Poniatowska explores and portrays their experiences as *flâneuses* of modernity, as seen from Poniatowska's vantage of postmodernity. In addition to the two novels studied here, Poniatowska's urban chronicles offer a new paradigm of the strolling artist who depicts our era of advanced capitalism and globalization in the Mexican megalopolis. Despite Poniatowska's privileged background, I agree with Judy Maloof's comment on the writer's daring choice of topics and narrative voices: "It is important to underscore that Poniatowska is a woman of remarkable courage who does not hesitate to publish criticism of the Mexican government" (149). Without a doubt, Poniatowska's literary vision is one of a *flâneuse* with a social conscience, walking down the city streets, focusing her gaze upon the life of its inhabitants, and creating works that transmit the scenes that she surveys, scenes of poverty, oppression, and suffering, but also ripe with possibility and even splendor.

NOTES

Translations are mine where English translations were not available and are not listed in the bibliography.

1. "Una ciudad es un valor espiritual, una fisonomía colectiva, un carácter persistente y creador... Formar 'ciudades', ciudades con entera conciencia de sí propias, y color de costumbres, y sello de cultura, debe ser uno de los términos de nuestro desenvolvimiento."

2. Poniatowska was born in Paris (1932) of Polish-Mexican origin, but at the age of ten she moved to Mexico City, which has been both her home and the constant focus of her written reflections.

3. "En la flanería el sujeto urbano, privatizado, se aproxima a la ciudad con la mirada de quien ve un objeto en exhibición" (128).

4. "Narrar es saber que ya no es posible la experiencia del orden que esperaba el *flâneur* al pasear por la urbe a principios de siglo. Ahora la ciudad es como un videoclip: montaje efervescente de imágenes discontinuas" (32).

5. "La escritora mexicana vincula en reiteradas ocasiones el carácter feminista de su obra con las condiciones de miles de mexicanos que no tienen peso" (95).

6. "La actual literatura de las mujeres ha de venir como parte del gran flujo de la literatura de los oprimidos, la de los sin tierra, la de los pobres, los que aún no tienen voz, los que no saben leer ni escribir... Ahora despunta, en ese gran silencio, en ese fuerte silencio latinoamericano ya no una literatura de confesión, intimista, de 'amor es una lágrima' sino una literatura de existencia y denuncia" (ibid.).

7. New Journalism arose in the 1960s with writers such as Tom Wolfe and Truman Capote, who began to incorporate novelistic elements in their journalism; these writers did not claim objectivity but rather interpreted, and participated in, the events that they documented. See, for example, Wolfe's *Kandy-Kolored Tangerine-Flake Streamline Baby* (1965).

8. "El sentimiento de inferioridad tan viejo que tenemos los mexicanos, lo debemos cuestionar. Los mexicanos no somos inadecuados, el inadecuado es el sistema. Vimos que si trabajamos juntos lo hacemos bien" (172).

9. "Si me hice periodista es porque sólo he tenido preguntas, nunca certezas. De lo que sí estoy segura es de mis intenciones... Muy pronto descubrí a las minorías y me identifiqué con ellas. Son mi legión" (157).

10. "Para todas las mujeres sería mejor ser hombre, seguro, porque es más divertido, es uno más libre y nadie se burla de uno" (186).

11. "En esa época no podía uno andar a deshoras de la noche, de mujer, porque no me acuerdo qué presidente, creo que Obregón, ordenó que dando las nueve de la noche, mujer que anduviera por la calle, mujer que se llevarían a la cárcel" (189).

12. "Al llegar a la casa me puse a pintar, estaba carburada y me senté frente a tu caballete, bajé la tela que dejaste a la mitad... y tomé una blanca y comencé. Es imposible no llegar a tener talento cuando se tienen revelaciones como la que experimenté ayer. Pinté con ahínco una cabeza de mujer que sorprendí en la calle ayer de regreso del Louvre, una mujer con ojos admirables, y ahora que se ha ido la luz te escribo mi conmoción y mi alegría" (21).

13. "El lograr mi independencia económica ha sido una de las fuentes de mayor satisfacción y me enorgullece haber sido una de las mujeres avanzadas de mi tiempo. Incluso cuando fui expulsada de la Academia de Bellas Artes por participar en una huelga estudiantil, mis padres no perdieron su confianza en mí" (66).

14. "Me siento mexicana" (55).

15. "Desde la cabeza a los pies, tenemos todo lo que requiere un caballero para vestir elegante" (112).

16. "Abría dentro de ella un flujo de energía creativa antes desconocido o apenas intuido, y las placas de gelatina y plata, el celuloide, la emulsión y la luz para fijar la imagen, eran los elementos del descubrimiento que él, sin más, había puesto en sus manos" (141).

17. "Fíjate Eduardito, antes que el sol, van a salir las muchachas a regar la banqueta. Cada una barre su pedazo de la ciudad. ¿No es éste el reparto equitativo de la belleza una ciudad engalanada entre todos? En México cada piedra está viva, habla, voy a hacerme un lugar en esta tierra" (ibid.).

18. "Este país me llama todos los días a ser mejor... Mejor amante, mejor discípula tuya, mejor fotógrafa, mejor ser humano. Aquí me construyo y me reinvento" (145).

19. "México es de quien nace para conquistarlo. Yo nací para México. México es mío; yo soy de México" (ibid.).

20. "Súbitamente Tina ya no es fotógrafa, ni tiene obra. No es nadie salvo un apellido que se deletrea trabajosamente, con displicencia, casi con asco, lanzándose además miradas de desprecio que subrayan que ella es ex-tran-je-ra, y por tanto capaz de inmiscuirse en la política y de hacer declaraciones falsas" (50).

21. "En México se desprecia a las mujeres, se les consume, se les desecha, se les estigmatiza, se les cuelga para siempre al árbol patriarcal y allí se les ahorca. Se bambolean durante años con la lengua de fuera, el sexo al aire" (618).

22. "Nahui le dijo que había envejecido, bendita vejez, bendita travesía que está por terminar" (ibid.).

23. "Aunque a nosotros nos parezca mejor una choza campesina, por más humilde que sea, a un tugurio proletario, ellos, los que vienen del campo, siguen creyendo en la bondad de la gran ciudad que algún día les dará lo que no les ha dado la tierra: la lotería, los premios del radio y de la televisión, las canciones dedicadas a mi mamacita porque hoy es el día de su santo, los aparatos domésticos que regala Pelayo, las fotonovelas" (*Todo México*, 23).

WORKS CITED

Baudelaire, Charles. *The Painter of Modern Life and Other Essays*. Ed. and trans. Jonathan Mayne. New York: Da Capo Press, 1986.

Baudrillard, Jean. *Simulacra and Simulation*. Trans. Sheila Faria Glaser. Ann Arbor: University of Michigan Press, 1994.

Bencomo, Anadeli. *Voces y voceros de la megalópolis: La crónica periodístico-literaria en México.* Madrid/Frankfurt: Iberoamericana/Vervuert, 2002.

Benjamin, Walter. *Arcades Project.* New Haven: Yale University Press, 1999.

———. *Charles Baudelaire: A Lyric Poet in the Era of High Capitalism.* Trans. Harry Zohn. London: Verso, 1989.

Franco, Jean. "Going Public: Reinhabiting the Private." In *On Edge: The Crisis of Contemporary Latin American Culture,* ed. George Yúdice, Jean Franco, and Juan Flores. Minneapolis: University of Minnesota Press, 1992. 65–83.

García Canclini, Néstor, Alejandro Castellanos, and Ana Rosa Mantecón. *La ciudad de los viajeros: Travesías e imaginarios urbanos. México 1940–2000.* Mexico City: Grijalbo, 1996.

Jörgensen, Beth. *The Writing of Elena Poniatowska: Engaging Dialogues.* Austin: University of Texas Press, 1994.

Maloof, Judy. "The Construction of a Collective Voice: New Journalistic Techniques in Elena Poniatowska's Testimonial: *Nada, nadie: Las voces del temblor.*" *Hispanófila* 135 (May 2002): 137–51.

Massey, Doreen. *Space, Place, and Gender.* Minneapolis: University of Minnesota Press, 1994.

McLaren, Peter. "The Ethnographer as Postmodern *Flâneur.*" In *Representation and the Text,* ed. William Tierney. Albany: State University of New York Press, 1997. 143–77.

Parsons, Deborah. *Streetwalking the Metropolis: Women, the City, and Modernity.* Oxford and New York: Oxford University Press, 2000.

Pollock, Griselda. *Vision and Difference: Femininity, Feminism, and the Histories of Art.* London: Routledge, 1988.

Poniatowska, Elena. *Dear Diego.* Trans. Katherine Silver. New York: Pantheon Books, 1986.

———. *Fuerte es el silencio.* Mexico City: Ediciones Era, 1980.

———. *Hasta no verte, Jesús mío.* Mexico City: Ediciones Era, 1969.

———. *Here's to You, Jesusa!* Trans. Deanna Heikkinen. New York: Farrar, Straus and Giroux. 2001.

———. "La literatura de las mujeres es parte de la literatura de los oprimidos." *Suplemento Cultural de Últimas Noticias* 1.146 (May 6, 1990): 1–3.

———. *La noche de Tlatelolco.* Mexico City: Ediciones Era, 1971.

———. *La piel del cielo.* Mexico City: Alfaguara, 2001.

———. *Las mil y una... (la herida de Paulina).* Barcelona: Plaza y Janés, 2000.

———. *Luz y luna, las lunitas.* Mexico City: Ediciones Era, 1994.

———. *Nada, nadie. Las voces del temblor.* Mexico City: Ediciones Era, 1987.

———. *Nothing, Nobody: The Voices of the Mexico City Earthquake.* Trans. Aurora Camacho de Schmidt and Arthur Schmidt. Philadelphia: Temple University Press, 1995.

———. *Paseo de la Reforma.* Mexico City: Plaza y Janés, 1996.

———. *Querido Diego, te abraza Quiela.* Mexico City: Biblioteca Era, 1978.

———. *Tinísima.* Mexico City: Ediciones Era, 1992.

———. *Tinísima: A Novel.* Trans. Katherine Silver. New York: Farrar, Straus and Giroux, 1996.

———. *Todo empezó el domingo.* Mexico City: Editorial Océano, 1997.

———. *Todo México.* Mexico City: Editorial Diana, 1990.

Ramos, Julio. *Desencuentros de la modernidad en América Latina.* Mexico City: Fondo de Cultura Económica, 1989.

———. *Divergent Modernities: Culture and Politics in Nineteenth-Century Latin America.* Trans. John D. Blanco. Durham, N.C.: Duke University Press, 2001.

Rodó, José Enrique. "Ciudades con alma." In *El camino de Paros.* Barcelona: Editorial Cervantes, [1917] 1928. 176–81.

Tester, Keith. *The Flâneur.* London: Routledge, 1994.

Wolff, Janet. *Resident Alien: Feminist Cultural Criticism.* New Haven: Yale University Press, 1995.

PART IV
Other Cities

11

Modernity, Flirting, Seduction, and Urban Social Landscape in Carmela Eulate Sanjurjo's El asombroso doctor Jover

ÁNGEL A. RIVERA

The pleasures and politics of flirting are a topic that may awaken passionate debates, particularly among feminist scholars. Would contemporary feminist theoreticians condemn women's performance of flirting, because it could be considered a stereotypically feminine act that exploits traits that have been considered vain and superficial? Or could it be considered an effective strategy of those who are socially "weaker"? Many of the novels written by the Puerto Rican intellectual Carmela Eulate Sanjurjo (1871–1961), also published under the pseudonym Dórida Mesenia, explore the controversies of flirtation within the context of modernity, modernization, and the city, both in Puerto Rico and in Spain, during the late nineteenth and early twentieth centuries.

Traditionally, scholars have studied modernity and the processes of modernization by considering how nineteenth-century intellectuals positioned themselves within that phenomenon. The studies produced by Aníbal González-Pérez (*La novela modernista*) and Julio Ramos (*Desencuentros de la modernidad*) provide good examples of this methodology. However, a topic that recently has aroused interest among literary critics is the gender of modernity. This study will take such an approach to Eulate Sanjurjo's novel: how is modernity constructed with respect to gender, particularly in the urban context?

I can begin my analysis with Ben Singer's definition of modernization, as an "array of profound socioeconomic and cultural transformations that developed in a remarkably compressed time frame over roughly the last two hundred years. This essentially factual way of defining modernity generally is designated with the term" (20–21). He explains that this concept of modernization corresponds to the developments of capitalism. Among a useful list of social and cultural transformations associated with this process we can find the following: rapid urbanization and population growth; the proliferation of new technologies and forms of transportation; the rise of the nation-state, popular nationalism, and colonialism; the expansion of heterosocial public circulation and interaction (including concerns for the participation of women in those spaces); and the transformation of traditional family ties.

In the context of Spanish and Latin American modernities one must consider the modern/tradition dyad, usually equated, respectively, with the urban and the rural and where one could find an exacerbation of the transformations just mentioned. In the case of Latin America, this conflict is well explored in the works of Domingo Faustino Sarmiento and his concern with *civilización* versus *barbarie*.[1] In Spain, for example, Benito Pérez Galdós and Emilia Pardo Bazán mapped similar conflicts by focusing mostly on urban and rural transformations produced by the conflicts of modern life.[2] However, owing to the new possibilities of social interactions and freedom that a city might offer, the novels written by Eulate Sanjurjo focus mostly on urban spaces.

Rita Felski has further enriched our understanding of these modern transformations with her observations on the contradictions inherent in the masculinist constructions of modernity. To be modern is "to be on the side of progress, reason, and democracy or, by contrast, to align oneself with 'disorder, despair, and anarchy.' Indeed, to be modern is often paradoxically to be antimodern, to define oneself in explicit opposition to the prevailing norms and values of one's own time" (11). Evidently, this is related to a consciousness of the passing of time, an experience of "temporality and historical consciousness" (9). In other words, to be modern is to develop a critical consciousness. However, as Felski points out, modernity has been implicitly defined as male and urban. In fact, Marshall Berman has presented a catalog of behaviors and individual practices in the city that show the many subjectivities (technologies of the self) produced to deal with the demands and rapid transformations that capitalist societies imposed on the male subject by the end of the nineteenth century and the beginning of the twentieth. Among those forms of behavior one can identify, for example, the *flâneur*, the dandy, the marginalized intellectual, the degenerate or social misfit, and the hypersensitive man.

Although Berman's catalog hints at male writers' inconformity with coetaneous society, his list nevertheless suggests that modernity is, in essence, masculine, and that female subjectivity has no space for representation within modernization, particularly within the public spaces of the city. However, while the representation of modernity as male was emerging, a group of female writers were simultaneously devising discursive and representational strategies that placed them in the midst of modernity. Writers such as Gertrudis Gómez de Avellaneda (Cuba, 1814–73), Salomé Ureña de Henríquez (Dominican Republic, 1850–97), Concepción Arenal (Spain, 1820–93), and Emilia Pardo Bazán (Spain, 1851–1921), among many others, thought about the position of their female characters (and of their own political selves) in the larger context of modern society.

Carmela Eulate Sanjurjo fits well within this emerging group of women writers. Her literary production, like that of many Caribbean, Latin American, and Spanish intellectuals, can best be studied within the urban context, as it was from these cosmopolitan areas that intellectual leaders led or, conversely, resisted the transformations of capitalism. It is in the imaginary of the urban space (at the expense of the rural) that the most important struggles took place on behalf of political power and social control of the nation. Thus, for this generation of women writers and intellectuals, many of the models of behavior for the modern subject revolve around the context of the city as the place for the centralization of power, services, and industry; as the location for intellectual renovation and (re)definitions of the national; as the place of political struggles and hegemony; and as the place where traditions are revisited and re-created.

Eulate Sanjurjo's novels *La muñeca* (The doll, 1896), *El asombroso doctor Jover* (The amazing doctor Jover, 1930), *Las veleidades de Consuelo* (Consuelo's fickleness, 1930), and *Teresa y María* (Teresa and María, 1936) offer an intellectual commentary about the many female subjectivities that helped construct modernization processes. Particularly in the novels *El asombroso doctor Jover, Las veleidades de Consuelo,* and *La muñeca,* Sanjurjo theorized about the sociological roles of the flirt and the frivolous woman.[3] These novels not only represent nineteenth-century Caribbean and Spanish women within the context of the city, they also explore the kind of

intellectual endeavors that would allow female writers to express or to construct their subjectivities. In this study, I will focus on *El asombroso doctor
Jover* and the phenomenon of the flirt as one of a variety of female characters able to transgress accepted norms of behavior, while also confirming many of the traits traditionally associated with the feminine within
the modern. Flirtation is a modern psychological and social phenomenon
mainly associated with inducing a simultaneous feeling of desire and hesitation in those who respond to coquettish behavior.[4] In spite of its apparent connotations of weakness and manipulation, the flirt's coy playfulness
allowed a gendered positioning within the context of modernization, especially in the urban context. I argue that it is primarily through the motif
of the flirt that Sanjurjo envisioned the possibilities of women as urban
professionals and intellectuals in the nineteenth century.

The themes of the flirt and of flirtation, as addressed in this essay, connect with the social and political changes of the period, changes linked in
turn with other issues of the social imaginary of the time, such as eugenics, as we shall see later. In this sense, we will find that although the protagonist of the novel is revealed to be a model of conduct for the urban
professional woman of modernity, she is not free from contradictions,
both in her own interpretations of eugenics and in her problematic strategies of flirtation, intrigue, and manipulation. In a parallel fashion, the
Spanish government and many Latin American states were engaged in a
contradictory process of modernization. On the one hand, those nations
were concerned with the improvement of living conditions and the expansion of circles of power, but on the other, this meant a greater intromission
of the state in personal and family affairs. Although on one side the state
was interested in the democratization of power, on the other, one can encounter systemic efforts to control the growing social and political demands
of female intellectuals. Of course, in each country, modernization happened at different levels and rates.

Eulate Sanjurjo devoted most of her career to exploring the problems
women faced in the late nineteenth and early twentieth centuries in the
Hispanic world, and many scholars have focused on the feminist aspects
of her work:[5] "As a feminist, she defended a woman's right to have access to
an education that would allow her to interact intelligently with males and
to climb the ladder of social opportunities. She defended a woman's right
to participate in political decisions through universal suffrage" (Santos-
Silva).[6] Eulate Sanjurjo studied female forms of representation not only

within a political framework but also within Caribbean and Spanish literary contexts. In many of her writings she devised representational strategies that made use of traditional forms of representing women within modern metropolitan cultural spaces: the flirt, the frivolous woman, the consumer of goods, the femme fatale. In this essay, I will analyze the reasons that provoked Eulate Sanjurjo, as a female and feminist writer, to use the image of the flirt within the context of her novel *El asombroso doctor Jover* (1930). In other words, I am interested in how she manipulated existing female representational forms to create a discourse that would place female urban intellectuals in the midst of modernity.

Eulate Sanjurjo was one of the few known female intellectuals who appeared in the cultural panorama of late-nineteenth- and early-twentieth-century Puerto Rican and Spanish literature. She was born in San Juan in 1871. Her father was a Spanish naval commander and admiral, and her mother was a Spaniard who moved to Venezuela, and later to Puerto Rico, because of the wars of independence. While certainly not the only woman intellectual of her time, she was considered a rare female thinker amid the plethora of male writers and intellectuals in her milieu.[7] Among her many vocations, she was a musicologist, a literary critic, a polyglot, and the creator of an enormous body of literary work. Of her best novels written in Puerto Rico, one can mention *La muñeca* (The doll, 1895), with a foreword by Manuel Zeno Gandía (one of Puerto Rico's best-known intellectuals at the turn of the twentieth century).[8] However, most of her intellectual work was written and published in Spain, particularly in Barcelona, where she resided until her death in 1961. In spite of having lived in Spain for a long time, her social background and national heritage always affected the reception of her work. According to Loreina Santos Silva, "her critics argue that although her work is comparable to that of the greatest female Spanish writers such as Emilia Pardo Bazán, her Latin American and Creole identity did not allow her to enjoy a well-deserved fame, since Spaniards considered her a foreigner."[9] Due to her foreign status and intellectual inclinations, she was considered an *ave rara* (a rare bird) both in Spain and in Puerto Rico.

Eulate Sanjurjo's eccentric literary persona results in part from her transitions among the romantic, realist, and naturalist literary traditions, and certainly from her straddling two cultures and two continents. Her literary characters, evolving from one novel to the next, ultimately resemble modernist characters as she approaches her intellectual maturity. However, her literary style was envisioned within the scope and interests of the realist and naturalist novel. In particular, Eulate Sanjurjo inherited the influences of the realist/naturalist novel in concomitance with a melodramatic imagination. During Eulate Sanjurjo's time, urban spaces in Spain and Puerto Rico were undergoing tremendous changes in response to modernity, and this is reflected in the melodramatic aspects of her novels.

One could argue that, with its emphasis on courtship rituals, *El asombroso doctor Jover* refers to an apparently superficial or vain reality. However, this novel is deeply embedded in the rich tradition of Spanish novelists who attempted to construct a national reality through their writings (Pérez Galdós, Valdés, Pereda, and Pardo Bazán). At the same time, Eulate Sanjurjo's novels are also produced in the context of the dilemmas presented to female intellectuals during early and late modernity in Latin America and Spain: How could female intellectuals make use of cultural artifacts that a male-oriented society offered to them? How did they envision themselves within the process of modernization, particularly within the urban landscape? It seems that for Eulate Sanjurjo, a melodramatic imagination and flirtation were useful tools for a woman intellectual to negotiate urban modernity.

Before developing any further these questions regarding modernity and the flirt, and in order to put her writings into context, I will pause to briefly summarize *El asombroso doctor Jover*.[10] The novel takes place in Barcelona during the late 1930s; the protagonist is an unusually beautiful and intelligent pediatrician, Dr. María Francisca Jover, or Francis for short. Although she has received many offers of marriage, she has decided to remain single until she finds the perfect male. But he must be physically perfect and mentally appealing. She bases her idea of beauty and perfection on images by the Greek sculptor Praxiteles. Despite her own beauty, however, she faces difficulty in finding that perfect partner; her intellectual ability keeps suitors at bay. Most of the men she befriends cannot accept that she is a doctor and a highly educated woman. Furthermore, most of the women she meets do not welcome her for the same reason. Therefore, in order to navigate the mazes of power in a city such as Barcelona, she must continuously recur to her provocative abilities as a flirt, along with her intellectual prowess.

The novel is thick with incidents of intrigue and jealousy. For example, adultery is an important component in the plot. We soon learn that Francis has fallen in love with Maximiliano, a young poet and intellectual trained as a lawyer, who fulfills her expectations of male physical beauty. However, because he is part of an apparently wealthy and aristocratic family, he has not taken the time to seek a firm where he can practice law. Like the other men, Maximiliano feels intimidated by Francis's intelligence and beauty. To complicate matters further, and in a bold move, Francis openly declares her love to Maximiliano and asks him to marry her. Her aggressiveness repels him. Not discouraged, Francis then starts to calculate ways of winning him back.

If it is true that all texts carry within themselves the psychological imprints of their own times, one must wonder, then, about the literary and cultural import of a novel, such as *El asombroso doctor Jover*, that seems to be purely *folletinesque*, a frivolous novel based on romance and affairs. However, in her important book *The Gender of Modernity*, Rita Felski has argued that intimate relationships emerge as modernity's central arena.[11] She echoes Gail Finney's ideas that familiar ties and personal identities and relationships are central in the construction of a modern subjectivity. According to Hans Medick and David Warren Sabean "family mediates social differentiation and class formation" (19). Therefore, private emotions and sexuality have a deep historical nature.[12]

Felski is particularly interested in demonstrating how the modern has had an influence on feminist thought. Her study explores "some of the different ways in which women drew upon, contested, or reformulated dominant representations of gender and modernity in making sense of their own position within society and history" (21). However, she cautions about the dangers of developing overarching theories about the role of women, which could simplify the complexities of the relationship between women and the modern. She argues that although "the figure of woman pervades the culture of the *fin de siècle* as a powerful symbol of both the dangers and promises of the modern age" (3), modernity has been perceived as a masculine endeavor, identified with dynamic activities, the development of unlimited desire, and the control and possession of nature. In other words, it is identified with a Faustian impulse. On the other hand, Felski also explains that "woman is aligned with the dead weight of tradition and conservatism that the active, newly autonomous, and self-defining subject must seek to transcend. Thus she functions as a sacrificial victim exemplifying the losses which underpin the ambiguous, but ultimately exhilarating and seductive logic of the modern" (2). Thus womanhood, allied with tradition, must be sacrificed for the sake of the masculine progress of the modern. This is one of the contradictions in the definitions of modernity, which Felski views as a discursive practice that is a necessarily conflictive response to social change.

El asombroso doctor Jover, in spite of its apparent frivolity, is deeply connected to Spanish history and to the multiple responses to social change that Felski describes. The main character, Francis, on many occasions establishes her difference from women who are "vain and tasteless."[13] She also claims that she is not a romantic woman at all. Along with these declarations, Francis is aware of her abilities as a flirt: "In Barcelona, I had and have many flirts, not as straightforward and fun as those of my student years."[14] As a matter of fact, the word *flirt,* as a marker of its structural and meaningful presence, is produced many times throughout the novel. In addition, Francis is very much aware of the mechanics of erotic love. Interestingly, her desire for love is coupled with a strong desire of physical perfection in a man: "I adore beauty in all its manifestations, and there is nothing more beautiful than a perfect human body; it is well said that man is the masterpiece of God's creation."[15] However, this desire for perfection is not innocent and it is very much related to her flirtatious behavior. It is related also to a disturbing impulse among European intellectuals during the early twentieth century: eugenics, a science that dealt with the improvement of the genetic qualities of a race (Galton, 1). Despite her egalitarian desire to seek social inclusion and political participation, Francis's visions of beauty in male genetic perfection have antidemocratic repercussions. Apart from the repulsion that today's readers may experience when confronting this theme, in Eulate Sanjurjo eugenics refers not to issues of ethnic selection but rather to the construction of an alternative space of power (not free of contradictions, as we have mentioned) for the protagonist, Francis.

During this period, Spanish novelists, including Eulate Sanjurjo, were concerned with what they understood as a social problem in Spain and in other Spanish-speaking countries as well, particularly in urban areas: mental and physical degeneration.[16] When Francis speaks about the art of sculpture with one of her friends, she interjects: "We lack models, my dear doctor. . . . Humanity degenerates, men and women are short, ugly, and ridiculous, if we compare their proportions with the eternally classical models."[17] This she views as decadence, and as a physician Francis is concerned about what she interprets as a medical and social problem.

This question of decadence launches the novel into historical and intellectual debates about the Spanish nation after the 1898 *desastre* (disaster) of the Spanish-American War, and in the context of the approach of Primo de Rivera's dictatorship (1929). As a matter of fact, the production of the Spanish novel around the turn of the century is an exploration of Spain's identity and of its historical significance. According to Jo Labanyi, realist novels did not construct a tradition of a national past, but rather created the space for a forum that would foster critical debates on topics that concerned modern Spanish intellectuals: "The novel is better placed than other public-sphere institutions to air collective anxieties, for it can invent its stories, tailoring to highlight specific concerns" (5).[18] Realist and naturalist novels, then, were concerned with the composition of civil society and how the government could intervene for the betterment of Spanish culture. That is why the realist/naturalist novel was interested in ambiguous spaces or spaces yet to be defined—such as the emerging modern city: those were areas that modern society did not yet know how to approach. The realist/naturalist novel was especially preoccupied with women's roles in civil society and the public sphere. Both cultural realms were exploring what to do with a new social sector that was demanding attention and enfranchisement through increased political activity (feminism and the right to vote) and through increased economic participation (consumerism and the professionalization of new sectors), which required a constant presence of females in the streets of any major city. Females went public. This change in women's roles in turn was connected with the lower social classes, which were also disenfranchised by a contractual and capitalist society.

As one can imagine, many of the responses to the presence of new sectors expressed concern on behalf of males and upper-class intellectuals. Many Latin American and Spanish intellectuals thought that women's emancipation was a regression to a lower stage of evolution. For that reason, the Spanish government created the Comisión de Reformas Sociales (Social reforms commission) in the late nineteenth century.[19] This institution was in charge of assessing and compiling information of every aspect of daily and national life. The interest in documenting everyday life in detail corresponded to the interest in reconstructing society and also explained the extensive narratives that the realist novel produced. The documentation of social activities was accompanied by the creation of hygiene manuals and legislation aimed at increased social control and larger intervention by the state in family affairs.

It is not surprising, then, that a novel such as *El asombroso doctor Jover* would be concerned with issues of degeneration and eugenics. At one point in the novel, an old flame of Francis's asks her to marry him at the same time that an old American millionaire approaches her with the same proposition. She responds negatively to both of them because of her ideal of beauty and her faith in eugenics. Francis prefers a man who is young and physically perfect: "I have always had an ideal of physical beauty that I considered unattainable" and "When I marry, it will be with a young man, handsome, like that one (she pointed at the reproduction of a statue of Praxiteles); my ideals respond to eugenics."[20] What she needs is a genetically perfect man, as evidenced by his physical appearance.

Later, based on the same ideals, Francis indirectly asks for a stronger intervention of the state in family affairs: "It is necessary that we have laws prohibiting marriage between men and women whose health does not allow them to have robust families free of hereditary problems. The majority of these little creatures visiting my office, one after another, should never have seen the light of day."[21] This is only one example where Dr. Jover insists on the necessity of physical perfection in order to produce offspring. Nevertheless, despite her interest in influencing public health legislation, she is also aware of her weak position as a woman in society, which tells her that she cannot make this kind of demand publicly and that she alone cannot achieve political change. As Labanyi explains, in Spain, as elsewhere during this period, the construction of the abnormal led to the realization of the normal. In the context of national discourses, theories of degeneration emphasized familial history.

Eulate Sanjurjo's novels take interest in familial relationships as they relate to societal wellness. *El asombroso doctor Jover* is a good example of her concerns with this kind of social interaction. In this novel, Maximiliano (Francis's object of desire) is intimidated by her strong sexual advances, flirtation, and seduction. But he decides to escape her powers by becoming engaged with the young girl that his family told him is the best candidate for him and his family. Her name is Adelita Soler: "Beautiful and frail, like one of those tempting bibelots," she was like "a little idol."[22] On many occasions, in a sarcastic and accusatory manner, Francis refers to Adelita as *puber* (pubescent). It is clear that in the novel Maximiliano's family lost everything in bad business deals, as did many other families in Barcelona at that time. Although the novel takes place during the relatively prosperous "years of hope" (Ubieto et al.),[23] the crisis of 1929 was also having an impact on Spain. The colonial disaster (in Latin America and the Caribbean) brought many financial readjustments. In the same fashion, the

Spanish-American War, in which the colonies were lost, and the ongoing war in Morocco, represented financial disorder and chaos for Spanish society as a whole.

For that reason, as in Latin America, bourgeois Spanish families opted for the creation of new alliances to protect their class integrity and patrimony. Therefore, arranged marriages within the same social circles, or other wealthy groups, would ensure continuity in the midst of strong social changes. One must remember that the accelerated capitalist changes in the modern world modified many forms of social interaction, including the composition and interaction of social classes. Even though it is clear that Francis belonged to an emerging professional and privileged economic sector, she was not considered the best alliance for Maximiliano's family. Maximiliano's kinship favored the Soler family, because they were from a rich industrial sector in Barcelona. Francis lacked the social enfranchisement to effectively intervene in what she considered to be a problem. Her object of desire will be taken away from her as a result of social conventions or marriage by convenience. Francis's only weapon is her intellect and the manipulation of men by flirting, a technique that she continuously uses to navigate through the mazes of power in Barcelona.

According to Adam Phillips, "Flirts are dangerous because they have a different way of believing in the Real Thing" (xvii). Flirting is calculated behavior, but its effect is one of uncertainty. The cherished vocabulary of commitment and the promise of happiness implicit in beauty are to be exploited and undermined by the ambiguities of flirting. It is also a way of cultivating one's own desires by buying time to enjoy power in the form of postponing any fulfillment or final decision. Phillips also comments: "Flirtation is the game of taking chances, of plotting illicit possibilities" (xxiv). Given the context of modern culture and the possibilities of choosing between multiple paths, flirting gives a chance to explore new avenues of action without making a final commitment. Focusing his theory on heterosexual relationships, Phillips argues that a flirtatious woman offers her sexuality in ambiguous ways, with a possible promise that entices men to pay attention to her. With her flirtatious behavior, she becomes the object of attention and desire. In other words, she is making room for possibilities in the realm of fiction.

Georg Simmel, a German sociologist from the turn of the twentieth century, argues that the act of flirting generates value or desirability and that this is achieved by a simultaneous game of refusal and consent. However, according to Kevin Yelvington, this action may be just a reinforcement of cultural values, because implicit in this game is the recognition of a disadvantage that must be overcome by approaching obliquely an objective: "While women's flirting may bring them pleasure or buy them time, over time it tends to reinforce the society's gender double standards; men's reputations, on the other hand, are made, not besmirched by flirting" (Yelvington, Osella, and Osella, 457).[24] In spite of the clash between Simmel's and Yelvington's arguments, one could argue also that social phenomena are usually not monolithic, and that in the interstices of the game of flirting exists the possibility of gaining the upper hand, particularly when what is sought after or desired remains controlled by its owner (from women's point of view: the female body). This game may give power to women, but it requires a willing or interactive participation that could modify the tone, extension, and intensity of flirting. Simmel takes his ideas further by asserting that females engaged in this kind of social behavior exhibit a fascination with liberty (141), and that liberty is related to the acquisition and use of power: "The power of woman in relation to the man is exhibited in consent and refusal" (ibid.).[25] I argue in this essay that Carmela Eulate's Sanjurjo's novels share Simmel's views on flirting.

Francis's interactions with men provide an example of this power of refusal and consent. She clearly acknowledges in the novel that the exercise of flirting makes her a more desirable woman: "I will flirt as necessary to protect my social ascension, and when you see that other males desire me, I will be even more desirable to you."[26] For Simmel, this inaccessibility increases the power of the coquette: "In the behavior of the flirt, the man feels the proximity and interpenetration of the ability and the inability to acquire something. This is the essence of 'price'" (134). This is the meaning of value. Also, this would be evidence of a desire to enjoy power in an enduring form.

However, the reader may question the purpose of exercising the wiles of flirting if it only seeks attention from the object of romantic desire but does not provide broader social control. At this point, it is important to comment on how many critics have seen intimate relationships as a metaphor or marker of wider social interactions (Jo Labanyi, Doris Sommer, and Hans Medick and David Warren Sabean, for example). For Spanish and Latin American intellectuals, familial and intimate relationships do reflect a selected societal model and propagate an ideal form of public behavior. In the case of *El asombroso doctor Jover*, the families portrayed in the novel, involved in the trading of their respective heirs for the sake of keeping their fortunes and names, act unwittingly and to the detriment of their own offspring and the national future. Those families are not models to follow. The narrator, who assumes Francis's point of view, criticizes Maximiliano's attitude toward work by characterizing him as "a parasite on his own kind."[27] At a time when the state was unsuccessfully intervening in the family through the creation of innumerable institutions throughout the Hispanic world, and at a time when families were reflecting the chaotic state of the nation, Carmela Eulate Sanjurjo presents through this novel her own solution: professional females in the city were to revitalize or regenerate a failing system that in practice excluded them from participation in any modernization process.

We can view Francis's intervention in Maximilano's family affairs as an example of her efforts to revitalize the nation. In the middle of the novel, and after the rejection by Maximiliano, Francis discovers that Maximiliano's sister, who has also been married for convenience, is involved in a sexual scandal. A Polish man is blackmailing her by threatening to reveal her affair with him. He has in his possession several letters she wrote to him, and to buy his silence, Mónica (Maximiliano's sister) must pay an enormous sum of money (ten thousand pesetas). Francis finds out by accident when her masseuse offers her a jewel that is being sold by a lady in trouble and who needs money desperately. After using her charms to investigate the problem, she decides to take action to protect Maximiliano's family.

Since the beginning of the novel, and thanks to her flirting skills, all male characters have flocked to Francis's side whenever she needs help or attention. Aware of her powers of attraction, she carefully has been constructing a network of people prepared to come to her rescue when needed. One only has to take account of all the males interested in her well-being and, of course, her beauty. Toward the end of the novel, she acknowledges her own ambition, as well as her use of flirtation to achieve success. The following dialogue highlights this tactic:

> You have climbed to a pedestal that we, simple mortals, cannot reach.
> I always have been an ambitious woman.
>   And you obtained what you wanted. Today you are a woman well known in Spain.[28]

Her power is further increased by her success as a doctor. After she publishes a book about pediatrics, she wins an award and with it the admiration of the medical community. Therefore, her social enfranchisement comes from the combination of intellectual work and her flirting abilities. As a sociological phenomenon, flirting fulfills its function; it attracts the attention of the intended audience in order to select. According to Simmel, the purpose of flirting with simultaneous partners is to increase one's selling value, and to stimulate the chosen male's desires and wants. However, in *El asombroso doctor Jover* flirting goes beyond this mere principle, thus acquiring social and political implications important to the development of the modern urban woman: Francis transforms sexual desirability into a metaphor of social interaction and reconstruction.

Francis is determined to solve Mónica's situation both out of solidarity with her and out of interest in Maximiliano's family. Again, this is not an innocent act. The realist novel was very much concerned with foreign influences, and also reflected the view that all social transactions, including marriage, corresponded with monetary transactions. In the realist novel, marriage was being interpreted as a contract. Equally problematic was that state policies were inundated by a market-like logic. Jo Labanyi indicates that Pérez Galdós's novels were concerned with this capitalistic approach to social interactions, but also, as a logical consequence, with the role of women in the modern public sphere. Pérez Galdós's novels also expressed the conflicts that intellectuals had about the dissemination of a market ideology. These concerns, owing to the ambiguous position of many intellectuals toward capitalism, created debates among many intellectuals who were attempting to define the role of women in society. Eulate Sanjurjo proposed her own solution to this debate through fiction.

As one might expect, Francis decides immediately to plot against the Polish thug. Realist novels were particularly concerned with adultery; the adulterous woman entered into a realm of strangeness, by being simultaneously inside and outside of the public sphere, and by violating the contract of marriage. In order to help Mónica, Francis has recourse to the army of men who adore her and that she has put together by using her charms. First, Francis contacts a worker, Felipe (a socialist), who owes her a favor because, as a doctor, she had saved the life of his daughter. She also recruits her friend Andrés Roig, the owner of a bookstore and the boyfriend of Francis's best friend. Felipe lives in the area of Badalona, which was, perhaps, the most important working-class district in Barcelona. The novel makes a veiled reference to the tragic workers' strikes during the earlier twentieth century. Francis's solidarity with this social class is made evident when she decides not to charge him anything for the medical treatment she provided for his daughter. She declares: "Rich people cannot understand such things";[29] this comment not only implies an alliance with Felipe, but also indicates that the bourgeoisie would not be able to understand her lack of interest in exploiting him. Felipe has in common with Francis a certain social marginality. He is an intellectual who has been under police surveillance because of his political and socialist beliefs, while she is an independent urban professional during a period when such a role was rare for a woman, or at least frowned upon.

The solution that Francis and Felipe employ to recover the letters in question is an illegal one that may require deceit and the use of violence. Francis herself is the owner of a Browning pistol, which she is ready to use, if necessary. Felipe, with Francis's assistance, enters the house of the Polish man and steals the letters from him, but not without a scuffle that almost results in Felipe being shot. Once she recovers the letters, Francis takes them to their rightful owner, Mónica. She thereby obtains the attention and respect of Maximiliano's family, as their money and reputation have been saved.

In Eulate Sanjurjo's novels, issues of money and capital are important topics threading the narrative. As I have indicated, many novels of the era were concerned with the introduction of capitalist logic into the sphere of the family. For many Krausists this was a modern social problem. They understood that marriage was a target of contractual regulation and commercialization. Carmela Eulate Sanjurjo echoes this problem by utilizing parody, especially when speaking about Maximilano's older sister, Lulú: "When she was sixteen, when her sister Mónica got married, she was introduced to society by being thrown into the Marriage Stock Exchange at a time when the older of the Albalena's daughters was being valued in that market."[30] In this case, marriage is criticized by being equated with a capitalist exchange, and it points to the modifications that cultural values were experiencing in Spain. This was evidence of an increasing level of anxiety about the nature of private property and how it changed hands.

Krausism attacked the generalization of contracts, including in marriage. For Krause's followers, the family institution should be a "natural" enterprise, based on the good nature of humankind, and on the overcoming of personal interests for the good of the collective (the nation). Krausism was concerned that society was being governed by a market ideology. In *El asombroso doctor Jover*, bourgeois families were feeding off each other and marriages were arranged in relation to profits or material gains. However, Maximiliano's family is bankrupt. A detective Francis hires discovers this fact:

> Don Luis did not contribute to the marriage. The 3 million pesetas that came with the pubescent bride, far from gaining value, by harvesting the farms the family had in the province of Tarragona, and especially the cork farm, in the county of San Feliú de Guixols, served as collateral for the enormous mortgages, which I consider to be impossible to pay.[31]

Therefore, there is a mathematical equation of imbalance and discredit: "The specific information for which you will pay extra makes me believe that such is not the case, since it is demonstrates an imbalance between earnings and expenditures, which explains the constant selling of valuables, the mortgages on the big cork farm, and the expected sale of that farm, which is the core of their capital."[32] These two examples from the novel represent a clear concern about how increased capitalist activity affects social relations.

However, as an independent woman of the city, Francis will endeavor to fix all these social problems. First, she destroys Adelita and Maximilano's engagement by revealing bankrupcy information to Adelita's father. She then rescues Maximiliano's sister and family from sure social damnation and scorn by recovering the compromising letters and chasing away the perpetrator. She makes clear that her flirtation results in the involvement of one admirer (a government official) who helped to expel the foreigner from Spain. Finally, she succeeds in mesmerizing Maximiliano and induces him to marry her. But first, she clearly indicates that she expects a husband willing to move beyond old social practices and commit to the development of a modern society. She actually describes a new bourgeois ethos by explaining that she did not inherit her material goods but rather earned them with her own work: "the fancy furniture, the fine porcelain table service, the Baccarat glassware, the silverware, and the flowers complementing the tablecloth and napkins made with fine figured silk damask, an ensemble of comfort and well-being."[33] In the same manner, and again as a result of her flirting and intellectual abilities, she manages to find a job for Maximilano: "My friend, the minister, will give him a well-paying job, and even tomorrow, if he wants to, he can start working for the Baró's firm, one of the premiere law practices of Barcelona."[34] In an evident inversion of gender roles, Francis uses her feminine wiles to create her new modern family life.

Maximiliano is persuaded, truly mesmerized by "such feminine audacity,"[35] even more so when the scene finishes with Francis asking permission from Don Luis Soler (Maximiliano's father) to marry his son: "Mr. Luis, will you grant me your son Max's hand in marriage?"[36] Francis's intervention in this idealized social realm ends by transforming Maximiliano's soul. He finally rejects the money his family wants to give him as a dowry, expresses his desire to work as a lawyer, and vows to dedicate his life to profitable activities: "I offered her, in exchange, to quit literature, since she says that poetry is shoddy and a waste of time. I will follow her advice and will translate from French some law book. Then, I'll compile ideas from several writers, will contribute something of my own, and will print an original piece of work for my profession."[37] One must observe the instrumental reason operating here and the acceptance of the professionalization of Maximiliano's social class in order to better participate in capitalist exchange.

Although we might argue that the novel plays against the introduction of capitalist rule in daily existence, this work accepts capitalist exchange and the work ethic of a new bourgeois community, as defined by Francis. At this point we must go back to the issue of the role of female intellectuals in Spain during modernization. Since the nineteenth century, Spain was struggling to turn itself into a modern nation by creating a strong central state that would turn its inhabitants into citizens. The symbols of modernity were mainly masculine, and women writers had to devise strategies to use and manipulate those images and symbols that the culture had already created. For that reason, intimate relationships are important to Eulate Sanjurjo. Critics such as Rita Felski and Jo Labanyi have demonstrated how females were reduced to the libidinal and repressed Other. Georg Simmel argued that women, owing to their condition of physical and spiritual unity and their marginalization from capitalist society, could not experience the contradictions and alienations of modernization. Nevertheless, this implied that females could not participate in processes of modernization and were relegated to mere observers or guardians of a tradition that would become the symbol of resistance and refuge from the drastic changes of modernity.

However, Felski argues that one should not create idealized spaces of resistance, especially in relation to the female figure. She also warns against producing an overarching theory of modernity to explain everything, because this will produce a caricaturized image of females and of modernity itself. Sanjurjo's novels are the best example of this warning, for her characters' relationship with modernity is complex. In fact, those characters installed themselves in the midst of Spanish modernity. One must not assume as superficial the fact that Francis is precisely a modern woman who surrounds herself by modern technology; she owns a car and a Browning pistol, practices modern medicine, smokes, enjoys fashion, and owns her own house. But more important, she is involved in a process of transformation of a sclerotic social group. For that transformation she uses her well-honed powers of flirtation for the manipulation of intimate relationships and of men in particular. Although coquetry may be considered as a trick of the weak, conversely, flirtation aids Francis in achieving positions of overt power, both through a marriage of her choosing and through professional respect. Francis's professional success is not a result of flirting (there is no question of her intellectual abilities), but flirtation can be considered, in this case, an important element in the process of enhancing her social and political franchise. With her medical practice and with her social actions, Francis attempts not only to achieve a progressive feminist version of marriage, but also to fix the degenerative tendency she sees in Spanish society and culture.

Francis's intervention on social issues originates within the qualities she offers as a foreigner who can operate both in the center and at the margins of modern and urban society, and it is specially brought into being by her gender transgressions in taking an active role in matters of sex and marriage, and in her desire to fix social problems. It has been argued that when women engage in the reformation of social sectors, they are also speaking or dealing with the reformation of themselves. One can think, for example, of antislavery literature in the Caribbean. In the case of Eulate Sanjurjo, that reformulation takes place within the possibilities of democratization and professional advancement that Spanish modernity was able to offer. Therefore, Francis, through her apparently innocuous social behavior, has created the possibilities of a transformation: "By unsettling preferences and priorities flirtation can add other stories to the repertoire by making room for them" (Phillips, xxv). However, whatever possibilities are proposed or invented in *El asombroso doctor Jover,* they can only make sense under the umbrella of the modern and linked to the urban environment. Although one must not interpret modernity as an intrinsically liberating phenomenon, the possibilities expressed by Francis in the context of one of the most important and vibrant cities of Spain do have elements of liberation. Evidently, that liberation takes place in the sexuality that Francis exhibits, her gender transgressions, and the social impact she has in the manipulation of cultural codes in her favor.

Nevertheless, she is conservative in her endorsement of a capitalist logic, in the co-optation of the working class (Felipe), and in the expulsion of the foreign element causing havoc in Barcelona (the Polish foreigner). The foreign element is also excluded when Francis rejects an American millionaire who proposed marriage to her. In addition, Francis criticizes anarchist ideologies, also considered foreign to the nation, and, contradictorily, she supports eugenics as a medical and social ideology. The period between 1917 and 1923 was a period of constitutional crisis (Ubieto et al., 855–76), and during the 1920s and 1930s Spain was losing its bipartisan political system. Neither liberals nor conservatives had the power or ability to appeal to, or to integrate, social or political sectors at the margins of the system. Spain was clearly losing its unity and becoming increasingly fragmented. By the end of the novel one can say that a formula for defragmentation has been proposed: all the elements foreign to Spain have been expelled, and Maximiliano (the son of old aristocracy) has been turned into a man of benefit to society. Adelita, the young woman and daughter of an industrialist initially destined to marry Maximiliano, will now marry the son of another industrialist family. And, of course, Francis, the new professional woman, makes an alliance with old aristocracy.

With all these actions, Eulate Sanjurjo proposes a closure to an old debate: What is the place of women in modern Spain? What should their role be in relation to marriage, the public sphere, and private property? The idea of bringing peace and order to chaos in the social and economic sphere diminishes the exaggerated and melodramatic threats that the Spanish novel connected to female mobility in the city. To the question raised by the novels of the time regarding who can or should intervene in society's affairs, Eulate Sanjurjo responds with a new female subjectivity: the urban female professional. This new woman, with her intellect and vitality, would regenerate Spanish society. This new woman, or this new family, would be the model for social integration, for a society governed by persuasion instead of coercion and by new alliances between classes.

NOTES

1. See *Facundo* (1845).

2. See the novels by Pérez Galdós, *La familia de León Roch* (1879) and *La desheredada* (1881), and by Pardo Bazán, *Los pasos de Ulloa* (1886).

3. See my study, "Relectura de la *femme fatale* en el contexto de la modernidad decimonónica: *La muñeca* de Carmela Eulate Sanjurjo," *Chasqui: Revista de Literatura Latinoamericana* 27.2 (1998): 54–69.

4. I am aware that flirting is an interactive process that requires active and consensual participation. However, in interpreting the Social Issues Research Institute research on flirting (based in the UK) one can conclude that women are better skilled both at flirting and at responding appropriately to flirtation: "Research has also shown that men have a tendency to mistake friendly behaviour for sexual flirting. This is not because they are stupid or deluded, but because they tend to see the world in more sexual terms than women. There is also evidence to suggest that women are naturally more socially skilled than men, better at interpreting people's behaviour and responding appropriately. Indeed, scientists have recently claimed that women have a special 'diplomacy gene' which men lack" (http://www.sirc.org/publik/flirt.html).

5. See her essay *La mujer en la historia* published in Seville in 1915.

6. "Como feminista, defendió el derecho de la mujer a obtener una buena educación que le permitiera compartir inteligentemente con los hombres y escalar un lugar apropiado en la sociedad. Defendió el derecho de la mujer a participar en las decisiones políticas a través del sufragio" (128). All translations are my own.

7. In addition to the writers already mentioned, one must place her in the company of Cecila Boh (1797–1877), Dolors Monserdà (1845–1919), Ana Roque de Duprey (1853–1933), María de Teresa Claramunt (1862–1931), Caterina Albert (1869–1966), and Luisa Capetillo (1879–1922), among many others.

8. Manuel Zeno Gandía's *La charca* (The cesspool, 1894) is one of the most important naturalist novels in Puerto Rico. The title refers to a stagnant and emaciated peasantry.

9. "sus críticos sostienen que, a pesar de que su obra está a la altura de las grandes escritoras de España, como Emilia Pardo Bazán, su sentimiento de criolla americana no le permitió gozar de la fama que ella mereciera porque los españoles la consideraban extranjera" (125).

10. Notice that the title of the novel is gender ambiguous: *el asombroso doctor* instead of *la asombrosa doctora*. In the same manner, the nickname of the protagonist is unisex: Francis. Her name could be an indication that her actions are, from the onset, ambiguous, confusing, and socially challenging, or that many of her actions will be male-like, in particular when those actions are related to taking the initiative about love. It also could be an argument that in naming (a cultural action) one adjudicates new properties and qualities to an individual. However,

right from the beginning Francis's femaleness is announced and stressed, for it is the main focus of the novel.

11. We must also recall Doris Sommer's theories on the relationship between romance and nation consolidation in Latin America. Her book *Foundational Fictions* is a good example of this approach to nationalist discourses.

12. Michel Foucault's theories on sexuality clearly indicate the connectedness of sexual practices, power, and historical contexts. See his *History of Sexuality*.

13. "vanidosas e insulsas" (8).

14. "En Barcelona tuve y tengo muchos flirts, no tan candorosos ni divertidos como los de mis años de estudiante" (9).

15. "Adoro la belleza en todas sus manifestaciones, y nada hay tan bello como un cuerpo humano perfecto; bien dicen que el hombre es la obra maestra de la creación" (10).

16. This was a concern for the realist/naturalist literary movement.

17. "Faltan modelos, querido doctor... La Humanidad degenera, los hombres y las mujeres son pequeños, feos, ridículos si comparamos sus proporciones con los eternos modelos clásicos" (ibid.).

18. For example, Benito Pérez Galdós was interested in the fate of the middle classes. For him, as for Emilia Pardo Bazán, Leopoldo Alas Clarín, and other Spanish writers of the period, the realist novel represented the study of society, and necessarily focused on the role that new or emerging social sectors should have in Spain at that time. Many of Pérez Galdós's novels were interpretations of this process, and also announced the construction of a modern national subject or subjectivity.

19. The *Comisión de Reformas Sociales* was created in 1883 by parliamentary decree. This action was supported and initiated by Krausist followers and supporters. Karl Christian Friedrich Krause (1781–1832) was a German-born philosopher who had an enormous impact on modern Spanish thought. His ideas influenced Latin American and Spanish intellectuals (educators and politicians such as Eugenio María de Hostos) during the nineteenth century. Krausism, as a philosophy, was interested in the creation of citizenship, the idea of scientific progress, and the betterment of humanity. Krausist ideology understood marriage as a natural expression and thought that it should be protected against contractual expressions. Having a contract would imply that it was mutable, therefore its natural quality was contested. In Spain, Julián Sanz del Río was one of Krausism's major exponents with his *Ideal de la humanidad* (Humanity's ideal, 1860).

20. "he tenido siempre un ideal de belleza física que consideraba irrealizable" y "Cuando me case, será con un hombre joven, guapo como ese (le señaló la copia de la estatua de Praxiteles), tengo un ideal de eugenesia" (96).

21. "A que es preciso que se legisle prohibiendo contraer matrimonio a hombres y mujeres cuya salud no los capacite para formar familias robustas y libres de

taras. Estas criaturitas que desfilan unas tras otras por mi gabinete, en su mayoría no debieran haber visto la luz del sol" (100).

22. "Linda y frágil cual uno de los bibelots tentadores" (28), "idolillo" (28).

23. "años de esperanza" (862).

24. His arguments are based on a revision of Simmel's theories and in the context of a critique to an article on flirting and romance in Kerala, South India.

25. All the theories consulted for this essay focused mostly on heterosexual relationships. However, the study of homosexual forms of flirting could lead into new interpretations of the phenomenon, but I suspect that forms power and the ability to give or to take away, in any case, could be an important component of its understanding.

26. "flirtearé de preciso para no disminuir mi ascendente social y viendo tú que me desean los otros hombres, te resultaré más deseable" (115).

27. "rémora para los suyos" (108).

28. "—Te has subido a un pedestal al que no alcanzamos los simples mortales. —Siempre fui ambiciosa. —Y conseguiste lo que te proponías: hoy eres una mujer célebre en España" (28).

29. "Los ricos no comprenden estas cosas" (34).

30. "Al cumplir los diez y seis, cuando se casó su hermana Mónica, la presentaron en sociedad lanzándola a la Bolsa de Cotización de Matrimonios en el momento en que se recogía la emisión de papel de la mayor de las señoritas de Albalena" (82).

31. "Don Luis no aportó nada al matrimonio. Los tres millones de pesetas llevados por la pubilla, lejos de aumentar, cultivando las fincas que poseía en la provincia de Tarragona y especialmente en la corchera de la jurisdicción de San Feliú de Guixols, soportan hipotecas crecidísimas que considero imposible que puedan ser levantadas" (62).

32. "La información particular que abonará usted extra, me hace creer que no, pues acusa un desnivel entre los ingresos y los gastos, lo que explica la venta constante de valores, las hipotecas sobre la gran finca corchera, y la venta proyectada de esa finca, que es el núcleo del capital" (ibid.).

33. "el rico mueblaje de la estancia, la fina vajilla de porcelana, la cristalería de Baccarat, los cubiertos de plata y las flores que completaban con el mantel y las servilletas de finísimo damasco, un conjunto de confort y bienestar" (114).

34. "Mi amigo el ministro le concederá un destino bien remunerado, y mañana mismo, si quiere, entrará de pasante en casa de Baró, uno de los primeros bufetes de Barcelona" (ibid.).

35. "tanta audacia femenina" (ibid.).

36. "Señor don Luis, ¿quiere usted otorgarme la mano de su hijo Max?" (116).

37. "le ofrecí en cambio renunciar a toda labor literaria, pues dice que los versos resultan inútiles y cursis. Seguiré su consejo, traduciré del francés alguna obra

de Derecho, luego recopilaré ideas de diversos autores, pondré algo propio, y daré a la estampa una obra original de mi profesión" (119).

WORKS CITED

Berman, Marshall. *Todo lo que es sólido se desvanece en el aire.* Mexico City: Siglo XXI, 1991.

Eulate Sanjurjo, Carmela. *El asombroso doctor Jover.* Barcelona: Ediciones Edita, 1930.

———. *La muñeca.* San Juan: Editorial del Instituto de Cultura Puertorriqueña, 1994.

———. *Las veleidades de Consuelo.* Barcelona: Editorial Juventud, 1950.

———. *Teresa y María.* Barcelona: Talleres Gráficos de la Sociedad General de Publicaciones, 1936.

Felski, Rita. *The Gender of Modernity.* Cambridge: Harvard University Press, 1995.

Foucault, Michel. *The History of Sexuality.* Trans. Robert Hurley. New York: Vintage Books, 1988.

Galton, Francis. "Eugenics, Its Definition, Scope and Aims." *American Journal of Sociology* 10.1 (July 1904): 1–25.

González-Pérez, Aníbal. *La novela modernista hispanoamericana.* Madrid: Gredos, 1987.

Labanyi, Jo. *Gender and Modernization in the Spanish Realist Novel.* New York: Oxford University Press, 2000.

Medick, Hans, and David Warren Sabean, eds. *Interest and Emotion: Essays on the Study of Family and Kinship.* New York: Cambridge University Press, 1984.

———. "Interest and Emotion in Family and Kinship Studies: A Critique of Social History and Anthropology." In *Interest and Emotion,* ed. Hans Medick and David Warren Sabean. New York: Cambridge University Press, 1984. 9–27.

Phillips, Adam. *On Flirtation: An Introduction.* Cambridge: Harvard University Press, 1994.

Ramos, Julio. *Desencuentros de la modernidad: literatura y política en el siglo XIX.* Mexico City: Fondo de Cultura Económica, 1989.

Santos-Silva, Loreina. "Esquema biográfico." In *La muñeca* by Carmela Eulate Sanjurjo. Río Piedras: Editorial de la Universidad de Puerto Rico, 1994.

Simmel, Georg. "Flirtation." In *Georg Simmel, On Women, Sexuality, and Love.* New Haven: Yale University Press, 1984.

Singer, Ben. *Melodrama and Modernity: Early Sensational Cinema and Its Contexts.* New York: Columbia University Press, 2001.

Social Issues Research Institute. "SIRC Guide to Flirting." January 15, 2005. http://www.sirc.org/publik/flirt.html.

Sommer, Doris. *Foundational Fictions: The National Romances of Latin America.* Berkeley: University of California Press, 1991.

Ubieto, Antonio, Juan Reglá, José María Jover, and Carlos Seco. *Introducción a la historia de España.* Barcelona: Editorial Teide, 1979.

Yelvington, Kevin A., Caroline Osella, and Filippo Osella. "Power/Flirting." *Journal of the Royal Anthropological Institute.* 5.3 (September 1999): 457–60.

12

Woman between Paris and Caracas

Iphigenia by Teresa de la Parra

NAOMI LINDSTROM

The 1924 novel *Iphigenia (The Diary of a Young Lady Who Wrote Because She Was Bored)* by the Paris-born Venezuelan writer Teresa de la Parra (1889–1936) is first and foremost the self-portrait of a young woman. María Eugenia, the narrator-protagonist, is torn between the respectability of traditional Caracas and a free-spirited, risk-taking approach to life. The latter is linked in her mind to an idealized vision of Paris as a space of complete personal liberty, where everyone, male or female, is free to come and go as he or she pleases. As *Iphigenia* begins, María Eugenia is eighteen, just back from a short stay in Paris, and mildly rebellious. At its end she is twenty and declares herself resigned to marriage to a family-approved suitor and absorption into traditional Caracas society. She records her experiences and confides her feelings, first in an immensely long letter to a friend, then in a diary. The heroine neglects the diary for months and then resumes it. In this way, her self-account is divided into a period before and an era after she has become outwardly socialized into the old-line Caracas bourgeoisie and has apparently relinquished her dreams of "Parisian" freedom. The long letter and the two sections of the diary make up the text of *Iphigenia*.

At the same time, the novel offers a highly judgmental characterization of Caracas, where, with the exception of three months in the country, the heroine is situated as she writes down her memories and reflections. (Paris only appears in characters' accounts drawn from memory.) Like the protagonist-narrator, Caracas appears as a divided entity with competing forces seeking to retain their traditional dominance or become the new prime factor. As Barbara Probst Solomon summarizes the novel's portrayal of the city, it is "a Caracas in social transition, a society trapped between a disintegrating land-owning aristocracy and the new bourgeoisie created by oil money" (22). In addition to the old and new elite groups that Solomon mentions, poor people and impoverished zones appear in *Iphigenia*'s portrait of the city. The novel also presents a clique of wealthy bohemians who physically reside in Caracas, but identify with Paris, or at least with their mental image of the French capital.

At the time of its publication as a book, *Iphigenia* aroused indignation among many readers in Venezuela. Part of what would become the novel *Iphigenia* had appeared in 1922 in the Caracas magazine *La Lectura Semanal* (Weekly reading), apparently without creating a scandal. However, its first edition as a book was printed in Paris, where the author had joined the sizable population of Venezuelan expatriates, and was soon exported back to South America. The novel's daring features include the disparagement, by various figures, of the institution of marriage. In addition, characters allude to certain widely whispered secrets of Caracas. The heroine's Uncle Pancho, from the nonconformist paternal side of the family, enjoys airing gossip about the city's elite, such as long-ago infidelities and likely African ancestry.

Apart from provocative remarks by the novel's characters, an important point of controversy in 1920s Venezuela was *Iphigenia*'s depiction of Caracas, both the city and the society. Gabriella Ibieta summarizes contemporary reaction to the novel in Caracas: "Even though an excerpt from *Iphigenia* had been published to great acclaim by *La Lectura Semanal,* the work in its entirety presented problems that the reading public could not accept at that time. For instance, de la Parra's acute and often negative observations about the suffocating atmosphere of Caracas's upper-class society did not go unnoticed" (423). According to Velia Bosch, Enrique Bernardo Núñez remarked that de la Parra had "bad luck when she got the idea of placing her characters in Caracas," leading many local readers to take personal offense (xxx). Ibieta observes: "Interestingly, however, the Venezuelans and other Latin Americans then living in Paris were generally enthusiastic about the novel" (ibid.). One may conjecture that, as expatriates, they were more sympathetic to, and perhaps shared, María Eugenia's vision of Caracas as a place that stifled individual freedom.[1]

The physical city of Caracas seemed, to *Iphigenia*'s detractors, to appear represented in an unflattering light. At a time when Venezuela was striving for modernization, *Iphigenia* focused attention on Caracas's older, and in some episodes decaying, urban zones. María Eugenia makes use of negatively charged terms, such as "drowsy" (38), to refer to the city.[2] An example that particularly stands out, and which upset contemporaries, is María Eugenia's vivid recollection of her disappointing first sight of Caracas after a lengthy absence in Europe:

> The city seemed bowed down by the mountains, by the eaves, by the telephone lines whose endless fibers, strung low, immutable,[3] sketched streaks across the bright blue of the sky and the undefined gray of some distant hills . . . Oh! yes . . . Caracas, of the delightful climate, of gentle memories, the familiar city, the intimate and distant city, turned out to be that flat town . . . a kind of Andalusian city, like a melancholy Andalusia, without a shawl or castanets, without guitars or music, without flower-pots and flowers on the balconies . . . a drowsy Andalusia that had dropped off to sleep in the sultry heat of the tropics! (*Iphigenia*, 37–38)[4]

Julieta Fombona describes de la Parra's exchange with a critic who objected to this image of Caracas that *Iphigenia* offers:

> To someone who reproached her with presenting Caracas in her novel as a backward, provincial city, she answered that she was perfectly aware of the existence there of a society that was very au courant, very refined and sophisticated, that played golf and danced the Charleston, but that what interested her as a novelist was the other Caracas: "that of those old houses, temples of boredom, through which, as in ancient, musty churches, there floated the age-old smell of traditions and blood lines (*raza*)." (xvi)

María Eugenia's observations in the novel concerning the staid conservatism of everyday life in Caracas are part of a tradition of Spanish-American intellectuals lamenting what they perceive as a resistance to change in Spanish-American society. It is easy to think of celebrated examples beginning with Domingo F. Sarmiento's foundational essay of 1845, *Civilización i barbarie: Vida de Juan Facundo Quiroga* (English versions: *Life in the Argentine Republic in the Days of the Tyrants; or, Civilization and Barbarism* and *Facundo; or, Civilization and Barbarism*), in which the author expresses frustration over Argentina's slowness to modernize its infrastructure and social institutions. Another fundamental figure in the Spanish-American essay, the Cuban national hero José Martí, perceived Spanish America as shrinking from participation in the excitement of new cultural tendencies.

An example closer to Teresa de la Parra, because her critique includes the element of gender, is the Cuban poet and novelist Gertrudis Gómez de Avellaneda. In her *Autobiografía,* composed in 1839 and included in the English-language volume *Sab and Autobiography,* Avellaneda evokes the superficial and intellectually stagnant existence of wealthy young Cuban women, who had little to occupy their minds beyond dressing fashionably, maximizing their beauty, and appearing at dances until they could be married off as advantageously as possible. Avellaneda portrays herself as at first immersed in this archaic conventionalism, but eventually able to rise above it and form part of her era's intellectual and cultural life.

Iphigenia also portrays the protagonist's struggles to rise above social conventions. The novel's characterizations of its central character and of its urban setting are closely linked. The struggle over María Eugenia is waged between one set of characters identified as defenders of tradition and another composed of anticonventional figures who, in diverse ways, militate in favor of individual freedom. The traditionalists are a strikingly homogeneous group, all being either members of, friends of, or individuals handpicked by María Eugenia's starchy maternal relatives. A much more varied cast of characters, including a paternal uncle, a laundress, a child, various local nonconformists, and (in the heroine's memory) the entire population of Paris, stands in opposition to the maternal relatives' attempt to domesticate the protagonist. The conflict involves, among other questions, the issue of where a woman can go in a city and under what circumstances. Throughout the narrative, different neighborhoods of and sites in Caracas, and even various areas within a single house, appear in contrast to one another. For a marriageable, upper-class young woman like María Eugenia, Caracas is divided into certain areas where her family is intent on placing her, a second set of areas that are merely disapproved of, and the rest of the city, which is forbidden.

In addition, Caracas as a whole stands in contrast to the memory of Paris, where the young protagonist has spent the three months immediately preceding her return to Venezuela. The novel's characters often refer to Paris in moments of stress. In particular, those figures associated with "free ideas" treasure their remembrances of Paris as an elegant, modern place in which they at one time took more pleasure in life than they now do in straitlaced Caracas. The characters who support Caracas tradition refer to Paris less frequently. When they do, it is at times with horror, as a place of rule-breaking, if not as "one huge house of corruption let loose on the streets" (32).[5]

María Eugenia is among those longing for Paris. During her most recent stay in the city, housed with liberal family friends, she traveled about the city without a chaperone. In Paris she could rely on perennially available taxis to gain access to locations of her own choosing. For María Eugenia, the most desirable places to be in Paris are, on the one hand, high-end women's-wear shops and, on the other, public spaces like the Place de la Concorde, Champs-Élysées, Bois de la Boulogne, and the cities' major boulevards (141). She prizes the latter, open-to-all urban areas as show-cases where she could believe herself the focus of all eyes in her newly acquired, up-to-the-minute chic. María Eugenia's memories of this stay in Paris cross the line into fantasy as she rapturously recalls herself and her new clothes arousing universal admiration in the French capital. Of her hats, she remarks, "Just imagine, they attracted attention in Paris!" (49).[6] As Gabriela Mora observes, María Eugenia inadvertently reveals that, far from creating a citywide stir as she claims, she interacted with very few people during her stay in Paris (133).

One item of María Eugenia's Parisian wardrobe on which she especially dwells is a black hat with a veil that, a saleswoman tells her, is of a type worn only by widows. When she wears this headdress on the street or in shops, it confers upon her an "assumed widowhood" (15).[7] On one shopping trip, she strengthens the effect of widowhood with another accessory, a borrowed three-year-old. María Eugenia never says why she derives pleasure from impersonating a widow and hearing saleswomen address her as "Madame" rather than "Mademoiselle" (15).[8] Nonetheless, I would conjecture that the young woman is savoring, via this fiction, the often-noted exceptional independence of financially comfortable widows compared with other women. Married women were subject to husbands; those who had yet to be married were perceived as constantly in danger of losing their virginity.

When María Eugenia speaks of her recent stay in Paris, it is clear that in her mind a woman's freedom to move about a city is commingled with a different form of liberty: free spending in shopping districts. During her first days back in Caracas, her proper relatives express horror over her recent unfettered movement and unrestrained spending in Paris, but she defends both. Reproached with squandering the last of her inheritance in high-end Parisian shops, she produces a justification of her actions in which she equates expenditure with personal autonomy: "Do you think, do you think, Grandmother, that I would trade those days of freedom just to have twenty wretched pesos a month? . . . Oh! No, no, no!" (30).[9]

Readers of the novel are likely to view favorably María Eugenia's desire to navigate the urban space without interference and to judge much less positively her closely linked campaign to spend all available funds on luxuries. Mora comments that some readers have always been disconcerted by *Iphigenia* and its main character because of María Eugenia's frequent lapses into vanity and superficiality, even when she is trying to confront a serious matter. Mora reminds readers to stay aware that de la Parra is not writing a frivolous novel: "The superficial comments about matters of no importance are part of the realism with which the character is portrayed. One must not forget that the person writing is an eighteen-year-old, upper-class girl, first corresponding with a friend of a similar type, and then later lost in the sentimental vagaries of her first love, circumstances that would justify her frivolity" (135–36). The author is thematizing frivolity as an aspect of the personality of a very young protagonist.

Significantly, María Eugenia recounts her activities in Paris only after months have gone by and nostalgia has magnified events. As the title of the novel indicates, she sets pen to paper to compensate for lack of stimulation in her current existence in Caracas. Although María Eugenia longs to return to Paris, and in two episodes other characters offer to take her with them to the French capital, she is never able to return to the place that she associates with personal fulfillment. Paris figures in the novel purely as it has been reconstructed, and often greatly embellished, in the minds of the characters, especially those who are experiencing dissatisfaction with Caracas.

Critics have characterized María Eugenia's self-account in *Iphigenia* of her unsatisfactory life in Caracas as a narrative of failure. For example, Edna Aizenberg argues that the entire novel may be viewed as a "failed bildungsroman." Elizabeth Garrels notes that María Eugenia "is a person who at several moments is on the verge of lucidity, but always backs away from a full awareness of her situation" (51). María Eugenia's attempt to attain some measure of at least mental independence through her exploration of Caracas is another tale of defeat.

María Eugenia quickly realizes that her maternal grandmother and maiden aunt, in whose care she has been placed, have made it their mission to break her independent spirit and maximize her value on the marriage market. Although she is aware of their campaign, she eventually capitulates to it. Her guardians achieve apparent success during the months in which María Eugenia neglects her diary, because, in the "after" sections, she shows greater concern with maintaining a show of propriety. As Mora points out, though, "what María Eugenia has really learned is to pretend skillfully" (141), rather than to share the outlook of her more respectable relatives. In the first months after the protagonist's return to Caracas, however, she openly resists control by struggling to gain access to spaces deemed unsuitable for a young lady.

Particularly attractive to María Eugenia in her early days back in Caracas are areas associated with people of African ancestry, whether classified as black or as mulatto. At various moments, angered by her own situation as a young woman with elite lineage but no inheritance, she expresses her alienation from her own class by drawing nearer to poor people of African descent.

While her resentment is at its height, María Eugenia spends considerable time in a milieu that, while lowly, is still on the grounds of her grandmother's house. This space is the corral, the purview of Gregoria, the family's elderly African-Venezuelan laundress who cared for María Eugenia during the latter's earliest years. It is no mere convention to call Gregoria "black." Her skin actually is black. María Eugenia frequently observes, with pleasure, how black Gregoria's skin appears in contrast with white soapsuds and bleached linen. Of the characters who encourage María Eugenia to break with established mores, Gregoria is the only one who has no connection with Paris. What links her to the other anticonventional figures is outsider status in relation to the ultrarespectable faction of the Caracas bourgeoisie. The extreme darkness of Gregoria's skin reassures María Eugenia that the laundress, though a member of the household, is very different from the grandmother and aunt and does not share their plans for the young woman.

Spending time in the corral, in the company of Gregoria is, as María Eugenia puts it, "a delight" (101).[10] One reason that this space attracts her is that, although it is part of the home and not off-limits, her presence there provokes disapproval. The heroine's maiden aunt says to her every day, "A young lady's place is not in the corral, not in the society of servants"

(102).[11] In addition to providing the thrill of a disapproved-of locale, the corral stands out in María Eugenia's mind as an open space. She contrasts the corral and other fenced-in yards as a redeeming feature of an otherwise constricted and confining city (101).[12] One of her reflections begins with praise for "our forebears, who founded the city of Caracas" (ibid.), for leaving these small open areas within the urban space.[13] As María Eugenia critiques the city's layout, she identifies features that limit or discourage movement, such as narrow streets paved with sharp pebbles and window bars that protrude out onto the already cramped roadways. The private yards provide "a way to live in a community without renouncing the rustic and bucolic charms of country life" (ibid.).[14]

After María Eugenia assumes a more docile persona, she seldom visits the corral. Yet, in a moment of crisis, in her account, "I came to seek relief in the outdoor peace of the corral, which is the only generous space in this poor, cramped house" (286).[15] In addition, María Eugenia enjoys the corral as a place where otherwise suppressed information can circulate freely. Out of earshot of the heroine's grandmother and aunt, who seldom venture out of doors, Gregoria is quick to air the proverbial dirty laundry. The longtime laundress and Uncle Pancho are María Eugenia's main sources of information about aspects of the family's past over which the others draw a veil.

Issues of race also figure in the episode in which María Eugenia most dramatically violates the rules meant to govern her whereabouts. On this occasion, she seeks access to a poor neighborhood of the city, La Pastora, whose population is predominantly black and mulatto. This transgression occurs shortly after she discovers that an especially annoying uncle, who cultivates the appearance of a solid citizen, is now owner of a country estate that should have been three-quarters hers. She then persuades Uncle Pancho to take her on a tour of La Pastora. After reassuring her grandmother that she is heading to a destination suitable for moments of quiet contemplation (163), she demands: "Take me down the oldest streets, Uncle Pancho, take me down the poorest, the ugliest, the dirtiest, the saddest, because I want to see them all, all of them!" (69).[16] However, the trip hardly results in a breakthrough in racial understanding. Pancho expounds some poorly conceived theories about the ill results of racial mixing while María Eugenia, commenting like a tourist on the picturesque charm of the impoverished neighborhood, reduces the intended journey of learning to a slumming jaunt.

As Mora points out, María Eugenia's effort to assert her independence, while upsetting to her grandmother, "does not go far enough for her behavior to qualify as rebellious" (134). This generalization applies to the protagonist's very limited success in exploring Caracas beyond the spaces to which she is allowed access. A major hindrance is that, to gain entry to forbidden zones, she is dependent on an ally, Uncle Pancho, who is a drinker in shaky health. The antiauthoritarian, uninhibited Pancho enjoys loosening the restrictions that her maternal relatives try to maintain over María Eugenia. In the early parts of the novel, while he is still well enough to ramble about the city, Pancho is consistently associated with means of transportation. Appearing at various moments in a beat-up automobile and a horse-drawn carriage, and in addition given to lengthy strolls, he allows the young woman to cover a range of territory to which she would otherwise be denied access.[17] Other family members tell the protagonist where they will take her and at what time. Pancho is the only one who will come at María Eugenia's bidding and allow her to dictate the itinerary (69).[18]

Garrels (51) singles out the visit to La Pastora as an example of María Eugenia's habit of approaching an insight about the workings of society, then backing away from it. In this critic's interpretation, after discovering that her inheritance has been diverted, "Sensitized by the awareness of her own lack of independence, of her own enslavement to what it means in her social class to have a woman's body and at the same time lack money, she momentarily glimpses a fraternity that unites her with others who also suffer because of their bodies—people of color" (51). The mulatto women are "condemned by the racial identity of their bodies," while María Eugenia is "condemned by the sexual identity of hers" (52). However, this identification is only momentary, as she returns to her grandmother's control.

In direct opposition to Pancho, familiar with all of Caracas and Paris, is the protagonist's maternal grandmother, Eugenia. The grandmother attempts to keep María Eugenia inside her house as much as possible. To support her efforts to restrict the young woman's movements, she cites not only general norms of propriety but also the circumstance that her granddaughter is observing a period of mourning, with the special protocols that it entails. The etiquette of mourning becomes a pretext for control. Although María Eugenia's father has died several months ago, he kept his daughter in boarding schools and only saw her occasionally. She has positive memories of him, especially in that he figures among the family members who represent personal freedom. But, as her letter and diary reveal, she rarely thinks of him and it is almost a conventional fiction that she is mourning him. The grandmother's fundamental motive appears to be to preserve María Eugenia's marriageability—her last remaining asset—by preventing her from acting on her desire to explore.

Toward the end of the novel, when the protagonist's beloved Uncle Pancho dies, readers discover that mourning customs, which the grandmother earlier invoked as absolute, are flexible. María Eugenia is rebuffed when she requests to postpone her imminent wedding in observance of mourning. Her family-approved fiancé allows only ten days between Uncle Pancho's death and the ceremony. During these ten days María Eugenia, exhausted from nursing her uncle, is prompted by her grandmother and aunt to keep on schedule with such worldly activities as adjustments to her wedding gown. María Eugenia, her grandmother, and her aunt accede to the fiancé's demand out of fear of losing the opportunity for an advantageous marriage. The contrast between the artificial period of mourning for the father and the denial of needed mourning time for the uncle illustrates a major theme of the novel, the arbitrary character of social conventions.

Starting with María Eugenia's return to Caracas, the grandmother's goal is not to isolate her, but to invite exclusively selected individuals to meet and admire her granddaughter in an environment that the older woman can control. The young woman, formally dressed, is made the centerpiece of what she calls "a kind of exhibit before Grandmother's Gothic friends, that is to say, before a small number of people of both sexes more or less uniform as far as their ideas, dress, and age" (43).[19] Uncle Pancho offers María Eugenia this explanation of her grandmother's behavior: "Eugenia is very vain about you. You are her pride now, rather like what a new hat brought from Europe must have been in her youth. She wants to show you off to everyone, as a part of herself, I mean, in her house" (79).[20] Uncle Pancho omits from this explanation another of the grandmother's motives, one that Eugenia does not disguise. Eugenia and the other conformist members of the family are striving to situate her granddaughter in the path of an eventual prestigious suitor who can shore up the young woman's depleted finances. Their appraisal of the situation is that, as the ceaselessly mercantile Uncle Eduardo puts it, "in Caracas there are few eligible bachelors" (221)[21] and therefore the family should do everything possible to lead one of them to María Eugenia and secure his attachment via marriage.

In pursuit of this goal, Eugenia is almost obsessed with situating her granddaughter's body in the right part of the house and the correct posture.

María Eugenia's spontaneous tendency is to perch on any type of support, including tabletops and a pedestal designed to hold a potted palm. Her grandmother is intent on limiting her to conventional seating, especially the drawing-room sofa. The sofa, which is mentioned many times in the course of the novel, is the spot on which the young woman is displayed to visitors and, later on, courted by her ultraconservative fiancé. María Eugenia remembers this piece of furniture from her childhood. It seems to be unfailingly positioned in an invariable location and covered in blue damask. The sofa figures as the official site of courtship in the house. María Eugenia recalls her then-young aunt occupying the same place on the same sofa to receive a gentleman caller. The older woman failed to retain the affection of her suitor and ended up as the classic "old maid" with no prospects of marriage or independent income, living out her years as a dependent in other people's houses. The sofa carries, for María Eugenia, a reminder of the urgency of contracting marriage to a good husband before opportunity passes her by.

As well as placing her granddaughter in optimal locations, Eugenia is obsessed with controlling the disposition of the young woman's limbs. María Eugenia's spontaneous postures are censured because of their association with low social class, with masculinity, or with both: "you assume the manners of a [male] street urchin" (47).[22]

The grandmother's campaign to pose and display María Eugenia reaches an extreme when she decides that it is time for the heroine, who by now is twenty and to outward appearances thoroughly domesticated, to "sit in the window" (215).[23] At the same time every afternoon, María Eugenia and her maiden aunt don their finery and, with a pet poodle for an accessory, arrange themselves at the window in what at first strikes the protagonist as "immobile and solemn attitudes that were horribly false" (216).[24] Although the grandmother suggests the window-sitting sessions and serves as stage manager, she finds that she cannot participate directly because she "has a fear of the drafts and the dust from the street" (218–19).[25] This is another reminder that the character who serves as spokeswoman for concepts of female propriety, striving to restrict her granddaughter to highly selected spaces, herself lives as a virtual agoraphobic. As María Eugenia observes, "she never sets foot in the street" (128).[26]

After María Eugenia realizes that passers-by are admiring her beauty, without ceasing to find the ceremony ridiculous, she takes pleasure in it. In Mora's analysis, although the young woman is at moments a shrewd

observer of social customs, "vanity . . . is very evident in the protagonist
of the novel," making the accuracy of her observations and judgments
problematic (135). At the same time that María Eugenia perceives herself
as a figure of admiration, she comes to understand that the sessions spent
sitting by the window are another of her grandmother's strategies to showcase her in the sight of a well-off suitor. In fact, her future fiancé is first
attracted to her as he passes by in his new automobile. María Eugenia for-
mulates her insight through an apt analogy: "I found that seated like this,
in the lighted room, at the window wide open to the bustling street, my
person acquired a notable likeness to those luxury items that are exhibited
at night in store windows to tempt shoppers" (218).[27]

In contrast with the restrictive space of her grandmother's window,
María Eugenia lovingly evokes in her diary the house, and especially the
boudoir, of Mercedes Galindo. Before the unconventional Mercedes appears
in the novel, María Eugenia begins hearing of her. In the protagonist's
lengthy letter, she gives a portrait of the still-unseen Mercedes: "In Caracas
there is a married lady, between thirty and thirty-five years old, lovely,
elegant, very distinguished, a distant relative and close friend of Uncle
Pancho and Papa" (85),[28] that is to say, affiliated with the paternal—and
more bohemian—side of María Eugenia's family. Despite resistance from
her grandmother, according to whom, besides being married to a libertine,
"Mercedes herself had very liberal ideas, a wrong concept of life" (207),[29]
María Eugenia finally succeeds in meeting this talked-about person. The
young woman soon becomes a frequent visitor to Mercedes's elaborately
decorated home.

Mercedes's house figures ambiguously in the geography of the novel,
being neither an entirely proper space for a young lady nor expressly taboo.
The young woman's grandmother cannot actually forbid her to visit a member of her own family, though she can inveigh against "the atmosphere of
Mercedes's home" (116).[30] Yet Mercedes's dwelling is on the far edge of the
respectable zone, partly because of her husband's widely rumored dissi-
pation and partly owing to the outlook of the mistress of the house and the
liberal crowd to whom she plays hostess. To gain initial access to this place
of suspected danger, María Eugenia must again depend on her most read-
ily available ally, Uncle Pancho. Pancho is happy to help his niece escape
temporarily from her grandmother's tight grip.

Caracas is the location of Mercedes's house. Yet once María Eugenia is
inside this special space, which features one of the sumptuous interiors

favored in *modernista* writing, she feels as if she were no longer in a South American city. The link to Europe is strengthened by the knowledge that the furnishings were not merely purchased from an import house. Rather, as Mercedes enjoys pointing out, they were part of her residence in Paris. The up-to-date French décor contrasts with the interior of the grandmother's home. Although the latter's house has been remodeled, it still looks like a place where time stands still. The décor features mosaic tiles, wicker chairs, potted plants on pedestals, a sewing basket, mahogany heirlooms, and, of course, the sofa designated for the family's marriageable young women. María Eugenia immediately judges the grandmother's house as "such an out-of-date ambience, one so old-fashioned" (41).[31]

Fleeing this stultifying environment, the young woman reflects euphorically: "What a delicious atmosphere one breathes in the house of Alberto and Mercedes! It's as if, along with the pictures, tapestries, and Sèvres porcelains, they had also filled their house with that divine atmosphere that I was only allowed to breathe for a few days during my last and all-too-short stay in Paris" (110).[32] The characterization of Mercedes exemplifies the connection, made throughout the novel, between dissatisfaction with the traditionalism of Caracas and a rose-colored memory of Paris. The unhappy Mercedes is given to "alluding to the time she lived in Paris in a beautiful, exclusive hotel, rich and surrounded by influential friends like a princess" (110).[33]

Not only is the décor brought over from Paris. In Mercedes's house, conversation has a Continental sophistication. For the sake of amusement, the hostess allows guests to air daringly anticonventional views and permits the conversation to assume, from time to time, a mildly risqué character. The above-mentioned rumors about the ancestry of old-line Caracas families, which created a shock effect at the time of the novel's publication, appear as a topic of lighthearted gossip during soirées at Mercedes's house.

Inside this miniature Paris is an Oriental refuge, Mercedes's boudoir. This room is distinguished from the rest of the house by its Asian décor and by its special status as women's space. The boudoir is where Mercedes retreats after unpleasant encounters with her husband, who apparently is not allowed into the room. Mercedes draws María Eugenia into "the intimacy of her make-believe Orient" (162),[34] where the two share confidences. Since the 1978 publication of Edward Said's *Orientalism,* many readers pay particular attention to the artificial Orients that non-Asians construct, suspecting that they may betray a racist or imperialist mind-set. However, it would be difficult to subject Mercedes's boudoir to an analysis along these lines, especially given the scant information readers have about it. *Iphigenia* provides extremely few details concerning this room or the characteristics that identify it as Oriental. Its principal feature, or at least the one that María Eugenia mentions, is a Turkish divan with numerous pillows. María Eugenia delights in the boudoir, and there is nothing in the novel that would indicate that Mercedes is being critiqued for her version of the Orient. Instead, her devotion to this room is a measure of the unhappiness that she feels in her marriage and in Caracas, driving her to take comfort in exoticism. Although the novel barely sketches in the room's Oriental characteristics, its exceptionality as gendered space is treated more fully. It is in the boudoir that the two women confide in one another with the fewest inhibitions.

Mercedes and the oasis of relative freedom that her house provides to María Eugenia eventually disappear from the novel. When it becomes known that Mercedes is ending her marriage, the protagonist's grandmother seizes the opportunity to shift this distant cousin's home from the category of disapproved-of destinations to the forbidden zone. María Eugenia loses not only a friend and confidante but also a rationale for venturing out of her grandmother's house and moving about Caracas. When Uncle Pancho's health worsens, María Eugenia's movement is further circumscribed, because he was able to accompany her to places that would otherwise have been inaccessible to her. After these events, the protagonist has little opportunity to be in spaces where she is not controlled by the family traditionalists.

The process of limiting María Eugenia's movements is reprised during the three months she spends in the country. Alarmed by her interest in a somewhat bohemian man that Mercedes has selected for María Eugenia, the family whisks her off to the same estate to which she should rightly have been principal heiress. During her stay in the country, she achieves a small triumph over her maternal relatives. While throughout most of the novel they are a uniformly straitlaced tribe, the rebellious niece temporarily wins one of them, her smitten cousin, over to the side of the rule-bending and -breaking characters. María Eugenia roams all over the grounds in the company of the younger cousin who has a crush on her. However, her young admirer, in an unguarded moment, reveals their freedom of movement to her starchy relatives and the same conflict erupts. María Eugenia has been writing while sitting by a natural pool in the river, but the older women now attempt to restrict her composition to the supervised environment of the house. Her young male cousin is allowed to remain outdoors, but required to perform purposeful chores rather than wander idly.

María Eugenia's movement, then, is restricted in both the country and the city. Immediately upon her return to Caracas from Europe, her grandmother tells her that she cannot go out into the city alone. María Eugenia appears to obey this directive fully. At no point in the novel does she describe herself as venturing beyond the borders of family property without some type of chaperone. As she spends more time under the control of her grandmother and aunt, the area of the city that she is able to cover steadily shrinks. Her boldest foray, the expedition to La Pastora, occurs only a short time after she comes back from Paris. The events recorded in the latter portions of her diary take place inside her grandmother's house.

The major turning point in the novel's plot occurs near the end. At this juncture, the forces promoting conventionality and those favoring risk taking appear equally likely to prevail in determining the course of María Eugenia's future life. The struggle that has been going on throughout the novel is now encapsulated in the rivalry of two men attempting to win over the protagonist. Tradition is incarnated by the pompous fiancé who has her family's backing. A more daring approach is represented by the young man that Mercedes had earlier selected for María Eugenia. The latter, though by now married, tries to persuade the protagonist to run away with him.

The two men's appeals to María Eugenia bring up again the question of her liberty of movement. The official fiancé makes it clear that he wants his wife at home and prohibited from such displays of modern independence as bobbed hair. The honeymoon he has planned involves very little travel. The newlyweds will stay in a rented country house before settling definitively into their home in Caracas. In contrast, María Eugenia's other admirer, in a secret letter, paints for her a future of constant movement and adventure if she is willing to join him. In the letter, he informs her that he has already booked passage for them both on an ocean liner (324).[35] In the course of his rapturous portrayal of their future travels together, he invokes the names of various cities. He goes beyond the usual Western European tour to name cities like Baghdad, Alexandria, and Constantinople, which few Venezuelan women of María Eugenia's generation would ever have the opportunity to visit. But the couple's first destination and primary home base in Europe is specified as, predictably, a highly idealized Paris: "Like all lovers . . . we will weave our first nest under some eave in the shadow of a tree, in that Parisian springtime, always rosy and blooming with flowers" (325).[36]

According to the letter, María Eugenia can attain this glamorous existence and become "an exquisite Parisian" (327)[37] only if she follows the letter's step-by-step instructions for carrying out the rendezvous with her married admirer. In the novel's next-to-last sequence, María Eugenia begins to follow the instructions to the letter but becomes unnerved and abandons the plan halfway through. The protagonist characterizes her decision to accept her conventional suitor as a sacrifice. Almost at the novel's end, she makes explicit the allusion that has been present in the novel's title and the subtitles of its third and fourth parts, referring to the daughter that Agamemnon sacrificed for favorable winds to set sail and invade Troy: "As in the ancient tragedy, I am Iphigenia" (353).[38] In notable contrast, critics have viewed the protagonist's change of plans less as a sacrifice than as a capitulation to social pressure and fear of life without marriage.

Critics, and readers generally, have long striven to interpret the protagonist's motives for backing out of the escape (for example, Fombona, xvi–xvii). Another question that critics have taken up is whether María Eugenia's capitulation to a conventional marriage makes *Iphigenia* more or less of a feminist novel. In her study, Siegel argues that the disappointing outcome of the central conflict sharpens readers' awareness of the few options open to women in María Eugenia's situation. Moya-Raggio, in contrast, suggests that the protagonist's last-minute decision to accept a traditional marriage reflects a lingering conservatism in the mind of the real-life author. In her judgment, de la Parra's "critical vision is limited and bounded by her own origin and social position" (170).

Although there may be little left to add to the discussion of the meaning of the protagonist's swerve back toward conformity, I would like to note that this moment of crisis again draws attention to María Eugenia's difficulty in making her way through the city. The escape plan requires the young woman to do something she has not done since returning to Venezuela: step out alone onto the Caracas street. Her would-be lover will wait for her in a car standing at a nearby street corner. He foresees that sneaking out of her house when it is barely daylight and making her way unaccompanied down the street will be exceptionally frightening. He imagines that she will reach him "trembling with fright . . . pale" (324).[39] In the letter he encourages her to perform "one act of moral courage" (ibid.) and assures her that once she reaches his car he will protect her, emphasizing the idea that a woman out in the city needs an escort.[40]

After setting the projected escape in motion, María Eugenia's means of aborting the plan is to stay at home and take to bed. While packing, she encounters her aunt in the still-dark house. María Eugenia realizes that she could easily explain away her activities and continue with her plan. Instead, she behaves alarmingly, crying out, "I want to stay here,"[41] begging her aunt to stay with her. She turns herself into a distraught, ill creature who needs to be put to bed.

Iphigenia does not contain an explanation of María Eugenia's behavior at its crucial moment, and her actions cannot fairly be attributed to a single motive. While respecting the novel's reticence, I would still point out that the attempted escape from an especially confining marriage runs into a problem that María Eugenia has encountered ever since her return to Caracas from Paris. Lacking any opportunity to move about the city without supervision, she has suffered a loss of the ability to independently enter and navigate the urban space.

NOTES

1. Along similar lines, Bosch observes: "But despite its contemporary triumph in Europe, in Venezuela, and in Colombia, in that first quarter of a century the novel *Iphigenia* was the center of a scandal" (xxix).

2. "soñolienta" (*Iphigenia,* 122).

3. In the published translation, this word is translated as "innumerable," but I have changed it to "immutable."

4. "La ciudad parecía agobiada por la montaña, agobiada por los aleros, agobiada por los hilos del teléfono, que pasaban bajos, inmutables, rayando con un sinfín de hebras el azul vivo del cielo y el gris indefinido de unos montes... ¡Ah!, ¡sí...! Caracas, la del clima delicioso, la de los recuerdos suaves, la ciudad familiar, la ciudad íntima y lejana, resultaba ser aquella ciudad chata... una especie de ciudad andaluza, de una Andalucía melancólica, sin guitarras ni coplas, sin macetas y sin flores en las rejas... una Andalucía soñolienta que se había adormecido bajo el bochorno de los trópicos" (*Iphigenia,* 122).

5. "una gran casa de corrupción que estuviera suelta por las calles" (113).

6. "¡Figúrate que llamaban la atención en París!" (141).

7. "supuesta viudez" (86).

8. Spanish original, 85.

9. "¿Crees, crees, Abuelita, que cambio esos días de libertad por tener veinte miserables fuertes mensuales...? ¡ah! ¡no, no y no!" (143).

10. "una delicia" (218).

11. "El puesto de una señorita no es el corral, ni su sociedad es la de las sirvientes" (218).

12. Spanish original, 217.

13. "nuestros antepasados, los fundadores de la ciudad de Caracas" (ibid.).

14. "la manera de vivir en ciudadana comunidad sin renunciar a los encantos agrestes y bucólicos de la vida campesina" (ibid.).

15. "me fui a buscar alivio en la paz campesina del corral, que es el único lugar amplio de esta casa angosta y pobre" (516).

16. "Llévame por las calles más viejas, tío Pancho, llévame por las más pobres, por las más feas, por las más sucias, por las más tristes, que quiero conocerlas ¡todas!" (173–74).

17. One of the many transitions that Caracas is undergoing during the time of the novel is that from horse-drawn to motorized vehicles. ·

18. Spanish original, 173.

19. "una especie de exhibición ante las relaciones góticas de Abuelita, es decir, ante un reducido número de personas de ambos sexos más o menos uniformadas en cuanto a ideas, vestimenta y edad" (131).

20. "Eugenia está muy vanidosa de ti. Vienes a ser hoy para su amor propio algo así como lo que debió ser en su juventud un sombrero nuevo traído de Europa. Quiere mostrarte a todos, pero puesto en ella, es decir, en su casa" (190).

21. "en Caracas no abundan los buenos partidos" (418).

22. "tomas estos modales de muchacho de la calle" (137).

23. "ponerse en la ventana" (408).

24. "unas actitudes inmóviles y solemnes que eran horriblemente falsas" (ibid.).

25. "le teme mucho al aire y al polvillo de la calle" (412).

26. "ella no pone jamás los pies en la calle" (264).

27. "Me pareció que sentada así, en el salón alumbrado, junto a la reja abierta de par en par sobre la animación de la calle, mi persona adquiría un notable parecido con esos objetos de lujo que se exhiben de noche en las vidrieras de las tiendas para tentar la codicia de los pasantes" (411).

28. "Hay en Caracas una señora casada, de treinta a treinta y cinco años, preciosa, elegante, distinguidísima, pariente lejana y amiga íntima de tío Pancho y de papá" (199).

29. "la misma Mercedes tenía ideas muy libres, un concepto de la vida muy errónea" (396).

30. "ese ambiente de casa de Mercedes" (243).

31. "un medio ambiente tan atrasado, tan añejo" (128).

32. "¡qué ambiente delicioso se respira allá en la casa de Alberto y de Mercedes!

No parece sino que con los cuadros, los tapices, y las porcelanas de Sèvres se hubiesen traído también, para llenar su casa, aquel divino ambiente que sólo me fue dado respirar algunos días, durante mi última y cortísima permanencia en París" (233).

33. "aludiendo a los tiempos en que vivía en París, en un precioso hotel propio, rica y bien relacionada como una princesa" (ibid.).

34. "la gran intimidad de su fingido Oriente" (321).

35. Spanish original, 574–75.

36. "Como todos los enamorados, iremos a tejer nuestro primer nido, bajo algún alero o a la sombra de algún árbol, en esa primavera de París siempre rosada y florecida" (576).

37. "una exquisita parisiense" (579).

38. "Como en la tragedia antigua soy Iphigenia" (624).

39. "trémula de espanto... pálida" (575).

40. "un acto de valor moral" (574).

41. "quiero quedarme aquí" (605). This line does not appear in the published English translation.

Works Cited

Aizenberg, Edna. "El *Bildungsroman* fracasado en Latinoamérica: el caso de *Iphigenia,* de Teresa de la Parra." *Revista Iberoamericana* 132–33 (July–December 1985): 539–46.

Bosch, Velia. "Estudio crítico." In Teresa de la Parra, *Obra,* xxvii–xxxvii, subsection "*Iphigenia,* entre la crónica lírico-psicológica y la tragicomedia novelada." xxix–xxx.

de la Parra, Teresa. *Ifigenia.* 1924. Madrid: Anaya & Mario Muchnik, 1992. [Complete title, not used on this edition, *Ifigenia. Diario de una señorita que escribió porque se fastidiaba.*]

———. *Iphigenia (The Diary of a Young Lady Who Wrote Because She Was Bored).* Trans. Bertie Acker. Foreword by Naomi Lindstrom. Austin: University of Texas Press, 1993.

———. *Obra: narrativa, ensayos, cartas.* Ed. Velia Bosch. Caracas: Biblioteca Ayacucho, 1982.

Fombona, Julieta. "Teresa de la Parra: las voces de la palabra." In Teresa de la Parra, *Obra,* ix–xxvi.

Garrels, Elizabeth. *Las grietas de la ternura: nueva lectura de Teresa de la Parra.* Caracas: Monte Ávila, 1986.

Ibieta, Gabriella. "Teresa de la Parra." In *Spanish American Women Writers: A Bio-Bibliographical Source Book,* ed. Diane E. Marting. Westport, Conn.: Greenwood Press, 1990. 415–26.

Mora, Gabriela. "La otra cara de Iphigenia: una reevaluación del personaje de Teresa de la Parra." *Sin Nombre* (San Juan) 7.3 (1976): 130–44.

Moya-Raggio, Eliana. "El sacrificio de Iphigenia: Teresa de la Parra y su visión crítica de una Sociedad criolla." *La Torre: Revista de la Universidad de Puerto Rico* 2.5 (January–March 1988): 161–71.

Siegel, Rebeca. "Iphigenia vs Iphigenia: el problema del anticlímax en la novela de Teresa de la Parra." M.A. thesis, University of Texas at Austin, 1991.

Solomon, Barbara Probst. "Una señorita que escribía porque estaba fastidiada." Trans. Víctor Polanco. *Quimera* 130 (1994): 19–25.

13

Amateurs and Professionals in Ena Lucía Portela's Lexicon of Crisis

JACQUELINE LOSS

> in an underhanded manner, the verbs *resolve* and *obtain* had been replacing the verb *to buy* in the lexicon of the crisis.[1]
>
> Ena Lucía Portela

Beginning in the early 1990s, following the 1989 collapse of the Soviet Union, there have abounded lurid narrative descriptions of Cuba's capital city in a crisis nominally attenuated by its official term "Special Period in Times of Peace." The crisis exacerbated racial and economic differences, but the drastic nature of the change also saw the emergence of revised discourse on ethnic, religious, and sexual difference that related to Cuba's new and varied relation with an elaborate external sphere, no longer dominated by the USSR. Writers created other means to deal with this crisis; most internationally successful of the literary expressions of this crisis are Pedro Juan Gutiérrez's realistic portraits of Pedro Juan, a picaresque-like protagonist who, impoverished, sexed, and dirty, captivates the reader through his performance of an unabashedly "authentic" Havana life, as construed through the author's establishment of equivalences between himself and the protagonist.[2]

A lengthy debate has ensued around the topic of whether Cuban writers on and off the island must adhere to this formula if they are to become one of the fortunate who, like Gutiérrez, have published numerous novels with international publishing houses. In an article titled "¿Pathos o marketing?" published in the journal of the Juventud Cubana (Cuban youth), *El Caimán barbudo,* Rafael de Águila takes Cuban writers to task for what he sees as lowering their literary standards for the foreign press: "Now what we're talking about is inserting our insular dirtiness in the universal market."[3] However, this process of intersecting economy, sexuality, and literary success is much more multidirectional and orchestrated than Águila suggests.[4]

Furthermore, while the debate concerning extraterritorial audiences and Cuban literature has reached new heights in post-Soviet Cuba, the notion that it is through the international sphere that national writing becomes a text is not entirely new. Describing the restrictions implanted by socialist regimes, in "Grito, luego existo" (I scream, therefore I exist), Reinaldo Arenas, the renowned Cuban novelist, states: "There is a golden rule common to all writers under the Communist system: *a manuscript that has not crossed the border is a manuscript that has yet to be written*" (18).[5] Although Arenas blames the Communists for impeding the evolution of literature, in post-Soviet Cuba it is the capitalist dollar that obliges texts to travel if they are to have an impact on a global perception of a national literary canon.

Considering the number of representations of decay and sexuality in Havana today, in order for Cuban novelist Ena Lucía Portela's (Havana, b. 1972) "lexicon of crisis" to still be heard, it must reinvent itself. Only this way can Portela's language articulate differently the experiences of living in the Special Period, in general, as well as the experiences of positioning oneself as a writer within it, in particular. Ending in the year 2000, the novel distances itself temporally from the most difficult early years of adversity. The ability for writers to continue challenging readers' horizons of expectations for the crisis in Cuba and Cuban literature is presently at stake, particularly because many of these readers do not live on the island. This essay explores how Portela's *Cien botellas en una pared* (One hundred bottles on a wall) responds to this need, amplifying the "lexicon of crisis" through a technique of doubling that intricately links a discussion of female writers, readers, and geographic space.

For a few fortunate Cuban writers, the nation-state's ideological and economic orphanage in the wake of the Soviet Union has translated into new partnerships: individual negotiations with foreign suitors. Portela's career showcases this process. Even more fascinating is the way in which her own writing and the story she tells about it mirror this courtship between Cuban writers and the foreign press. Among the many prizes awarded to her are the national UNEAC "Cirilo Villaverde" prize for her first novel *El pájaro, pincel y tinta china* in 1997, the "Juan Rulfo" prize from French

International Radio for her short story "El viejo, el asesino y yo" in 1999, the Spanish Premio Literario Jaén in 2002, and the French Dos Océanos prize in 2003, both for her third novel, *Cien botellas en una pared*. First published outside the island by Mondadori in 2002, *Cien botellas* was republished by Unión in Cuba the next year.

In an interview with Cuban poet Marilyn Bobes, Portela responds to the "market question" as if she were doubling as a critic of her own career. This doubling is, in fact, characteristic of an emerging lexicon that splinters the terms "here" and "there," representative of what are commonly, but frequently erroneously, conceptualized as the local and the global spheres:

> Well, you see, the idea of an "international market" is an abstraction. There's no such thing. What there are are different linguistic regions and different countries. . . .
>
> Look, it can go something like this: an unknown thirty-year-old Cuban writer writes her third novel; in Spain, she receives a prize and a few positive reviews come out in *Lateral* and in *El Mundo*. This is fine, although, in truth, you wouldn't say that they've paid her a lot of attention. Then Seuil, in France (where the Spanish prize doesn't count for anything), gets her a top translator, none other than François Maspero, and they arm a publicity campaign. Our little friend is going to be "the revelation of the year" and in this sublime moment . . . bang! The war in Iraq explodes and all the media revolve around it, taking away from cultural news. The campaign is done in the same way, of course, but it's just not the same . . . And this is how things go—in each place, a different story. So I can't imagine how a Cuban writer, from *here* and without knowing very well what is happening *there*, could arrange everything to please people that are so distinct from one another. So, writing with the "international market" in mind seems to me to be rather schizophrenic. . . .
>
> How to write and be successful without making concessions? Ah! This oft-treated little topic of "market concessions" always makes me think of the writer as a heroic character, constantly chased by a band of malignant publishers that try to bribe him into renouncing his sacred beginnings.[6]

Portela's commentary suggests that the marketability of national products depends greatly on happenstance and on the continued plurality of local markets—some with more power to transform chance into a fortune. She is aware of the erroneous grouping together of disperse places under the rubric of the "market" and recognizes the power of a variety of forces—one of which, she soon reveals in the interview, is a professional reader, employed by the principal promoter of the "Boom Cubano," the Carmen

Balcells Literary Agency in Barcelona, Spain. The sacred nature of those
beginnings is exaggerated in a country that views itself as ideologically
exceptional and economically avenged. All these negotiations would not be
of such grave importance if it were not for the overall national regulations
on exterior travel and for the U.S. blockade. Portela's insights require further explanation. The so-called local sphere is itself heterogeneous. Its heterogeneity emerged even more so in the Special Period, as identity politics
is construed, in part, through external theoretical frameworks. Official celebrations of distinct heritages on the island have become more frequent,
as the government also courts external benefactors. This is to say that individual and national monetary and cultural relations combine; subjects perform their hybrid identities for themselves, but also with distinct publics
in mind. For that matter, the so-called global sphere already penetrates the
insular space through courtships at the Havana Book Fair, the Film Festival,
contacts through state institutions and publishing houses. The Internet
also breaks up the uniformity of space in the sense that even those artists
who are not yet sufficiently professional to have made those formal contacts sometimes encounter ways to market themselves as cultural producers
on the Internet, through personal informal contacts abroad. One instance
of this more informal traveling of culture is manifest on the "Cuba Under-
ground" Web site, where its U.S.-based Cuban proprietor houses a fascinating array of Cuban insular culture that has no other exterior outlet but
this one.

A metacritical discourse, similar to Portela's interview voice, operates
in the novel *Cien botellas en una pared,* where the author holds up a mirror to the creative and marketing processes. The narrative offers a highly
nuanced representation of *here* and *there; here* as a Havana that is varied
in ways that elude the somewhat antiquated and nationalistic code of syncreticism, and *there* as an outside world that is similarly heterogeneous.
The novel illustrates that, on one level, the Afro-Cuban is upheld as a
sacred component of Cuban identity, and another, not only racial but also
sexual and religious prejudices are pervasive. Furthermore, the lesbian and
gay populations are segregated; such notions as syncretism and transculturation do not apply to them.[7] In *Cien botellas,* they congregate in a home
in the sociologically marginal yet geographically central neighborhood of
Centro Havana, where they invert the power structures to their liking.
Although the neighbors are not pleased with the lesbians' parties, this does
not make gratuitous the detail that it is in the heart of Havana's center, the

marginal neighborhood of Centro Havana, rather than outside of Cuba, that yet another *there*—a more permissive *there*—is constituted. We follow *there* to a gathering of principally women, to meet Linda Roth, a Jewish lesbian Cuban writer who is one of the novel's principal protagonists. Linda is doubly marginalized, but she is able to utilize these differences to her professional advantage. She arrives in a taxi so as not to damage her Mercedes on the potholed streets. The lesbian community that welcomes her is "a little island within an island"[8] where desire can be expressed, and it is in this urban island that Roth elaborates her novels. In addition to the world of Centro Havana, other *theres* that exist outside the island also make an appearance in the novel. Besides New York and Barcelona, chief agents in the trafficking of Cuban art, can be found the presence of the Austro-Hungarian Empire and Nazi Germany, two spheres that also influence Roth's sense of persecution and entitlement.

This multiplicity of spaces suggests the necessity to look beyond already reified versions of difference within distinct topoi. Beginning in 1991, religious adherents could officially join the Communist Party, and increasingly throughout the 1990s, particularly after Pope John Paul II's visit to the island, the importance of religion within this Communist society became a publicly debated subject. The narrator of Portela's *Cien botellas* is not the Jewish Linda, however, but Zeta, who conveys her own experience, as an inhabitant in a decaying mansion-turned *solar* in the Vedado section of Havana, living with her abusive partner, the misanthropic, bearded, older, and richer Moisés, who suffers from paranoia, a practically collective disease in authoritarian regimes. Zeta employs a vast venue of religious figures, beyond the more characteristically Afro-Cuban orishas and Catholicism. Although traditional Christian confession remains her modus operandi, she seeks refuge in a diverse religious repertoire that includes the Virgin of El Cobre; Obbatalá, the chief of the Yoruba pantheon; and, to top it off, Odin, the chief of the Scandinavian pantheon. Her spiritual curiosities also lead her to palm reading, Ouija, the I Ching, and tarot. When Zeta conveys that a dear friend is suffering from a pulmonary illness and that several of her friends experience hunger daily, it becomes obvious that these extraworldly realms are her only solace. Portela's eclecticism interrupts the versions of syncreticism of Afro-Cuban and Christian religions that are expected of representations of *cubanidad* or Cubanness today, both nationally and internationally. Furthermore, confession is an integral part of Zeta's religious practice; she confesses to Padre Ignacio, to her friends, and to readers as well. While this technique cross-references the authoritarian aspects of Catholicism and Communism, it more importantly involves a more fluid and oral expression of storytelling that contrasts with Linda Roth's more distant, yet highly successful literary modalities.

The imagined formula for a writer's success is as much followed as it is acutely manipulated in *Cien botellas*. Numerous unresolved whodunits are woven into the narrative as a strategy "to hook" the distant reader, who was expected to hold particular preconceived notions of a socialist, tropical, hot, and decaying paradise. Nevertheless, what occurs in the novel is quite different; these whodunits actually pass into the hands of local denizens who confront their own realities through narratives that publishers intend for others. Whether, to some extent, writers create with a particular audience in mind is undeniable in a Cuba whose book market, like the rest of the society, was, until 2004, stratified according to purchases in dollars or in Cuban currency.[9] The divisions between characters' experiences of Havana and Linda Roth's literary representations of them are not as discrepant as Portela's characters assume they might be because the whodunits are published outside the island. Portela's characters wonder out loud whether, in fact, Havana at the end of the century is as dirty and violent as the internationally renowned author and Mercedes-driving Roth paints it. Nevertheless, it becomes apparent that the stories told by Zeta leave readers hanging at least as much as Linda's intercalated novels.

Zeta's description of Linda's novels also sheds light on the key to success, the successful bridge from *here* to *there*. That bridge is potentially forged through a combination of a certain degree of explanatory material about place, and, of course, professional connections. "Her agent negotiated translations. And perhaps a cinematographic version."[10] The dream of a film adaptation inspires Linda's writing process. Regarding her friend's first detective novel, *El año próximo en Jerusalén* (Next year in Jerusalem), Zeta asks if such a crime could have occurred "*in reality*, in fin de siècle Havana,"[11] or whether, in fact, Linda "had successfully achieved what she announced ten years before: to become a consummate fake, a sublime liar."[12] The consensus among the readers in Portela's novel of Roth's fictitious works is "yes" to both questions, a response that challenges the notion that successful authors have portrayed a nonauthentic Havana for tourist consumption.

Through the novel's characterizations of Havana's neighborhoods—primarily Vedado, Miramar, and Centro Habana—diverse political, gender, and economic games can be seen. The principal anecdote about homophobia in the novel is also an anecdote about social space. For instance, more angered by his gay son's residence in Centro Habana than by his sexual activities, a father ships his son to the richer suburb, Miramar, and tries to normalize him with a wife. At the same time that the population is consumed by performing for the outside, it experiences severe rationings not only of essential commodities, but also of urban space. The decay on the surfaces that is frequently seen to be aesthetically pleasing occurs alongside the "provincialization" of the city, but such a provincialization may not be entirely negative.[13] We cannot ignore the following interwoven whodunit, narrated by the character named Zeta, when we think about this process. Moisés dies, having fallen out the window "accidentally" on the Gran Día de la Literatura Cubana, also the birthday of the great Cuban writer José Lezama Lima and, coincidentally, of Linda Roth. Whether the death was an accident is questionable; that same evening a forsaken scholarship girl from the provinces—who has left the communal residence and now lives with Zeta and her partner—had told the pregnant Zeta that she would resolve her problem. It is possible, although not definitive, to compare the abusive lover, once a jurist, called the Antichrist by the narrator, to Fidel Castro, who himself was a jurist, and to think of this young lesbian scholarship girl from the provinces as the instigator of a familiar revolution. The provincial girl's possible revenge is exceptionally personal. Although this action is intimate, the importance of spatial, social, economic categories is undeniable. Four and a half decades after the revolution attempted to do away with economic and social differences, race, gender, religion, and origins continue to map out the way the characters in the novel imagine the nation.

The novel suggests a discrepancy between the actual circumstances of a diverse city and the singular narrative of progress and equality taught in the schools. The following passage featuring the cultural hodgepodge of Vedado foregrounds the strange poetics of the revolution. Its introduction of "progress" is meant to dominate the unruly forces of nature and geography:

> On account of optimism or habit, there are people who come up with strange ideas about Vedado. It's true that in the 1950s it was a bourgeois neighborhood. . . . It's true that in this city, there are some that are much worse. Centro Havana, for example, is really screwed. Now, when I was born (in the Sagrado Corazón, a hospital in the sacred heart of the city), Vedado was already filled with citadels and you could see anything, from the daughter of the large estate owner who decided not to emigrate, to

the ex-convict swindler who was planning to run down the estate's
daughter in order to rob her of paintings and lamps. It was already the
hodgepodge, the stew, the carnival. Even then, behind the mask of false
respectability, characteristic of a zone of contrasts, in the street there was
a certain roughness. But in school, there wasn't any. School was progress.
There one went to advance, to take advantage of opportunity . . . to get on
the good side of the battle of civilization against barbarism.[14]

At the same time that the narrator refuses a regressive nostalgia (this is not
a novel about the magnificence of pre-Castro Cuba), Zeta's exposure of
citizens' brute behavior in the present critiques the belief that barbarism
could be entirely eliminated across the population.

The interweaving of Linda's novels with Zeta's oral-like narration dra-
matizes the debates concerning the cultural effects of the legal implementation of the dollar in 1993 and, in turn, dissects both the nation's and
readers' conceptualizations of authenticity, local customs, and difference.
The relationship between the *habanera* Zeta and the worldly Linda become
emblematic of the differences between local and global literature. The *solar*
where Zeta lives, La Esquina del Martillo Alegre, was previously the residence of an oligarch, likely the owner of sugar mills. He disappeared and
all that remained was a Cadillac and a maid named Petronila. Zeta asserts
that this absence provides a space for fiction to develop: "There is the first
hole in the story of the Esquina, a broken string . . . where emerges . . . the
propensity to fictionalize."[15] Fictionalization contrasts with the historici-
zation on which local/national claims envision themselves as being based.
In contradictory fashion, the grittiest of local spaces provide a wealth of
material on which to fictionalize. Although Linda Roth usually occupies
the position of "fictionalizing," undoubtedly both Zeta and Linda partake
in this process. Zeta's imaginative digressions concerning her residence
lead her to numerous hypotheses until a small engraved stone grounds her
in the historical presence of the Pythagorean society of 1954–61. With the
downfall of the esoteric society, the building became state property, and
because of its proximity to the newly founded ICAIC, the Cuban Institute
of Cinematographic Art and Industry, it was filled with young artists en-
thralled by a variety of trends and movements in cinema. Zeta's description of this period is especially important because of its sharp contrast
with the present day. "It must have been a moment of hope."[16] Then, eventually it becomes a disheveled housing project, a *solar,* called, among other
names, "The Cave of Whores and Queers."[17]

The novel's detailed attention to different lifestyles in Havana is especially fascinating considering that the very notion of lifestyles is inherently antagonistic in a socialist society. Lifestyles relate to purchasing power and capitalistic concepts of desire. The case of *The H Magazine: Havana's Essential Lifestyles Magazine,* launched in 2004, manifests these contradictions extraordinarily. With offices in Madrid, London, and Havana, an international coterie of contributors that include some of Cuba's stars, such as Pedro Juan Gutiérrez, the concept catapults socialist Havana into the transition through a biopsy-like identification of lifestyles. Although *H* may appear to be an extreme case of distorted representation, Portela's fiction also splices Havana, capturing the disparate lifestyles where ordinary denizens may yet have fixated their gazes or reflected on their meaning. Roth possesses bourgeois luxuries. Although, from this limited depiction, readers may assume that, from Linda's heights, she is unable to adequately know or represent Havana, the novel questions the accuracy of this assumption on various levels. She is able to convincingly defend her perspective:

> If one tells these things in the form of a chronicle, a report, or something like that, many people don't believe it. They say that they're exaggerations, that Havana is the most boring city, where nothing ever happens. Some son of a bitch might even accuse you of doing political propaganda in favor of the enemy and, you already know the game, the stupid bullshit. . . . For this reason, there are novels. They tell something true as if it were false, they reorganize facts, invent a bit. . . . Everyone buys it. . . . They say one is sensationalist, morbid, gruesome, commercial, that she writes literature for tourists and all that crap.[18]

Here, Linda exposes the implications of writing for readers who are caught in between: formed within a socialistic and nationalistic state and now experiencing certain aspects of capitalism up close, even if they merely do so as witnesses or have-nots, rather than as actual consumers. In this sense, like the more bizarre *H,* art serves to tear readers away from the nation's more comfortable (and I say this, even as I am aware that they may be so inward-looking that they become paranoid) journalistic accounts of their lives and into other ones that, though not lacking in verisimilitude, readers have hardly come to accept as their own.

Cien botellas's exploration of the city with regard to the craft of writing is especially evident in the comparison of Linda's and Zeta's "rooms of their own." Zeta's explicit reference to Virginia Woolf's 1929 extended and groundbreaking essay places her within a feminist tradition that she sometimes critiques when it pertains to Linda. Linda's "room of her own" has access to a terrace that she does not utilize, but that right of entry is symbolic of her facile admittance to the world. If she were to go up on the terrace, she could observe what Zeta does one day when she visits:

> The city, so white and beautiful from a distance, from the height that hides the devastation that covers the misery and the horror with a veil of modesty, Havana—iridescent and in the rose twilight, with its cars like beetles, its passerbys the size of ants, the Malecón interrupted by the Fosca tower, and further on, the bay. Pure air, sensation of plenitud. Vertigo.[19]

Linda sits crouched inside surrounded by books. How Zeta and Linda experience the external world and transform it in their storytelling is revealing. Zeta calls her friend Linda a "professional" writer. "She is a professional writer, a *true* writer, a traveler, ambitious and energetic, at times a feminist, with a wide scope of ideas."[20] Zeta calls herself "una amateur" (46), with a "room of her own" nonetheless. Hers does not block out the ruckus of the *solar* "Compay Segundo, el Médico de la Salsa, NG La Banda . . . the bellowing of the goat along with the ding dong of the little bell . . . folkloric expressions."[21] The pervasiveness of these sounds in Zeta's space of creation prevents her from being fully conscious of her role in that creation. Her positionality is defined by the degree to which she is the recipient of the urban everyday. The commonalities between the scribe and those she represents in her storytelling are significant for determining the effects about the claims that she makes. As Linda Alcoff affirms in "The Problem of Speaking for Others," "a speaker's location (which I take here to refer to their *social* location, or social identity) has an epistemically significant impact on that speaker's claims and can serve either to authorize or disauthorize one's speech" (7). The case of Zeta's modest room of her own, representative of her social location, inclines us as addressees to more easily accept what she delivers as accurate and ethical; however, the manner in which the novel reenacts these theoretical questions with respect to Linda's novels obliges us to consider how context and positionality bear on our interpretation of information.

More characteristically literary forms of intertextuality also pervade Zeta's world. Never having traveled outside of the island, Zeta comes to know it principally through her immense contact with literature, which she studied at the University of Havana, and through the stories told to her by Linda, who is, by the way, author of a novel within the novel titled *Cien botellas en una pared.* Among many other details, Linda Roth's and Portela's novels' common title nuances the novel's critique of and admiration for Linda Roth, and establishes a mirroring effect between the two writers. Linda is a Jewish and worldly citizen with a degree of privilege unbeknownst to any of the other characters in Portela's novel by the same name. Because *Cien botellas* is Linda Roth's third novel, as it is for Ena Lucía Portela, it is difficult to avoid comparisons between Portela and her character Roth. Even the chronology of Roth's literary trajectory roughly parallels Portela's. For instance, a small editing house in Barcelona is central to both Roth's and Portela's careers. Zeta's envisioning of Linda Roth as different from other Cubans—for, among other reasons, Roth exits from and returns to Havana—is most fascinating to keep in mind, as part of this intricate portrait of the character as a Jewish, lesbian, Cuban professional writer.

Among these roles, it is the final one through which Linda Roth primarily defines herself; however, in particular situations of marginalization, other aspects of her identity become more pronounced. While Portela may scoff at the notion of making concessions in an interview, her autobiographical character Roth realizes she must do so with the leftist Catalan publisher of her first novel circa 1997, as she is "a young writer . . . almost unknown and from a peripheral country, yes, peripheral, underdeveloped, primitive, wild, because she was Cuban, although her passport said otherwise."[22] This passage suggests that artistic visibility depends on the successful negotiation of one's national identity. Although progress and civilization are the mainstays for Cuban revolutionary existence, even in the context of a leftist publisher, Roth must conform to this other, colonizing view of Cuba, one of underdevelopment and strangeness.

Some aspects of identity are less inescapable than others. Portela portrays this situation using remarkable physical descriptions. At first glance, Zeta's depiction of Linda appears highly prejudiced, but it must be understood in the context of her more general portraits of a collective sphere that functions upon having superficially transformed the prejudices of a Catholic society into the syncretic workings of a Communist one:

> The person was a little girl from our class. A skinny girl with curly hair
> and a prominent witch's nose, with glasses like Quevedo's, Italian
> moccasins, and a gold Rolex on her wrist (in our country, a gold Rolex
> is not only a luxury watch, it is more, much more, a myth, a legend, a
> symbol of power. I identified it because I had seen it once in a magazine),
> a stiff and arrogant creature who sat in the first row and did not talk with

anyone and didn't look at anyone and got good grades in all her classes
and responded to teachers' questions in detail, as if she were saying:
"I know it all. You don't have to teach me . . ."

I confess—I was afraid of her. I'm not sure why. Maybe because
I found her too smart, too cold, too adult, distant, mysterious, like a
foreigner. *Different*.[23]

This stereotypical portrait of the wandering and solvent Jew, the *polaca*
who writes *Cien botellas,* directly reflects back on Portela. The portrait of
Linda Roth as set apart continues with the scene of a hostile incident in
ninth grade involving Linda, the slightly chunky Zeta, and the black and
striking Yadelis. This incident reveals to Zeta how far away from the rest of
the population Linda imagined herself to be, and this distance has immediate ethical consequences for Linda's interpretations of local life. When
the girls have injured a clerk, the authorities single out Linda for blame
rather than the more characteristically Cuban Zeta or Yadelis. Nevertheless, she does not reveal her friends' complicity. In this case, Linda's different appearance isolates her, to her detriment, but she is also automatically
associated with an external sphere. On account of this difference, the adolescent Linda is enabled to *novelar*—to fictionalize and emphasize some
parts of the story at the expense of others—with the knowledge that she
has the security of a father who, if need be, could send her off on an international plane. In fact, he becomes infuriated by the authorities' utilization
of Linda as a scapegoat and threatens to call on the United Nations.

These details relate to a complex discussion of persecution and rescue.
As referenced by the Jewish detective protagonist of one of the novels within
the novel, *El año próximo en Jerusalén,* many Jewish immigrants arrived
in Cuba with the hope that it would merely be a stopover on the way to
somewhere else. Although a large percentage of Jews emigrated out of
Cuba with the revolution, international agencies' involvement in response
to the crisis of the 1990s have increased somewhat the visibility of the
few who remained.[24] Roth's genealogy may not be Hispanic, but she speaks
Spanish, among several other languages, and is invited to the congress of
female Hispanic writers in New York at Hunter College. Traveling with an
Austrian and then a European Union passport, she walks easily through
customs. Linda's heritage is composed of a series of negations. "Regarding
ancestors, hers are very curious. In Cuba, we call them 'Poles,' but they do
not have anything to do with Poland. They lived in Prague, but they were
not Czechs. They spoke German, but they were not German."[25] The novel

suggests that globalism, considered as an array of discrepant and peripheral belongings, accompanied by greater financial security, provides Linda with the freedom to create. Nevertheless, it is seen that her financial security is not unquestionable; for instance, she leaps at the possibility of trafficking cigars. In this way, Portela opens up the classic revolutionary question regarding both the definition of an authentic Cuban novel and the exceptionality of the Cuban diaspora.

While the luckier of Havana's denizens are negotiating deals with foreign contractors, others are engaged in the most provincial of survival strategies. For example, Zeta explains, "Like many people, I had tried to raise a pig. A gloomy initiative. . . It lived in my room, very protected. . . . The thing is that I was dying of hunger in the center of a city with some millions of inhabitants without anyone to go to for help."[26] Nevertheless, during the period when the novel is set, this degree of despair has passed. The city and its inhabitants have been transformed by the crisis, but this splintering is not only cast in a negative light. Zeta's playful narration of this final story in quotations, as if she were Roth, comments on how to proceed. Visibility is important, but so is disguise, of the sort that Portela offers her readers through complex doubling. To the degree that *Cien botellas* questions the role of visibility in the constitution of writers, it searches for a legitimate style—from within and from without—to narrate a city that is itself one and multiple.

In the same vein, the novel suggests that gossip, storytelling, and literature are not as far removed from one another as they are often imagined to be, and that the luck of timing and international marketing is instrumental in defining how writers are critically received. The "lexicon of crisis," as framed by Portela, probes the shifts within the unified category of the "Special Period" as well as the distinct geographic units that constitute local identities. In the last five or so years, the gaze of critics and publishers has been directed to female writers in Cuba, but in the midst of these successive promotions, Portela's writing begs questioning on what basis these categories are constituted and to what degree they continue to be useful for interpreting diverse and conflicting contemporary realities both on and off the island.

Notes

1. "de manera solapada los verbos 'resolver' y 'conseguir' habían ido desplazando al verbo 'comprar' en el léxico de la crisis" (76).

2. See Esther Whitfield, "Dirty Autobiography."

3. "Ahora de lo que se trata es de insertar nuestra suciedad insular en la suciedad universal" (3). My translation is figurative, taking universal dirtiness to signify market.

4. Esther Whitfield brilliantly elucidates this topic in her dissertation "Buying In, Selling Out: Fictions of Cuba in Post-Soviet Cultural Economics."

5. "Hay una regla de oro común a todos escritores bajo el sistema comunista: *manuscrito que no haya cruzado la frontera es un manuscrito por escribir.*" I might add that, for Arenas, borders were aggressively demolished with Julian Schnabel's independent/Hollywood film *Before Night Falls* (2001).

6. "Pues, verás, eso de 'el mercado internacional' es una abstracción. No hay tal. Lo que hay son diferentes áreas lingüísticas y diferentes países... Mira, puede ocurrir algo como esto: una escritora cubana desconocida de treinta años escribe su tercera novela; en España se gana un premio y salen un par de críticas positivas, en *Lateral* y en *El Mundo,* eso está bien, aunque en rigor no podría decirse que le hayan hecho demasiado caso; entonces Seuil, en Francia (donde el premio español no cuenta para nada), le consigue un traductor de lujo, nada más y nada menos que François Maspero, le prepara una campaña publicitaria con todos los hierros, nuestra amiguita va a ser 'la revelación del año' y en ese momento sublime... ¡zas! estalla la Guerra en Irak y todos los medios se giran hacia allá, restándole espacio a las culturales; la campaña se hace igual, claro, pero ya no es lo mismo... Y así van las cosas, en cada lugar una historia diferente. De modo que no imagino cómo podría un escritor cubano, desde *aquí* y sin saber muy a las claras lo que sucede *allá,* arreglárselas para quedar bien con toda esta gente tan distinta. Así, escribir en función de 'el mercado internacional' me parece una onda bastante esquizofrénica... ¿Cómo escribir y tener éxito sin hacer concesiones? ¡Ah! Este asuntico tan llevado y traído de las 'concesiones al mercado' siempre me hace pensar en el escritor como un personaje heroico, todo el tiempo acosado por una pandilla de malignos editores que tratan de sobornarlo para que él renuncie a sus sagrados principios" ("No sé para quién escribo," 37–38; emphasis added).

7. See celebrated Cuban anthropologist Fernando Ortiz's classic study of "transculturation," *Contrapunteo cubano del tabaco y el azúcar* (1940).

8. "islote dentro de la isla" (189).

9. See Jacqueline Loss and Esther Whitfield, "Art and Economics: Focus on Cuba."

10. "Su agente negociaba las traducciones. Y tal vez una versión cinematográfica" (25).

11. "*en la realidad,* o sea, en La Habana finisecular" (164).

12. "había logrado realizar el propósito que anunciara diez años atrás: convertirse en una consumada farsante, una sublime embustera" (166).

13. See Ana Dopico's "Picturing Havana" for a fascinating exposition on decay and "an international field of vision."

14. "Por optimismo o por hábito, hay personas que se hacen ideas extrañas acerca del Vedado. Cierto que en los años cincuenta fue un barrio burgués... Cierto que en la ciudad los hay mucho peores. Que Centro Habana, por ejemplo, está del carajo. Ahora, cuando yo nací (en el Sagrado Corazón, un hospital justo en el sagrado corazón de la barriada), ya el Vedado estaba repleto de ciudadelas y se veía cualquier cosa, desde la hija del latifundista que se había negado emigrar hasta el bandolero ex-convicto que planeaba atropellar a la hija del latifundista para robarle los cuadros y las lámparas. Era ya la mezcolanza, el ajiaco, el carnaval. Aun detrás de su máscara de falsa respetabilidad, característica de una zona de contrastes, en la calle había cierta dureza. Pero en la escuela no. La escuela era el progreso. Allí se iba a adelantar, a aprovechar la oportunidad... a ponerse del lado bueno en la lucha de la civilización contra la barbarie" (62).

15. "He ahí el primer hueco en la historia de la Esquina, un hilo roto... donde prolifera... el afán de novelar" (32).

16. "Debió ser un momento de ilusiones" (37).

17. "La Cueva de las Putas y los Maricones" (ibid.).

18. "Si una cuenta estas cosas en forma de crónica, reportaje o algo así, mucha gente no lo cree. Dicen que son exageraciones, que La Habana es una ciudad aburridísima donde nunca pasa nada. Capaz que hasta algún hijoeputa te acuse de hacer propaganda política a favor del enemigo y ya tú sabes, el rollo, la jodienda estúpida... Por eso las novelas. Se cuenta algo cierto como si fuera falso, se reorganizan los datos, se inventa un poquitín... Todo el mundo se traga la papa... Dice que una es efectista, morbosa, truculenta, comercial, que escribe literatura para turistas y toda esa mierda..." (176).

19. "Una ciudad, tan blanca y bella de lejos, desde la altura que oculta la devastación, que tiene un velo de recato sobre la miseria y el horror, La Habana tornasol y en el crepúsculo rosa, con sus carros como escarabajos, sus transeúntes del tamaño de hormigas, el Malecón interrumpido por la torre del Fosca y, más allá, la bahía. Aire puro, sensación de plenitud. Vértigo" (96).

20. "Ella es una escritora profesional, una escritora *de verdad,* viajera, ambiciosa y enérgica, a sus horas feminista y con pensamientos de gran envergadura" (22).

21. "Compay Segundo, el Médico de la Salsa, NG La Banda... los berridos del chivo añadidos al din don de la campanita... expresiones folklóricas" (46).

22. "una escritora joven... casi desconocida y procedente de un país periférico, sí, periférico, subdesarrollado, primitivo, silvestre, porque ella era cubana aunque su pasaporte dijera otra cosa" (158).

23. "La persona era una chiquita del aula de nosotras. Una flaca de pelo rizado

y nariz prominente, de bruja, con espejuelitos quevedo, mocasines italianos y un Rólex de oro en la muñeca (en nuestro país un Rólex de oro no es s[ó]lo un reloj muy lujoso, es más, mucho más, un mito, una leyenda, un símbolo de poder, yo lo identificaba porque lo había visto una vez en una revista), una criatura tiesa, arrogante, que se sentaba en la primera fila y no hablaba con nadie ni miraba a nadie y sacaba buenas notas en todas las asignaturas y respondía las preguntas de los profesores con mucha suficencia, como diciendo 'yo lo sé todo, no tienes nada que enseñarme...' Yo, lo confieso, lo que le tenía era miedo. No sé muy bien por qué. Tal vez porque la encontraba demasiado lista, demasiado fría, demasiado adulta, distante, misteriosa, como extranjera. *Diferente*" (54–55).

24. For a brief synopsis of Jews in revolutionary Cuba and current relation to the outside, see Dalia Acosta. "Religion-Cuba: Rumored Deal on Jewish Emigration to Israel."

25. "A propósito de los ancestros, los de ella son bien curiosos. En Cuba les llamamos 'polacos', pero no tienen nada que ver con Polonia. Vivían en Praga, pero no eran checos. Hablaban alemán, pero no eran alemanes" (214).

26. "Al igual que mucha gente, había tratado de criar un cerdito. Funesta iniciativa... Vivía dentro de mi cuarto, bien protegido... El caso es que me moría de hambre en el centro de una ciudad con varios millones de habitantes sin nadie a quien acudir en demanda de auxilio" (74–76).

Works Cited

Acosta, Dalia. "Religion-Cuba: Rumored Deal on Jewish Emigration to Israel." *IPS Inter-press Service,* October 12, 1999.

Alcoff, Linda. "The Problem of Speaking for Others." *Cultural Critique* 20 (winter 1991): 5–32.

Arenas, Reinaldo. "Grito, luego existo." In *Necesidad de libertad.* Miami: Universal, 2001.

de Águila, Rafael. "¿Pathos o marketing?" *El Caimán barbudo* 31.292 (1998): 2–3.

Dopico, Ana. "Picturing Havana: History, Vision, and the Scramble for Cuba." *Nepantla* 3.3 (2002): 451–93.

Loss, Jacqueline, and Esther Whitfield. "Art and Economics: Focus on Cuba." *ReVista: Harvard Review of Latin America* (October/November 1999). Accessible at drclas. fas.Harvard.edu/publications/tcontents_issue.php?issue=3&article=477.

Ortíz, Fernando. *Contrapunteo cubano del tobacco y el azúcar.* Havana: J. Montero, 1940.

Portela, Ena Lucía. *Cien botellas en una pared.* Barcelona: Mondadori, 2002.

Whitfield, Esther. "Buying In, Selling Out: Fictions of Cuba in Post-Soviet Cultural Economics." Ph.D. diss., Harvard University, 2001.

———. "Dirty Autobiography: The Body Impolitic of *Trilogía sucia de la Habana.*" *Revista de Estudios Hispánicos* 36.2 (2002): 329–51.

Contributors

Debra A. Castillo is Stephen H. Weiss Presidential Fellow and Emerson Hinchliff Professor of Romance Studies and Comparative Literature at Cornell University. She specializes in contemporary narrative from the Spanish-speaking world, women's studies, and cultural theory. She is author of several books, including *Re-dreaming America, The Translated World: A Postmodern Tour of Libraries in Literature, Talking Back: Strategies for a Latin American Feminist Literary Criticism, Easy Women: Sex and Gender in Modern Mexican Fiction* (Minnesota, 1998), and (cowritten with María Socorro Tabuenca Córdoba) *Border Women: Writing from La Frontera* (Minnesota, 2002). She also translated Federico Campbell's *Tijuana: Stories on the Border.*

Sandra Messinger Cypess is professor in the Department of Spanish and Portuguese at the University of Maryland. She has published numerous studies on the figure of "La Malinche," including *La Malinche in Mexican Literature: From History to Myth.* She is coeditor of the section on drama for *Handbook of Latin American Studies* and editor of *Studies in Romance Languages and Literatures: Essays Critical and Contextual.*

Elisabeth Guerrero is associate professor of Spanish at Bucknell University. Her essays on Argentine, Mexican, and Latino/a literature have appeared in several journals, including *Hispanófila, Chasqui: Revista de literatura latinoamericana, Arizona Journal of Hispanic Cultural Studies,* and *Latin American Literary Review.* She has recently completed a monographic study, *Confronting History and Modernity in Mexican Narrative.*

Guillermo B. Irizarry is assistant professor of Spanish and director of the Institute of Puerto Rican and Latino Studies at the University of Connecticut, Storrs. He has published articles on Caribbean literature and on the literature of Latinas/os in the United States in such journals as *Revista Iberoamericana, Chasqui, La Torre,* and *Latin American Theater Review.* He is the author of *El intelectual nómada: José Luis González y su emplazamiento del nacionalismo puertorriqueño,* and he is working on a project about questions of travel, translation, and community in the Caribbean and its diaspora.

Anne Lambright is associate professor of modern languages and literature in the Hispanic Studies Program at Trinity College in Hartford, Connecticut. Her book *Creating the Hybrid Intellectual: Subject, Space, and the Feminine in the Narrative of José María Arguedas* is forthcoming. She has published articles on Andean literature and culture in several journals, including *Revista Iberoamericana, Latin American Literary Review,* and *Hispanófila.*

Naomi Lindstrom is professor of Spanish and Portuguese at the University of Texas at Austin, where she is affiliated with the Program in Comparative Literature and the Jewish Studies Program. Her recent books are *Twentieth-Century Spanish American Fiction, The Social Conscience of Latin American Writing,* and *Early Spanish American Narrative.* She is manager of the electronic archive of the Latin American Jewish Studies Association and is one of the associate editors of *Latin American Research Review* and *Modern Jewish Studies.*

Jacqueline Loss is associate professor of Spanish at the University of Connecticut, Storrs. She is the author of *Cosmopolitanisms and Latin America: Against the Destiny of Place* and the coeditor of *New Short Fiction from Cuba.* Her essays have appeared in *Nepantla, Miradas, Chasqui, Mandorla,* and *New Centennial Review,* among other publications.

Dorothy E. Mosby is assistant professor of Spanish at Mount Holyoke College, where she specializes in Latin American and Afro-Hispanic literature. She is the author of *Place, Language, and Identity in Afro–Costa Rican Literature,* a study of works by Costa Ricans of Afro–West Indian descent. She has published in journals such as *Afro-Hispanic Review, PALARA: Publication of the Afro/Latin American Research Association,* and *College Language Association Journal.* She is writing a book-length study on the works of Costa Rican novelist and activist Quince Duncan.

Daniel Noemi Voionmaa studied Latin American literature at the Universidad Católica de Chile, Universidad de Chile, and Yale University. He has published several articles and the book *Leer la pobreza en América Latina: Literatura y velocidad*. He teaches Latin American literature and culture at the University of Michigan, Ann Arbor.

Ángel A. Rivera is associate professor at Worcester Polytechnic Institute, where he specializes in nineteenth-century Caribbean and Latin American literature. He is author of *Avatares de una modernidad caribeña: Eugenio María de Hostos y Alejandro Tapia y Rivera*. He has published several articles on nineteenth-century writers and their relationship to the process of modernization, cultural representations, identity strategies, and border/frontier theories.

Lidia Santos is associate professor of Brazilian and Latin American literature at Yale University. She is the author of *Tropical Kitsch: Media in Latin American Literature and Art,* which was awarded a prize from the Latin American Studies Association in 2003. She has contributed book chapters to *Contemporary Latin American Cultural Studies* and *Ritualidades latinoamericanas: Un acercamiento interdisciplinario*. She received the Guimarães Prize awarded by Radio France Internationale in 1992 and is author of two books of short stories, *Flauta e Cavaquinho* and *Os Ossos da Esperança*.

Marcy Schwartz is associate professor of Spanish at Rutgers University. She specializes in twentieth-century Latin American narrative and cultural studies, with particular emphasis on urban studies, exile, photography, and postcolonial theory. She is the author of *Writing Paris: Urban Topographies of Desire in Contemporary Latin American Fiction,* and coeditor (with Daniel Balderston) of *Voice-Overs: Translation and Latin American Literature* and (with Mary Beth Tierney-Tello) *Photography and Writing in Latin America: Double Exposures*.

Gareth Williams is associate professor of Spanish at the University of Michigan, Ann Arbor. He is the author of *The Other Side of the Popular: Neoliberalism and Subalternity in Latin America* and of numerous articles on contemporary Latin American literature, cultural politics, and political philosophy.

Index